THE UNFORMED CONSCIENCE *of* EVANGELICALISM

Recovering the Church's Moral Vision

J. DARYL CHARLES

InterVarsity Press
Downers Grove, Illinois

InterVarsity Press
P.O. Box 1400, Downers Grove, IL 60515-1426
World Wide Web: www.ivpress.com
E-mail: mail@ivpress.com

InterVarsity Press® is the book-publishing division of InterVarsity Christian Fellowship/USA®, a student movement active on campus at hundreds of universities, colleges and schools of nursing in the United States of America, and a member movement of the International Fellowship of Evangelical Students. For information about local and regional activities, write Public Relations Dept., InterVarsity Christian Fellowship/USA, 6400 Schroeder Rd., P.O. Box 7895, Madison, WI 53707-7895, or visit the IVCF website at <www.ivcf.org>.

Scripture quotations, unless otherwise noted, are the author's translation.

Passages from D. H. Williams, Retrieving the Tradition & Renewing Evangelicalism, *©1999, published by William B. Eerdmans Publishing Company, are reproduced by permission of the publisher.*

Cover photograph: ©Mark Oatney/Photonica

ISBN 0-8308-2691-2

Printed in the United States of America ∞

Library of Congress Cataloging-in-Publication Data
Charles, J. Daryl, 1950-
   The unformed conscience of evangelicalism: recovering the
church's moral vision / J. Daryl Charles.
     p. cm.
   Includes bibliographical references and index.
   ISBN 0-8308-2691-2 (pbk.: alk. paper)
   1. Christian ethics. 2. Evangelicalism. I. Title.
BJ1251.C474 2002
241'.0404—dc21
                                             2002009250

P	19	18	17	16	15	14	13	12	11	10	9	8	7	6	5	4	3	2	1
Y	17	16	15	14	13	12	11	10	09	08	07	06	05	04	03	02			

To Rosi and Melo

two women of virtue

Contents

Preface

There is no such thing as an evangelical social ethic. Let us be frank about the matter. Church growth we've made a science; our forays into the contemporary music scene are endless; inspirational books and Christian "breakthrough" literature are selling like there is (literally) no tomorrow; the number of our church programs knows no limit; and without question, we are as seeker-friendly as any group on the face of the earth. But the truth is, we simply cannot speak of an approach to ethics that is distinctly Protestant evangelical. Why is that?

This book represents an attempt to understand why contemporary American evangelicals are, by and large, absent from the great ethical debates of the day and, more fundamentally, why we tend not to think in terms of a viable social ethic. In many evangelical circles, to speak of virtue, of moral formation or of social ethics is to elicit a look of bewilderment from the listener, as if he or she has been addressed in some foreign language. But the fact of the matter is, we may need to learn this language.

Yet while the tone of this book is at times impassioned, *The Unformed Conscience* is by no means the "last word" on vice and virtue or on Christian ethics. It is but an introduction, a "first word." It is written to those who share a concern that within broader evangelicalism, business as usual as we presently know it is somehow deficient. It speaks to the congregation as well as the academy, to the layperson as well the technician, to those saints being equipped as well as those doing the equipping. It is a humble attempt to understand why the evangelical conscience is largely unformed and, in the end, to propose a different way of thinking.

The first order of business, it seems to me, is to consider the ethical challenges that confront not just evangelicalism but the Christian community as a whole. In this, we evangelicals are not alone; we join Roman Catholic and Orthodox Christians in facing a culture that is both hostile *and* indifferent to the exclusive claims of the Christian message. And it is to this cultural climate that we must initially turn our attention.

The subject of ethics represents something of a conundrum for Americans. On the one hand, interest in ethics would seem to be quite high. It is the focus of heated discussions in the academy (particularly in business and law schools); in politics, legislatures and Congress; in business and finance; and in public-policy circles. Numerous books are published every year on the subject, and it is a regular topic of concern among journalists and pundits. In a 1999 Gallup survey, "ethics and morality" were found to be the most important issues facing the nation. (They were followed in importance by crime, the economy, education and guns, respectively).[1] Similarly, a 1998 Roper poll established the "letdown in moral values" as a "major cause of our problems today."[2]

On the other hand, any serious discussion of ethics and moral standards tends to cause embarrassment and serves as an affront to our modern and postmodern sensibilities, making people uncomfortable, irritable, even paranoid. Christian claims to truth, for example, and the acknowledgment of any universally binding ethical standards are derided and (almost universally) deemed "intolerant." Meanwhile, tolerance in a most degraded form has become the cardinal virtue of American culture. Unceasingly praised and promoted, tolerance *as vice* bears no resemblance to its former self. Its makeover has facilitated our indulgence in "alternative" opinions, practices and lifestyles—to the point that we are comfortable with tolerating evil itself. Accord-

---

[1]"Ethics, Morality Tops Public's List of Concern for First Time in Half-Century," *Emerging Trends* 21, no. 7 (1999): 1-2.
[2]The results are reported in Karl Zinsmeister et al., "Is America Turning a Corner?" *The American Enterprise* 10, no. 1 (1999): 37.

ingly, whoever is perceived as "intolerant" is branded as insensitive and bears, as it were, the mark of Cain.

But this volume is not an exercise in handwringing; nor is it at bottom a lamentation of the state of contemporary culture (even though we shall engage in a bit of cultural criticism along the way). Its concerns lie elsewhere. Rather, it seeks to probe the reasons why Protestant evangelicals have been reticent to participate in the important ethical debates of the day. It also presents an argument for the necessity of moral formation, which, given the primacy of grace and faith in evangelical theology, may have received short shrift in our more recent history. Finally, it is an attempt to prod confessing evangelicals (and those with evangelical sympathies) toward responsible ethical thinking and engagement, wherever that might lead. To the extent that the Christian must understand the relativist assumptions that fuel various modes or "schools" of moral reasoning, these schools—be they utilitarian, emotivist, egoist, situationist, evolutionary or virtue-based—need to be identified, certainly. However, a summary of these schools does not constitute the trajectory of this book. Such can be found in any standard primer on philosophical ethics.[3]

This writer approaches the subject of ethics from a variety of perspectives. I teach at a Christian liberal arts university that draws students from a wide array of Protestant evangelical backgrounds. The role I fill in the religion department is interdisciplinary, which is to say that the courses for which I am responsible frequently wrestle with the intersection of faith and culture as well as with doctrine and ethics. Additionally, while serving a fellowship in the 1996-1997 academic year through the auspices of Princeton University's Center for the Study of American Religion, I was struck anew not only by the strident character of American religious pluralism, but also by the relative absence of evangelicals entering or engaging in serious theological and ethical conversation beyond the level of political reaction and protest.

Finally, I have personal reasons that account for my interest in ethics that extend above and beyond my own vocational calling. Ever since my own "conversion" to Christian faith three decades ago, I have been some-

---

[3]See, e.g., Arthur F. Holmes, *Ethics: Approaching Moral Decisions* (Downers Grove, Ill.: InterVarsity Press, 1984); Scott B. Rae, *Moral Choices: An Introduction to Ethics,* rev. ed. (Grand Rapids, Mich.: Zondervan, 2000); and Steve Wilkens, *Beyond Bumper-Sticker Ethics: An Introduction to Theories of Right and Wrong* (Downers Grove, Ill.: InterVarsity Press, 1995).

thing of a student of American evangelical culture—intrigued by its bewil-
dering diversity, troubled by its relative lack of unity, and on occasion
stupefied by its conspicuous absence from the great moral debates raging
within society. (This last tendency stands in marked contrast, for example,
to the visibility of Roman Catholics,[4] who for over two decades have ben-
efited from the moral leadership of Pope John Paul II, one who has *not*
been reticent to offer penetrating ethical and social commentary in the
form of regular major encyclicals.)

In their recent history, American evangelicals have been known for their
commitment to biblical authority and tenacious affirming of what "the Bible
says." In and of itself, this is commendable. At the same time they have *not*
been particularly known for their contributions to theology and philosophy,
ethics (i.e., moral philosophy), law, economics, statecraft, the social sciences
or public policy—which is to say, areas that require considerable reflection on
the interaction between Christian faith and pluralistic society. Happily, there
are indications now, at the cusp of the third millennium, that this is changing.
But evangelicals in the main will need to step back, learn to think historically
with the whole of the church and begin training their own based on a vision
that is long-term in nature. This project will entail, among other things, the
hard work of learning and articulating moral persuasion. No stopgap political
and legal measures (to which a previous generation of evangelical "religious
right" involvement has been inclined to resort) will be adequate. Educating for
the future requires vision that extends to future generations. Theologically and
ethically speaking, the present generation of American evangelicals is a generation that "knew not Joseph"; thus, we must begin to reason, reflect and edu-
cate at the level of "first principles."

This process will mean several things relating to the task of ethics:

- It will require learning to approach biblical theology and biblical ethics
  as a unified, coherent and consistent whole spanning the entirety of
  scriptural revelation.[5]
- In addition, it will necessitate acclimating ourselves to think historically
  and becoming acquainted with the width and breadth of the entire

---

[4]This is not to deny the great diversity—and in some circles, the considerable heterodox dissent to the
church's teaching—that exists among Roman Catholics.
[5]Chapter eight identifies hermeneutical issues in this regard.

Christian moral-philosophical tradition. We must be willing to take into account *all* of church history—not merely the Protestant Reformation—as a reference point. Evangelicals will thereby discover that there is much to be gleaned from generations of Christians past who also wrestled with questions of Christian exclusivity amidst pagan inclusivity.

• Furthermore, it will mean taking seriously the church's cultural mandate, which compels the Christian community toward responsible and strategic cultural engagement.[6]

In recent years much has been written concerning the legacy attending Protestant fundamentalism in North America and evangelicals' evacuation from the cultural mainstream during the century just concluded. These trenchant critiques of our recent history are indispensable for understanding our identity. But merely being reminded of the past does not equip us for the present and future; reconstructive moral vision must be birthed and come to fruition. That vision has two parts: Negatively, it will not turn a deaf ear to important questions raised by the past and present. In all humility it will seek to understand which inherent tendencies in evangelical thinking, whether at the turn of the twentieth century or the turn of the twenty-first, shape and dominate the ethos of the evangelical church. Positively, it will seek to identify and lay hold of the foundations in which Christian moral vision is anchored—foundations that will aid us in overcoming prevailing weaknesses in the evangelical ethos, however debilitating in the recent past they may have been. It will also acknowledge important resources at our disposal for equipping the believer who lives in the context of pervasively pagan culture.[7]

Before assuming a full-time academic post, I spent a season doing social- and public-policy work in Washington, D.C., a primary focus of which was criminal justice. What I had observed to be generally true about the evangelical contribution to mainstream culture was particularly true at the level of policy research and debate. Several tendencies were striking. Evangelicals, with some notable exceptions, were prone to being theologically deficient. That is, they seemed to have an inherent bias against theology and Christian doctrine,

---

[6]The goal, it must be stated, is faithfulness, *whether or not* the church achieves any measure of "success" in moral transformation.

[7]It is a fundamental assumption of this writer that evangelicals will need to look beyond their borders for helpful resources if they are serious about Christian social ethics.

as if the task of theology were the exclusive domain of the theologian, the seminarian or the technical expert. This theological deficiency inhibits our ability to work constructively over the long term; we are creatures of the moment, reacting to issues and dilemmas on the basis of stopgap measures rather than developing the implications of our worldview (which, truth be told, is hard work). A related tendency among evangelicals was (and remains) our inability to relate biblical theology to ethics, which would seem to suggest a rather tragic *divorce between belief and practice,* in the end revealing a faith-works dichotomy that is roundly condemned in the epistle of James.[8]

By contrast, more often than not Roman Catholics were the ones who seemed to be making the most significant contributions to social and political thought. Where were evangelical Protestants? And why were evangelicals conspicuously absent among vocational ethicists, legal consultants and theorists, economists, social scientists and policy analysts? Did this suggest a basic flaw in our evangelical worldview?

As the reader of this book will likely conclude, reasons for this void have both theological and sociocultural roots. Now that I am situated in the classroom and attempting to equip young adults who hopefully will be part of the emerging generation of Christian leadership, I find myself still grappling with these basic questions. At times I am somewhat discouraged by the lack of coherent thinking that characterizes pan-evangelicalism, and at times I am greatly encouraged and invigorated by the fresh hunger and vision I sense among these young adults. Amidst this process, there is perhaps one question that continues to haunt me most: Why is the influence of American Protestant evangelicals—a subculture thought by many social analysts to be dominating the American religious landscape at the close of the twentieth century—*disproportionate to its reputed numbers?*

One clue might emerge from a perusal of textbooks on ethics written by evangelical authors over the last several decades. Since the publication of *Principles of Conduct: Aspects of Biblical Ethics* (1957) by John Murray and *Aspects of Christian Social Ethics* (1964) by Carl Henry (neither of whom was writing as an ethicist), one is able to cite only a limited number of works devoted to ethics that have been authored by self-confessing evangelicals and even fewer that

---

[8]Faith that is not evidenced or validated by works, writes James, is "dead" (*nekros,* Jas 2:17, 26) and "useless" (*argos,* Jas 2:20).

have been published by the major evangelical publishing houses.[9] This list in-
cludes Norman Geisler's *Ethics: Issues and Alternatives,* Stephen Charles Mott's
Biblical Ethics and Social Change, Arthur Holmes's *Ethics: Approaching Moral De-
cisions,* John Jefferson Davis's *Evangelical Ethics: Issues Facing the Church Today,*
John and Paul Feinberg's *Ethics for a Brave New World,* David Jones's *Biblical
Christian Ethics,* Scott Rae's *Moral Choices: An Introduction to Ethics,* Steve Wilkens's *Beyond Bumper-Sticker Ethics: An Introduction to Theories of Right and
Wrong,* Stanley Grenz's *The Moral Quest* and theologian David Wells's *Losing
Our Virtue: Why the Church Must Recover Its Moral Vision.*[10] While each of these
volumes makes a significant contribution, many are dated and most are devot-
ed primarily, if not exclusively, to a "Christian position" on specific moral is-

---

[9]John Murray, *Principles of Conduct: Aspects of Biblical Ethics* (Grand Rapids, Mich.: Eerdmans, 1957);
Carl F. H. Henry, *Aspects of Christian Social Ethics* (Grand Rapids, Mich.: Eerdmans, 1964). This list
does not include recent (and much needed) volumes on bioethics (e.g., collected essays from annual
bioethics conferences sponsored by the Center for Bioethics and Human Dignity in Deerfield, Illinois,
that have been published by Eerdmans since 1995). Neither does it include surveys of Old Testament
or New Testament ethics (e.g., Walter C. Kaiser Jr.'s *Toward Old Testament Ethics* [Grand Rapids,
Mich.: Zondervan, 1983], Christopher Wright's *An Eye for an Eye: The Place of Old Testament Ethics*
[Downers Grove, Ill.: InterVarsity Press, 1983], his more recent *Walking in the Ways of the Lord: The
Ethical Authority of the Old Testament* [Downers Grove, Ill.: InterVarsity Press, 1995]; and Jonathan
Wilson's *Gospel Virtues* [Downers Grove, Ill.: InterVarsity Press, 1998]). Nor does it take into account
works published over the last two decades on sexual ethics and love, which are legion. Finally, also
excluded from this list are works by Protestant mainline ethicists who have evangelical sympathies
(e.g., Lutheran ethicist Gilbert Meilaender, whose books *The Theory and Practice of Virtue* [Notre
Dame: University of Notre Dame Press, 1984] and *Faith and Faithfulness: Basic Themes in Christian Ethics* [Notre Dame, Ind.: University of Notre Dame Press, 1991] are essential reading for anyone interested in Christian social ethics; or Methodist Stanley Hauerwas, author of works such as *Vision and
Virtue* [Notre Dame, Ind.: Fides, 1974]; *A Community of Character* [Notre Dame, Ind.: University of
Notre Dame Press, 1981]; *The Peaceable Kingdom: A Primer in Christian Ethics* [Notre Dame, Ind.: University of Notre Dame Press, 1983]; and with Richard Biondi and David B. Burrell, *Truthfulness and
Tragedy: Further Investigations in Christian Ethics* [Notre Dame, Ind.: University of Notre Dame Press,
1977]).
[10]Norman Geisler, *Ethics: Issues and Alternatives* (Grand Rapids, Mich.: Zondervan, 1971); Stephen
Charles Mott, *Biblical Ethics and Social Change* (New York: Oxford University Press, 1982); John Jefferson Davis, *Evangelical Ethics: Issues Facing the Church Today* (Phillipsburg, N.J.: Presbyterian & Re-
formed, 1985); John Feinberg and Paul Feinberg, *Ethics for a Brave New World* (Wheaton, Ill.:
Crossway, 1993); David Jones, *Biblical Christian Ethics* (Grand Rapids, Mich.: Baker, 1994); Stanley
Grenz, *The Moral Quest* (Downers Grove, Ill.: InterVarsity Press, 1997); and David F. Wells, *Losing Our
Virtue: Why the Church Must Recover Its Moral Vision* (Grand Rapids, Mich.: Eerdmans, 1998). (The
books by Holmes, Rae and Wilkens are cited above.) A revision of Geisler's book was published by
Baker in 1989 under the title *Christian Ethics: Options and Issues.* The revised edition of Rae's book
(first published in 1995) appeared in 2000. Mott's and Wells's books, it should be noted, were published by Eerdmans. Another very important work, authored by British evangelical Oliver O'Donovan, *Resurrection and Moral Order: An Outline for Evangelical Ethics* (1986), was also published by
Eerdmans.

sues. Few grapple with biblical ethics in terms of a *unified biblical theology*,[11] and none adequately assesses *both* the theological *and* cultural factors that are formative in—and that impinge upon—evangelical thinking.

This relative void, reflected in the literature, can be seen to refract in evangelicals' cultural engagement. In contrast to Protestant evangelicals, Roman Catholics over the last three decades have by and large taken the lead in addressing ethical matters, most notably since the abortion issue became something of a cultural watershed in the late 1960s and early 1970s. Modeling this ethos, of course, has been John Paul himself, who has been nothing short of prolific in confronting critical social and ethical issues facing Western culture. The 1990s alone have been witness to a breathtaking series of commentaries by the pontiff: for example, *Centesimus Annus* ("The Hundredth Year"), *Ut Unum Sint* ("That They May Be One"), *Redemptoris Missio* ("The Mission of Redemption"), *Veritatis Splendor* ("The Splendor of Truth"), *Evangelium Vitae* ("The Gospel of Life") and *Fides et Ratio* ("Faith and Reason").[12] These encyclicals have combined timely and incisive cultural criticism with much-needed analysis of questions as diverse as the value of work, a free society and the threat of class warfare; the church's evangelistic mission; beginning-of-life and end-of-life issues; the necessity of Christian unity for comprehensive cultural witness; the nature of truth and moral agency; Christian proclamation in the context of radical pluralism; and the symbiosis of faith and reason.[13]

As we head into the new millennium, the verdict on evangelicalism is still out, reports of its vitality and resilience notwithstanding. What legacy will we leave to future generations of evangelicals? What example will we set now that

---

[11]Notable exceptions are Jones, Holmes and Rae.

[12]As the title indicates, the encyclical *Centesimus Annus* is a centennial commemoration—and development—of the argument put forth a century earlier by Leo XIII in *Rerum Novarum*. This list, of course, does not take into account John Paul II's best-seller *Crossing the Threshold of Hope* (New York: Alfred A. Knopf, 1994).

[13]It is only fair to note that long before he became pope, Karol Wojtyla had written his doctoral thesis on Max Scheler's *Ethics of Values* and had published a work on sexual ethics (which subsequently has been translated into English and published as *Love and Responsibility,* trans. H. T. Willetts [San Francisco: Ignatius, 1993]). Also, in his book *The Acting Person* [Toronto: D. Reidel, 1979], Wojtyla investigates the psychology of making moral decisions while reflecting on the sources of moral knowledge and our ability as rational agents to choose. During his pontificate, John Paul has been described as "unabashedly counter-cultural," even when cultural witness for him will mean at times drawing out the implications of truth and at other times confronting culture head-on. It is not, therefore, surprising that both secularists as well as nominal and erstwhile Catholics (i.e., those who wish to retain their Catholic identity while rejecting Christian orthodoxy and the church's teaching authority) find the current pontiff disquieting, to say the least.

will strengthen or diminish evangelicalism's witness? And to what extent will we contribute in meaningful ways to the church's overall cultural witness to the world? As Robert Webber has recently argued, "The road to the future runs through the past."[14] This means evangelicals will need to recover a "universally accepted framework of faith" that will serve as a guide for present and future generations. Nowhere is this recovery more critical than in the sphere of Christian ethics.

This book is written by an evangelical to those who confess evangelical faith in its many expressions. If the questions raised in the following chapters induce fellow believers to reflect on both the past and the future, the modest goals of this writer will have been achieved.

---

[14]Robert E. Webber, *Ancient-Future Faith: Rethinking Evangelicalism for a Postmodern World* (Grand Rapids, Mich.: Baker, 1999), p. 7.

1

The Cultural Moment
and the Cultural Mandate

—

Much has been said and written in recent years about our having entered a post-Christian era. The prevailing mood, at least among some social observers, is disjunctive—even terminal.[1] There is literally something for everybody in the laundry list of one cultural critic, who, in summarizing social commentary of our time, describes ours as "post-traditional," "post-modern," "post-literary," "post-historic," "post-collectivist," "post-bourgeois," "post-capitalist," "post-industrial," "post-Protestant," "post-civilized" and, above all, "post-Christian."[2] Christian ethicist Vigen Guroian has posed the intriguing question, "Is Christian ethics any longer possible?" in a volume

---

[1]Thus, for example, Francis Fukuyama can speak of "the great disruption" in order to depict the disintegration of social bonds and moral values that have long held together Western societies (*The Great Disruption: Human Nature and the Reconstitution of Social Order* [New York: Free Press, 1999], pp. 3-26). A helpful antidote to the doom and gloom that haunts historians at the end of the twentieth century is Richard J. Evans, *In Defense of History* (New York: W. W. Norton, 1999). Blessedly free of technical jargon, Evans's book comes at a time when, in the author's words, "growing numbers of historians themselves are abandoning the search for truth, the belief in objectivity, and the quest for a scientific approach to the past" (p. 4). See my review of Evans's book in *Academic Questions* 13, no. 1 (1999-2000): 93-96.

[2]Richard John Neuhaus, *Time Toward Home: The American Experiment as Revelation* (New York: Seabury, 1975), p. 1. Neuhaus captures the mood of the present cultural moment with poignancy: "Whether in melancholia, in panic or in religious-revolutionary ecstasy, many experience our time as a sense of ending" (p. 3).

with the equally intriguing title *Ethics after Christendom*.[3] In this age of disjunction, is it an overstatement to say, or to suggest, that Christian ethics is no longer possible? And how might Protestant evangelicals in particular react to Guroian's question?

Cultural critics have responded in a variety of ways. According to theologian George Lindbeck, Christianity is in "the awkwardly intermediate stage of having once been culturally established but . . . not yet fully disestablished."[4] This position seems to imply that while no outright moral collapse is upon us, morals degenerate where people do not consciously deliberate over moral ideas. Few would argue with the notion that Christian religion, accompanied by Christian ethical influence, has sharply abated in the latter part of the twentieth century. A more pessimistic view is taken by moral philosopher Alasdair MacIntyre, who compares the present time with the fourth through sixth centuries, the period of decline into the "Dark Ages." In MacIntyre's opinion, we are moral cave-dwellers who have undergone a catastrophic shift in our understanding that has warped our ability to do moral reasoning at all.[5] Johns Hopkins cultural historian Morris Berman as well believes that the United States is headed for its own "dark age," wherein cultural conservatives will play a key role in transmitting what is enduring to successive generations.[6] Sociologist James Davison Hunter's assessment of our moral landscape bears some resemblance to that of MacIntyre and Berman. In his postmortem examination of moral character, Hunter concludes, "The social and cultural conditions that make character possible are no longer present."[7] The position taken by social critic Herbert Schlossberg would appear to be somewhere between Lindbeck's and MacIntyre's position: we are not yet fully established as moral cave-dwellers but are well on the way to becoming so. Schlossberg writes:

---

[3]Vigen Guroian, *Ethics After Christendom: Toward an Ecclesial Christian Ethic* (Grand Rapids, Mich.: Eerdmans, 1994). The question posed is the title of Guroian's introductory chapter.

[4]George Lindbeck, *The Nature of Doctrine* (Philadelphia: Westminster Press, 1984), p. 134.

[5]Alasdair MacIntyre, *After Virtue: A Study in Moral Theory,* 2nd ed. (Notre Dame, Ind.: University of Notre Dame Press, 1981), p. 263. Understandably, those ethicists for whom tolerance and pluralism are pivotal issues in Christian ethics—for example, Jeffrey Stout (*Ethics After Babel: Languages of Morals and Their Discontents* [Boston: Beacon, 1988]) and Ian Markham (*Plurality and Christian Ethics,* rev. ed. [New York: Seven Bridges Press, 1999])—disagree strongly with MacIntyre's gloomy analysis of modernity.

[6]Morris Berman, *The Twilight of American Culture* (New York: W. W. Norton, 2000).

[7]James Davison Hunter, *The Death of Character* (New York: BasicBooks, 2000), p. xiii. Hunter is speaking foremost of moral discipline, the prime ingredient of which is the inner restraint of one's appetites (p. 16).

After biblical faith wanes, a people can maintain habits of thought and of self-restraint. The ethic remains after the faith that bore it departs. But eventually a generation arises that no longer has the habit, and that is when the behavior changes radically.[8]

Ethicist Gilbert Meilaender, acknowledging "a good measure of truth to the diagnosis of our cultural predicament offered by Lindbeck and MacIntyre," nevertheless confesses, "I am not myself persuaded that ours is as fully post-Christian a culture as these diagnoses suggest." Around us Meilaender sees "at least partial bits of evidence for a resurgent ability of Christians to shape the moral life of our society."[9] The writings of British evangelical theologian Alister McGrath, by contrast, mirror a cautious optimism tempered by a sober realism vis-à-vis both opportunities and obstacles that the present cultural moment presents. While McGrath fully acknowledges that ours is a postmodern and postliberal society, he does not use the term *post-Christian,* suggesting that the church has always to contend with pluralistic thinking and amoralism, whatever its historical location.[10]

As we consider the cultural moment and what American evangelicals might contribute to ethics at the beginning of the third millennium (whatever our social prognosis might be), we must avoid two extreme positions. On the one hand, an optimistic synthesis between secular culture and Christian values, such as that espoused by twentieth-century Protestant liberalism, is untenable. We might call this the vision of a "de-Christianized" society. It is one that views throwing off "repressive" restraints of Christian orthodoxy *as necessary;* alas, it has made its peace with surrounding culture.[11] One social critic has summarized this mindset well:

People [thinking thusly] fail to appreciate the worth of society's Christian underpinnings, because they are unconscious recipients of its blessings. The

---

[8]Herbert Schlossberg, *Idols for Destruction: The Conflict of Christian Faith and American Culture,* rev. ed. (Wheaton, Ill.: Crossway, 1990), p. 296. In the penultimate chapter of his book, Schlossberg does speak of "ethics in a post-Christian society" (p. 287).

[9]Gilbert Meilaender, *Faith and Faithfulness: Basic Themes in Christian Ethics* (Notre Dame, Ind.: University of Notre Dame Press, 1991), pp. 8-9.

[10]Representative of McGrath's thinking are *Evangelicalism and the Future of Christianity* (Downers Grove, Ill.: InterVarsity Press, 1995) and *A Passion for Truth: The Intellectual Coherence of Evangelicalism* (Downers Grove, Ill.: InterVarsity Press, 1996).

[11]This position bears resemblance to the "Christ of culture" model described by Richard Niebuhr, *Christ and Culture* (New York: Harper, 1951).

most vigorous atheist in the world has grown up in a world in which love and justice are ideals. But such ideals have no objective referent outside of the biblical accounts.[12]

On the other hand, equally flawed is the extreme vision of a "re-Christianized" America, a vision based on a false or romantic reading of our nation's history, with its corresponding dismissive attitude toward culture in general.[13] Many evangelical readers will doubtless be well acquainted with this mindset in its varied expressions. (An appeal to a *third position* is made by some, but in its premises it shares a good deal with the first position, while in its practice it underestimates or ignores culture in much the same way as does the second position. It is the Anabaptist or "free church" position that seeks to offer a "radical" assessment of the flaws of Constantinianism and, consequently, tends to encourage by way of this "radical" critique a withdrawal from the institutions of the cultural mainstream.[14])

Our intellectual culture, all in all, has not assisted ordinary men and women in making moral judgments.[15] Intuiting the need to take stands on ethical issues of the day, people often feel like refugees living in a land captured by hostile forces, as social critic James Q. Wilson has remarked.[16] When they speak of virtue, they must do so privately, in whispers, lest they be charged with the grievous crime of being "unsophisticated" or, if they press the matter, "fanatics." Many in surrounding culture go as far as to deny the very *possibility* that moral judgments can be made.[17]

The ethical challenges that confront the Christian community, it goes

---

[12]Schlossberg, *Idols for Destruction,* p. 288.

[13]While no serious contemporary ethicist promotes this vision, it animates much of evangelicalism on a popular level. One of the most well-balanced assessments of America's past and present is found in Robert W. Jenson, "The Kingdom of America's God" (in his *Essays in Theology and Culture* [Grand Rapids, Mich.: Eerdmans, 1995], pp. 50-66), which endeavors to reconcile the breadth of Puritan vision and hopes with the spiritual vacuity and hopelessness one finds today.

[14]This position can be found, e.g., in the writings of John Howard Yoder.

[15]Thinkers of previous generations believed that moral judgments arose out of universal norms, "self-evident truths," and that these judgments should shape our behavior.

[16]This is the introductory lament of James Q. Wilson, *The Moral Sense* (New York: Free Press, 1993), p. x.

[17]Richard Neuhaus summarizes the business of Christian social ethics well: "The enterprise we call ethics is always posited against despair. Ethics is the hope for meaning, despair the logical conclusion to be drawn from meaninglessness. We speak ethically in the hope that there is some ontological support system for the 'oughtness' we posit against 'wasness' and 'isness.' Serious ethics can only be done in the hope that we are not spitting against the wind" (*Time Toward Home,* p. 157).

without saying, are enormous. This is all the more true for the challenges facing Protestant evangelicals. At present, one might plausibly argue that Protestant churches in North America (in contrast to recipients of Roman Catholic moral teaching, which finds consistent application to pressing ethical issues of our day) lack the conviction necessary to persuade their own— much less, broader culture—of the need for basic Christian morality. Moreover, when the personal conduct of professing Christians no longer gives evidence of a consistent moral teaching that is rooted in sturdy and timeless theological reflection, the Christian community should not be surprised when it is not taken seriously or when it seems to exercise no measurable influence on society at large.

ASSESSING CULTURE

Not long ago, Boston College education professor William Kilpatrick noted in his book *Why Johnny Can't Tell Right from Wrong* that students in his graduate classes were unable to list the Ten Commandments.[18] Although some columnists at the time scoffed and took Kilpatrick to task, his observation strikes us today as rather unremarkable. Kilpatrick's findings are in keeping with those observed elsewhere. Reported in the December 1998 issue of *The American School Board Journal* were the following rather unflattering results of a nationwide poll among high-school-age and middle-school-age students:[19]

- 92 percent admitted having lied to their parents in the last twelve months
- 70 percent admitted having cheated on an exam
- 47 percent admitted having stolen something from a store
- 45 percent said they believe a person has to lie or cheat sometimes in order to succeed
- 36 percent said they would be willing to lie if it would help them get a good job
- 25 percent said they have stolen something from a friend

Surely, these students, upon arriving at college, would feel at home in Professor Kilpatrick's classes.

---

[18]William Kilpatrick, *Why Johnny Can't Tell Right from Wrong: Moral Illiteracy and the Case for Character Education* (New York: Simon & Schuster, 1992).

[19]Cited in "How Ethical Are Today's Kids?" *The American School Board Journal* 65 (December 1998): 18. The survey, "1998 Report Card on the Ethics of American Youth," was taken by the Josephson Institute of Ethics <www.josephsoninstitute.org>.

Kilpatrick went on to argue that the absence of a moral component in education has created dire social problems—a conclusion that also strikes us as uncontroversial. In truth, the United States, more than any other developed country, is paying dearly—and literally—for its social and behavioral problems: from costs incurred in the emergency rooms and intensive care units of hospitals, to the costs associated with the breakdown of the family, to the staggering costs of crime, to the escalating cost of medical insurance and health-care.[20]

In his 1995 encyclical *Evangelium Vitae* ("The Gospel of Life"), Pope John Paul II observed a profound confusion between good and evil resulting from the corruption of conscience that is taking place in our "culture of death"[21]— a culture that, in the view of some, is becoming "repaganized."[22] His comments, it should be noted, came *after* the extraordinary events in Eastern Europe that took place in the 1990s and were directed at those living in Western democracies:

> Today, when many countries have seen the fall of ideologies which bound politics to a totalitarian conception of the world—Marxism being the foremost of these—there is no less grave a danger that the fundamental rights of the human person will be denied and that the religious yearnings which arise in the heart of every human being will be absorbed once again into politics. This is the risk of an alliance between democracy and ethical relativism, which would remove any sure moral reference point from the political and social life, and on a deeper level make the acknowledgment of truth impossible.[23]

Was John Paul overstating the potential for "an alliance between democracy and ethical relativism"? The pontiff was reiterating what has been a common theme in his writings. He cautions that if there is no ultimate truth to guide

---

[20]In a 1991 op-ed piece published in the *Wall Street Journal*, Dr. Leroy L. Schwartz, president of Health Policy International, a nonprofit research organization, presented mind-boggling statistics reflecting the toll that moral illiteracy has had in the realm of health care alone. Schwartz argued that the U.S. must make the commitment to resolve our social problems *before* they become medical problems. See Schwartz, "The Medical Costs of America's Social Ills," *Wall Street Journal*, June 24, 1991, p. A23.

[21]John Paul has spoken frequently of our culture as a "culture of death." This may be applied in the more restricted sense of end-of-life issues but also in the broader sense of a culture that tends to dehumanize, and thus devalue, life in general.

[22]See, e.g., Schlossberg, *Idols for Destruction*, pp. 268-70; Michael Novak, "Awakening from Nihilism: The Templeton Prize Address," *First Things* 45 (August-September 1994): 18-22; and Benjamin D. Wiker, "The Repaganization of the West," *New Oxford Review*, May 1996, pp. 19-22. See also my observations in "Engaging the (Neo)Pagan Mind," *Trinity Journal* n.s. 16 (1995): 47-62.

[23]*Veritatis Splendor* ("The Splendor of Truth"), par. 101.

and direct the activity of a society, then ideas and convictions are easily manip-
ulated for the purposes of corrosive political power. In drawing this conclusion, John Paul seems to have in mind the lessons of recent history when he
reiterates that "a democracy without values readily turns into open or thinly
disguised totalitarianism."[24]

THE THERAPEUTIC MODEL

Ours has been described by one cultural critic as the "Age of Sentiments"[25]—an age that gives birth to "therapeutic culture" and a "sensate society." A society is sensate to the extent that its habits, its aims and its
technologies are aimed at increasing physical comforts while ignoring the
transfiguration of the soul and perennial transcendent values.[26] Implied in
the word *sentiment* are a person's private feelings, emotions and psychological state. The present generation, in expressing its convictions, will say
something like this: "We *feel* that human rights are being violated," or "We
feel that a particular situation is unfair," or "We *feel* that two plus two equals
four." Not infrequently I will tell my students in class, "I am not particularly
interested in what you *feel* at the moment; how you currently *feel* may be
the direct result of the pizza you ate late last night. I am more interested in
what you *think* and *believe*."

Such a distinction is all the more important as we live in and interact with
surrounding pagan culture, which fancies itself as postmodern. We encounter
people around us who reject the notion that certain things can be truly known,
that truth has a universal character about it and that language can effectively
convey meaning. Our dilemma is this: What if some people *feel* that two plus
two—whether in the *mathematical* realm or the *moral* realm—does *not* equal
four? Are all sentiments valid? Who or what should adjudicate between competing sentiments? What if particular odious sentiments—for example, bestiality,
mercy killing or artificial human breeding—become enshrined in public policy?

Such are the dilemmas facing those living in an Age of Sentiment. The
majority of people will believe what they *feel*, what their *appetites dictate*,

---

[24]Ibid.

[25]Russell Kirk, *Redeeming the Time*, ed. Jeffrey O. Nelson (Wilmington, Del.: Intercollegiate Studies Institute, 1996), p. 128.

[26]This is the definition offered by Pitirim Sorokin and Walter Lunden in *Power and Morality: Who Shall
Guard the Guardians?* (Boston: Porter Sargent, 1959), p. 118.

what they observe by way of *images and entertainment*.[27] An Age of Sentiment is emotive and will tend toward the irrational. This raises important
questions about education, about the development of moral character and
about what we will pass on to the next generation. More immediately, however, it raises questions about how we will handle deviant and socially unacceptable behavior.

In an important essay that appeared in the *American Scholar,* New York Senator Daniel Patrick Moynihan noted what is a truism among sociologists: deviant
behavior is like many social goods (at least in developed nations) whereby the
supply often exceeds the demand. Given the possibility that there can be too
much crime, circumstances may cause a society to choose *not to notice* behavior
that otherwise would be unaccepted, controlled or punished. Moynihan's thesis
was simply this: over the past thirty years deviant behavior in American society
"has increased beyond the levels the community can 'afford to recognize' "; accordingly, we have been "re-defining deviancy."[28] This means that behavior
which previously had been stigmatized was being exempted from sanction, thus
lowering the standard for what was considered "normal." This redefining, wrote
Moynihan, accounted for much of the so-called culture war that many social and
religious conservatives were lamenting. While the senator stopped short of suggesting anything remedial, his framing of this ethical phenomenon in terms of
"defining deviancy downward" is worth pondering.[29] It suggests that we are engaged in a curious form of cultural denial.

In describing a collapse of the distinction between the normal and the
pathological, Moynihan was reminding us of what sociologist Philip Rieff had
observed over three decades ago. In *The Triumph of the Therapeutic: Uses of
Faith After Freud,* Rieff examined evidences for what he called "the emergence

---

[27]Kirk, like Neil Postman (*Amusing Ourselves to Death: Public Discourse in the Age of Show Business* [New
York: Viking, 1985]), believes that the bombardment of visual images and stimuli to which Americans are regularly and indiscriminately exposed has the effect of curtailing reflection and dialogue—
sweeping critical thinking, critical engagement and, ultimately, public involvement in the great debates of the day into oblivion. See Kirk, *Redeeming the Time,* pp. 128-40.

[28]Daniel Patrick Moynihan, "Defining Deviancy Down," *The American Scholar* 62 (winter 1993): 18-19.

[29]Shortly after the publication of Moynihan's essay, syndicated columnist Charles Krauthammer, writing in *The New Republic,* extended Moynihan's thesis one step further. Krauthammer argued that to
redefine deviancy downward is also to *redefine normalcy upward.* Hence, not only does deviant behavior escape our sanction, but also what was previously honorable or praiseworthy is now held up
as dangerous, undesirable and needing to be vilified (an example of which would be the stereotypical
"Ozzie and Harriet" family arrangement of two generations ago). See Krauthammer, "Defining Deviancy Up," *The New Republic,* November 22, 1993, pp. 20-25.

of psychological man" in Western society.[30] Ours, he noted, was a "period of deconversion," characterized by "the dissolution of a unitary system of common beliefs." The dynamics and values emanating from a Christian culture were now becoming obsolete, with a notable shift occurring: religious leaders had given way to the psychologizers, who were now recognized as "the pacesetters of cultural change." In our quest to be free of "inherited morality" with its creedal mentality, writes Rieff, we needed a new center of "anti-religion." This new center is self-worship.[31]

At stake in this emerging therapeutic model was nothing other than a manipulation of the sense of well-being. This quest for personal well-being had become (note that Rieff was writing in the mid sixties) "the unreligion of the age."[32] It afforded modern humanity "culture without *cultus*." In contrast to the traditional mode of morality, informed by Christian religion and expressed through varying degrees of self-restraint and self-accountability, the new model was permissive, allowing the self to be indulged. Whereas the religious person was born to be saved, the psychological person is born to be pleased. *How one feels,* not *what one believes,* was now understood to be the spiritual and ethical guide.[33] The locus of moral authority began to shift from external, objective criteria to private, subjective experience.[34] As a result, the moral grammar of vice and virtue, of right and wrong, was being eclipsed by a grammar of psychological well-being that was self-referential. Given the central place in the universe reserved for autonomous self, it was only natural that "self-esteem" should replace traditionally accepted notions of moral character as society's "cardinal" virtue.

As the subtitle of Rieff's work indicates, it was left to post-Freudian thinkers to develop fully the implications of self-orientation, self-actualization, self-realization and, ultimately, self-worship. Whereas in previous eras socially unacceptable behavior was understood to be the fruit of deliberate choices made by morally responsible people, several generations of Freud's disciples have

---

[30]Philip Rieff, *The Triumph of the Therapeutic: Uses of Faith After Freud* (New York: Harper & Row, 1966), pp. vii, 25.

[31]Ibid., pp. 1-12.

[32]Ibid., p. 13.

[33]It was Rieff's conviction that "psychological man" was more native to American society than even the Puritan sources of early American culture might indicate, given the emphasis on individualism rather than community.

[34]More recently, Hunter has offered a penetrating critique of this shift in *Death of Character* (see n. 7 above); see esp. chap. 4 ("The Progressive Turn in Moral Education") and chap. 5 ("The Psychological Regime").

helped us to see that our deep-seated psychological needs and pathological behaviors (e.g., shoplifting, alcoholism, mugging, lying, incivility, smoking,
promiscuity,[35] obesity and drug abuse) are really "addictions"; that is, we are
compelled to behave the way we do *irrespective* of our inclinations.[36] Roman
Catholic psychologist Paul Vitz, in his classic work *Psychology as Religion: The
Cult of Self-Worship,* has done the Christian community a great service by
drawing out the implications of "psychological man" by examining the influence of several important post-Freudian therapists.[37] Four practitioners—Rol-
lo May, Erich Fromm, Abraham Maslow and Carl Rogers—are the focus of
Vitz's study, in which the reader finds a penetrating and witty critique of the
self-worshiping and narcissistic character of modern psychology. Vitz, a man
of strong faith, does not spare the Christian community either, since countless
Christians, in his view, worry more about losing their self-esteem than about
losing their souls. The worst sin of the church, according to Vitz, is that it has
allowed therapists to usurp the traditional role of the clergy in matters of mind
and soul. Americans, thus, have installed a "new priesthood."

  One can find ample evidence to confirm Vitz's thesis. One need only walk
into any bookstore and take note of recent best-sellers in order to see the grip
that therapeutic culture has on our way of thinking. These best-sellers have titles like *Codependent No More, Revolution from Within: A Book of Self-Esteem* and
I'm Dysfunctional, You're Dysfunctional. New support groups constitute the
ever-shifting "ecclesiastical" bedrock of this culture, and surely there is something out there for everyone: one might find a group for "children of bisexual
parents who smoke anonymously" and, of course, "children of adult children."

---

[35]While no one denies that there is a psychological element in sexual pleasure, what must be acknowledged is the degree to which idiosyncratic sexual experiences contribute to one's sexual predilections.
For homosexuals to insist that they are "programmed" to be attracted to persons of the same gender
is to acknowledge that they have no choice in their sexual partners, their sexual practices or the development of their sexual proclivities. The homosexual is thus caught in a web of inconsistency. "Bisexuality" presents a case in point, for it suggests that heterosexuality and homosexuality are choices
rather than compulsions, insofar as the individual *prefers* either homosexual or heterosexual relations, depending on the inclination.

[36]Indeed, the range of behavior now being deemed "addictive" or "compulsive" is growing exponen-
tially. In fact, it is encroaching on territory inhabited by deviant acts that heretofore have been considered heinous crimes—crimes such as child molestation, rape, sexually taboo behavior and torture.
A masterful commentary on contemporary American "addictions" is found in Jackson Toby, "Medicalizing Temptation," *The Public Interest* 130 (winter 1998): 64-78.

[37]Paul C. Vitz, *Psychology as Religion: The Cult of Self-Worship,* 2d ed. (Grand Rapids, Mich.: Eerdmans,
1995). This book was originally published in 1977.

It is not at all difficult to argue that American society desperately needs to re-cover from the recovery movement.

As we head into the twenty-first century, Americans have indeed discovered themselves to be one big (un)happy family of adult children. The broader cultural trend toward self-worship, with its attendant victimization syndrome, would be comical were it not shown to be a cancer that eats away at the moral foundations of civil society. And nowhere is this tragedy more on display than in the domain of law and criminal justice. Who can forget some of the "unfor-gettable," highly televised moments of the 1990s that invaded our lives? As a nation we were richly entertained by court jesters like Lorena Bobbitt ("Let the healing begin") and the brothers Menendez ("It was only a preemptive strike") as well as by athletes such as Tonya Harding and O. J. Simpson. The question of Harding's complicity in the mugging of fellow skater Nancy Kerrigan ("I know I let you down," Harding confessed to the American public, "but I've also let myself down") was front-page news and barely took a back seat to the episode involving former All-Pro football player O. J. Simpson. In retrospect, the "Free the Juice" campaign was extraordinarily successful, particularly after Simpson's heart-rending confession in his pseudo-suicide note (doubtless penned during his getaway on the Santa Monica Freeway), which read, "At times I've felt like a battered husband."

Receiving less coverage by news and media outlets, but just as telling, was the reemergence of double-felon Kathleen Powers. A fugitive of the law for twenty-three years, Powers surrendered September 15, 1993, after her lawyers had ar-ranged a plea bargain for her role as an accomplice in a September 1970 bank robbery and shooting of a policeman (and father of five) in Boston. Powers stunned the nation by turning herself over to the authorities with the announce-ment that "I have finally learned to forgive myself." By her account, she was a "victim of revolutionary idealism." Following the plea bargain arrangement, part of which prohibited Powers from telling her story for profit, she submitted a re-quest to the Supreme Court asking that the ban on writing for profit be lifted.[38]

If there is nothing to restrain oneself, then there is nothing to restrain the next person. "I feel," wrote Sigmund Freud, "that the irrational forces in man's nature are so strong that the rational forces have little chance of success against

---

[38]Frank J. Murray, "Powers Asks High Court to Let Her Profit from 1970 Crime," *Washington Times*, August 22, 1995, p. A6.

them." Thus, for human beings, one's neighbor is

> not only a potential helper and sexual object, but also someone who tempts them to satisfy their aggressiveness on him, to exploit his capacity for work without compensation, to use him sexually without his consent, to seize his possessions, to humiliate him, to cause him pain, to torture and kill him.

That Freudian and post-Freudian psychotherapy has altered society's moral mindset is hardly debatable. What is screaming for debate is whether Christian notions of morality have a place in culture as we presently understand it.[39]

Jonathan Imber, who teaches sociology at Wellesley College, has summarized the recent trend well: given the fact that American adults are increasingly encouraged to abdicate responsibility for their actions and delve into their childhood to find exculpation, American holocausts, we are now being told, begin in the home.[40] Indeed, every instance of pathological behavior that now becomes public, whether it involves people in high places or death-row felons, seems to be linked to an unfortunate childhood.[41]

Sadly, the same therapeutic zaniness to which we have grown accustomed in broader culture is every bit a part of church life as well. "Christian recovery" and "Christian self-help," as a perusal through any Christian bookstore will in-

---

[39]It is worth noting that social commentators of differing political persuasion agree that in the next fifteen years American society will be deluged with a wave of violent crime perpetrated by young "predatory" males, the likes of which we have not yet seen. This conviction is based statistically on the incidence of juvenile crime presently being committed in which offenders come from fatherless homes. See, e.g., Peter Yam, "Catching a Coming Crime Wave," Scientific American 274, no. 6 (1996): 40-44; and John J. DiIulio, "The Coming of the Super-Predators," The Weekly Standard, November 27, 1995, pp. 23-28. Although statistics from the U.S. Department of Justice (based on the National Crime Victimization Survey as of June 13, 2001) indicate that violent-crime rates have decreased since the mid 1990s—when the aforementioned predictions were made—this recent trend seems to correspond to several factors: increased visibility in policing urban neighborhoods, increased incarceration and tougher sentencing. Time will tell whether this is just a blip on the screen, postponing a forthcoming violent crime wave. See <www.ojp.usdoj.gov/bjs>. There is nothing to indicate that their prognosis is off-target.
[40]See Jonathan B. Imber, "American Therapies and Pieties," The American Enterprise 4, no. 3 (1993): 20.
[41]A corollary to the childhood-victimization syndrome is the attempt by some therapists to "locate" sins perpetrated by others in the past in a patient's memories. In fact, a debate in recent years has been raging—in courtrooms, in journals and in the popular press—about the validity of recovering memories from events that occurred long ago. Something of this debate can be seen in the literature, which contains such titles as Making Monsters: False Memories, Psychotherapy and Sexual Hysteria; The Myth of Repressed Memory: False Memories and Allegations of Sexual Abuse; and Victims of Memory: Incest Accusations and Shattered Lives. A good overview of this controversy is found in Daniel L. Schacter, "Memory Wars," Scientific American 272, no. 4 (1995): 135-39.

dicate, are *very* big business, particularly among evangelicals. Should one examine the contemporary preaching issuing from Protestant pulpits, one would find the spiritual and the psychotherapeutic, the transcendent and the pragmatic, walking curiously hand in hand. This phenomenon is what sociologist Marsha Witten has referred to as "the Janus face" of American Protestantism—one side bearing the visage of traditional piety, the other the face of secular psychology. While this split image may indicate that certain cherished core beliefs are still found among some American Protestants, it also reveals the extent to which Protestant churches have been penetrated by cultural forces such as privatization of belief, psychologizing of the faith and theological relativism.

The findings that Witten reports in her book *All Is Forgiven: The Secular Message in American Protestantism* are telling.[42] God is portrayed exclusively in terms of positive services that he renders to human beings. Especially emphasized in today's sermons are God's inner psychological state, empathy and feelings toward us. This is particularly dramatized by two recurring figures of speech— "God as daddy" and "God as psychological sufferer." In much Protestant preaching, God appears as an "extravagant lover." Contemporary Protestants prefer to think of God as "friend" rather than "Lord." All told, the author discovers a "softening" of God's demeanor in American Protestant thought, much in contrast to the awesome transcendence that characterized Protestant visions in the preaching of Reformers. Furthermore, God is thoroughly democratized, dispensing kindnesses and freedoms to humans with immense liberality.[43]

Witten also found that the notions of sin, suffering and human depravity are frequently mitigated in the pulpit by the language of humanistic psychology. Rarely was evil identified as a source of human problems. Tolerance, acceptance and cultural accommodation rather than cultural resistance typified

---

[42]Marsha Witten, *All Is Forgiven: The Secular Message in American Protestantism* (Princeton, N.J.: Princeton University Press, 1993). Witten's study, while not exhaustive, is highly illustrative. Witten has chosen approximately fifty sermons preached by Presbyterian Church (USA) and Southern Baptist pastors for content analysis. All the sermons are based on the same text: that of Luke 15 and the parable of the prodigal son. Witten's goal is to observe the degree to which these sermons, thought to be representative of American Protestant preaching, mirror contemporary theological commitments. She has limited her investigation to the two aforementioned denominations because, in her view, together they tell us much about American Protestantism's encounter with secular culture—in their differences and in their similarities. What makes her analysis refreshing is that she writes as an "outsider," i.e., as one who genuinely wishes to observe American religion from a stance that *suspends* rather than *denies* belief.

[43]See in this regard ibid., chap. 3, "God as Daddy, Sufferer, Lover and Judge."

most of the sermons analyzed. Correlatively, in many of the sermons conversion is transformed into self-discovery and self-fulfillment, so that the trajectory of most preaching is "psychological self" rather than moral self.[44]

The general picture that Witten paints of American Protestantism—inclusive of evangelicals—should give us pause. Like the former treasurer of the Episcopal Church in the United States, who embezzled $2.2 million and blamed her actions on a psychiatric "breakdown" caused by "workplace stress" and "the pain, abuse and powerlessness I have felt,"[45] no one bears moral responsibility any longer. In the end, even religion exists to serve the self-life. Left to itself, the psychotherapeutic model promises a glorious liberation from the nagging effects of free will and moral agency. It effectively contributes to the condition C. S. Lewis described as "the abolition of man."

The Biological Model

Curiously parallel to our culture's psychological excuse-making is the emergence of the biological model for explaining human behavior. In the ongoing debate over nature versus nurture, nature would currently seem to have the upper hand. Biology is destiny—at least, the scientific pendulum is swinging in that direction.[46] Given recent advances in genetic research (e.g., mapping the human genome, identifying criminals' DNA, and gene splicing[47]), the gene is becoming, if it has not already become, a cultural icon. This development can be measured by the gene's iconic status not only in scientific and

---

[44]See ibid., chap. 4, "Images of Christian Faith in the Contemporary World"; chap. 5, "Images and Mitigations of Sins"; and chap. 6, "The Transformed Self."

[45]Laurie Goodstein, "Episcopal Church Accuses Ex-Treasurer of Embezzling," *Washington Post*, May 2, 1995, p. A9, 10. The "victim" here, Ellen Cooke, had a reported salary at the time of her "bust" of $125,000 annually.

[46]The received wisdom of the behavioral sciences concerning the importance of genetics as opposed to environment in explaining human behavior has changed dramatically in the last two decades. In 1992, for example, the American Psychological Association identified genetics as one of several themes best representing the present and future of psychology. See R. Plomin and G. E. McClearn, eds., *Nature, Nurture and Psychology* (Washington, D.C.: American Psychological Association, 1993).

[47]Only a few years ago scientists would spend weeks searching the library for gene sequence and protein information. Thanks to the Internet, however, scientists presently can access innumerable databases of technical information on the structure, sequence and function of genes and proteins. See, e.g., M. Hendricks, "Presto! Genetic Sequencing Information at Your Fingertips," *Johns Hopkins Magazine*, September 1994, p. 33, and I. Peterson, "NSF Funds New Computing Partnerships," *Science News* 151 (April 5, 1997): 204. On new quantitative and molecular genetic techniques (which even as of this writing may be obsolete!) as they contribute to behavior correlation, see R. Plomin et al., "The Genetic Basis of Complex Human Behaviors," *Science* 264 (June 17, 1994): 1733-39.

medical journals but also in popular culture and political discourse as well.[48] One writer quips:

> The whole culture is metaphorically awash in genes, which are depicted as pervasive and powerful agents central to understanding both everyday behavior and the secret of life. Foraging through countless specialty periodicals and mass-culture sources, [one uncovers] references to selfish genes, pleasure-seeking genes, violence genes, gay genes, couch-potato genes, celebrity genes, depression genes. Everything but the kitchen sink gene.[49]

Increasingly diverse social critics maintain that we stand on the threshold of the "biological century." University of California at Irvine physicist Gregory Benford writes that beyond 2000, "the principal social, moral and economic issues will probably spring from biology's metaphors and approach, and from its cornucopia of technology."[50] Evidence already indicates that this prediction has come true.

What shall we make of the vaunted bio-genetic advances that are breaking upon us? What do they portend for theology and ethics? Can people be held morally responsible for their actions as we enter the "biological century"?

Ongoing progress in the biomedical field confronts contemporary society with inherent and perplexing ethical dilemmas—dilemmas that will need to be addressed against the backdrop of scientific materialism on the one hand and postmodern nihilism on the other hand, both of which engender their own form of moral skepticism. Increasingly, the gene offers an explanation for human behavior that is too readily appropriated, too seldom criticized and too frequently misused in the service of socially destructive ends. Ultimately, the gene is not *merely* a cultural metaphor; it holds sway over foundational assumptions that drive behavioral theorists, and these assumptions trickle down to influence common culture.[51]

The relationship between biology and free will—fully apart from recent advances in science—has long occupied moral philosophers. Are human beings

---

[48]See D. Nelkin and M. S. Lindee, *The DNA Mystique: The Gene as a Cultural Icon* (New York: W. H. Freeman, 1995), for a lucid commentary on this development.

[49]Jeff Reid, "The DNA-ing of America," *Utne Reader,* September-October 1995, pp. 26-27.

[50]Gregory Benford, "Biology 2001: Understanding Culture, Technology and Politics in 'The Biological Century,'" *Reason,* November 1995, p. 23.

[51]A healthy and much needed skepticism is found in Nelkin and Lindee, *DNA Mystique,* and E. F. Keller, *Refiguring Life: Metaphors of Twentieth Century Biology* (New York: Columbia University Press, 1995).

capable of moral reason and free choice, and thus responsible for their actions?[52] Is there a dimension of human existence that transcends the gene and biology, thereby allowing humans to define themselves morally and spiritually? Is human behavior *determined* by one's genetic makeup? Given the new genetic twist to the question of moral self-responsibility, author Renée Mirkes summarizes the issues that stand before us:

> According to chemical reductionism central to biological determinism, the causal laws of a tightly structured nexus of human biology—a nexus that is becoming ever more refined through the advances of human genetics—dictate human behavior. *It is illogical within this view of human behavior to require personal responsibility for the moral quality of one's actions; moral accountability makes sense only if actions [proceed] from a free agent.*[53]

This observation, already a decade old, remains intact and should give us pause. Given the present cultural climate, people cannot be held accountable for their actions. A significant consensus is growing around the biological model. It is a consensus to which social and behavioral scientists are coming as America loses it patience with the criminal justice system in its present form. Considered by most cultural critics as *the* issue of the nineties, crime will doubtless retain its position as a cultural factor in the years ahead.[54]

Forty years ago, in a small but important volume titled *Progress and Religion,* historian Christopher Dawson wrote tellingly about the contradiction of the secular mindset.[55] Dawson observed that the most enthusiastic supporters of the doctrine of human progress on the whole have been the people who are most impatient with the purported injustices of existing social institutions. At the end of twentieth century, this insight is finding validation in unsettling ways, particularly in the field of criminal justice.

Shortly after its publication in 1993, James Q. Wilson's *The Moral Sense* set

---

[52]If sexual orientation is biologically determined, then bisexuality would be rare to nonexistent; moreover, any change in one's sexual orientation, whether from homosexual to heterosexual or vice versa, would be even rarer yet. The fact that homosexual behavior is chosen is further illustrated in the AIDS epidemic, which from time to time has resulted in dramatic changes in sexual-behavior patterns simply due to the awareness that one risks contracting a fatal disease.

[53]Renée Mirkes, "Programmed by Our Genes?" *Ethics and Medics* 16, no. 6 (1991): 1, emphasis added.

[54]Only the economy and terrorism (a subset of crime) will receive greater attention. In a Gallup survey that was instituted fifty years ago and is taken every five years, crime topped the list public concerns in 1995 and was second only to ethics and morality in 1999. See "Ethics, Morality Tops Public's List of Concerns for First Time in Half-Century," *Emerging Trends* 21, no. 7 (1999): 1-2.

[55]Christopher Dawson, *Progress and Religion* (Garden City, N.Y.: Doubleday, 1960).

off a veritable firestorm of criticism among criminologists, social scientists and behavioral theorists. This strong reaction was not, however, due to Wilson's failure to interact with interpretive paradigms in philosophy, the social sciences and biology. Indeed, the book is an ambitious synthesis of philosophical, biological and social-scientific insight. Rather, its assumptions about morality appear to have caused the most controversy. Wilson, who is James Collins Professor of Management and Public Policy at the University of California at Los Angeles, takes the position that moral judgments begin with intuitions about what one *ought* to do (hence, "*the* moral sense," as the title has it). This thesis implies what for most academics is nothing short of scandalous: that human beings by nature arrive at moral judgments about any given act on the basis of innate moral sentiments and, in the end, are self-responsible.[56]

A good example of the strong reaction to Wilson was contained in the summer/fall 1994 issue of the journal *Criminal Justice Ethics,* which devoted its pages to a very spirited symposium on *The Moral Sense.* Invited to respond to Wilson were three philosophers, three anthropologists, two political scientists, a psychologist and two criminologists. The tone of the responses is indicative of how academics tend to respond to the notion that there is a normative standard for morality. Ironically, it was one of the criminologists who dissented most vigorously from Wilson's thesis of a universal "moral intuition." Perhaps sensing in Wilson a sympathetic note toward religious commitments that undergird moral intuition,[57] the criminologist objects by citing past missionary atrocities on indigenous peoples—an objection that constitutes the "hammer" in any skeptic's toolbox. Waxing critical of Wilson's unsympathetic critique of ritual cannibalism in some cultures, he observes that the consumption of human flesh also can be "a physical channel for communicating social value," since it "ties together one generation to the other by virtue of sharing certain substances" and can be regarded as "binding the living to the dead in perpetuity."[58] In the end, the criminologist sides with the tribal chieftain: "Christianity spoils our feasts."[59]

Charting trends in behavioral science, W. Wayt Gibbs reports in the March

---

[56]Wilson's argument is not without its problems, and I have noted these elsewhere.

[57]Wilson's is the language of a social scientist, and Wilson takes great pains to avoid writing from any sort of religious viewpoint.

[58]Gilbert Geis, "Moral Innatism, Connatural Ideas and Impuissance in Daily Affairs: James Q. Wilson's Acrobatic Dive into an Empty Pool," *Criminal Justice Ethics* 13, no. 2 (1994): 81.

[59]Ibid.

1995 issue of *Scientific American* on the optimism among a growing number of social theorists that science will identify markers of deviant behavior, which, within the decade, could revolutionize our criminal justice system.[60] One of those interviewed, psychologist and author Adrian Raine, believes that after nearly two decades of biological research on crime that the following scenario could be with us in the very near future: Given the accuracy of statistical measurements available, we will be able to predict with 80 percent certainty that someone's son will become seriously violent by the time he is a young adult. Therefore, as a society we are under obligation to offer a series of biological, social and cognitive intervention programs on his behalf. Stuart Yodofsky, chairman of the psychiatry department at Baylor College of Medicine, is one of those who welcomes this development. "We are now on the verge of a revolution in genetic medicine," Yodofsky notes. "The future will be to understand the genetics of aggressive disorders and to identify those who have greater tendencies to become violent. . . . We're going to be able to diagnose many people who are biologically brain-prone to violence."[61] Author Raine avows in his book *The Psychopathology of Crime* that "a future generation *will* reconceptualize nontrivial recidivistic crime as a disorder."[62]

A frightening eventuality presents itself. When the "disease" reaches a socially intolerable level, will "treatment" become compulsory, even for those who are innocent? C. Ray Jeffery, a criminologist at Florida State University, is assertive: "Science must tell us what individuals will or will not become criminals . . . and what law enforcement strategies will or will not work."[63]

Do Raine and Yodofsky represent an isolated minority in their conviction that crime will necessitate biomedical "answers"? Commentary by Jeffery suggests that this viewpoint is gaining wider acceptance. Jeffery has argued elsewhere that the traditional model of criminal justice, which is based on retribution, has failed to achieve its stated objective. Neuroscientific research, accordingly, suggests the propriety of turning to a biomedical approach to crime:

> What we call "free will" is the activities of the brain in controlling the somatic nervous system. . . . Since behavior is dependent on the serotonin levels of the

---

[60]W. Wayt Gibbs, "Seeking the Criminal Element," *Scientific American* 272, no. 3 (1995): 100-107.
[61]Quoted in ibid., p. 107.
[62]Adrian Raine, *The Psychopathology of Crime: Criminal Behavior as a Clinical Disorder* (San Diego: Academic Press, 1993), p. 319, emphasis in original.
[63]Quoted in Gibbs, "Seeking," p. 104.

brain, whether or not one is rational depends on the serotonin levels of the brain. . . . My moral self is thus defined by my serotonin level.[64]

Thus follows Jeffery's recommendation on dealing with crime: "We must shift the emphasis from punishment to treatment and prevention. Crime prevention must replace the police-courts-prison system."[65] Alas, on Jeffery's view, ethics reduces purely to biology and neuroscience. Murder? Well, blame it on the knife.

Writing over fifty years ago, C. S. Lewis fully expected that some day society would abolish punishment per se while at the same time viewing religion as neurotic. Both crime and religious conviction would be treated as a mental health disorder. Treatment, of course, would be "humanitarian" and therapeutic in nature. With the ascendancy of determinism and scientific technique in his own day, Lewis foresaw the eclipse of rationality and moral agency. Lewis was writing precisely at the time B. F. Skinner was trumpeting, "If man is free, then a technology of behavior is impossible. . . . I deny that freedom exists at all. I must deny it—or my program would be absurd."[66]

Moral acts, and their immoral counterpart, are inconceivable apart from freedom. Social or genetic determinism, dialectical materialism, astrology, evolutionism and, to a certain extent, fanatical Islam[67] all have one thing in common: in pleading that human actions are externally compelled, they facilitate a flight from ethical accountability in the temporal realm. In our own day, the sciences are only too glad to bolster this assumption.[68] But if science is being pressed to provide sociological and biological answers to pathological behavior, whence will come the *necessary moral constraints* that hold bad science— let alone criminal behavior—in check? And if crime is an inherently moral is-

---

[64]R. D. Masters and M. T. McGuire, eds., *The Neurotransmitter Revolution: Serotonin, Social Behavior and the Law* (Carbondale, Ill.: Southern Illinois University Press, 1994), p. 177. See also Masters's earlier work, which argues for biology as the key to criminal justice (R. D. Masters, ed., *The Sense of Justice: Biological Formulations of Law* [Newbury Park, Calif.: Sage, 1992]).

[65]Masters and McGuire, *Neurotransmitter Revolution*, p. 174.

[66]B. F. Skinner, *Walden Two* (New York: Macmillan, 1948), pp. 213, 242.

[67]What extremist Muslim theism shares in common with the aforementioned brands of nontheism in this sequence is its *disavowal of human moral accountability* (irrespective of its theological justification) based on its justification of *jihad* (literally, "submission" to the divine will), thus showing itself to be inhumane. See Roland Jacquard, *In the Name of Osama bin Laden: Global Terrorism and the bin Laden Brotherhood,* trans. G. Heloch (Durham, N.C.: Duke University Press, 2002); see also "Iran-Backed Group Warns Sharon 'Holy War' Is Forever," *World Tribune,* February 12, 2001 <www.worldtribune.com/worldtribune/Archive-2001/me-mideast-02-12.html>.

[68]Schlossberg is right to suggest that the most damaging legacy we can bequeath to the next generation is a moral relativism "clothed with suitable scientific coverings" (*Idols for Destruction,* p. 272).

sue, as even most nonreligious people intuit, then thoughtful Christians will need to recognize the moral imperative of *exposing the ethical assumptions* that undergird the practice of science. It is incumbent upon the Christian community, evangelicals included, to remind secular culture of the "first principles" of human moral agency and the attendant ramifications for all of society.

HOLDING CULTURE ACCOUNTABLE

Few episodes reflect more graphically the moral challenges facing contemporary culture and the Christian community than recent political developments in Washington, D.C. In November of 1998, more than 140 professors of religion and public life convened in Orlando, Florida, at the annual meeting of the American Academy of Religion—a venue that by no means takes a sympathetic view toward Christian orthodoxy. The meeting was called for the purpose of discussing and signing a "Declaration Concerning Religion, Ethics and the Crisis in the Clinton Presidency." Shortly thereafter, Eerdmans published *Judgment Day at the White House: A Critical Declaration Exploring Moral Issues and the Political Use and Abuse of Religion*, a volume that included the declaration as well as numerous essays by signatories to the declaration.[69] While the political affiliations of the signers differed immensely, all were united around the conviction that, ethically speaking, recent political developments surrounding the White House—specifically, the president's moral failings and the illegitimate use of public office—constitute something of a watershed in American culture.[70]

---

[69]Gabriel Fackre, ed., *Judgment Day at the White House: A Critical Declaration Exploring Moral Issues and the Political Use and Abuse of Religion* (Grand Rapids, Mich.: Eerdmans, 1999). Contributors include Jean Bethke Elshtain, Max Stackhouse, Stanley Hauerwas, Matthew Lamb, Don Browning, Robert Jewett, Gabriel Fackre, Klyne Snodgrass and Troy Martin. Also included were op-ed pieces by Stephen Carter, Andrew Sullivan and Shelby Steele, which had previously appeared in *The Wall Street Journal* and *The New Republic*.

[70]To the credit of the editor, six essays written by dissenters to the declaration were incorporated into the volume. What is unfortunate is that these contributions, despite the authors' good intentions, are riddled with muddled ethical thinking, at times bordering on sloppy sentimentalism. Tragically, the line of thought adopted by this group of essayists proves disastrous when translated into the realm of public policy. Remarkably, the dissenters are teachers of Christian ethics and moral philosophy. Many of the contributors to *Judgment Day*, it must be emphasized, confessed Democratic over Republican political affiliation; thus, there is no room for objection by critics that the declaration was mirroring "conservative Christian" or "religious right" sympathies. What is stunning, however, is that many who have objected to religious criticism of Bill Clinton were (and are) themselves vocal in their criticism of Richard Nixon, the only other impeachable president in the last century. Among those who contributed to *Judgment Day* but dissented from the declaration are ethicists Donald and Peggy Shriver, ethicist Glen Stassen and philosopher Nicholas Wolterstorff.

What precisely were the prevailing concerns of this diverse group of religious liberals and conservatives? Summarized below are the declaration's six points:

(1) Many of us worry about the political misuse of religion and religious symbols even as we endorse the public missions of our churches, synagogues, and mosques. We fear that the religious community is in danger of being called upon to provide authentication for a politically motivated and incomplete repentance that seeks to avert serious consequences for wrongful acts.[71]

(2) We challenge the widespread assumption that forgiveness relieves a person of further responsibility and serious consequences. A wronged party chooses forgiveness instead of revenge or antagonism, but this does not relieve the wrongdoer of consequences.

(3) We are aware that certain moral qualities are central to the survival of our political system, among which are truthfulness, integrity, respect for the law, respect for the dignity of others, adherence to the constitutional process, and a willingness to avoid the abuse of power. We reject the premise that violations of these ethical standards should be excused so long as a leader remains loyal to a particular political agenda and the nation is blessed by a strong economy. We are particularly troubled about the debasing of the language of public discourse with the aim of avoiding responsibility for one's actions.

(4) We are concerned about the impact on our children and on our students. We maintain that in general there is a reasonable threshold of behavior beneath which our public leaders should not fall, because the moral character of a people is more important than the tenure of a particular political or the protection of a particular political agenda. Political and religious history indicate that violations and misunderstandings of such moral issues may have grave consequences.

(5) We urge the society as a whole to take account of the ethical commitments necessary for a civil society and to seek the integrity of both public and private morality.

(6) We are all convinced that extended discussion about constitutional, ethical, and religious issues will be required.[72]

---

[71]Reference here in the declaration is to two events in particular: (*a*) a nationally televised speech by President Clinton in August 1998 in which he asks the American public to put the Monica Lewinsky ordeal behind them and allow the president to move on; and (*b*) a "Presidential Prayer Breakfast" the following month in which the president was seeking forgiveness and absolution from select religious spokespersons whom the White House had invited. For copies of both speeches, see Fackre, *Judgment Day,* apps. A and B.

[72]Ibid., pp. 1-3.

It is telling that the above declaration should emerge from a consensus of mainline Protestant and Catholic teachers of religion and ethics. While, to their credit, a number of evangelical scholars were among the signers, this initiative began with those who represent mainline religious affiliation. The declaration, together with the essays contained in *Judgment Day,* in no way allows itself to be misconstrued as a *political* statement.[73] Rather, it represents a consensus, however hidden from the general public or Capitol Hill, that people of Christian conviction must be willing to take a stand—even when it is not popular or when it evokes knee-jerk cries of political "partisanship"—in reminding society of *moral markers that may not be transgressed.*[74]

The task of confrontation and of raising moral markers, however, will be difficult for many. Our drive for social respectability, coupled with our unwillingness to resist conformity and be ostracized from the cultural mainstream, causes us to become particularly susceptible to cultural trends and the idolatries of the present age. Chief among American idolatries is the wish to be perceived as tolerant and nonjudgmental.

An Intolerable Tolerance

Along with its siblings "diversity" and "compassion,"[75] tolerance has achieved

---

[73]This thoughtful collection of essays addresses issues that are critical to the nation's moral and political life: e.g., the public-private dichotomy, the role of social covenants, the debasement of language and political discourse, public office and public trust, and the use of religion for political gain. Given its apolitical stance, this volume should be required reading for any ethics class and for all who are concerned for the viability of Christian social ethics. It raises questions that are of an enduring nature.

[74]My concern here is not with the legal-constitutional complexities of the presidential crisis, over which there has been disagreement and room for debate. Rather, the signatories raise critical questions that invite earnest reflection—questions that concern *the preservation of civil society* as we have known it and the proper place of religion. Furthermore, as Notre Dame law professor Douglas Kmiec has wisely cautioned, Christians should refrain from attempting to lay too much of the nation's cultural conflict at the feet of the Clintons, who are merely representative of tendencies that are decades old ("America's 'Culture War': The Sinister Denial of Virtue and the Decline of Natural Law," *Saint Louis University Public Law Review* 13, no. 1 [1993]: 183-205). Indeed, forty years ago Roman Catholic political philosopher John Courtney Murray raised the question as to whether American democracy and Catholic faith were in fact compatible (*We Hold These Truths: Catholic Reflections on the American Proposition* [New York: Sheed & Ward, 1960], pp. ix-x). His answer was affirmative *only* to the extent that the republic was capable of acknowledging transcendent norms by which to be governed.

[75]I am referring here to the prostituted use of "compassion" that denies or condones the reality or effects of evil or wrongdoing. For example, a flood of sympathy for AIDS victims, automatically employed as a wedge for the purposes of normalizing homosexuality, becomes the instrument for ignoring or deliberately concealing the moral, physical and psychological degradation associated with sodomy.

the status of being our culture's reigning virtue. In the words of one commentator, the commandment "Thou shalt not judge" supersedes all revealed commandments—even rationally discovered ones.[76] But how far tolerance? And how is tolerance best understood?

Originally, tolerance denoted a policy of forbearance in the presence of something disliked or disapproved. It was foremost a political virtue, demonstrated by a government's readiness to permit a variety of religious beliefs.[77] The notion that government should not enforce a specific religion comes to expression in John Locke's *Letter on Tolerance* (1688) and *Two Treatises of Government* (1690). Removed from its political context, however, tolerance ceases to be a virtue; indeed, it becomes a vice if it ceases to care for truth, ignores what is good and disdains the values that uphold a community. The culture of tolerance in which we presently find ourselves is one in which anything goes. It is a culture in which people believe nothing, possess no clear concept of right and wrong and, ultimately, are indifferent to this precarious state of affairs. The challenge facing people of faith is learning how to purify tolerance so that it remains a virtue, without succumbing to the centripetal forces of relativism.

Any discussion of the notion of tolerance must first presuppose a context of pluralism. While Protestant evangelicals have been inclined to see a red flag at the mention of the "P" word, they would benefit from a more nuanced understanding of what, perhaps, is taken for granted. Pluralism can be defined in two ways: On the one hand, it can simply signify the phenomenological reality of differing cultures, ethnic groups and traditions: that is, pluralism is a social and cultural fact of life. It is out of this form of pluralism that the American experience emerged; hence, our nation's motto *E pluribus unum* ("out of many, one").[78] Herein different communities, different identities and different ethnic traditions agree to coexist; they do so because of a commitment to an overarching common cause.

---

[76]Adam Wolfson, "What Remains of Toleration?" *The Public Interest* 134 (winter 1999): 40.

[77]In a recently published volume with the fascinating title *The Long Truce: How Toleration Made the World Safe for Power and Profit* (Dallas: Spence, 2001), A. J. Conyers has traced the modern history of this notion (see esp. chaps. 2-7) in an attempt to answer the question of whether tolerance can be considered a virtue. Conyer's answer is that it is not, strictly speaking, a virtue in the classical sense, though it is conceived of as a secular virtue. It is, rather, to be viewed as a "strategy" or policy that directs virtues such as patience, humility, moderation and prudence to a desired end. In the end, the goodness of tolerance is understood as depending entirely on the nature of the goods that it serves.

[78]Markham (*Plurality and Christian Ethics*, pp. 5-6) refers to this as "plurality," to be distinguished from religious or philosophical pluralism.

On the other hand, pluralism can operate under the spoken or unspoken assumption that among competing religious viewpoints or worldviews, none has (or is permitted to have) a privileged place as a framework for interpreting reality. On this view, all religious positions possess an essential unity, and all religious viewpoints stand on equal terms. Therefore, arguing for the authority and supremacy of Christianity, we are told, amounts to religious and cultural imperialism. But this stance flies in the face of Christian uniqueness, and by this argument a wedge is driven between God and his self-revelation in Jesus Christ.

Thus, it is crucial to distinguish between pluralism as a fact of life and pluralism as an ideology.[79] The term *tolerance* is normally found in association with both understandings. In the context of the former, tolerance is a genuine manifestation of virtue. Social or cultural pluralism is to be welcomed and praised; it is the soil in which the gospel exists and furthers itself.[80] At stake in this form of pluralism are negotiable issues: for example, language, cultural customs, ethnic habits and group preferences. In the context of the latter form, however, the Christian is in fact being asked to tolerate alternative explanations of reality, while at the same time being pressured to negotiate and abdicate claims to ultimate truth. American culture has shifted in its understanding of tolerance—a shift that calls for Christians' vigilance. It has devolved into an indifference toward truth, often belligerently and intolerably so; and the result is a permissiveness toward all manner of evil.[81]

Tolerance, it should be emphasized, has private as well as public or communal dimensions. While we may disagree with another's opinion, vice or lifestyle, we extend (in principle) that person's "right" to a specific opinion or behavior we find objectionable. Christians and non-Christians of *all* varieties tolerate one another's differences because of what they *all* share in common—the laws of nature. When, however, that person, in the name of tolerance, is making claims on the *public square,* tolerance must cease, for we tolerate what we dislike *until it begins making claims on the wider community in a way that undermines the common good.* Thus, the Christian is required to

[79]A helpful summary of this important distinction is found in McGrath, *Passion for Truth,* esp. chap. 5, "Evangelicalism and Religious Pluralism."

[80]Of all people, Christians in particular should treasure cultural pluralism, simply because of the enormous opportunities it affords us to bear witness to Christ's lordship.

[81]In this regard, I must agree with Markham that the greater threat today seems to come from the militant secularist, not religion (*Plurality and Christian Ethics,* p. 153).

draw a strict distinction between the freedoms of an individual, practiced in private, and the needs of the community, of which we all are contributing members. This distinction is not necessarily owing to Christian insight, for Locke himself makes the basic observation—an important one for contemporary Americans—that a great deal of difference can be tolerated *provided that it does not endanger social cohesion.*

Where exactly, then, do we draw the line? A well-worn bit of conventional wisdom among evangelical Christians is that we should "hate the sin while loving the sinner." Granted, there is some truth to this maxim. Nevertheless, as Lewis pointed out, this nice-sounding piece of piety can easily descend into sloppy sentimentalism. Lewis observes that to love the sinner in fact means that we feel toward him

> as we feel about ourselves—to wish that he were not bad, to hope that he may, in this world or another, be cured: in fact, to wish his good. That is what is meant in the Bible by loving him: wishing his good, not feeling fond of him nor saying he is nice when he is not.[82]

Lewis's advice appropriately parallels the Pauline admonition to speak the truth in love (Eph 4:15). Such moral honesty will refuse to compromise the moral consequences of ultimate reality, while simultaneously it is cognizant of the fact that fellow human beings are to be treated as bearers of the image of God. Love and truth are not mutually exclusive, despite the ethical propaganda that emanates from common culture. Those who would call us to "love the sinner" frequently *really* mean that we should *sympathize nonjudgmentally* with him. That is, we should refrain from stigmatizing and expressing disapproval. The person, then, will feel better. But as one writer quipped, this attitude only "makes the world safe for moral dereliction."[83]

Tolerance and compassion that are not rooted in moral principle end up corrupting both the practitioner *and* the object.[84] Elevating compassion to a cardinal virtue but disengaging it from the unbending realities of truth sends the signal to the unscrupulous that

> a good strategy for getting their way is to play on other people's pity, which is

---

[82]C. S. Lewis, *Mere Christianity* (New York: Macmillan, 1960), p. 108.

[83]John Attarian, "In Dispraise of Tolerance, Sensitivity and Compassion," *The Social Critic,* spring 1998, p. 16.

[84]These vices feed off of other virtues such as fairness, generosity and good will.

dreadfully destructive to character. It encourages malingering, self-pity, and claims of victimhood. It encourages not self-sufficiency, but dependence . . . ; not strength, but weakness; not honesty and integrity, but shameless and vicious exploitation of others; not cheerfulness in adversity, but whining; not acceptance of life's vicissitudes, but a readiness to find fault.[85]

As to precisely where Christians are to draw the line, the answer must be this: we must draw the line *where private preferences that undermine the communal good make claims in the public sphere.* Are Christians called to tolerate an individual whose sexual behavior differs from their own? Indeed. Are Christians called to tolerate the theoretical and practical promotion of that behavior in the form of social or public policy? By no means. Whereas sexuality is a private matter, education on human sexuality (at least through a public, tax-supported institution) ceases to be private; it is very much a public and communal concern.[86] Thus, whatever the cost and inconvenience, not only are Christians free to contend, they are *required* to do so *for the purposes of preserving social cohesion and the moral order.*[87]

This, of course, will lead to charges that we are "imposing" our morality on those around us. Christians are reminded ad nauseum by secularists that because we live in a pluralistic democracy, we are *forbidden* from such imposition. But are we?[88]

If morality is in truth a *private* matter as some contend, then critics of Christianity would be justified in excluding the voice of Christian ethics from the public square. But since the square is *public,* that means that all *may* contend; this includes especially evangelical Christians, who (at least traditionally) have prided themselves in their "missionary" vision and believe that there is a direct correlation between doctrine and ethics, between what one believes and how one lives. In the last two decades vigorous debate has transpired between professors of law, political scientists and philosophers over interlocking questions of justice, the public square and moral neutrality. The

---

[85]Ibid., p. 18.

[86]A brief but excellent overview of the limitations of tolerance within the communal context as well as the contours of Christian responsibility are found in Kent Weber, "How Far Is Tolerance a Virtue?" *re:generation quarterly* 2, no. 1 (1996): 29-31.

[87]Adopting *the appropriate language* with which to contend, however, is of vital importance. See esp. the discussion of *natural* in chap. five, "Retooling the Evangelical Mindset: Ethics and the Permanent," below.

[88]See also the section "On Imposing Morality" in chap. five, below.

strongest advocates of tolerance insist on the idea that the public square is morally neutral. But, of course, as we know, there is *no such thing* as neutrality, just as we know that those voices screaming the loudest for neutrality are not neutral themselves.

It is here that the aforementioned reflections on tolerance are critical. Tolerance as an authentic *virtue* is rooted in a commitment to what is true and good for society; correlatively, as a *vice* it is indifferent to these realities. Therefore, tolerance must not—indeed, it cannot—be neutral toward what affects society.[89]

What we are prepared to tolerate pivots on what is ultimate—in our personal lives and in the life of culture. There is something ultimate before which every person and, in the end, every society will bow. Modern and postmodern idolatries abound, but there is no escaping the fact that everyone has a hierarchy of values. What we tolerate is predicated on this hierarchy, atop which sits something ultimate. Social consensus is possible where there are overlapping realms of agreed-upon moral-social capital. Where there is no overlapping agreement, consensus is impossible, and anarchy is invited.[90]

By contending that there is *no such thing* as moral neutrality, we are also declaring that *someone's morality will be imposed*. Thus, the public nature of the marketplace (of both ideas and goods) as well as of social institutions, coupled with the very public nature of requisite Christian witness, compels us to work for the common good using any and all means, so long as democratic pluralism resists the centripetal slide into a soft form of totalitarian statism.[91] The hard truth is this:

> [A society] cannot function well, cannot survive, and cannot protect the innocent . . . from harm and evil, without a large measure of intolerance. Yes, intol-

---

[89]Properly understood, tolerance is a moral virtue that exists between two extremes: it avoids what J. Budziszewski has depicted as softheadedness on the one hand and narrowmindedness on the other—the former referring to the excess of indulgence, the latter bespeaking an inability to engage people ("The Illusion of Moral Neutrality," *First Things* 35 [August-September 1993]: 34).

[90]Hence, as James Davison Hunter and Budziszewski have attempted to demonstrate, the metaphor of "culture wars" is no mere metaphor; at stake is the clash of two competing, all-encompassing visions for humanity and society. See Hunter, *Culture Wars: The Struggle to Define America* (New York: Basic Books, 1990), and Budziszewski, *True Tolerance: Liberalism and the Necessity of Judgment* (New Brunswick, N.J.: Transaction Publishers, 1992).

[91]In response to the potential objection that a balance of power—namely, judicial, executive and legislative—excludes the possibility of political tyranny of various degrees in the U.S., I would simply pose the following question: what if all three branches of "democratic" government, mirroring the values of elitist culture, are (more or less) committed to a bleaching of the religious viewpoint and an eradication of Christian participation in the moral, legal and political process?

erance—of theft, burglary, cruelty, classroom hooliganism, disrespect for parental authority, and violent crime of all sorts; of substance abuse, infidelity, illegitimacy, perversion, pornography, rape, and child molestation; of fraud, envy, covetousness, and knavery; of sloth, mediocrity, incompetence, maleducation, improvidence, irresponsibility and fecklessness. A society tolerant of those things would soon find itself in serious trouble, even facing dissolution, and many people in that society would be in peril of their lives.[92]

Everyone has claims—most notably, Christians—on the public square. It is not, however, a "given" that everyone's claim will be tolerated.

REDISCOVERING THE WHEEL

Standing on the stage of the Bolshoi in Moscow several years ago, I pondered the fact that for the first time after forty-plus years, I had undergone—musically speaking—something of a "conversion." I have lingering, vivid childhood memories of my father turning on the radio every Saturday afternoon, with religious devotion, to listen to that scourge of any red-blooded teenager—the New York Metropolitan Opera. *How can he possibly stomach such music?* I would wonder to myself over and over until I left home for college, where my musical tastes proceeded straight to hell.

Now a guest in this magnificent Russian city, I suddenly became aware of my cultural nakedness—an awareness that from time to time forced me to fight off tears. How drastically my musical perceptions had changed over the years! And how utterly bankrupt was my prior appreciation for art and culture. Now, too, with three children of my own (all of whom quite naturally despise and mock opera), I find myself in my father's shoes. I had learned to embrace musically what for years I had loathed. Try as he might, my father could not foist upon me an appreciation for classical expressions such as opera. I had to come to the point of appreciation on my own.

And so it is with morality. Every generation must rediscover (though not reinvent) the wheel, ethically speaking. Not only must each succeeding generation lay hold of this moral trust, a trust that is generational and binding in character; but every generation is *held accountable* for its relationship to this trust. Historically, moral truth—and thus jurisprudence—has been understood as divine law: that is, as revelation working in concert with natural-law

---

[92]Attarian, "Dispraise of Tolerance," p. 22.

theory, moral law grasped through reason.[93] Forged in the heat of social, political and cultural challenges that have confronted generation after generation, this moral trust is an abiding treasure. While existing independently of particular cultures and eras, it must be rediscovered and appropriated by each new generation. When one generation or multiple generations fail to draw from this imperishable deposit, moral-cultural poverty ensues. This poverty, though not *necessarily* a sickness unto death, nevertheless by its cancerous nature compels the church to rethink its cultural mandate.

Where previous generations possessed a common moral grammar informed by religious beliefs (even when these beliefs were not consistently followed), the same no longer holds true. Indeed, the most telling aspect of late twentieth-century Western culture is that it denies the *possibility* of making moral judgments. In the present state of affairs it will no longer suffice, if it ever did, for people of faith who assume a moral universe and the benevolent rule of a Lawgiver or Judge merely to remind society that "the Bible says . . . ." Even when the biblical tradition remains authoritative through the ages, it must be accompanied by a moral apologetic that argues for the existence of a universal moral sense. Whence derives the tendency to make moral judgments in the first place? Can or should humans distinguish murder, incest, rape or sadomasochism in the human experience? Should any surpassing value be attached to human over against nonhuman life? If so, why? And wherein lies the rationale?

Upon his 1992 induction into the Academy of Moral and Political Sciences of the Institute of France, Joseph Cardinal Ratzinger noted the underpinning of morality that alone makes human liberty possible.[94] To illustrate this, Ratzinger contrasts the life-views of the late Andrei Sakharov, whose place in the academy he was taking, and the American philosopher Richard Rorty.[95] Underlying Sak-

---

[93]Natural law is discussed at greater length in chap. five, "Retooling the Evangelical Mindset: Ethics and the Permanent," below.

[94]Joseph Cardinal Ratzinger, "Without Morality Liberty Is Impossible," *Crisis* 11, no. 5 (1993): 36-38.

[95]Rorty—the grandson of social gospel advocate Walter Rauschenbusch and son of Trotskyites who had broken with the Communist Party in 1932—has argued with considerable fanfare that the ancient-to-modern European quest for cultural "foundations" (e.g., a belief in objectivity, reason, meaning and truth) is mistaken and needs to be replaced. For a declaration of his philosophical stance, see his *Contingency, Irony and Solidarity* (Cambridge: Cambridge University Press, 1989) and for a more personal reflection his "Trotsky and the Wild Orchids," in *Wild Orchids and Trotsky: Messages from American Universities*, ed. Mark Edmundson (New York: Penguin, 1993), pp. 33-46. Millard Erickson has offered a very thoughtful intellectual biography of Rorty that helps the reader make sense of Rorty's views and influence. See Erickson's *Truth or Consequences: The Promise and Perils of Postmodernism* (Downers Grove, Ill.: InterVarsity Press, 2001), pp. 150-66, 222-27.

harov's work as a scientist, notes Ratzinger, was the conviction that to deny moral principle—that is, to deny that organ of knowledge we call *conscience*—is to deny humanity. Obedience to conscience, says Ratzinger, even at the cost of suffering, is a message that loses nothing of its relevance even when the political context in which this message was forged no longer exists.

In stark contrast to Sakharov stands Rorty, who has formulated with considerable success and notoriety a "new utopia of banality." Commenting on the fall of socialist utopian thought worldwide, Ratzinger observes the rise in Western thinking of a "banal nihilism," epitomized by Rorty. While Sakharov demonstrates at considerable personal cost the link between science and morality, Rorty advocates a society in which fixed moral principles no longer exist. Sakharov's example, argues Ratzinger, cries out to us today. How can the free world assume and assert its moral responsibility? The conclusion, while escaping Rortians, is for Ratzinger unavoidable: freedom, in the end, can preserve its integrity only to the extent that it is tethered to an abiding moral foundation.

In the conclusion of his address, Ratzinger emphasizes that Sakharov's moral seriousness and Rorty's playful promiscuity together show us that we need to reconsider the century lying behind us as we calculate the century before us. The tragedy of the human experience is that human freedom, when detached from moral accountability, can empty and annihilate itself.

THE ETHICAL "LAST WORD"

Missing from most books on Christian ethics is any discussion of divine judgment and a biblically informed understanding of history. In an age that prides itself in being nonjudgmental, this absence may seem salutary. However, in truth, it may be a serious omission. Judgment is not merely the domain of systematic theology; it is the domain of ethics as well.

The category of history, of which judgment is an important part, is indispensable to a theology based on God's reconciling the world to himself through his Son. Christ's incarnation fulfills historical conditions and promises that are part of God's covenant with Israel, just as Christ's return fulfills the same to both Israel and the church. To the extent that redemption in Christ is taken seriously, history must be taken seriously, especially in an age such as ours, which is known for its dogged relativism. Christian theology rests on irreducible core truths, and these truths are mediated through history. This bottom-line confession can be seen in Paul's speech to the Council of the

Areopagus, as recorded in Acts 17:

> While God has overlooked the times of human ignorance, now he commands all people everywhere to repent, because he has fixed a day on which he will have the world judged in righteousness by a man whom he has appointed, and of this he has given assurance to all by raising him from the dead. (Acts 17:30-31)

Upon reading Luke's account of Paul's address to the council, one can well imagine the audience—among the most well-educated people of the day—moving at these words from courteous toleration to seething irritation. Most likely, the audience comprised Stoic pantheists who operated within a worldview that denied the notions of creation by divine fiat and divine judgment. Thus, when the apostle to the Gentiles announces a cataclysmic day of moral reckoning, he is not merely waxing rhetorical, nor is he stating parenthetically what was uncontroversial; rather, he is "going for the jugular," as it were. According to Paul, the same God who created the cosmos ex nihilo and maintains it (Acts 17:24-28) is also the moral arbiter of the cosmos, before whom all must give personal account. One detects in Paul's Areopagite speech a calculated apologetic logic, and doubtless a disconcerting logic at that.[96]

The Christian doctrine of judgment cuts at the heart of the sundry idolatries of our era—whether the modernist myths of inevitable progress and human perfection or the postmodern myth that nothing in history can really be known. Because history, as seen biblically, has a beginning and an end that are superintended by a sovereign God, everything occurring between these two points is infused with meaning and purpose. This awareness allows both the present and the future to assume new significance. A biblically informed view of history does justice to both the present and the future. That is, it finds meaning in our present existential reality while preserving the significance of eschatological realities. Any view of history that is dismissive of either the present or the eternal distorts the reality of the kingdom of God.[97]

Although life is filled with constant flux and change, Christians are armed

---

[96]Chapter six, "Biblical Resources for Ethics: The Pauline Model," below, is devoted to an examination of Paul's strategy in Athens.

[97]The withdrawal of Christian faith and ethics from world history invites greater appeal toward false utopian hopes. And to ignore the eschatological element is to deny Christ's resurrection and the reality of our future hope. For a balanced discussion of history and the kingdom of God, see Carl E. Braaten, "Eschatology and History," in *History and Hermeneutics,* vol. 2 of *New Directions in Theology Today,* ed. Carl E. Braaten (Philadelphia: Westminster Press, 1966), pp. 160-79.

with the knowledge that their ultimate frame of reference *does not change*. As Herbert Schlossberg has argued, this awareness provides a value against which all values are to be judged.

> Judgment carries with it a certain inevitability because it is a consequence of man's attempt to live in a way inconsistent with his own nature. Cholera is a judgment on dirty living, not because God arbitrarily favors clean people but because of the structure of that element of the universe.[98]

To affirm the notion of divine judgment is to affirm that events in history, even cataclysmic events, are invested with meaning. For the nihilist, catastrophe is meaningless, since justice and judgment (and much more so divine retribution) are purely illusory. It should be emphasized, however, that to maintain a belief that there is purpose in divine intervention is *not* to have particular insight into predicting the future, contrary to evangelicals' infatuation with "Bible prophecy." Nor does it care to speculate *the manner* in which divine action might occur. What it does affirm is that there is a connection between human actions and human accountability.

We have already observed the degree to which the Christian message has been attenuated by a therapeutic gospel that simultaneously softens God's demeanor and accommodates itself to secular culture. Clearly, the message of repentance and judgment is an unpopular one. It will very likely not cause people to feel good about themselves or enhance their self-esteem. And yet the church itself is no less accountable to the Judge of the Universe than unbelieving society is. Before the church can remind surrounding culture of normative standards for ethics and morality, it will need to acknowledge that judgment first begins with the household of God (1 Pet 4:17).

My own viewpoint is that we who live in a pagan, post-everything culture find particular affinities with those Christians living in a pagan pre-Christian culture, mirrored in the pages of the New Testament.[99] If the eyes of contemporary Christians are opened to a fuller appreciation—and application—of biblical revelation, resulting in a more robust Christian social ethic, then the present moment holds promise.

Part of the ethical task of being "resident aliens" (cf. 1 Pet 1:1) in any era is

---

[98]Schlossberg, *Idols for Destruction*, p. 294. See especially Schlossberg's discussion of history from the biblical vantage point in chap. 1, "Idols of History," of his book.

[99]See chap. six, "Biblical Resources for Ethics: The Pauline Model," below.

that the Christian community must defy and expose the idolatries of its particular age. The preceding discussion, by no means conclusive, has attempted to outline the contours of several idols that dominate our contemporary world. Like Israel of old, the church too is custodian to the prophetic message. This message is that humans are held morally accountable to a Creator-Lawgiver-Judge who intervenes in and supersedes human history.[100] To the extent that the church is faithful to that message, it retains a "prophetic" role in society. This will mean that the church will dissent and extract itself from trends, fads and developments within culture that deny or vitiate its message.[101] It will resist the tendency to be conformed to this world while maintaining an outlook that avoids the twin errors of de-Christianizing and re-Christianizing society.

The aforementioned task set before the church is doubly challenging as it applies to moral education. This is because the social institutions that historically have worked with the church in promoting moral education have been weakened and have all but lost their capacity to contribute. In addition, much of the church itself is held utterly captive to the culture. Hence, a fundamental and radically countercultural commitment to biblical ethics is urgent.[102] Indeed, nothing less will be able to confront and resist society's embrace of assisted death, genetic tampering, infanticide and related moral evils that, within the next decade, have the potential to strip our culture of its humanity.

I believe that evangelical faith and practice in America, despite its deficiencies, can thrive in the years ahead (which is *not* to state that it necessarily *will* or to suggest in what cultural climate this will transpire). Such can occur especially where evangelicals rediscover their debt to the classical Christian tradition they—alongside Roman Catholics and Orthodox—have inherited.[103] This demonstrable unity, which will *not* necessitate like ecclesiologies and the

---

[100]Compare again in this regard Acts 17:30-31.

[101]This is particularly true, given the combination of "a steady evacuation of a cultural habitus" and "the weakening of key socializing institutions" that Hunter points out (*Death of Character*, p. 225).

[102]In using the term *radical*, I do not have in mind the word's frequently *political* connotations, connotations that emanate from the left as well as from the right. Rather, I have in mind the truest sense of the term—the adjective form of the Latin *radix* (root): hence, "of or from the root," "going to the foundation or source," "basic" or "fundamental." The final chapter in this book, "Thinking with the Church," is intended to offer some ideas as to what it might mean for evangelicals (or those like-minded) to "return to foundations" and thus be "rooted."

[103]Evangelicals would profit immensely from reading D. H. Williams's *Retrieving the Tradition and Renewing Evangelicalism: A Primer for Suspicious Protestants* (Grand Rapids, Mich.: Eerdmans, 1999), a volume written for and to those who remain largely suspicious of—or indifferent to—church history and the place of tradition.

setting aside of theological controversy, will be important for the transmission of Christian truth to future generations and for a comprehensive cultural witness.[104] Furthermore, it will assist evangelicals in resisting the temptation to either withdraw from culture or be absorbed by it. This tension, living between withdrawal and absorption, is, of course, nothing new. As in the first century and as in the fifth century (a period that witnessed the dissolution of dominant culture), Christians must learn to navigate between isolationism and capitulation.

While learning from the past has not always been an evangelical strength, perhaps the evangelical legacy indeed has something to teach us.

---

[104]My own views on common-cause cooperation are spelled out in "Evangelicals and Catholics: One Year Later," *Pro Ecclesia* 5, no. 1 (1996): 73-90, and "Two Evangelical Manifestos," *re:generation quarterly* 7, no. 3 (2001): 37-39.

2

Ethics and the
Evangelical Legacy

E vangelical social conscience, to the surprise of some critics, has a rich history. Standards works such as J. W. Bready's *England: Before and After Wesley* and Timothy Smith's *Revivalism and Social Reform* chronicle the moral impetus of our more recent heritage.[1] A century ago church historian F. J. Foakes-Jackson could write:

> No branch indeed of the Western Church can be refused the honor of having assisted in the progress of human ideas[,] and non-Christians have participated largely in diffusing the modern spirit of kindness; but the credit for the inception of the movement belongs without doubt to that form of Protestantism which is distinguished by the importance it attaches to the doctrine of the Atonement. . . . The later Evangelicalism, which saw in the death of Christ the means of freed salvation for fallen humanity, caused its adherents to take the front rank as champions of the weak. . . . Prison reform, the prohibition of the slave trade, the abolition of slavery, the Factory Acts, the protection of children, the crusade against cruelty to animals are all the outcome of the great Evangelical Revival of the eighteenth century.[2]

---

[1]J. W. Bready, *England: Before and After Wesley* (London: Hodder & Stoughton, 1938), and Timothy Smith, *Revivalism and Social Reform* (Nashville: Abingdon, 1957).
[2]F. J. Foakes-Jackson, "Christ in the Church: The Testimony of History," in *Cambridge Theological Essays,* ed. H. B. Swete (New York: Macmillan, 1905), pp. 512-14.

Much has been written in recent years concerning evangelicalism's marginalized status in the early twentieth century.[3] While there is no intrinsic merit to being absorbed with the past, reflecting on this period nevertheless affords valuable lessons for contemporary evangelicals who wish to take seriously the implications of their cultural mandate. For better or worse, it is a fact that fundamentalist evangelicalism, responding to the incursion of modernism, in large part withdrew from the mainstream of American culture. Such is part of our not-too-distant legacy.

An opposite tendency, however, has afflicted evangelicalism at century's end. More recently, authors as diverse as Marsha Witten and David Wells[4] have attempted to show that contemporary American evangelicalism has generally been absorbed by culture and is reflecting the values of surrounding culture in ways that should give us pause.[5] In her examination of contemporary Protestant preaching, Witten, a sociologist of religion, observes a rather disconcerting pattern: Protestant theology, as evidenced from the pulpit, bears little resemblance to its historic counterpart. A "softening" of God's demeanor can be detected in Protestant thought-life; gone are the exalted, transcendent visions that characterized the preaching of Martin Luther, John Calvin, Jonathan Edwards and John Wesley. Equally conspicuous, in Witten's view, is the concomitant softening of sin.[6] More often than not, Protestant preaching is clothed in the language of therapeutic culture. Not sin and self-denial, but self-actualization represents the staple of the Protestant diet. To use the words of novelist Dorothy Sayers, we have "very efficiently pared the claws of the Lion of Judah . . . [and] certified him 'meek and mild.' "[7]

---

[3]See, e.g., George M. Marsden, *Fundamentalism and American Culture: The Shaping of Twentieth Century Evangelicalism, 1870-1925* (New York: Oxford University Press, 1980); Grant Wacker, "The Demise of Biblical Civilization," in *The Bible in America: Essays in Cultural History,* ed. Nathan O. Hatch and Mark A. Noll (New York: Oxford University Press, 1982), pp. 121-38; James Davison Hunter, *American Evangelicalism: Conservative Religion and the Quandary of Modernity* (New Brunswick, N.J.: Rutgers University Press, 1983); and R. Handy, *A Christian America,* 2nd ed. (New York: Macmillan, 1984).

[4]Marsha G. Witten, *All Is Forgiven: The Secular Message in American Protestantism* (Princeton, N.J.: Princeton University Press, 1993); David F. Wells, *No Place for Truth, or, Whatever Happened to Evangelical Theology?* (Grand Rapids, Mich.: Eerdmans, 1993). Wells's sequel to this volume, *God in the Wasteland* (Grand Rapids, Mich.: Eerdmans, 1994), continues to examine this glaring deficiency.

[5]Witten's analysis encompasses both evangelical and nonevangelical Protestants. The upshot of Witten's investigation is to show that Protestant theology, reflecting accommodation to culture, has "softened" considerably. The aim of Wells's study is to ask the question "Why do evangelicals produce so little theology?"

[6]What is remarkable about this observation is that Witten, a sociologist, claims no religious conviction personally.

[7]Dorothy L. Sayers, *Creed or Chaos?* (reprint; Manchester, N.H.: Sophia Institute Press, 1974), p. 6.

The conclusions are difficult to avoid. Twentieth-century evangelicalism has been inclined toward two equal and opposite errors. The fundamentalist legacy serves as a reminder that responsible cultural engagement must accompany confession of the fundamentals of the faith. Present-day evangelicalism, by contrast, has become absorbed by culture, being marked, most notably, by its psychologizing of the faith, its consumerist mentality[8] and its theological relativism.[9] As we continue into the twenty-first century, several questions are worth pondering. What is inherent in American evangelical thinking that tends toward either isolation or capitulation? Why have American evangelicals, past and present, produced so little in the way of advancing Christian social ethics? And, ultimately, how is this scarcity to be overcome?

THE "UNEASY CONSCIENCE" OF FUNDAMENTALISM

Reacting to a decades-long bifurcation in Protestant churches between liberalism and evangelicalism, Carl Henry published in 1947 something of a manifesto in which he called fellow evangelicals to a deeper commitment to demonstrating the relevance of their faith. Mainline Protestant churches, in Henry's view, had disengaged themselves from Christian orthodoxy and, responding to the existential needs of persons, displaced it with a predominately political program. Not unlike some of Jesus' day, who envisioned the kingdom of God as being ushered in by social-political directives, many evangelicals in Henry's time fell prey to the view that a transformation of earthly institutions signals a realizing of the kingdom of God on earth. And yet while rejecting this politicizing of the kingdom of God, Henry felt simultaneously constrained to decry the reactionary tendency among conservative Protestants to neglect the existential needs of society around them, even while they reaffirmed Christian orthodoxy. For Henry, evidence of an "uneasy conscience" among conservative Protestants, given their social neglect, was growing. The hour had come to demonstrate the credibility of one's convictions.

It was not the assault on central doctrines of the Christian faith that trou-

---

[8]By this I refer to two tendencies: picking and choosing what we want to believe as well as focusing on what will meet our personal "needs."

[9]See also Mark A. Noll, Cornelius Plantinga Jr. and David Wells, "Evangelical Theology Today," *Theology Today* 51, no. 4 (1995): 495-507, in which the authors argue that despite its dynamism and success at a popular level, modern American evangelicalism has largely failed in sustaining serious intellectual life, part of which accounts for the lack of strong evangelical theology.

bled Henry, since such resistance will always accompany genuine Christian discipleship. Rather, it was the concern that the church "needlessly invited criticism and even ridicule" by a tendency in some quarters to "parade secondary and sometimes even obscure aspects of our position as necessary."[10] In the end, worried Henry, Protestant fundamentalism was in danger of being reduced to "a tolerated cult status."[11]

Fundamentalists were quick to criticize modernist Protestants, but they did this without critically reflecting on their own problems. Chief among these, in Henry's view, was the fact that fundamentalism had no social impetus or agenda, in addition to its unwitting repudiation of practical ethical standards.[12] This moral-social absence, Henry warned, was nothing less than a "defection" by the evangelical church from culture. The practical and humanitarian aspect of Christian faith, sadly, had "evaporated."[13] This defection, moreover, was complicated, as Henry saw it, by prevalent eschatological views among Protestant conservatives. Premillennial thinking regarding the kingdom of God, which held no hope for change within society, had induced a pervasive mood of "prophetic despair," whereas Protestant liberalism was at least concerned to address the problems attending social evil.[14] Fundamentalists had shown themselves to be world-resisting, not world-changing; consequently, out of this mindset it was impossible for any contemporary version of Augustine's *City of God* to emerge.[15]

Fundamentalism's failure to "work out a positive message within its framework," coupled with its doom-and-gloom attitude toward world history, made evangelicalism, for all intents and purposes, socially irrelevant. In revolting against the social gospel that they decried, fundamentalists "seemed to revolt against the Christian social imperative" itself.[16] And, seemingly, any creative thought toward affecting a moral impulse was being done *solely by nonevangelicals.*[17]

---

[10]Carl F. H. Henry, *The Uneasy Conscience of Modern Fundamentalism* (Grand Rapids, Mich.: Eerdmans, 1947), p. ii.
[11]Ibid., p. i.
[12]Ibid., pp. 16-17, 22, 26.
[13]Ibid., p. 23.
[14]Ibid., p. 29.
[15]Ibid., p. 30.
[16]Ibid., p. 32.
[17]Ibid.

Most embarrassingly, for the first time in recent church history, evangelical Christianity stood "divorced from the great social reform movements," thereby ensuring the loss of apostolic authority.[18] For Henry, it was inexcusable that fundamentalism had failed to demonstrate the relevance of its redemptive message to the great moral problems in the twentieth century.

Evangelicals, ironically, had divorced themselves from Hebrew thought, of which they were heirs. In the Hebrew thought-world, metaphysics and ethics go hand in hand.[19] This symbiosis continues to be biblically normative, argued Henry; the ethical values and norms remain unchanged. In neither the Old Testament nor the New is the ethics of belief suspended.[20] John the Baptist remains as ethically alert as Moses; in fact, John prophesied that the Messiah would come, above all, *doing good works* (Mt 11:4-5).[21]

Henry was not about to deny the evangelical confession that the kingdom of God has a future component. *But what about the present?* What is the church to demonstrate *in the here and now?* Henry was painfully aware of a pharisaical spirit that could be detected in the evangelical community; while it might be doctrinally attuned, it was ethically unsound.[22]

Henry's critique of the "fundamentalist" tendency within evangelicalism was not merely negative, however. It was accompanied by the call for a positive agenda. Evangelicals were admonished *not to miss the present opportunity.* Specifically, the program for evangelical resurgence entailed two important academic changes. First, given their general lack of influence, Henry was convinced that evangelicals should be producing competent literature in all fields of academic study: hence, his call for broader and more sophisticated involvement in the academy. Second, at a more fundamental level, evangelicals were in need of *developing a robust Christian world- and lifeview*—what Henry called an "interim world program."[23] This program was understood to be all-inclusive (cf. Eph 1:10), willing to oppose moral evil and possessing the wherewithal to propose a higher ethical standard.[24] Henry correctly observed that Christian ethics not only is related to but *issues out of* Christian metaphysics.

---

[18]Ibid., p. 36.
[19]Ibid., p. 38.
[20]Ibid., p. 39.
[21]Ibid., pp. 40-41.
[22]Ibid., p. 63.
[23]Ibid., pp. 70-71, 76.
[24]Ibid., p. 76.

Unquestionably, this would mean for the evangelical community a rethinking of its relationship to the world. Within this vision, education, rather than being derided, would be prized, not distrusted as simply "other-worldly."[25]

Henry concluded his critique with the admonition that the great dilemmas we face are moral-spiritual in nature; thus, they demand a moral-spiritual response. Worldview and ethics cannot be divorced, and if evangelical churches would be willing to promote a gospel message that resulted in social influence, they would see the "dawn of a new reformation."[26]

How successful were Henry's efforts to reinvigorate evangelical thinking? Theologian Donald Bloesch has described the years between 1942 and 1956 as a "renaissance" of evangelical social concern.[27] Others have referred to this period as "watershed years" in evangelical conscience building.[28] During these years it was Henry, more than any individual, who led the way in helping to mold an evangelical moral conscience. His attempts to stir the "uneasy conscience" of fundamentalist evangelicalism bore precious fruit. It is significant that Henry's calls for reinvigorating evangelicalism were not merely calls to pious activity. Rather, they were calls to develop *a theoretical and technical basis for Christian ethics.* Appalled that evangelicals lacked the intellectual tools to formulate a worldview capable of influencing morality and intellectual thought, Henry also wrote during this time *Remaking the Modern Mind,* a critique of prevailing naturalistic assumptions.[29] In his view, Christians living with a ghetto mentality were ill-prepared to do intellectual combat and raise an alternative:

> Protestant Fundamentalism, although heir-apparent to the supernaturalist gospel of the Biblical and Reformation minds, is a stranger, in its predominant spirit, to the vigorous social interest of its ideological forbears. Modern Fundamentalism does not explicitly sketch the social implications of its message for the non-Christian world; it does not challenge the injustices of the totalitarianisms, the secularisms of modern education, the evils of racial hatred, the wrongs of current labor-management relations, the inadequate bases of international dealings.[30]

---

[25]Ibid., p. 72.

[26]Ibid., pp. 84-89.

[27]Donald G. Bloesch, *The Evangelical Renaissance* (Grand Rapids, Mich.: Eerdmans, 1973), pp. 26-37.

[28]Augustus Cerillo and Murray W. Dempster, "Carl F. H. Henry's Early Apologetic for an Evangelical Social Ethic, 1942-1956," *Journal of the Evangelical Theological Society* 34, no. 3 (1991): 365.

[29]Carl F. H. Henry, *Remaking the Modern Mind* (Grand Rapids, Mich.: Eerdmans, 1946).

[30]Henry, *Uneasy Conscience,* pp. 44-45.

Nothing less than re-entrance into the mainstream of American life and culture was acceptable if evangelicals were to take their calling seriously.

Significantly, it was Henry who legitimated the study of social ethics in some evangelical circles, although at the seminary level over the last two decades this emphasis, more often than not, has been eclipsed by a focus on counseling and church-growth concerns. Nevertheless, Henry's early moral-apologetic work had important long-term results and inspired two subsequent generations of evangelicals. It may well be that as we head into the twenty-first century, the uneasy conscience of evangelicals again needs stirring so that they might be capable of responding to the challenges of neopagan culture.

ON "PRACTICAL CHRISTIANITY"

A decline in civility and morality in England during the last half of the 1600s and the early 1700s is well attested both by public documents and private testimony. The tenor of lamentation by the churchmen who drafted the *Presentation of the Present State of Religion* in 1711 is illustrative: "We cannot without unspeakable grief reflect on that deluge of impiety and licentiousness which hath broken in upon us and overspread the face of this church and kingdom."[31] Writing in the year 1707, Isaac Watts confirms this sense of moral illiteracy amidst common culture:

> Though perhaps some particular sins were not so much talked of before, yet sinners of various kinds were much more numerous, more public and more shameless. The streets rung with oaths and blasphemy: the taverns were nightly witnesses of lust and drunkenness: open houses of abomination were maintained with many inhabitants, and the fields were polluted with lewdness in the very face of heaven in the sight of the sun or stars. . . . You may most effectually convince yourselves that crimes will grow numerous and shameless, if you forbear the prosecution.[32]

The most significant evil of this period, however, which would reach its apex at the end of the eighteenth century, seemed to find its most fertile soil in the British Empire, even though its roots predate England's greatness. It was an evil nonetheless that would meet its match in the form of fearless and persistent evangelical witness.

---

[31]Quoted in Gordon Rupp, *Religion in England 1688-1791* (Oxford: Clarendon, 1986), p. 295.
[32]*The Works of the Rev. Isaac Watts,* ed. E. Parsons, 7 vols. (Leeds: A. Hawes, n.d.), 1:626.

During the 1400s and corresponding with the Age of Discovery, the European powers began discovering the vast territory of Africa that lay past the Sahara. Over the next two centuries colonies stretching from North to South America, including the West Indies, would be settled. Abundant supplies of sugar, tobacco, precious metal and other exotic commodities from the New World presented opportunities for lucrative commerce. The chief problem, however, appeared to be a shortage of laborers in the burgeoning intercontinental trade—that is, until the Portuguese discovered something in Africa other than gold. With this discovery, the first cargo of black slaves was brought to Lisbon in 1440, signaling an economic development with which the Spanish and French would soon be aligned. From the mid 1600s onward the English expanded slave trade in accordance with mounting commercial and naval interests.

Born on August 24, 1759, in the English city of Hull, William Wilberforce was the third son of a wealthy merchant family. After his father died, William, who was nine years old, stayed with a childless aunt and uncle who, providentially, happened to be friends of evangelist George Whitefield. Significantly, it was also at this formative time that Wilberforce was exposed to the evangelical preaching of John Newton, the former slave trader. While this early spiritual influence would reap fruit in the years to come, the demands of being a member of the British aristocracy, at least at present, meant that religion was subservient to a "gentleman's" education.[33]

Wilberforce entered St. John's College, Cambridge, in the fall of 1776. Three years later he would graduate, as would future prime minister William Pitt, with whom he had cultivated a growing friendship. At the ripe age of twenty-one the ambitious Wilberforce embarked on a campaign for election to the British Parliament and, remarkably, beat all of his opponents. Equally remarkable is the fact that for the next forty-five years he would remain a member of Parliament without being unseated. Notes in his personal diary suggest his growing awareness of the very public nature of his vocational calling. And he was becoming keenly aware that Providence had a role in this. It is not insignificant that Wilberforce's tenure in Parliament coincided precisely with the period of time in which the most heated battles over the question of slave trading were fought.

[33]In particular, it appears to have been the newly emergent religion of Methodism that was offensive to his immediate family.

Quakers seem to have been the first group of Christians in England who concerned themselves with the problem of slavery.[34] Six Quaker abolitionists met in London in 1783 to consider what steps might be taken both for the discouragement of slave trade on the African coast as well as for the relief and liberation of slaves who had been transported to the West Indies. Wilberforce was to join in this two-pronged battle.

The first necessity was to attempt to stop the trade of slaves across the Atlantic, and it was to this goal that Wilberforce devoted himself tirelessly. Ultimately, abolitionists persisted in their efforts to outlaw plantation slavery within the British colonies, but achieving this ban would prove extremely difficult and would take many years to come to pass. For example, year after year, Wilberforce would deliver his annual denunciation of slave trading—and would do so eloquently[35]—while introducing yet another abolition bill in Parliament, only to watch it be voted down. Several factors contributed to this state of affairs. On one level, most English citizens were not aware of the harsh realities associated with slavery; and on another level, few possessed much interest in the far-away people of Africa. Even the colorful figure Newton, the slave-trader-turned-hymn-writer and son of a shipmaster who eventually sailed his own ship, demonstrates from his own correspondence that slave trading was widely regarded as a "respectable" vocation.

> During the time I was engaged in the slave trade, I never had the least scruple as to its lawfulness. I was upon the whole satisfied with it, as the appointment Providence had marked out for me. . . . It was, indeed, counted a genteel employment, and very usually very profitable. . . . However, I considered myself as a kind of gaoler [jailor] or turnkey, and I was sometimes shocked with an employment that was perpetually conversant with chains, bolts, and shackles. In this time I had often petitioned in my prayers that the Lord, in his own time, would be pleased to fix me in a more humane calling.[36]

---

[34]Quakers also appear to be the first in the American colonies who questioned slavery, and this happened around 1700, even when Quakers, as a group, also participated in slave trade in the triangle of New England, West Africa and the West Indies. See J. C. Furnas, *The Americans: A Social History of the United States 1587-1914* (New York: G. P. Putnam's Sons, 1969), p. 120.

[35]Wilberforce's abilities as an orator are no secret. According to Edmund Burke, considered the most eloquent British orator of the day, Wilberforce was unequaled in rhetorical skill. Burke's assessment of Wilberforce's rhetorical giftedness is cited by the editor of William Wilberforce, *The Enormity of the Slave-Trade and the Duty of Seeking Moral and Spiritual Elevation of the Colored Race,* ed. B. Hazlitt (New York: American Tract Society, n.d.), p. 6.

[36]*The Works of the Rev. John Newton,* ed. B. Martin, 4 vols. (London: J. Murray, 1839), 1:24-28.

Interestingly, Newton himself remained a trader for eight years following his conversion to Christ.[37]

But the fact that he remained a trader is too easy an explanation. The greater story doubtless lies in the economics of the slave trade coupled with the tragic reality that leaders in the church, many of whom well knew of slave trading, did nothing. Why the silence?

Consider alone the possibilities and margins of profit, put into perspective by historian Mark Galli:

> First, the slave trade was a profitable business. Liverpooler slavers, for instance, between 1783 and 1793, carried over 300,000 slaves to the West Indies, sold them for over 15,000,000 pounds, and pocketed a net profit of 30 percent. The productivity of the West Indies was on the line. "The impossibility of doing without slaves in the West Indies," wrote a London publicist in 1764, "will always prevent this traffic being dropped. The necessity, the absolute necessity, then, of carrying it on, must, since there is no other, be its excuse."[38]

Galli notes a second powerful factor contributing to the society's, and the church's, silence in the face of slavery: reasons of state. Were Britain to withdraw from this growing field, it stood the chance of placing its maritime strength in jeopardy. Moreover, if England were to interfere with the slave trade it could possibly arouse considerable resentment in the colonies, where economic interests were present as well. And it was further argued by some that populating the islands with slaves would keep colonists loyal to the mother country.[39]

Thus slave agents, colonial planters, naval officers, officers of state and politicians together formed a powerful vested interest.[40] The formidable degree of resistance to the abolitionist cause comes to expression in the testimony of Lord Nelson, admiral of the British navy, at a time when England was fighting for its life against Napoleon Bonaparte. Nelson wrote from his ship, the *Victory,* that neither abroad nor at home in the senate would the interests and "just

---

[37]Newton speaks, for example, of frequent hours of divine communion aboard ship on his trips to the African coast. See further testimony in *The Works of the Rev. John Newton,* ed. Richard Cecil, 6 vols. (Boston: Farrand & Mallory, 1810), 1:62-63, 75-86.

[38]Mark Galli, "A Profitable Little Business," *Church History* 53 (1997): 22.

[39]Ibid.

[40]Christopher D. Hancock has captured the force of this unrelenting resistance well in his assessment of Wilberforce's tireless efforts ("The 'Shrimp' Who Stopped Slavery," *Christian History* 53 [1997]: 12-19). See also Michael Craton, *Testing the Chains: Resistance to Slavery in the British West Indies* (Ithaca, N.Y.: Cornell University Press, 1982).

rights" of the West Indian sugar planters be infringed upon, as long as he possessed the will to defend or a voice to denounce what he considered the "damnable doctrine" of Wilberforce and his allies.[41]

Criticism of Wilberforce—a man of impeccable character—was by no means isolated, nor was it sparing. Even the distinguished biographer of Samuel Johnson, James Boswell, who is so generous in his praise of Johnson, characterized Wilberforce in a manner that drips with disdain:

> Go, Wilberforce, with narrow skull,
>   Go home and preach in Hull.
> No longer to the Senate cackle
>   In strains that suit the tabernacle.
> I hate your little wittling sneer,
>   Your pert and self-sufficient leer.
> Mischief to trade sits on your lip,
>   Insects will gnaw the noblest ship.
> Go, Wilberforce, be gone, for shame,
>   Thou dwarf with big, resounding name.[42]

Alas, the pathway to abolition was exceedingly difficult. Deeply entrenched political and economic vested interests presented themselves at every turn, so that it would be years before Wilberforce and a minority of Christian abolitionists would see any success to their efforts whatsoever.

Following his initial three-and-a-half-hour speech in Parliament on May 12, 1789, in which Wilberforce condemned slavery, he made a motion that it be abolished—a motion that was roundly defeated. His eloquent parliamentary speeches, followed by the defeat of his motion, became a regular pattern. And so it continued: defeats in Parliament in 1789, 1792, 1793, 1797, 1798, 1799, 1804 and 1805. To his immense credit, throughout the frustrating ordeal of continued resistance to his cause, Wilberforce seems to have remained every bit the gentleman. He never developed a martyr's complex, and he resisted any temptation to become shrill, bitter or fanatical.

And yet, amazingly, Wilberforce persisted. (Wilberforce would die literally hours before final passage of the emancipation bill that had been drafted by the House of Commons, which took place July 26, 1833.) No little credit for

---

[41]See Roger Norman Buckley, *Slaves in Red Coats* (New Haven: Yale University Press, 1979), p. 79 n. 64.
[42]Samuel Johnson, *Works*, 16 vols. (Troy, N.Y.: Heinemann, 1903), 7:202.

Wilberforce's perseverance must go to John Wesley, one of the few churchmen for whom social conscience and spiritual regeneration went hand in hand. While Wesley was not alone, he represented a distinct minority among the clergy of his day. It behooves the modern reader to consider the dramatic change that came over England during the half century of Wesley's preaching, including his influence on Wilberforce.[43]

For Wesley there was no cleavage between evangelical belief and ethical responsibility. Theology and ethics fit together as hand and glove: "A scheme to reconstruct society which ignores the redemption of the individual is unthinkable, and a doctrine to save sinning men, with no aim to transform them into crusaders against social sin, is equally unthinkable."[44] If a tree is judged by its fruit, Wesley has much to teach contemporary evangelicals.

For forty years Wesley's London headquarters was known as "the Foundry," an old abandoned iron-works mill where the king's royal cannon had been cast. The building, which had stood empty following an explosion years earlier, was leased by Wesley and repaired for use as a church, a medical clinic and dispensary, and a ministry to the poor. Adjacent to the Foundry was a house that Wesley used as a refuge for orphans and widows.

Although there is no indication that abolition was Wesley's central burden, given his evangelistic and "apostolic" commission, he nonetheless devoted considerable energy to the cause. In 1774 he published *Thoughts Upon Slavery*, which ran through three editions the first year.[45] In this tract, Wesley notes that with the rise of Christianity in the West, slavery as an institution had declined and become almost extinct, until the early 1500s brought the increase of navigation and the discovery of the Americas. Wesley traces the reemergence of slavery among the Portuguese and Spanish to its present manifestation in the British Empire. By Wesley's day, England was supplying approximately 100,000 slaves a year to America; of these, roughly 30,000 died either en route or once there.[46] Wesley decries the treatment of slaves and cries out for justice in the face of such barbaric cruelties toward those created in the

---

[43]In the view of historian Earle Cairns, English evangelicals accomplished more than any reform movement in history (*Christianity Through the Centuries: A History of the Christian Church,* rev. ed. [Grand Rapids, Mich.: Zondervan, 1996], pp. 398-402).
[44]John Wesley, *Christian Perfection,* ed. T. S. Kepler (New York: World, 1954), p. 120.
[45]John Wesley, *Thoughts Upon Slavery* (London: A. Hawes, 1774).
[46]Ibid., p. 22.

image of God; slave holding is incompatible with the justice and mercy of God.[47] One motive, and one motive alone, stands behind this wretched state of affairs: "trade, wealth and glory of our nation."[48] Wesley's response is that of a thundering prophet:

> Better no trade, than trade procured by villainy; It is far better to have no wealth, than to gain wealth, at the expense of Virtue. Better is honest Poverty, than all the Riches bought by the tears, and sweat, and blood of our fellow-creatures. . . . Is there a GOD? You know there is. Is He a Just GOD? Then there must be a state of Retribution: A state wherein the Just GOD will reward every man according to his works. Then what reward will He render to *You?* . . . Think now, *He shall have Judgment without mercy that shewed no mercy.*[49]

Thoughts concludes with Wesley's appeal to merchants to forsake exploitation for the sake of wealth and recognize that they have blood on their hands.[50]

Fittingly, Wesley's final correspondence, written February 24, 1791, on his deathbed, was to Wilberforce, encouraging the public warrior in what would be a long campaign against slavery. "Dear Sir," he wrote,

> Unless the divine power has raised you up to be as Athanasius *contra mundum* [against the world], I see not how you can go through your glorious enterprise in opposing that execrable villainy, which is the scandal of religion, of England, and of human nature. Unless God has raised you up for this very thing, you will be worn out by the opposition of men and devils. But if God be with you who can be against you? Are all of them together stronger than God? O be not weary in well-doing! Go on, in the name of God and in the power of His might, till even American slavery (the vilest that ever saw the sun) shall vanish away before it. . . . That He who has guided you from youth up may continue to strengthen you in this and all things is the prayer of, dear sir,
> Your affectionate servant.[51]

The cause of abolishing the slave trade and freeing slaves was not Wilberforce's sole concern, however. His second "great object" was to work for moral reform in English society, what he called a "reformation of manners." It was his conviction that Christianity calls on us "not merely in *general,* to be *religious*

---

[47]Ibid., pp. 22-31.
[48]Ibid., p. 38.
[49]Ibid., pp. 38-39, 46, emphasis in original.
[50]Ibid., pp. 47-51.
[51]Frederick C. Gill, ed., *Selected Letters of John Wesley* (New York: Philosophical Library, 1956), p. 237.

and *moral,* but *specially* to believe the doctrines, and imbibe the principles, and practice the precepts of Christ."[52] Wilberforce was convinced that the majority of orthodox Christians in his day suffered from a "scanty and erroneous system" of belief, a "poverty" of "superficial religion," a "defective scheme" that in truth was a contradiction of "real Christianity."[53] At bottom, wrote Wilberforce, "it signifies little what a man believes; *look to his practice.*"[54]

When one examines both the work and the writings of Wilberforce, several themes emerge which constitute the foundation of his ethical vision.[55] Chief among these are the absence of virtue in society, the decadence of the wealthy and the apathy of the clergy. Perhaps Wilberforce's greater contribution—even when overshadowed by the slave issue and, consequently, often overlooked—is that he made *private morality a matter of public concern.*[56] Wilberforce made common cause with other members of the Clapham Sect[57] (so named by later historians because of the district of London in which many of them lived), all of whom shared a robust commitment to a very *public and integrated* evangelical faith.[58] In point of fact, Christopher Hancock estimates that at one point in his life Wilberforce actively supported as many as sixty-nine philanthropic causes, noting that he

> gave away a fourth of his annual income to the poor. He also gave an annuity to Charles Wesley's widow from 1792 until her death in 1822. He fought the cause of "climbing boys" [chimney sweeps] and single mothers. He sought the welfare of soldiers, sailors and animals, and established Sunday schools and orphanages for "criminal poor children." His homes were havens for the marginalized and dispossessed.[59]

---

[52]William Wilberforce, *A Practical View of Christianity,* ed. Kevin C. Belmonte (Peabody, Mass.: Hendrickson, 1996), p. 6, emphasis in original.

[53]Ibid., pp. xxxi, 4.

[54]Ibid., p. 7.

[55]For a bibliography of Wilberforce's writings, see the editor's "Recommended Bibliography" in ibid.

[56]See Hancock, "The 'Shrimp,' " esp. pp. 17-19, for a very helpful summary of this accomplishment.

[57]Other notable members included Hannah More, Henry Thornton, Isaac Milner and John Venn. Claphamites were writers, politicians, bankers, diplomats and businessmen. Their efforts are thought to have been responsible for the establishment of the Church Missionary Society as well as the British and Foreign Bible Society, and the legalization of missionary outreach in India, fully apart from any successes in the abolition of slavery among British colonies.

[58]As the reputation of this small but influential group grew, one politician warned, "I would counsel my lords and bishops to keep their eyes upon that holy village" (quoted in Hancock, "The 'Shrimp,'" p. 18).

[59]Ibid., p. 17.

Among the various groups whose establishment could be traced to his influence were the Society for Bettering the Cause of the Poor (est. 1796), the Church Missionary Society (est. 1799), the Africa Institution (est. 1807) and the Anti-Slavery Society (est. 1823).

In 1787 Wilberforce founded the Society for the Reformation of Manners, which set out to work "for the encouragement of piety and virtue" and "for the preventing of vice, profaneness and immorality."[60] As a recent biographer of Wilberforce writes, "The reformation of manners grew into Victorian virtues and Wilberforce touched the world when he made goodness fashionable."[61] The theoretical basis for Wilberforce's Christian ethic is found in his book carrying the rather intimidating title *A Practical View of the Prevailing Religious System of Professed Christians, in the Higher and Middle Classes in This Country, Contrasted with Real Christianity,* published in 1797. Speaking of vice and virtue, Wilberforce finds it necessary to counter a prevailing notion regarding human nature:

> The bulk of professed Christians are used to speak of man as of a being, who naturally pure, and inclined to all virtue, is sometimes, almost involuntarily, drawn out of the right course, or is overpowered by the violence of temptation. Vice with them is rather an accidental and temporary, than a constitutional and habitual distemper.[62]

And yet in practice, Wilberforce observes, there is enough empirical evidence to demonstrate that human nature is naturally *tainted* and not pure:

> How is his reason clouded, his affections perverted, his conscience stupefied! How do anger, and envy, and hatred, and revenge, spring up in his wretched bosom! How is he a slave to the meanest of his appetites! What fatal propensities does he discover to evil! What inaptitude to good![63]

---

[60]This is the chief burden of Wilberforce, as indicated in the opening chapters (pp. 1-30) of *Practical View.* Significantly, the Christian alternative to social rehabilitation in Wilberforce's day was three-pronged: (1) instruction in Scripture accompanying (2) practical help that is undergirded by (3) education.

[61]John Pollock, *Wilberforce* (New York: St. Martin's, 1977), p. 43. Wilberforce belonged to the Anglican Low Church (as distinct from the High Church, which represented the political status quo), where abolitionist sentiment was to be found. In addition to Quakers, Baptists and independents also fostered resistance to slavery. Wilberforce's theological orientation has been described as "mildly Calvinistic" (Hancock, "The 'Shrimp,' " p. 18), while his spirituality and intellectual stimulation appear to be owing in large part to the writings of Richard Baxter, John Owen and Jonathan Edwards.

[62]Wilberforce, *Practical View,* p. 12.

[63]Ibid., p. 14.

Moreover, if human nature is essentially good, as is commonly argued, why is there so little progress in virtue? Why is it that "habits of vice grow up of themselves, while those of virtue, if to be obtained at all, are of slow and difficult formation"?[64] If human corruption is proved by the mode of reasoning, as Wilberforce skillfully maintains, then corruption is corroborated by the witness of divine revelation, as attested to by the Old and New Testaments: "The inclination of the human heart is evil from youth" (Gen 8:21); "The heart is devious above all else; it is perverse" (Jer 17:9); "The tongue is placed among our members as a world of iniquity" (Jas 3:6).[65]

Speaking to those who profess a religious commitment, Wilberforce is pained by a particular observation: in the church the "sanctifying operations of the Holy Spirit" are "too generally undervalued and slighted."[66] Some individuals are unabashedly carnal in their appetites; others do not avail themselves (for whatever reasons) of the divine grace that is theirs through Christ. Cultivating virtue, for Wilberforce, is no mere works-righteousness. The fruits of holiness in ours lives are "*the effects, not the cause,* of our being justified and reconciled."[67] This is precisely as Jesus taught and as James reiterates: a tree is to be known by its fruits. Wilberforce writes,

> True faith (in which repentance is . . . involved) is in Scripture regarded as the radical principle of holiness. If the root exist, the proper fruits will be brought forth. An attention to this consideration would have easily explained and reconciled those passes of St. Paul's and St. James' Epistles, which have furnished so much matter of argument and criticism. St. James, it may be observed, all along speaks of a man, not who has faith, but who says he has faith.[68]

While it is true that Wilberforce was vilified by many influential contemporaries (part of the cross he had to bear as a "public warrior" for the cause of morality), prominent persons of his day nonetheless praised him for his virtuous life and his remarkable achievements. Playwright Hannah More's opinion of Wilberforce was hardly restrained: "That young gentleman's character is one of the most extraor-

---

[64]Ibid., p. 16.

[65]Ibid., pp. 19-20.

[66]Ibid., p. 61.

[67]Ibid., p. 64, emphasis in original.

[68]Ibid., p. 73. Wilberforce is at pains to expose distorted views of the Christian ethic. See esp. ibid., chap. 4, "On the Prevailing Inadequate Conceptions Concerning the Nature and the Strictness of Practical Christianity."

dinary I have ever known for talent, virtue and piety."[69] Statesman Edmund Burke, who spent the final days of his life reading Wilberforce's *A Practical View of Christianity,*[70] confessed: "If I live, I shall thank Wilberforce for having sent such a book into the world."[71] Similarly, John Newton, whose former career was part of the mainstream Wilberforce was seeking to reform, praised Wilberforce for writing his book: "I deem it the most valuable and important publication of the present age. . . . I shall be glad to look to you . . . to strengthen my motives for running the uncertain remainder of my race with alacrity."[72]

It is not easy to measure the scope of Wilberforce's influence and accomplishments.[73] Largely forgotten,[74] this public warrior exercised influence in ways direct and indirect. His example beckons evangelicals who, living on the cusp of the third millennium, are confronted with enormous ethical challenges. Realizing that the social evils of his day could not be eradicated without simultaneously addressing public morality, Wilberforce along with fellow evangelicals adopted calculated and creative strategies of moral persuasion—strategies that can inspire two centuries later.

THE MORAL FUNCTION OF DOCTRINE

Figures such as John Wesley and William Wilberforce, two centuries removed, and, more recently, Carl Henry illustrate the fact that evangelical faith must be ethically sound to be viable. They also serve to remind us that theology and

---

[69]Hannah More, *1787 Thoughts on the Importance of the Manners of the Great,* 5th ed. (Worcester, England: Isaiah Thomas, 1797), p. 83. More concurs with Wilberforce: Christianity, she writes, is "a religion of *motives* and *principles*" (p. 13, emphasis in original). And like Wilberforce, she was concerned to expose what she called "fashionable character" of her day, "whose false brightness is still more pernicious" than the "destructive vices" it seeks to cover (p. 19).

[70]See the editor's preface of Wilberforce, *Practical View,* p. xiv.

[71]R. B. McDowell, ed., *The Correspondence of Edmund Burke,* 9 vols. (Chicago: University of Chicago Press, 1970), 9.100-09.

[72]Quoted in Robert Isaac Wilberforce and Samuel Wilberforce, *The Life of William Wilberforce,* 5 vols. (London: John Murray, 1838), 2:207.

[73]It is generally acknowledged by historians of the nineteenth century that *Practical View* played a role in the Second Great Awakening.

[74]Tragically, despite the hyperconsciousness of contemporary Americans toward race and race-related issues, Christian contributions to race from the past are all but ignored in both secular *and* religious discourse. Why are the contributions of people like John Wesley, William Wilberforce, Thomas Clarkson, Harriet Beecher Stowe and Harriet Tubman so conveniently (perhaps deliberately) forgotten? For a helpful reminder of Christian influence that stands behind the abolition of slavery and the slave trade on both sides of the Atlantic Ocean, see Vincent Carroll and David Shiflett, *Christianity on Trial: Arguments Against Anti-religious Bigotry* (San Francisco: Encounter, 2002), pp. 24-53.

ethics are indivisible. When we acknowledge this symbiosis, we are confronted with a certain unmistakable realism. Doing theology takes effort: it is work
and it entails personal struggle. In the same way, ethical formation is hard
work and no less of a struggle. But whatever their vocational calling in the
marketplace, evangelicals will need to rediscover the place of theology (assuming they rediscover a *will* to do theology), which in turn will equip them—
along with the next generation—to think and live ethically. A recovery of
Christian doctrine is foundational to the restoration of Christian ethics.

Christian doctrine is what sets Christian ethics apart from every competing
ethical system. It defines what is distinctive about our worldview and lifeview.[75]
To lose sight of the importance of doctrine is to lose the backbone of faith we
profess and to invite spurious alternatives. Alister McGrath has stated it well:

> Every movement that has ever competed for the loyalty of human beings has
> done so on the basis of a set of beliefs. Whether the movement is religious or
> political, philosophical or artistic, the same pattern emerges: A group of ideas,
> of beliefs, is affirmed to be in the first place true and in the second [place] im-
> portant. It is impossible to live life to its fullness and avoid encountering claims
> for our loyalty of one kind or another. Marxism, socialism, atheism—all alike
> demand that we consider their claims. . . . In order for anyone—Christian, athe-
> ist, Marxist, Muslim—to make informed moral decisions, it is necessary to have
> a set of values concerning human life. Those values are determined by beliefs,
> and those beliefs are stated as doctrines. Christian doctrine thus provides a fun-
> damental framework for Christian living.[76]

As one charts the development of university learning since the medieval period, one can detect that academic study of theology has tended to divorce the
theoretical from the practical. The effects of this separation, down to the
present day, have been by no means innocuous. It has robbed the Christian
church of one of its central tasks: namely, the formation of character.[77] Con-

---

[75]One work that does precisely this Oliver O'Donovan's *Resurrection and Moral Order: An Outline for Evangelical Ethics,* 2nd ed. (Grand Rapids, Mich.: Eerdmans, 1994).

[76]Alister E. McGrath, "Doctrine and Ethics," *Journal of the Evangelical Theological Society* 34, no. 2 (1991): 145-46.

[77]Protestant liberalism of the late nineteenth century up to the present day has believed it possible to embody a Christian social ethic while dismantling or rejecting its fundamental doctrines. Even in evangelical seminaries, the split between the dogmatic and the ethical can be seen in seminary cur-ricula: dogmatic and historical theology are done separately from practical theology, which is pastoral and ethical in its trajectory. For a fuller examination of this separation, see Ellen T. Charry, "The Moral Function of Doctrine," *Theology Today* 49, no. 1 (1992): 31-45.

sider the doctrine of divine providence, for example. Our awareness—however finite and imperfect—of God's providence, comfort and care opens up to us the moral dimensions of Christian doctrine. The ethical implications of God's sovereignty are enormous. Theology and ethics show themselves to be interrelated. They anchor the Christian in attitude and in behavior. In the end, they produce a quiet and humble confidence, a dependent yet responsible trust.

Responding to the religion of her day that advocated a faith bleached of doctrinal content, Dorothy Sayers was adamant. In her view, it is

> worse than useless for Christians to talk about the importance of Christian morality, unless they are prepared to take their stand upon the fundamentals of Christian theology. It is a lie to say that dogma does not matter; it matters enormously. It is fatal to let people suppose that Christianity is only a mode of feeling; it is virtually necessary to insist that it is first and foremost a rational explanation of the universe. It is hopeless to offer Christianity as a vaguely idealistic aspiration of a simple and consoling kind; it is, on the contrary, a hard, tough, exacting and complex doctrine, steeped in a drastic and uncompromising realism.[78]

At the risk of appearing melodramatic, Sayers offered a scathing rebuke of fellow Christians in her own day who had a distaste for doctrine and for whom pious feelings were enough. In her mind, what was at hand was nothing less than a battle of competing worldviews:

> We are waging a war of religion. Not a civil war between adherents of the same religion, but a life-and-death struggle between Christian and pagan. The Christians are, it must be confessed, not very good Christians . . . but the stark fact remains that Christendom and heathendom now stand face-to-face as they have not done in Europe since the days of Charlemagne. . . . People who say that this is a war of economics or of power politics, are only dabbling about on the surface of things; . . . at bottom it is a violent and reconcilable quarrel about the nature of God and the nature of man and the ultimate nature of the universe; it is a war of dogma.[79]

---

[78]Sayers, *Creed or Chaos?* p. 31.

[79]Ibid., p. 28. Sayers purposely used the term *dogma,* knowing how unpopular it was. "It is our own distrust of dogma," she noted, "that is handicapping us in the struggle." We may make the distinction between Christian dogma and dogmatic statements that Christians make. The former corresponds to the nonnegotiables of historic Christian orthodoxy, believed and confessed by all, everywhere and at all times. By the latter we mean our particular understanding or interpretation of Christian doctrine, an understanding that is always subject to change or modification. The distinction between these two is the subject of Avery Dulles's helpful book *The Survival of Dogma,* rev. ed. (New York: Crossroad, 1987).

Christian theology, as Sayers understood, is an attempt to describe the nature of reality, which in turns causes people to act in particular ways.[80] It is, in the words of McGrath, "An expression of a responsible and caring faith, a faith prepared to give an account of itself and to give careful consideration to its implications for the way we live."[81] Given the public deficiencies of Christianity in her own day, Sayers was not particularly optimistic about the church's witness and moral fiber. "Theologically, " she wrote, "this country [England] is at present in a state of utter chaos, established in the name of religious toleration, and rapidly degenerating into the flight from reason and the death of hope."[82]

Ethics depends on one's worldview, and one's worldview rests on doctrine. This interconnection is underscored by theologian Basil Mitchell:

> Any world-view which carries with it important implications for our understanding of man and his place in the universe would yield its own distinctive insights into the scope, character and content of morality. To answer the further question "What is the distinctive Christian ethic?" is inevitably to be involved to some extent in controversial questions of Christian doctrine.[83]

Without a theological foundation, the church is utterly incapable of explaining, much less presenting, the outlines of Christian ethics.

At a point when the foundations of secular approaches to ethics are in disarray, it is high time that evangelical Christians rediscover the central place that theology and doctrine occupy. Doctrine defines who or what is obeyed, while demarcating between the true and the false church. It exposes the reigning Zeitgeist of contemporary culture and the idolatries of the age, and it purifies the Christian community that inhabits any age. Finally, it frees us from various bondages produced by the world, while placing us in the bondservice of the One who created all things.

Yes, doctrine is a tool that unpacks the creeds, reminding us of what Christians everywhere and at all times have believed. But it is more. It is also a practical vehicle of *ethical transformation* by which God is at work in the believer's life.

---

[80]In chap. 4 of her classic *Creed or Chaos?* Sayers lists seven areas of doctrine that should be constitutive of every person's worldview: a doctrine of God, of sin, of judgment, of human nature, of ethics, of society and of work.

[81]McGrath, "Doctrine and Ethics," p. 150.

[82]Sayers, *Creed or Chaos?* p. 32.

[83]Basil Mitchell, *How to Play Theological Ping-Pong* (London: Hodder & Stoughton, 1990), p. 56, emphasis in original.

3

The Necessity of
Ethical Formation

—

For a believing Roman Catholic, arguing for the necessity of ethical formation is a very natural expression of a rich moral-philosophical tradition that extends through the centuries. Not surprisingly, over the last fifty years Roman
Catholics, more than any other religious group in America, have contributed
most substantively to ethics, public-policy discussions and the development of
a "public theology" that concerns itself with the intersection of faith and culture.
Protestant evangelicals, at least in recent decades, are relatively new to this territory. Although evangelicals reentered the political mainstream in the 1970s and
have exerted notable political force since then, they have been inclined to prefer
the short-term approaches to social-ethical issues (viz., the ballot box and stopgap legislation) rather than the more tedious, long-term approach to affecting
social consensus that requires contending for a moral impulse. In their recent
history, evangelicals have typically opted for *protest* over moral *persuasion*.

To understand this culturally reactive tendency, at least in part, is to be cognizant of its roots, which can be located in the fundamentalist legacy of the
early twentieth century (as noted in the preface and discussed at some length
in chapter two). But while the explanation for the absence of an evangelical
social ethic is partly social-cultural, it is also theological in nature. Evangelicals
pride themselves in tracing their history to the Reformation, which was essen-

tially a "protest" movement, with its central cries of "scripture alone," grace alone" and "faith alone." The primacy of faith and grace accented by the Reformers was meant to counter what was perceived as a works-oriented righteousness based on human merit. To this day, evangelicals become wary when they sense that justification by faith, the merit of the cross and divine grace are being compromised. (The choice before us, it should be emphasized, is *not* between Pelagianism and grace; it is rather between Pelagianism and *cheap grace*.) Nevertheless, the theological priority of faith and grace has had consequences for a reading of the New Testament. For example, on this reading the apostle Paul has pride of place while James tends to be relegated to secondary importance within the canon. This attitude, of course, is in keeping with that of Martin Luther himself, who laid the groundwork for what biblical theologians call a "canon within a canon." Luther's distrust of books such as James, Jude and 2 Peter was based on his conclusion that such letters were insufficiently "christological."

Indeed, Luther's offspring, whether in the seminary or from the pulpit, whether among professional theologians or among the laity, continue to transmit this potentially fatal assumption—fatal insofar as letters such as James, Peter and Jude (i.e., the General Epistles) mirror *the heart of the Christian ethical tradition*. In these letters, ethics and "pastoral theology" rather than theological formulation of doctrine per se are accentuated.[1] While the letter of James shares a common theological basis with Paul's writings, it emphasizes the *ethics* of Christian belief. Any reading of the New Testament that is careful to take into account *both* doctrinal *and* ethical emphases is able to guard against the error of faith without validating either faith without works or a legalism devoid of grace. The priority of ethics over doctrine in the General Epistles has important implications for the Christian community and contemporary evangelicals in particular (which is not to minimize the importance of doctrine).

Sadly, strictly on a textbook level, there is a curious absence of the General Epistles in discussions of New Testament ethics, with virtually *no mention* of 2 Peter and Jude, which, along with James, are wholly devoted to ethical admonition. For example, Richard Hays's impressive *The Moral Vision of the New*

---

[1]This particular contribution of the General Epistles to the New Testament is explored in J. Daryl Charles, "Interpreting the General Epistles," in *Interpreting the New Testament: Essays on Methods and Issues,* ed. David A. Black and David S. Dockery (Nashville: Broadman & Holman, 2001), pp. 433-56.

Testament contains no reference to 2 Peter or Jude.[2] Willi Marxsen's *New Testament Foundations for Christian Ethics* omits any reference to 2 Peter.[3] In Wolfgang Schrage's *The Ethics of the New Testament,* described by one New Testament scholar as "the finest recent treatment of ethics in the New Testament that I have read," seven lines at the conclusion of the section devoted to 1 Peter are given to Jude and 2 Peter together in passing.[4] Jack T. Sanders's *Ethics in the New Testament* devotes just over a page to Jude and 2 Peter.[5] Ceslas Spicq's imposing *Theologie morale du Nouveau Testament,* Rudolph Schnackenburg's *The Moral Teaching of the New Testament* and R. H. Marshall's *The Challenge of New Testament Ethics* all contain no discussion of ethics in 2 Peter and Jude.[6] Wayne Meeks's very popular study of the grammar of early Christian morals, *The Moral World of the First Christians,* also omits any reference to the two letters.[7] This conspicuous gap in New Testament ethics and biblical interpretation is a telling commentary on the lingering influence of Luther,[8] whose prioritizing of books in the New Testament has had the unfortunate consequence of separating ethics from theology and relegating ethical books of the New Testament to secondary status.[9] In some ways Luther's spiritual heirs have perpetuated—and deepened—the cleft between doctrine and ethics, thereby neglecting New Testament books that are incomparably rich resources for ethics.[10]

---

[2]Richard B. Hays, *The Moral Vision of the New Testament* (San Francisco: HarperSanFrancisco, 1996).

[3]Willi Marxsen, *New Testament Foundations for Christian Ethics,* trans. O. C. Dean Jr. (Minneapolis: Fortress, 1993).

[4]Wolfgang Schrage, *The Ethics of the New Testament,* trans. D. E. Green (Philadelphia: Fortress, 1988).

[5]Jack T. Sanders, *Ethics in the New Testament* (Philadelphia: Fortress, 1975).

[6]Ceslas Spicq, *Theologie morale du Nouveau Testament,* 2 vols. (Paris: Gabalda, 1970); Rudolph Schnackenburg, *The Moral Teaching of the New Testament,* trans. J. Holland Smith and W. J. O'Hara, 2 vols. (Freiburg: Herder, 1965); R. H. Marshall, *The Challenge of New Testament Ethics* (London: SPCK, 1947).

[7]Wayne A. Meeks, *The Moral World of the First Christians* (Philadelphia: Westminster Press, 1986).

[8]This is true and exceedingly unfortunate even when Luther's motivation was purportedly to find the "christological" elements in these letters. Francis Watson's volume *The Text and the World: Biblical Interpretation in Theological Perspective* (Grand Rapids, Mich.: Eerdmans, 1994), which astutely questions the hermeneutical assumptions of standard historical-critical exegetes (and their children), is a useful step in the right direction to "freeing" the church's interpretation of the biblical text (though, in my opinion, in prescribing a way out of the dilemma it does not go far enough).

[9]Two mammoth untranslated German volumes further illustrate this curious phenomenon: Helmut Merklein, ed., *Neues Testament und Ethik* (Stuttgart: Katholisches Bibelwek, 1989), and Siegfried Schulz, ed., *Neutestamentliche Ethik* (Zuerich: Theologisher Verlag, 1987). Out of a combined 1,251 pages of text, *six* are devoted to ethics in 2 Peter, all of which appear in the latter volume.

[10]This neglect is by no means confined to New Testament ethics. It characterizes virtually all commentary on the General Epistles.

ETHICS AND THE WISDOM PERSPECTIVE

The necessity of moral formation is not merely lodged within neglected pages of the New Testament. It is abundantly and creatively on display in the Wisdom literature of the Old Testament in books such as Proverbs, Ecclesiastes and Job. Such literary works are the embodiment of "wisdom" because they concern themselves in large part with wisdom *(hokma)* by which to live. Old Testament studies in this fertile domain have shown that Israel was not alone in the development of a wisdom perspective. Significant parallels are to be found in Mesopotamia, Egypt and other ancient Near Eastern cultures.[11]

Determining the setting of Wisdom literature is difficult, given the dearth of information about its origins, and therefore we must yield to speculation. However, it is commonly assumed that the handing down of wisdom perspectives was didactic in nature, occurring in the home and, perhaps secondarily, in some sort of school setting:

> For learning about wisdom and instruction,
>   for understanding words of insight,
> for gaining instruction in wise dealing,
>   righteousness, justice, and equity;
> to teach shrewdness to the simple, knowledge and prudence to the young.
> (Prov 1:2-4)

> Listen, my child, to your father's instruction,
>   and do not reject your mother's teaching. (Prov 1:8)

> Listen, children, to a father's instruction,
>   and be attentive, that you may gain insight. (Prov 4:1)

> Hear, my child, and accept my words. . . .
> I have taught you the way of wisdom;
>   I have led you in the paths of righteousness. (Prov 4:10-11)

> My child, keep my words,

---

[11]The literature on the background of wisdom texts is voluminous. See, e.g., Gerhard von Rad, *Wisdom in Israel,* trans. James D. Martin (Nashville: Abingdon, 1972); R. N. Whybray, *The Intellectual Tradition in the Old Testament,* BZAW 135 (Berlin: de Gruyter, 1974); Claus Westermann, *Roots of Wisdom: The Oldest Proverbs of Israel and Other Peoples,* trans. J. D. Charles (Louisville, Ky.: Westminster John Knox, 1995); and, more recently, William P. Brown, *Character in Crisis: A Fresh Approach to the Wisdom Literature of the Old Testament* (Grand Rapids, Mich.: Eerdmans, 1996). Westermann's volume even contains examples of wisdom literature from African and Sumatran cultures. Consider the comment found in 1 Kings 4:30: Solomon's wisdom was "surpassed the wisdom of all the people of the east, and all the wisdom of Egypt."

and store up my commandments with you;
Keep my commandments and live. . . .
Say to wisdom, "You are my sister,"
  and call insight your intimate friend. (Prov 7:1-2, 4)

A wise child makes a glad father,
  but a foolish child is a mother's grief. (Prov 10:1)

The frequent address *my son* would appear to be no mere stylistic or rhetorical flourish; rather, it suggests that education in wisdom is the duty of—and is transferred from—a parent to a child, as well as a mentor to a student. Thus, biblical wisdom calls parents, guardians and teachers to take responsibility for the moral training of their own. Foundational to the wisdom perspective is the need for moral restraint (i.e., "discipline"), which is imposed on oneself as a consequence of understanding and insight. It goes without saying that in the home, parents' responsibility for the moral education of children would have been a *high* priority.

Keep these words that I am commanding you today in your heart. Recite them to your children and talk about them when you are at home and when you are away, when you lie down and when you rise. Bind them as a sign on your hand, fix them as an emblem on your forehead, and write them on the doorposts of your house and on your gates. (Deut 6:6-9)

The proverb or parable is the primary unit of instruction by which ancient ethical wisdom is encapsulated and taught. Such sayings may be exhortations, commands, prohibitions or simple comparisons based on observation. It is a given that personal instruction in wisdom is the foundation for Israel as a society. Personal standards of conduct become the bedrock of the community; there is no public-private dichotomy. The role of wisdom in the Old Testament generally and in the corpus of Wisdom literature particularly is that it reveals an *approach to life.* Lady Wisdom offers a catalog of lessons and insights gleaned from observation about *human conduct* and, for this reason, is to be treasured.[12] Hence, wisdom can be seen as a foundation of ethics. This wisdom, moreover, is unfolded to the individual *in the process of education.*

UNVIRTUOUS REALITY

In chapter one, above, I argued that the cultural moment in which we presently

---

[12]Wisdom is personified, for example, in Prov 3:13-18; 4:5-9; 7:1—9:18. In Proverbs 7—9 (NIV) Lady Wisdom is contrasted with the seducing adulteress named Folly.

find ourselves is one of extreme moral passivity and illiteracy. Hence, the challenge that confronts the Christian community is to develop a moral apologetic in the face of radical skepticism and moral atrophy. Philosopher Christina Hoff Sommers, in noting the absence of private charity in American culture, worries that good deeds have been given over to the "experts." Acts that constitute the social morality of our time are increasingly being performed by paid professionals in large public agencies. "Helping the needy, the sick and the aged," as Sommers sees it, has become "an operation whose scale and character leave little room for the virtuous private person."[13] A question worth pondering, from a Christian standpoint, is this: Is the federalization of charity a result of the loss of private virtue in people's lives, or is the loss of private virtue—which manifests itself in good deeds—the result of the federalization of charity? Or has society's moral atrophy resulted in both simultaneously?

Is it excessive to claim that American society has become morally passive, illiterate or atrophied? Abundant evidence exists to suggest that this is no overstatement. Writer Shelby Steele joins in Sommers's critique of public morality by contending that our culture's political diversion of moral energies has given rise to a new kind of hypocrisy. It is now possible to think of ourselves as morally exemplary *if we adhere to an "enlightened" social agenda.*[14] Steele finds this mindset prevalent, and troublesome, among the many people who consider Bill Clinton to have been "a somewhat flawed human being but a good president." This kind of moral schizophrenia, according to Steele, seemed to blossom rather notoriously in the baby-boom generation, for whom political and social virtue were (and remain) more important factors than is private morality in defining a person's character. By this ethic, public virtue becomes a *substitute* for individual responsibility—so much so, observes Steele, that "personal irresponsibility may not threaten the essential 'goodness' of a person whose politics are 'progressive' and 'compassionate.' "[15] It is a baby-boomer mark of

---

[13]Christina Hoff Sommers, "Where Have All the Good Deeds Gone?" in *Perspectives on Ethics,* ed. Judith A. Boss (Mountain View, Calif: Mayfield, 1998), pp. 13-16.

[14]Shelby Steele, "Baby-Boom Virtue," *Wall Street Journal,* September 25, 1998, p. W11. Compare Sommers, "Where," pp. 655-56.

[15]Steele, "Baby Boom Virtue," p. W11. Steele illustrates graphically the problem with virtue-by-identification: when moral self-responsibility is separated from ethics and virtue itself, then it is possible to have a much-celebrated male feminist who also gropes and harasses women. His feminist credentials are intact, not because of his personal virtue and self-government but because of his prior open support of feminist policies: i.e., through his identification with the feminist agenda. To the extent that virtue is sustained through identification with particular social causes, policies become iconographic.

sophistication that the politically virtuous person is *in essence* virtuous.[16]

But Steele is quick to remind us, whatever his objections to Clintonian ethics and whatever the political orientation of the reader, that we could not have had a Clinton presidency *without the generational corruption* that allowed virtue to be achieved through mere identification with social-political causes. And when we consider ourselves innocent, in the words of Albert Camus, we give birth to evil. For at the heart of virtue-by-identification lies a betrayal of self-responsibility.

What Steele calls "virtue-by-identification" and Christina Sommers calls "ethics without virtue" has been attributed by some to the deterioration, if not the wholesale abandonment, of moral education. Consider standard educational approaches that are taken to ethics. For decades the prevailing—and ironically, the most dogmatic—approach to ethics has been the much-vaunted "values clarification." Values clarification purposes to empower individuals to recognize what they *personally* value. Clarifying responses are found in an environment where there are no "right" answers; feelings, attitudes and preferences guide the student in the proper process of arriving at decisions. Boston University educator Edwin Delattre has summarized the ethos of "clarifying values":

> No virtue is really a virtue, no vice a vice; no action is really wrong, none right; no human achievement is really important, no failure is of consequence. . . . No purpose is genuinely good, none really evil; having a purpose is no better than being without one; betrayal of purpose is not wrong except for people who happen to believe it is wrong. Courage is no better than cowardice, wisdom than foolishness, temperance than intemperance, justice than injustice. Generous understanding of other people is no more right than manipulating them to your own advantage.[17]

Thus, in the end students are unlikely to learn anything of virtue and vice as a result of formal education, and they are assuredly unable to distinguish between good and evil, since the categories of right and wrong collapse and disappear into personal preference.

In similar fashion, college ethics courses typically contain nothing in the way of cultivating virtues such as personal self-responsibility, decency, integrity or honesty. Correlatively, wholly absent is any discussion of personal

---

[16]For the generation of the 1960s, issues such as racism, sexism and militarism were identified as chief sources of national shame. Thus, identification with those who oppose these meant, and continues to guarantee, a virtuous persona.
[17]Edwin J. Delattre, *Education and the Public Trust: The Imperative for Common Purposes* (Washington, D.C.: Ethics and Public Policy Center, 1988), p. 78.

vice and the need for countering such.[18] Most prevalent in these courses is the format of debating opposing sides of controversial ethical and public-policy issues while encouraging "social justice." This preoccupation with social- and public-policy issues confirms Steele's observations about virtue-by-identification. Moreover, it gives students an entirely wrong notion about what constitutes ethics; it fully avoids the *private dimension,* out of which issues *public* morality. While advocates of this approach to ethics would contend that we will not have ethical people until we have ethical institutions, the Christian acknowledges that the reverse is true: there can be no ethical institutions in society if a people will not govern themselves as private citizens.

The ensuing deadening of the moral impulse in the private life is reflected in the frequent invocation "Who is to judge?" or "Who is to say?"—an invocation normally designed to serve as a conversation killer, especially when Judeo-Christian values are in the vicinity. But the question is not so much *who* will judge as it is *how* anyone should judge. Once it is determined how any of us might judge (i.e., by what principles and criteria we are to judge), the question of who is to judge recedes.[19] In truth, the end of the question is that *each and every one of us must judge,* regardless of our willingness to admit such. The goal of wisdom, then, is to help us apply moral principles that will guide us in determining how we are to judge.[20] Hence, radical and dogmatic relativism, such as we encounter in post-Christian culture, leaves members of society ill-prepared to think well *and* live well.

This moral state of affairs finds a perfect illustration in a 1999 speech by Princeton University President Harold Shapiro. The timing of the address was dramatic because Shapiro was speaking about moral education to an audience at Cornell University precisely during the time Princeton was offering an endowed chair to controversial ethicist Peter Singer, known for his position on animal rights and his advocacy of euthanasia and infanticide. The question raised by Shapiro was this: Can—and should—a university teach its students to be better citizens and better

---

[18]In point of fact, most standard ethics textbooks are devoted to one of two areas—examining various approaches to or "schools" of ethics (utilitarian, egoistic, relativistic, etc.) or debating opposing sides of contemporary ethical issues.

[19]This point is eloquently made by Delattre in *Education,* p. 79, and by social critic Hans Oberdieck, "Who Is to Judge?" *Ethics* 87, no. 1 (1976): 77.

[20]See the excellent discussion of this question found in Delattre, *Education,* pp. 78-80.

people?[21] In his address, Shapiro wrestled with the possibilities and outlines of moral education against the backdrop of liberal education as we have come to know it. Shapiro noted that three elements anchor liberal education:[22]

- the need to "provide an understanding of the great traditions of thought"
- the need to "free our minds from unexamined commitments and un-questioned allegiances"
- the need to "prepare us for an independent and responsible life of choice."

In further elaborating these points, Shapiro made the rather remarkable statement that these tenets are

> especially important in a world where we increasingly depend on individual re-sponsibility and internal control to replace . . . the rigid kinship rules, strict re-ligious precepts, and other aspects of totalitarian rule that have traditionally imposed order on societies.[23]

The suggestion that "kinship rules" are "rigid" and that "religious precepts" belong to the category of "totalitarian rule" is rather frightening. And yet it explains why a prestigious American university, with very little protest, can present an endowed chair to an ethicist who has argued at great length in favor of rights for animals while denying those same rights to the newborn and the dying.

In turning to the rather knotty subject of moral education in the university, Shapiro acknowledges that "in a pluralistic world there will always be questions about whose values should dominate."[24] Perhaps feeling a bit of heat as a result of Singer's invitation to join Princeton's faculty, Shapiro asks rhetori-cally, "How tolerant are we of others' views?"[25] His own answer to that question is as disappointing as it is predictable:

> Questions about the role of ethics in the curriculum itself produce great uneas-iness that stems mostly from a reluctance to establish any particular moral or-thodoxy. To put the matter simply, many faculty feel it is not appropriate for the institution to decide what ethic or whose ethics ought to be taught. In my judg-ment this concern is valid.[26]

---

[21]Harold T. Shapiro, "Liberal Education, Moral Education," *Princeton Alumni Weekly* (January 27, 1999): 16-21.
[22]Ibid., pp. 18-19.
[23]Ibid., p. 19.
[24]Ibid., p. 20.
[25]Ibid.
[26]Ibid., p. 21.

What is uppermost in Shapiro's thinking is that all viewpoints be tolerated (with the exception, that is, of the "traditional" and the "religious" viewpoints). The most valuable thing we can derive from this exchange, in Shapiro's view, is that "we can learn from our disagreements in these matters"; out of this, "a great deal is gained."[27] In the end, Shapiro can only conclude that it is "totalitarian" for moral education to wrestle with or define moral markers. The best advice he can offer is rather limp: "Universities are not necessarily the places to come [sic] for answers."[28]

Meanwhile, the fact of the matter is that like Shapiro, college students rarely cope with evil and moral atrocity. Any perils that might attend ethical relativism are hypothetical. In contrast to university presidents, however, criminals—even hardened criminals—have a sense of fixed moral norms. In one study done of adult male criminal offenders, over 75 percent responded that they would be disappointed if one of their children were to commit a crime. While these men might not be fathers who are *good,* curiously they did not wish for their children to be *bad.*[29]

VIRTUES OR VALUES?

Interest in virtue-based ethics has been on the rise in the academy.[30] This may signal, as ethicist Gilbert Meilaender believes, a widespread dissatisfaction with a focus on duty, ethical dilemmas and borderline cases.[31] Such notable interest can be acknowledged even when the standard fare for teaching ethics *remains* "applied" or "dilemma" ethics. In fact, most colleges and universities today offer courses in ethics, some of which are even very well attended. But the influence of such courses is at best dubious, since in the end students will learn that *all* of ethics is controversial: that is, *all* moral questions have at least two sides—argument and counterargument.[32] The result is the inculcation of a skepticism about the notions of right and wrong (i.e.,

---

[27]Ibid.

[28]Ibid.

[29]Donald J. West and David P. Farrington, *The Delinquent Way of Life* (London: Heinemann Educational, 1977), p. 114.

[30]In virtue-based ethics, *being,* rather than *doing,* is focal.

[31]Gilbert Meilaender, *The Theory and Practice of Virtue* (Notre Dame, Ind.: University of Notre Dame Press, 1984), pp. 4-5.

[32]Gilbert Meilaender contends that twentieth-century ethics is "largely a history of metaethical disputes," characterized by "the seeming endlessness and futility of moral argument" (ibid., p. 23). Unfortunately, a perusal of most textbooks in ethics—and course curricula—would appear to confirm his assessment.

ethics in the end is only a matter of *choice*) without a necessary *edificatory effect* on the student.[33]

Alasdair MacIntyre believes that this revived interest in virtue-based ethics is ultimately doomed to failure, since our society has ceased being civilized and moral.[34] Similarly, though less pessimistically, Meilaender notes a problem at the most fundamental level: "Who today wishes to be virtuous? Who today even uses the word?"[35] Indeed, people tend to be uncomfortable speaking about virtues. If Christians are to live as fugitives in an amoral and alien culture, we find it necessary to speak of ethics and morality in a manner that *will not offend*. We need a code word for virtue and morality. That word is *values*.

But what do we mean by "values"? Most people, at least in public, shy away from answering that question. James Q. Wilson captures the tentativeness with which Americans approach the subject. In Wilson's opinion, the word *values* finesses all the tough questions. For most people,

> [their] instinctive and commendable tolerance makes them shun any appearance of imposing their philosophical orientation or religious convictions upon others. But beneath that tolerance there lurks among many of us a worrisome uncertainty—some of us doubt that we have a defensible philosophy or credible conviction that we would want to impose.[36]

Values—for example, industry, sincerity, tolerance, being true to oneself—are fluid and allow themselves to be conceived (or reconceived) without any inherent moral content. Values will differ from person to person and thus are subject to individual choice. Street gangs, Nazis and religious people all have their own values. Because values differ with every individual, they tend to be linked to self-expression and individualism. Hoodlums, therefore, can have high "self-esteem" and "feel good about themselves."

It is quite predictable, then, that values trump the virtues of duty, deferred gratification, esteeming the needs of the community and sacrifice. "Virtue," by contrast, still implies something of its traditional meaning; that is to say, it suggests universal standards or norms by which an individual's character and be-

---

[33]Thus Christina Hoff Sommers, "Teaching the Virtues," *The Public Interest* 111 (spring 1993): 7.

[34]Alasdair MacIntyre, *After Virtue: A Study in Moral Theory* (Notre Dame, Ind.: University of Notre Dame Press, 1981), p. 245.

[35]Meilaender, *Theory and Practice,* p. 4.

[36]James Q. Wilson, *The Moral Sense* (New York: Free Press, 1993), p. xi.

havior are to be measured.[37] It is important to restore to the word *virtue* its original meaning, since, as Servais Pinckaers has pointed out, it has been impoverished and deformed as a result of obligation-based morality.[38] In one recent experiment involving major Florida newspapers that was designed to see how the word *virtuous* is used in popular culture, the results are worth noting. The word was used infrequently, and when it did occur it was frequently employed outside of its traditional context. For example, in the seven years between 1989 and 1995, the *Orlando Sentinel* used the word *virtuous* ninety-two times—slightly more than once a month. Between 1987 and 1995, the *St. Petersburg Times* used the word 140 times, which is between one and two times a month. In most cases, according to authors of this survey, *virtuous* was "merely a term used to describe a character in a movie . . . or book, or, sometimes, a person in an obituary—in other words, non-people and dead people."[39]

Surely, I do not exaggerate when I contend that our cultural inability—or unwillingness—to speak of virtue and to define moral categories has amputated our ethical thinking and our ethical discourse at the knees.

Genuine virtue, it should be observed, is to be distinguished from the freedom to do anything one wants, on the one hand, and from boring conformism or legalism, on the other. The autonomy and freedom to be virtuous is perhaps best understood by way of analogy. It is comparable to the talent of an artist or the excellence of a craftsman. Two individuals are free to sit and play a piano. One of them has studied and learned to play the instrument through many tedious hours of practice; she possesses the "freedom" to play with great ease and fluidity, for she has interiorized the principles of music and has acquired the skills necessary to play beautiful music. The other may be "free" to strike whatever keys he wishes, yet he cannot produce good music that is pleasing to the ear.[40]

And so it is with the cultivation of virtue. Virtues may be said to be good habits or well-rooted dispositions that allow one to do good deeds with a willingness, without constraint. While virtue *involves* precept, it is not learned merely by precept *alone;* rather, it is learned by repetition. Over time we are in-

---

[37]Meilaender makes a similar comparison of the terms *character* and *virtue* (*Theory and Practice,* p. 4).

[38]See Servais Pinckaers, "Conscience, Truth and Prudence," in *Crisis of Conscience,* ed. John M. Haas (New York: Crossroad, 1996), p. 85.

[39]Jeb Bush and Brian Yablonski, "Virtuous Reality: Character-Building in the Information Age," *Policy Review* 75 (January-February 1996): 55-56.

[40]Gregory D. Gaston has very effectively employed this sort of analogy in the realm of chastity. See his "Sex Education and the Virtues," *Ethics and Medics* 23, no. 1 (1998): 3.

clined toward right action, if we *persist* in doing what is right. This is the inner logic of Aristotle's understanding of virtue,[41] and it undergirds Jesus' teaching that faithfulness in small things leads to faithfulness in greater things (Lk 16:10; 19:17)—a logic that reveals the utter falsehood of the public-private dichotomy that so often characterizes contemporary discussion of ethics. The nature of virtue is that it is never reduced to being *merely* the ability to perform acts through external conformity. Contrary to what many people think, virtue is not simply refraining from doing certain acts that are deemed bad; that is, it is not a *repressive* attitude or negative reality. Virtue develops our natural inclinations toward truth and goodness;[42] it is the peace of mind that issues from a desired moral self-governance. Virtue does not presuppose or require religious faith. But it does "require the conviction of truth made sacred"[43]—a conviction rooted in the transcendent, enabling a person to ward off expedience.

In its classical understanding, virtue denotes the quality or ability to achieve certain desired effects: for example, courage, strength, resilience. A virtuous man, to classical writers, was a leader in the art of statecraft or on the battlefield. How one develops this mark of moral excellence was the subject of much philosophical debate.

Virtuousness has learned to assimilate principles by which good arises. One's motivation for choosing and one's decision to be virtuous spring from within; they are not externally imposed. Josef Pieper's definition of virtue captures this sense of internal rather than external motivation: virtues may be thought of as those attitudes of excellence that enable the individual to "attain the furthest potentialities of his nature."[44] In this way, virtues may be thought of as skills that are learned and that require constant practice, in line with the aforementioned analogy of learning to play a musical instrument. But with such a definition of virtue we do not have in mind the mere learning of a *technique:*

A skilled craftsman (just as rare these days as a virtuous person) has not just

---

[41]Aristotle writes, "Surely, knowing about excellence or virtue is not enough: we must try to possess it and use it" (*Ethica nichomachea* 10.9 [1179b]; Aristotle, *Nichomachean Ethics,* 3rd ed., trans. Martin Ostwald [New York: Macmillan, 1986], p. 295).

[42]Thus, Pinckaers, "Conscience," p. 85. Writers such as Richard Foster (*Celebration of Discipline* [San Francisco: Harper & Row, 1978]) and Dallas Willard (*The Spirit of the Disciplines* [New York: Harper & Row, 1988]) offer much-needed introductions to the classical moral and spiritual disciplines that for too long have been neglected by evangelicals.

[43]Thus James Davison Hunter, *The Death of Character: Moral Education in an Age Without Good or Evil* (New York: BasicBooks, 2000), p. 19.

[44]Josef Pieper, *The Four Cardinal Virtues* (Notre Dame, Ind.: University of Notre Dame Press, 1966), p. 22.

mastered a technique—he has acquired a skill which permits him to respond creatively to new situations or unanticipated difficulties. . . . His skill is not usually taught in a classroom but is learned by apprenticeship.[45]

Ultimately, virtues engage the will—thereby showing themselves to be *moral entities*—in a manner in which skills do not. Thus, not merely skills or techniques, virtues are perhaps best thought of as character traits: traits that equip us for life by defining the kind of person we are. And because we are ever "on the way" in a quest for perfection of our character, the virtuous life is not something that is *possessed* or attained.

Virtue-based morality, though it may appear to some to be a recent development, was predominant in most of the church's history. Its strength and endurance lie in the fact that Christian moral thinkers took Greek and Latin philosophy—beginning with the question of human desire and happiness, around which the four cardinal virtues (justice, prudence, fortitude and temperance) were ordered—and infused it with new meaning.[46] Christian integration profoundly transformed the notion of virtue insofar as it was not solely predicated on human willpower but on the grace of God. Inspired by the writings of Augustine, Thomas Aquinas gave the virtues perhaps their most elevated categorization.

Aquinas believed that the doctrine of virtue implies the idea of progressive *growth*—he distinguishes between people who are beginning, those who are proficient, and those who have "perfected."[47] Meilaender captures the notion of "becoming" quite adequately:

> When we shape and mold character we are not creating an artifact which is forever fixed. There can be no preconceived blueprint of what a person ought to be, no science of morals. To attempt virtue is to set out on a quest which lasts as long as life does.[48]

---

[45]Meilaender, *Theory and Practice*, p. 9.

[46]This is not to suggest that catalogs of virtues found in pagan and Christian writers were identical or compatible. Stoic conception of the virtues, for example, was that the virtues are all predicated on knowledge (*gnōsis*)—to know is to be virtuous—and they omitted the Christian distinctive of faith (*pistis*). (Where *pistis* is included in Stoic lists, it conveys the idea of friendship, not faith per se.) Christian thinkers, by contrast, assume the priority of faith and grace over against knowledge. On rival notions of the virtues, see the chapter "The Nature of the Virtues" in MacIntyre, *After Virtue*, pp. 168ff. On the contrast between Stoic and Christian approaches to virtue, see J. Daryl Charles, *Virtue Amidst Vice: The Catalog of Virtues in 2 Peter 1*, Journal for the Study of the New Testament Supplement Series 150 (Sheffield, U.K.: Sheffield Academic Press, 1997), pp. 99-119.

[47]Thomas Aquinas *Summa Theologica* 1-2.Q24.

[48]Meilaender, *Theory and Practice*, p. 7.

The virtues, moreover, are understood by Aquinas to be interconnected, regardless of their number, diversity or classification; this interdependence, in his view, is guaranteed by charity.[49] Building on Aquinas's understanding of organic unity, Pinckaers uses the anatomical metaphor to emphasize that, regardless of their number and diversity, all the virtues constitute a whole, much the same as many members and organs constitute the human body;[50] they do not act in isolation. This seems to concur with the logic of virtue in 2 Peter 1, where a catalog of virtues finds faith as the basis and charity (love) the goal. That the virtues—for example, knowledge, reverence, endurance—are distinct does not mean that they are divorced from one another.[51] If Aquinas (along with those following his line of thinking) is correct about love's guaranteeing the integrity and unity of the virtues, then virtue, properly understood, avoids the dangers of self-preoccupation and self-absorption that are so characteristic of our narcissistic age, for by its very definition virtue is not self-centered in its motivation.[52] One cannot be ordered by truth in some areas of one's life while ignoring or rejecting truth in others. Jesus' maxim concerning the heart rings true in this regard: a tree is known by its fruit.[53]

But does it really matter whether the virtues constitute a unity? While the age-old question of the virtues' organic unity may seem academic, it has practical implications. There is a tendency to compartmentalize human existence.[54] This pattern, to be sure, is not found only in the secular mind. In

---

[49]Aquinas *Summa Theologica* 1-2.Q65.

[50]Pinckaers, "Conscience," p. 86.

[51]See chap. six, below, which examines the catalog of virtues employed in 2 Peter 1.

[52]Meilaender helpfully distinguishes between genuine virtue and monastic preoccupation with the "disciplined" life. Meilaender observes that the *task* might readily be substituted for the *goal,* whereby the ascetic could easily become more concerned with his relation to the discipline than to the end for which discipline exists. Therefore, an ethic of virtue will necessarily "find its place within some larger pattern of faith" that resists the temptation to see the virtues as human achievements (*Theory and Practice,* pp. 15-16).

[53]The fruit-bearing metaphor is also used by Paul. His allusion to the "fruit of the Spirit" (Gal 5:22-23) implicitly suggests that these virtues are not isolated; they grow together and are indivisible. Here it should be stated that I am assuming continuity between natural virtues (such as courage, loyalty, justice and courtesy) and the theological virtues. Love, hope and faith—entities rooted in the grace of God—simply go beyond the natural virtues; the former presuppose, while perfecting, the latter. The ultimate reality toward which we as creatures are open, as Meilaender reminds us, is directed toward God, *whether or not we know it* (*Theory and Practice,* p. 34). Hence, we find Scripture using the language of *death and dying* to describe the process of spiritual conversion. To come to the realization, and the confession, that *we cannot become what God intends apart from grace* entails no less than a dying to self.

[54]Fragmentation is one of the disordering effects of sin.

fact, evangelicals who have not worked out the implications and consequences of their worldview are notorious for privatizing faith and compart-
mentalizing their lives.[55] (In fact, it can be argued that Christian churches in
general are not well placed or predisposed to help bring about a revival of
interest in the concept of virtue. Even current graduates of seminaries, at
least seminaries of the Protestant variety, would appear to be ill-equipped to
discuss the merits of a virtuous life, or individual virtues, with any sort of
theological or philosophical insight.) The net result of this sort of thinking
is fragmentation, rather than transformation, of the self. In addition, understanding virtue in a holistic fashion also counters the public-private dichotomy that so dominates contemporary thinking about ethics, whether
religious or secular in its form. Americans wrongly assume that moral
knowledge and virtuous activity are divisible.

The Imperative of Self-Government

The framers of this nation's charter documents understood well, even though
their vision of reality was essentially deist, that a people can be a free people only
to the extent that they learn to control their passions, appetites and prejudices.
For them it was unthinkable that a republic could be created without virtue, inasmuch as virtue is a *social* achievement, not just a personal one. Consider the
base assumptions that are lodged in the words of Alexander Hamilton:

> It seems to have been reserved to the people of this country, by their conduct
> and example, to decide the important question whether societies of men are re-
> ally capable or not . . . of establishing good government from reflection or
> choice, or whether they are forever destined to depend, for their political con-
> stitutions, on accident and force.[56]

If individual people cannot govern themselves, what hope is there that a
people collectively can govern itself as a republic? Or, as Templeton Prize win-

---

[55]Examples of this abound: parents might teach their children how to pray, but if they do not teach them
how to be fair, work hard or be hospitable, their children may miss something of prayer's significance
and depth; believers who are continually told—expressly or implicitly—that "full-time Christian service" is the most noble goal toward which to strive end up thinking of a "regular job" in the workforce
as mundane, second-tier and less important than a ministry position; believers who are not taught that
Christ's lordship is cosmic in scope, entailing the reconciliation of *all things,* tend to operate on a notion
of "faith" that distrusts reason, underestimates education and discourages responsible temporal engagement in society.
[56]Alexander Hamilton, *Federalist Papers,* no. 1.

ner Michael Novak asks, how can they be sovereigns of the nation if they are not sovereigns of themselves?[57]

At the beginning of the twenty-first century, some doubts are being raised as to whether a society's members can be expected to govern themselves. Do people have the capacity for self-government? Should they be held responsible for their actions? Heated debates over this very question can be found today to be raging among behavioral scientists at the theoretical level, as well as among political and legal analysts at the policy level.

When in early 1998 Lindy Boggs, the United States' newly designated ambassador to the Vatican, paid Pope John Paul II a visit, the pontiff deemed it fitting to remind her that America's experiment in national self-government left the nation with a "far-reaching responsibility, not only for the well-being of its own people, but for the development and destiny of peoples throughout the world."[58] America's founding fathers, John Paul observed, "asserted their claim to freedom and independence on the basis of certain 'self-evident' truths about the human person: truths which could be discerned in human nature, built into it by 'nature's God' for the purpose of maintaining an 'ordered liberty.' "[59] The fathers clearly understood

> that there could be no true freedom without moral responsibility and accountability, and no happiness without respect and support for the natural units or groupings through which people exist, develop, and seek the higher purposes of life in concert with others.[60]

Contained in this rather remarkable address by John Paul to Ambassador Boggs is a rejection of the prevalent view of citizenship: the understanding that I am free to do as I wish. In its place is the emphasis on self-mastery based on "self-evident truths." The conclusion to be drawn is as clear as it is offensive: national self-government is directly and inescapably linked to personal self-government. Without the moral "freedom" to commit ourselves to the moral ordering of our lives, there can be no political freedom.[61]

---

[57]Michael Novak, "The Causes of Virtue," The New Character of Crime conference, Washington, D.C., January 31, 1994.

[58]Quoted in Michael S. Joyce, "On Self-Government," *Policy Review* 90 (July-August 1998): 41.

[59]Ibid., pp. 41-42.

[60]Ibid., p. 42.

[61]This connection, of course, is the critical emphasis of John Paul's 1993 encyclical *Veritatis Splendor* ("The Splendor of Truth").

And what are these "self-evident truths" to which John Paul, following the framers, was alluding? The framers show themselves to have possessed a realistic and clear-sighted understanding of human nature; thus, for example, James Madison writes,

> [just] as there is a degree of depravity in mankind which requires a certain degree of circumspection and distrust, so there are other qualities in human nature which justify a certain portion of esteem and confidence. Republican government presupposes the existence of these qualities in a higher degree than any other form.[62]

Madison understood that a society incapable of governing itself morally required "nothing less than the chains of despotism [in order to] restrain [its members] from destroying or devouring one another."[63]

IDEAS AND THEIR (ETHICAL) CONSEQUENCES

There exists a curious, divided way of thinking that is mirrored in the way we Westerners speak of reality. It is a split that often—and almost unconsciously—distinguishes between the classroom and "the real world," between the theoretical and the practical. This dichotomy is disastrous in terms of its effects on our thinking and on the way we live our lives. While this dualism is characteristically American, it is particularly widespread among American Protestant evangelicals.

Underlying this schism in our mindset is the assumption that ideas and values are not "real," or that how we think about things and how we behave are two distinct worlds. This tendency, as Edwin Delattre has astutely observed, encourages an intellectual schizophrenia among students, whom we are training for leadership in the next generation. Are indeed the classroom and the real world two separate spheres? Is the instructional and theoretical mode any less real? What about tutorials? training sessions? apprenticeships?

The unwitting distinction between theory and practice is by no means benign. It helps to foster, even when unintended, a disdain for the intellectual and moral life in favor of more immediate and "real" pleasures.[64] Thus, things that we "think" or "believe" to be important are relegated to the second shelf

---

[62] James Madison, *Federalist Papers,* no. 55.
[63] Ibid.
[64] See esp. the chapter "Attitudes about Reality," in Delattre, *Education,* pp. 69ff.

as it were, eclipsed by sensory impulses that are more immediate and "real" to our own experience. Ultimately, study, hard work, investigation, reflection, time-intensive examination, and academic rigor are viewed as *relatively* unimportant in life. Grades, degrees, diplomas and credentials are consequently viewed as nothing more than means to a more immediate, and more important, goal. Is it any wonder, then, that education today tends to produce students who are increasingly self-indulgent and utilitarian, as well as intellectually and morally lax?

This false dichotomy needs to collapse, whether in a Christian or secular context. Students must be reminded that education in the classroom, in the laboratory or in the library is every bit a part of the real world, and that to shortchange this aspect of reality is to pay a price at the other end. The price to be paid is that students will forfeit the opportunity to develop a rigorous mind as well as a rewarding life of virtue. Instead, they will likely fall victim to a life of drab, unimaginative (when overstimulated) self-interest—bouncing in daily life from sensory overload to sensory overload and very much resembling the "fool" in the book of Proverbs who has taken no time to reflect on what is important in life. The character of relativism, which immediately fills the vacuum that should be inhabited by solitude and mental sobriety, is that it effectively eradicates any basis for meaningful reflection, self-criticism and self-improvement. There is at bottom no more incentive to lead a life of wisdom, virtue and self-restraint than to lead a life of addiction and crime.

How we approach the world of ideas, then, and how we view education are not unrelated. Americans must free themselves from the mistaken belief that *doing* equals being, that the academy is not as important as the marketplace, that education in its theoretical understanding is of lesser importance than material and financial benefits to which education might in time lead. This imperative will grow as educational institutions become *even more market and media driven* in the twenty-first century, discouraging—perhaps even preventing—students from thinking at the basic level.

The implications of our cultural bias against the theoretical are enormous. If, for example, values are colorless and morally neutral and ideas are illusory and less real, it therefore only remains that *nothing we do has any ethical import.* At bottom, it matters nothing what I believe, since beliefs, which are ideas, are less real. Consequently, all action becomes arbitrary (and justifiable), since no social consensus exists as to what is right and wrong, proper and improper, acceptable and unacceptable. In the realm of criminal justice, one man's misfortune becomes another man's good time. No ethical restraints can be reasonably enforced. Duty and responsibility vanish in the interest of private rights, personal entitlement and immediate gratification. In broader culture, the development of *any* social consensus becomes all but impossible, as we are presently witnessing. In the end, such a society is destined to be come barbaric and ungovernable. And as the twentieth century tragically illustrates, political power inevitably steps, whether abruptly or gradually, into the moral vacuum that has been created, with the result being a soft or hard form of (totalitarian) statism.[65] Tyranny, after all, is the end game when a society manipulates truth and embraces falsehood.[66]

WHEN MORAL FORMATION FAILS: THE TOTALITARIAN OPTION

Why is it that people, at least in American society, do not seem to wrestle in an intentional manner with the question of good and evil? That they do not is curious, since who among us does not fear—whether for ourselves or our loved ones—being robbed, mugged, beaten, raped or murdered? And given the horrors and bloodshed of the century just completed (considered the bloodiest century due to war, political atrocity and mass murder), should the reality of evil not be foremost on our minds?

Strangely, this is not the case. But why? Perhaps a partial explanation can be found in a biblically mediated realism about human nature. Humans, in their essence, are fallen, self-centered, depraved and unable to do consistently what is morally right. G. K. Chesterton's oft-quoted observation remains intact: the doctrine of human depravity *is* the most empirically verifiable belief that confronts humanity. Jesus' explanation is straightforward: *men love darkness.* But this is too easy an answer; at the very least, it does not account for those people who, apart from Christian faith, *can* bring themselves to ac-

---

[65]It is this message that Alexander Solzhenitsyn, with considerable unpopularity, attempted to bring to the West. See Ronald Berman, ed., *Solzhenitsyn at Harvard: The Address, Twelve Early Responses and Six Later Reflections* (Washington, D.C.: Ethics and Public Policy Center, 1980).

[66]For this reason, George Orwell's *1984* is a compelling reminder to liberal democracies (for whom the novel was intended) that how we speak is reflective of how we think. In Orwell's world, it is impossible to speak against falsehood because society has embraced a lie. Orwell's theoretical explanation of the slide into tyranny is found in his essay "Politics and the English Language," in vol. 4 of *The Collected Essays, Journalism and Letters of George Orwell*, ed. S. Orwell and I. Angus, 4 vols. (New York: Harcourt, Brace & World, 1968).

knowledge the categories of good and evil and can then *do* the good.

If people are in fact willing to take moral issues seriously, this will necessitate, of course, that they will then begin to judge actions in themselves and in others. As soon as people embark on this path, they quickly find that friends are few; in no time, they begin making enemies. Once an action, a person, a group or a government is judged as evil, something must be done to counter it.[67] And confronting evil, as anyone who has attempted such will vouch, is at best unpleasant and at worst dangerous.

Given the fact that *tolerance* has been elevated to a cardinal virtue in American culture, it is not surprising to encounter a number of ingenious rationalizations for *not* confronting and judging evil. Social critic Dennis Prager has identified five; they are worthy of some consideration and comment:[68]

- deny that evil exists
- minimize evil
- reduce evil to personal opinion
- posit moral equivalence
- accuse people of judgmentalism

In fulfillment of Isaiah's frightening prophecy "Woe to those who call evil good and good evil" (Is 5:20 NIV), contemporary culture reminds us that denying evil is not a new phenomenon. Just as Western intellectuals and journalists in the 1930s and 1940s denied that Stalin's reign was one of terror and that a famine in the Ukraine took the lives of 5 to 10 million people (intellectuals and journalists who, in the end, defended the Soviet regime as "progressive"), there are those today who would deny that a Jewish Holocaust took place, that the unborn possess personhood or that crime is a moral decision. Perhaps the greatest treachery that exists is not simply to commit barbarian acts that are overtly evil but rather to *deny that evil exists*.

Not only can evil be denied, it is possible, as Anglican Archbishop Desmond Tutu did in January of 1990, to *minimize evil*. Tutu, after visiting Yad Vashem, an Israeli memorial dedicated to the 6 million Jews murdered in the Holocaust, exclaimed that what he saw reminded him of the black experience

---

[67]Who can forget the outcry among pundits and political contrarians when in the 1980s Ronald Reagan declared the Soviet Union to be an "evil empire"? Though correct, Reagan could *not* be forgiven for speaking the unspeakable.

[68]Dennis Prager, "Why Aren't People Preoccupied with Good and Evil?" *Ultimate Issues* 7, no. 2 (1991): 6-9.

in South Africa. Unjust as apartheid was, it is no overstatement to say with Prager that "any one of the six million Jews would have prayed to be a victim of apartheid rather than of the Nazi genocide."[69] Unjust as apartheid may have been, statements like that of Tutu are simply morally impermissible. But where there is no outright denial or minimizing of evil, people are inclined to *reduce evil to personal opinion.* As we have already observed, such is achieved in moral decision-making through values clarification and dilemma ethics, whereby students are taught that ethics reduces to personal choice; to issue authoritative claims about right and wrong is to be bigoted or imperialistic.

Yet another tactic of rationalizing evil is by using *moral equivalence,* examples of which are the conflation of the attack on Hiroshima with the Jewish Holocaust or the common argument that the United States and the former Soviet Union were two superpowers threatening peace. This tactic can be applied at any level to any actions and is extremely elusive. When nothing is ethically better than anything else, good and evil cannot exist.

A final strategy, frequently used to silence the public expression of religious conviction, is to *accuse people of judgmentalism.* This has a powerful effect on people, since it plays on their self-perception, in the end paralyzing them in the face of true evil. Jesus' words "Do not judge, or you too will be judged" (Mt 7:1 NIV) are hereby prostituted to mean we are not allowed to judge anybody else at all for any reason; otherwise, we are narrow-minded and intolerant. In the hands of most contemporaries, what this *really* means is that we are not allowed to judge *anyone's behavior,* however repugnant.

In light of society's strategies for rationalizing and avoiding evil, a crucial question emerges: Can a person be good without belief in God? While this question is the stuff of good debates,[70] it identifies inescapable assumptions that support conflicting views of reality. The short and unqualified answer to the question of whether God is necessary for a person to be good is no. There

---

[69]Ibid., p. 7.

[70]Consider, for example the debate that took place on March 3, 1993, under the auspices of Oxford's Chabad Rabbi Shmuel Boteach at the L'Chaim Center, between Jonathan Glover, lecturer in moral philosophy at Oxford, and social commentator Dennis Prager. (For a transcript of the debate see Dennis Prager and Jonathan Glover, "Can We Be Good Without God?: A Debate at Oxford University," *Ultimate Issues* 9, no. 1 [1993]: 3-22.) Also, see Paul Chamberlain's *Can We Be Good Without God?* (Downers Grove, Ill.: InterVarsity Press, 1996), which takes two questions lying at the center of traditional debate—"Is there an objective moral standard?" and "If so, on what basis?"—and places them in the format of what the author calls "dramatic interaction."

are good pagans everywhere, in all societies and in every sociocultural milieu, just as there are religious people who are bad, obnoxious, immoral and hypocritical. End of debate. But the more important question that people must confront is whether people are *likely to be good* without God,[71] which is to ask, can morality survive without God?

A convenient, ever-ready argument raised against the need for and viability of religion is the misuse of religion throughout the ages. Here the Crusades and sundry forms of religious fundamentalism past and present are normally trotted out as proof positive that religion can be cruel and inhumane.[72] That people can misuse or misrepresent God is, of course, nothing new; in and of itself this acknowledgment constitutes no argument against the necessity of God. Working with analogies may help preserve some intellectual honesty on this point. Does the counterfeiting of paper money automatically disqualify either our need for cash or the utility of money in our culture? Or, on the basis of the dark fact that the German Medical Association did not stop medical experiments on Jews sixty years ago, are we at liberty therefore to conclude that medicine is unnecessary? Correlatively, does food poisoning render people permanently inoculated against the need to eat? It is interesting to note that common sense often is the first victim when people are confronted with the claims of religion and morality. In virtually no other realm is the flight from reason so predictable—and violent!

In light of cultural anthropologists' broad-based assumption that morality is socially constructed and culturally specific,[73] an inescapable question presents itself: Is there a universal moral code? More recently James Q. Wilson, in his book *The Moral Sense,* has sought to present a compelling affirmative argument based on the best social-scientific and biological-scientific research.[74] Wilson describes this "moral sense" as an "intuition" that begins developing at

---

[71]Prager, in his debate with Oxford philosopher Glover, identifies this weakness in the atheist argument in a commendable manner. See Prager and Glover, "Can We Be Good?"

[72]We witnessed variations on this argument in response to the terrorist attacks in America of September 11, 2001.

[73]Two errors of thinking are to be avoided: the view that culture is everything and the view that culture is nothing. If culture is everything, then the human element counts for nothing, and one cannot legitimately speak of human "nature." If culture is nothing, then ethics, morality and law need no contextualizing or nuancing in their definition and application. Anthropologists will need to acknowledge that in all societies murder constitutes unjustifiable homicide and that, similarly, incest, rape, torture and theft are condemned. A reasonable explanation is required.

[74]Wilson, *Moral Sense.*

"a very young age" about "how one ought to act when one is free to act voluntarily."[75] For Wilson, this intuition expresses itself in four characteristic ways: through sympathy, fairness, self-control and duty.[76]

It must be recognized that Wilson's attempt to identify normative moral sentiments is important because of his considerable stature as a social scientist. In the end, his critique of human nature is both a help and a hindrance. His argument is hindered by a fundamental commitment to Darwinian evolutionary theory,[77] which in the final analysis fails to lead the way out of the crisis of contemporary ethical theory. And yet despite its inherent naturalistic fallacy,[78] Wilson's argument is useful to the extent that it seeks to get people to think about morality in universal terms.

Virtue has acquired a bad name, Wilson observes in the opening sentence of his book. To the politician it is a symbol to exploit for partisan purposes; to young and old alike it is a set of rules that intolerant bluenoses impose on other people.[79] Wilson's reason for writing is to help people "recover the confidence with which they once spoke about virtue and morality," to reestablish "the possibility and the reasonableness of speaking frankly and convincingly about moral choices."[80] Wilson contends that we all have a "moral sense"[81] but that most of us have tried to talk ourselves out of it:

> Many people have persuaded themselves that no law has any foundation in a
> widely shared sense of justice; each is but the arbitrary enactment of the politi-

---

[75]Ibid., pp. xi, 25.

[76]Ibid., pp. 40-45, 70, 82, 100-101. Wilson writes, "The most remarkable change in the moral history of mankind has been the rise—and occasionally the application—of the view that all people, and not just one's own kind, are entitled to fair treatment" (p. 191).

[77]Thus, people are "*naturally* endowed with certain moral sentiments" (ibid., p. 37, emphasis added). By this Wilson means that "infants and young children are prepared, biologically, for sociability" (p. 126). Theories of natural selection and inclusive fitness, according to Wilson, explain why caring for one's own young has been adaptive—that is, useful—for the human species.

[78]Waxing supremely critical of Wilson is Paul Knepper, professor of criminal justice at East Carolina University. Knepper, who welcomes faith-based approaches to criminal justice that transcend the naturalistic confines of the social sciences, believes that Wilson's argument (based on evolutionary psychology) is "hopelessly tautological." To say that moral intuitions reflect biological processes at work, as Knepper sees it, "is to say that there is a certain inevitability about human behavior," which Knepper rejects out of hand. In pursuing a biological basis for moral judgment, Wilson mistakenly reduces qualities of human behavior to animalistic tendencies and "blind forces" (Paul Knepper, *Explaining Criminal Conduct: Theories and Systems in Criminology* [Durham, N.C.: Carolina Academic Press, 2001], pp. 93-97).

[79]Wilson, *Moral Sense*, p. vii.

[80]Ibid.

[81]That Wilson speaks of moral "sentiments" rather than moral "law" weakens rather than strengthens his argument.

cally powerful. This is called "legal realism," but it strikes me as utterly unrealistic. Many people have persuaded themselves that children will be harmed if they are told right from wrong; instead they should be encouraged to discuss the merits of moral alternatives. This is called "values clarification," but I think it [is] a recipe for confusion rather than clarity. Many people have persuaded themselves that it is wrong to judge the customs of another society since there are no standards apart from custom on which such judgments can rest; presumably they would oppose infanticide only if it involved their own child. This I sometimes called tolerance; I think a better name would be barbarism.[82]

Several generations removed, C. S. Lewis also addresses the perennial question of a universal moral sense in his essay "Right and Wrong as a Clue to the Meaning in the Universe."[83] Lewis argues that the law of nature or natural law, what he calls "the law of oughtness," is a coordinate of revealed religion.[84] For Lewis, the ethical *likenesses,* not the ethical differences, among various cultures force us to ask why heinous crimes such as murder, rape, torture, theft and child molestation are *universally* proscribed. The Nuremberg trials were predicated on the assumption that there exists a universal transcendent moral law. And if one does not exist, then *there is no authority beyond reason and personal preference to decry moral atrocity.*

Can good and evil be identified and named by reason alone? Many would argue that indeed reason is sufficient to the task. The problem with this thinking, however, finds ample illustration in the twentieth century. Reason can be darkened and justify horrendous evil. Evil, as it turns out, can be perpetrated by supremely rational people.[85] In the end, reason alone does not bring us to ethical action. If there is no God, then morality becomes a state of mind, a personal choice, a feeling or the arrangement of physical matter and molecules. The perpetrators of modern evils—the burning of widows in India *(suttee),* the killing of (female) newborns in China, Soviet death squads and prison camps, Chinese purges under Mao, female genital mutilation in Africa, genocide in Europe, the killing fields of Southeast Asia, slavery in the Middle East and North Africa, genocide in Rwanda, not to mention murder and violent crime

---

[82]Knepper, *Explaining,* p. ix.

[83]C. S. Lewis, *Mere Christianity* (New York: Macmillan, 1943), pp. 17-39.

[84]A fuller discussion of the "moral impulse" and Lewis's argument can be found in chap. five, below.

[85]This is precisely the argument of G. K. Chesterton in chaps. 2 ("The Maniac") and 3 ("The Suicide of Thought") of *Orthodoxy,* rev. ed. (Wheaton, Ill.: Harold Shaw, 1994), pp. 9-44.

on the streets of America—were not motivated by their belief in God. Nor can we blame terrorists' belief in God, despite Muslim fanatical claims to the contrary, for their flying jetliners into skyscrapers and government buildings. Rather, *a rejection of religion-based morality* has resulted in the mass murders and killings of the twentieth (and early twenty-first) century that few have dared to adequately document. If there is no God who declares "You shall not murder" (Ex 20:13) and none before whom we ultimately must give account, then morality is impossible. Any ban on murder is at best a pragmatic rule, to be set aside when personal preference or political interest requires.

If a person does not believe in God, which is to say, if there is no God who exists, only one question remains: What are the alternatives? If there is nothing transcendent outside of ourselves in which to ground standards of conduct and morality, then there can be no good and evil. The alternative is one: namely, that *we make ourselves the source and standard of morality.* In so doing we declare that *nothing* can be the source of morality for *anybody.* At this point, the game, as it were, is over, and we have arrived at "the abolition of man" and the grim lament of Fyodor Dostoyevsky: (without God) all things become permissible. Totalitarian darkness awaits.

4

Retooling the Evangelical Mindset
Ethics and Worldview

—

In his highly acclaimed book *Ethics After Babel,* ethicist Jeffrey Stout, who does *not* write from the standpoint of religious faith, disapproves of what he sees as a "complete breakdown" of interaction between secular and religious ethics. Clearly this fissure has been caused by several factors, including an unwillingness among secular philosophers to dialogue with religious ethicists. But this is not the lone story. Just as troubling for Stout is the failure of religious ethicists to develop the implications of their beliefs in contradistinction to their secular counterparts and to state them with sufficient clarity and cogency. Stout writes,

> To gain a hearing in our culture, theology has often assumed a voice not its own and found itself merely repeating the bromides of secular intellectuals in transparently figurative speech. . . . Meanwhile, secular intellectuals have largely stopped paying attention. They don't need to be told, by theologians, that Genesis is mythical, that nobody knows much about the historical Jesus, that it's morally imperative to side with the oppressed, or that birth control is morally permissible. The explanation for the eclipse of religious ethics in recent secular moral philosophy may therefore be . . . that academic theologians have increasingly given the impression of saying nothing atheists don't already know.[1]

---

[1]Jeffrey Stout, *Ethics After Babel: Languages of Morals and Their Discontents* (Boston: Beacon, 1988), p. 163.

While Stout's critique of theology and religious ethics is not aimed solely—or even primarily—at evangelicals, his observation, spoken as an *outsider* to the faith, should give us pause and is eminently worth pondering.

Most Christians—evangelicals included—have not been taught to understand faith and life in terms of worldview, that is, in terms of an overarching framework for interpreting all of reality. Most believers would be unable to articulate what they believe in terms of a unified world- and life-view perspective. One symptom of this state of affairs is that most evangelical colleges and seminaries speak liberally of integrating faith and knowledge while offering few courses to show precisely *how* integration proceeds; correlatively, the same institutions typically devote numerous courses to Christian doctrine but a limited number to Christian ethics (or, at least, to demonstrating the indivisible link between doctrine and ethics).

Why is this? Part of the reason, it would seem, is the pietistic strain that is such an integral part of American evangelical history. This inward focus of a faith that is chiefly devotional and inspirational in character has unwittingly and not infrequently contributed to the neglect of the Christian mind.[2] Because evangelicals pride themselves in their emphasis on direct experience with God through Christ, they tend to think and act as if cultivating the life of the mind, studying Christian doctrine, subordinating our beliefs and traditions to the consensus of history, and learning from the early church fathers are unnecessary at best or a waste of time at worst.

THE EVANGELICAL SPIRIT

Frequently, pietism in this nation and in Europe has been the expression of religious renewal in protest against dry, arid ritualism, legalism or pharisaism. But although *piety* is the bona fide expression of true religious devotion, *pietism* represents an inward turn, which, if unmediated, results in a privatizing of faith and a distrust of the intellect. The result has been an unnecessary polarization between "head and heart," faith and reason, intellect and feeling, and countless other polarities. Critics such as historian Richard Hofstadter and, more recently, social commentator Os Guinness are correct to point out

---

[2]Perhaps the most eloquent cry in recent years for appreciation and recovery of the Christian mind has been Mark A. Noll's *The Scandal of the Evangelical Mind* (Grand Rapids, Mich.: Eerdmans, 1994). See also the symposium on "The Scandal of the Evangelical Mind," with contributions by Grant Wacker, Robert Wuthnow, Keith Pavlischek and Daryl Charles, that appeared in the March 1995 issue of *First Things*, a journal of religion and culture.

that false antagonisms of the either/or sort have become standard fare in evangelicalism.[3] Hofstadter summarizes the dilemma, which is by no means a recent development:

> The case against intellect is founded upon a set of fictional and wholly abstract antagonisms. Intellect is pitted against feeling, on the ground that it is somehow inconsistent with warm emotion. It is [also] pitted against character, because it is widely believed that intellect stands for mere cleverness, which transmutes easily into the sly or the diabolical.[4]

Sadly, most evangelical pulpits deepen rather than bridge this tragic divide.

In American life, the anti-intellectual strain would seem to manifest itself most often in politics and religion. In the latter realm, an excessive emphasis on piety is frequently the culprit.[5] Religious piety, given its inward and private focus, needs an intellectual counterweight to keep it from degenerating into pietistic irrelevance. When pietism is combined with the primitivistic strain in American evangelicalism (i.e., the desire to return to the pristine beauty of Christian beginnings), the result is more often than not a repudiation of the intellect.[6] Given the tendency of those in American evangelical pulpits to encourage *distrust* of the intellect and to stress subjective experience over objective proposition, very often evangelicals have been their own worst enemy. It goes without saying that this unfortunate scenario is exacerbated by the climate of postmodern skepticism toward reason and logic that is so prevalent today.

One historian of American intellectual life has written that because religion was the first arena of American intellectual life, it was accordingly the first arena to generate an anti-intellectual impulse.

> The feeling that ideas should above all be made to work, the disdain for doctrine and for refinements in ideas, the subordination of men of ideas to men of emotional power or manipulative skill are hardly innovations of the twentieth century; they are inheritances from American Protestantism.[7]

---

[3]Richard Hofstadter, *Anti-Intellectualism in American Life* (New York: Alfred A. Knopf, 1963), esp. pp. 55-141; Os Guinness, *Fit Bodies, Fat Minds: Why Evangelicals Don't Think and What to Do About It* (Grand Rapids, Mich.: Baker, 1994), p. 30.

[4]Hofstadter, *Anti-Intellectualism*, pp. 45-46.

[5]Thus ibid., pp. 29-30.

[6]Ibid., pp. 48-49.

[7]Ibid., p. 55. To be fair, it must be said that Hofstadter himself is far from being unbiased. "There seems," he writes, "to be such a thing as the generically prejudiced mind. Studies of political intolerance

It is not merely incidental that American society became fertile soil for religious enthusiasm, particularly in light of the Protestant conviction of personal access to God. The authority of evangelical enthusiasm is personal and charismatic rather than consensual and institutional. Thus, the need to validate religion by inward experience contains within it, at least potentially, "the threat of anarchical subjectivism," and with it a "total destruction of traditional and external religious authority."[8]

But is this too strong an indictment of the evangelical spirit?[9] Are we not hereby condemning that which has bred life and vibrancy in evangelical circles? Certainly, our Puritan forebears (even though their image has suffered) are a forceful reminder that it was not always so. Many from among the initial generation of American Puritans were people of learning.[10]

RECOVERING SANCTIFIED REASON

That a distrust of the intellect is both endemic in and confined to Protestant evangelical circles is confirmed by a comparison to Catholic thought, both past and present. Few things illustrate this better than Pope John Paul II's *Fides et Ratio*, an encyclical devoted to the relationship between faith and reason, delivered at Saint Peter's Basilica in Rome on September 14, 1998. John Paul understands both the incompatibility of most modern and postmodern thinking with Christian theism as well as the frequent rupture within Christian thinking that tends to divorce faith and reason. Hence, in the pontiff's view, Christians who occupy teaching and pastoral positions are obligated to address this gulf.

In this encyclical John Paul wishes to emphasize the unity of thought and being, reason and faith, objective and subjective faculties. Behind this urgency is the awareness that contemporary culture demonstrates an inordinately deep-seated distrust of reason. Within the community of faith, this divorce can readily lead to fideism, thus eliminating any need for doctrine, catechetics and

---

and ethnic prejudice have shown that zealous church-going and rigid religious faith are among the important correlates of political and ethnic animosity" (ibid., p. 133).

[8]Ibid., p. 57.

[9]A penetrating look at the role that evangelical religion has played in American thought-life is found in part 2 ("The Religion of the Heart") of Hofstadter's book. See esp. chaps. 3 ("The Evangelical Spirit") and 4 ("Evangelicalism and the Revivalists").

[10]An eloquent statement of their cultural accomplishments can be found in Samuel Eliot Morison, *The Intellectual Life of Colonial New England* (New York: Macmillan, 1956). See also Kenneth Murdock, *Literature and Theology in Colonial New England* (Oxford: Oxford University Press, 1949).

reflection on moral theology.[11] Nowhere, according to John Paul, is the need for reason more evident today than in the realm of ethics; the church has desperate need of a moral theology that possesses a "found philosophical vision of human nature and society, as well as of the general principles of ethical decision-making."[12]

What is John Paul's agenda for philosophy and reason? Historic Christian belief requires that we articulate the biblical vision of humanity both as created in the image of God and as fallen. Consequently, the "crisis of meaning" that afflicts contemporary culture can only be addressed authoritatively when justice is done to both extremes of the biblical vision.[13] The church also needs to wrestle with basic questions surrounding the meaning of life. The search for ultimate truth involves reason and must not be short-circuited or circumvented by the explosion of technology and society's obsession with information and data.[14] In this regard, John Paul is a realist: "If this technology is not ordered to something greater than a merely utilitarian end, then it could soon prove inhuman and even become [a] potential destroyer of the human race."[15] A third requirement is to move past mere experiential evidence of reality and to lay hold of what is "absolute, ultimate and foundational." "We cannot stop short at experience alone," John Paul asserts, for to do so is to render ourselves incapable of addressing the great pathological problems of our day.

Reason unaided by faith has led to numerous errors in our time and, in terms of ethics, has yielded disastrous results. These fallacies go by various names: for example, eclecticism, scientism and pragmatism. Despite the advent of postmodern skepticism, scientism is notable for its refusal to admit the validity of forms of knowledge other than those of the natural sciences; rather, it "relegates religious, theological, ethical and aesthetic knowledge to the realm of mere fantasy" and "consigns all that has to do with the meaning of life to the realm of the irrational or imaginary."[16] Science would thus be poised to dominate all aspects of human life through technological progress.[17] No less dangerous, in John Paul's view, is the pragmatic spirit of our age. As a mindset, it makes choic-

---

[11] John Paul II, *Fides et Ratio*, sec. 55, 68.
[12] Ibid., sec. 68.
[13] Ibid., sec. 80.
[14] Ibid., sec. 81.
[15] Ibid.
[16] Ibid., sec. 88.
[17] Ibid.

es that preclude theoretical and ethical judgments based on ethical principles. The ethical consequences of this line of thinking should not escape us:

> In practice, the great moral decisions of humanity are subordinated to decisions taken one after another by institutional agencies. Moreover, anthropology itself is severely compromised by a one-dimensional vision of the human being, a vision which excludes the great ethical dilemmas and the existential analyses of the meaning of suffering and sacrifice, of life and death.[18]

John Paul sees a logical development of ethical eclecticism, scientism and pragmatism in the direction of nihilism, which is a denial of all foundations and the negation of all objective truth and, therefore, a denial of human identity. Once the truth of human dignity is denied to human beings, it is pure illusion to attempt to set them free: "Truth and freedom either go together hand in hand or together they perish in misery."[19]

If this the task of sanctified reason (and hence the domain of Christian philosophers), what is required in the realm of faith? As John Paul sees it, the chief task of the church is theological: that is, it must instruct and form its members in the contours and certainties of unchanging Christian doctrine, without which the church will be ill-prepared to meet the needs of our time.[20] It is this word of exhortation that evangelicals in particular are in need of hearing. The purpose of theology is to provide an understanding of revelation and the content of faith. It is little wonder that evangelicals are incapable of articulating a social ethic; our churches would rather give their time to entertainment and quantitative growth than to instructing our own in the "certainties of unchanging Christian doctrine."

Still another task of the church is to develop the implications of revealed truth, the *intellectus fidei*.[21] Authentic faith is one that seeks understanding, a faith that is informed and takes seriously the intellectual or cognitive element of Christian confession. Although reason is not to be equated with faith, reason exists *in the service of* faith. The two should not be divorced.

A final and urgent task of the church is to develop a robust moral theology. It is critical, in John Paul's view, that the Christian community recover an un-

---

[18]Ibid., sec. 89.
[19]Ibid., sec. 90.
[20]Ibid., sec. 92-93.
[21]Ibid., sec. 97.

derstanding of faith that identifies *how it is linked to the moral life:* "Faced with contemporary challenges in the social, economic, political and scientific fields, the ethical conscience of people is disoriented."[22] Once the idea of a universal good, accessible to human reason, is lost, it is inevitable that the notion of conscience also changes. In its place arises a tendency "to grant to the individual conscience the prerogative of independently determining the criteria of goods and evil and then acting accordingly."[23] Thus, given the pressing ethical issues of the day, faith must develop a moral theology that is capable of "careful enquiry rooted unambiguously in the word of God" and "which is neither subjectivist nor utilitarian."[24]

It is impossible to overstate the significance of this recent papal encyclical. In *Fides et Ratio,* John Paul tackles an age-old question—the question of how faith seeks understanding. It is a question that the early church father Tertullian raised and one that has been posed again and again throughout the church's history: "What does Athens have to do with Jerusalem?" By Athens, Tertullian means the life of the mind, the intellectual life, the realm of reason; by Jerusalem, he is identifying salvation history and the redemptive work of Christ. Of course, what Tertullian wishes to ask rhetorically is worth pondering. If we are new creatures in Christ, having been delivered from the powers of the present age, and if the heritage of the Greeks is to go up in smoke anyway on the Last Day, why concern ourselves with the wisdom of the world? Is not intellectual refinement nothing but a luxury at best? Are we not simply fiddling while Rome burns?[25]

Protestant evangelicals readily empathize with Tertullian's sentiments. And they are correct to assert, as they have in their brief history, that Athens cannot save. Yet they would do well to affirm what some Catholic theologians have described as "incarnational humanism." Incarnational humanism is a view of the regenerate life that understands not just the soul but man in his composite unity (as well as the material universe) to have been affected by the fall. Therefore, redemption properly conceived is universal in scope. That is, all things natural are to be restored.

---

[22]Ibid., sec. 98.
[23]Ibid.
[24]Ibid.
[25]A most penetrating examination of Tertullian's question—coupled with a responsible Christian reply— is John F. Crosby's "Education and the Mind Redeemed," *First Things* 20 (December 1991): 23-28.

Human civilization, though it is something less than justification and union with God, is not simply irrelevant to Christian faith. On the basis of the incarnation, whereby we see that the Redeemer was willing to be the goal of human civilization, the Christian believer is reminded that culture and civilization, while not ultimate, are to be taken seriously.[26] The fruit of our earthly labor is not to be blotted out in eternity; rather, it is to remain, even when it stands transfigured. Christ's kingship, as the apostle Paul reiterates, is not merely rooted in the economy of souls that are saved; it has its foundation in the original plan of creation (Col 1:15-18). John Paul's recent encyclical underscores this Pauline truth: faith and reason together will enable the people of God to realize the full potential of their humanity—a humanity regenerated in Christ. To concern ourselves with ethics is to take seriously the task of theology as well as the implications of theology for the cultural context in which we are located. To pit faith against reason, as evangelicals have frequently been inclined to do, is to amputate ourselves at the knees and render the Christian faith inviable.

CONTOURS OF WORLDVIEW THINKING

Evangelicals tend not to think of life and faith in terms of a coherent philosophy of reality. Simply put, a worldview is a set of beliefs about life's ultimate issues. It is comprehensive in nature, offering an explanation to foundational questions that each person must face: Who am I? Why am I here? What constitutes being human? What purpose does my life serve? In what relation does my life stand to others? What is the meaning of suffering? Is there a grand scheme to the universe? Humans have an extraordinarily deep-seated need to be able to explain their own lives in relation to the universe in which they live; thus, one's worldview transcends opinions or feelings and entails certain baseline convictions.[27] An inability to explain reality with minimum coherence can lead, literally, to self-destruction. Humans instinctively avoid or react against a fragmented life that does not offer some sort of meaningful explanation of coherent human activity. Worldviews are very much like climates insofar as they affect us regardless of whether or not we are aware of them. One cannot

---

[26]Thus ibid., p. 26.

[27]As Albert M. Wolters writes, feelings do not lay claim to knowledge, nor can they be argued (*Creation Regained: Biblical Basics for a Reformational Worldview* [Grand Rapids, Mich.: Eerdmans, 1985], p. 2).

fully escape their influence. Every person possesses a worldview, as did Aristotle, Epicurus, Paul, Attila the Hun, Henry VIII, Martin Luther, Friedrich Nietzsche, Adolf Hitler and Mother Teresa.[28]

Formulating and articulating a biblical worldview in contemporary culture entails biblical revelation, but it does not subsist in or end with a mere formula, such as "The Bible says . . . ." A neo-pagan culture such as ours, typically denominated "post-Christian," has numerous points of connection with the pre-Christian culture that Paul encountered in the mid first century. In both pre-Christian and post-Christian cultural climates, the believer can reasonably assume that people are biblically illiterate. Therefore, to argue purely on the basis of what "the Bible says" may be meaningless for the audience; one must back up and begin with the "first things" of a biblically informed and philosophically robust apologetic for theistic faith.

Why is it that the knottiest disagreements between people are typically thought to arise over issues of politics and religion? In the realm of personal belief and public policy, the clash between competing worldviews becomes apparent. What is not immediately obvious in these disagreements is the level of presupposition or base convictions. Every worldview—whether theistic, deistic, pantheistic, atheistic or fatalistic—is supported by basic assumptions: assumptions about God (theology), human nature (anthropology), how humans derive knowledge (epistemology), human behavior (ethics), human relations (sociology) and the universe (cosmology). Thinking in terms of a worldview is not something that is reserved merely for philosophers or theologians; it is the responsibility of *every Christian*.

Many people, Christians included, are inclined to conceive of life (both generally and personally) as being similar to a pie that is cut up into individual slices. These units tend to be viewed as isolated, without any unifying factor or element. Perhaps a better model for understanding our lives might be the wheel with its hub as the core that causes all parts to cohere. The religious and

---

[28]Ronald Nash describes a worldview as "a conceptual scheme by which we consciously or unconsciously place or fit everything we believe and by which we interpret and judge reality" (*Worldviews in Conflict: Choosing Christianity in a World of Ideas* [Grand Rapids, Mich.: Zondervan, 1992], p. 16). Helpful articulations of a Christian worldview can be found in F. G. Oosterhoff, *Postmodernism: A Christian Appraisal* (Winnipeg: Premier, 1999); Brian J. Walsh and J. Richard Middleton, *The Transforming Vision: Shaping a Christian World View* (Downers Grove, Ill.: InterVarsity Press, 1984); Wolters, *Creation Regained;* and James W. Sire, *The Universe Next Door* (Downers Grove, Ill.: InterVarsity Press, 1976).

philosophical commitments, whatever they may be, constitute the core and thus affect all realms of life. William Abraham has captured the nature of life's unity and totality in similar terms:

> Religious beliefs should be assessed as a rounded whole rather than in stark isolation. Christianity, for example, like other world faiths, is a complex, large-scale system of belief which must be seen as a whole before it is assessed. To break it up into disconnected parts is to mutilate and distort its true character. We can, of course, distinguish certain elements in the Christian faith, but we must still stand back and see it as a complex interaction of these elements. We need to see it as a metaphysical system, as a worldview, that is total in its scope and range.[29]

IDENTIFYING CORE COMMITMENTS: THE ROLE OF PRESUPPOSITIONS

Any party who enters into the excitement and challenges of building a house knows how utterly critical the laying of the house's foundation is. In 1992 my wife and I decided to have a house built for us. Though wholly (and blissfully) unfamiliar with the mind-numbing detail that is part of the home-building ordeal, I recall my nervousness as the house's foundation was laid. This was magnified by the fact that *forty-five truckloads* of dirt were needed to help raise the building site that was among the lowest in the neighborhood (and what seemed like the lowest on the East Coast).

I can distinctly recall my deep anxiety when I arrived at the building lot to inspect the foundation that had been poured the morning before. Holding my breath, I walked around the perimeter of fresh concrete and steel on which the house was supposed to rest, looking for flaws. Instinctively I knew that everything in the house would be dependent on the quality of that slab. Any blemish or crack would affect the total structure of the house. If not discovered, the foundational weakness would render the house permanently flawed—flawed, that is, until the house was reduced to rubble and a new foundation was laid. The reality was unsettling: the foundation is the house.

Worldviews are supported at the foundation level by certain governing presuppositions about God, the world, human nature and reality. Typically, presuppositions are taken for granted. Even when most people do not consciously

---

[29]William Abraham, *An Introduction to the Philosophy of Religion* (Englewood Cliffs, N.J.: Prentice-Hall, 1985), p. 104.

work through these foundations, their lives are expressions of certain deeply held convictions. The natural sciences illustrate perhaps most clearly how important presuppositions are. All scientists work out of certain base assumptions; these assumptions, of course, interlock. Scientists assume, for example, that

> knowledge is possible and that sense experience is reliable (epistemology), that the universe is regular (metaphysics), and that scientists should be honest (ethics). Without these assumptions, which scientists cannot verify within the limits of their methodology, scientific inquiry would soon collapse.[30]

One might further compare the function of presuppositions in one's worldview to the function of the tracks on which a train runs and which determine the train's direction and destination.[31] A person's precommitment to a set of presuppositions leads, whether consciously or unconsciously, to inevitable and ineluctable results. This has profound implications for ethics, since moral convictions are formed out of one's convictions about ultimate reality.

For the pantheist, for whom God and creation (both human and material) are indistinguishable, there is no transcendent reality on which humans order their lives and before which they give account. Ethics becomes moralism based on sheer willpower, not obedience or conformity to a transcending standard. For the material atheist or naturalist, ultimate reality is matter, void of any spiritual-moral element. The naturalist, like the pantheist, conforms to no ultimate transcendent norm or standard. Authority resides in the autonomous self.

In considering the ethical implications of naturalism, we encounter the notable inconsistencies in modernist (as well as postmodernist) thinking. The Darwinian assumption of natural selection, the guiding law of nature, implies that for humans to evolve further, natural selection must continue. Such, in turn, assumes the struggle and elimination of the weak. It was only natural, then, that social Darwinists of the late nineteenth and early twentieth centuries would propose the need for eugenics and selective breeding. The poor, the infirm, the weak and the criminal elements of society were to recede. Where this naturalistic ethic flourished in the century past, incomparable harm was done.[32] Nevertheless, it is important to recognize that the philosophical foun-

---

[30]Nash, *Worldviews*, p. 23.

[31]Thus, ibid.

[32]The link between social Darwinism and ethics in pre-Nazi Germany is discussed in the epilogue to this volume and well illustrates the burden of this chapter.

dations of naturalism, in various forms, are still intact in Western culture. And they make possible the dehumanization of the human race at both ends of the life spectrum: at birth and at death. G. K. Chesterton was correct: when people stop believing in God, they don't merely believe in nothing; they will believe in anything.

While good and evil lose their meaning in both modernist and postmodernist accounts of reality, the Christian believer has grounds for *qualified* optimism with the advent of the postmodern era. After all, fruits of the modern era to which the twentieth century bears graphic and tragic witness (e.g., dialectical materialism/Marxism, methodological naturalism, God-is-dead religion) have produced moral atrophy and atrocity. The twentieth century has justified genocide, abortion and euthanasia in breathtaking proportions.

Certain presuppositions, however, particularly those governing one's understanding of human nature and ethics, die hard. Consider the work of Frans de Waal, a "primatologist" and professor of psychology at Emory University. In his recent book *Good Natured: The Origins of Right and Wrong in Humans and Other Animals,* de Waal applies evolutionary assumptions about human moral behavior to the concepts of justice and morality.[33] He contends that moral intuitions and notably our sense of "justice" are evident in higher primates and other social animals.[34] The use of examples from the animal kingdom supports de Waal's thesis that humans' framework for morality and justice may well have evolved from animals to humans. While de Waal stops short of calling animals moral creatures, he does argue for the presence in animals of emotional and psychological mechanisms that are involved in human morality.[35]

The author of a *Chronicle of Higher Education* article that evaluates de Waal's work writes, with some justification, that if de Waal's book persuades other social scientists that ethics has an evolutionary basis, our philosophical views of morality would be "changed dramatically."[36] What casts a shadow on de Waal's work, and thus requires that Christian ethicists be able to answer people like de Waal coherently and credibly, is his belief that we are now reaching a point

---

[33]Frans de Waal, *Good Natured: The Origins of Right and Wrong in Humans and Other Animals* (Cambridge, Mass.: Harvard University Press, 1996).

[34]Part of de Waal's definition of justice are hierarchy, reciprocity and mutual obligation.

[35]Among the book's weaknesses is the author's inability to give account of moral agency and the mechanism of the will.

[36]Kim A. McDonald, "A Primatologist Examines the Biological Basis for Ethical Behavior in Humans," *Chronicle of Higher Education,* March 15, 1996, pp. A10-11.

at which biology may finally be able to "wrest morality from the hands of philosophers."[37] With this comment de Waal reveals what the Christian knows intuitively: there is *no neutrality* when it comes to presuppositions. Our conflict at the level of assumptions exposes two competing notions of reality that vie for the hearts and minds of human beings.

Contrast the ethical implications of an atheistic or naturalistic worldview with those of the theist. For the naturalist, morality issues out of utility. No one's view can be said to be right or wrong.[38] For the Christian, because there is a Creator-God who reveals himself in intelligible and meaningful ways to humankind, the existence of the universe is not a mere "brute fact" and nature is not "all there is"; morality is thus not merely the rearranging of molecules, nor is it the realm of the "noumenal" that is separate and unrelated to the realm of the "phenomenal." The universe is understood to consist of material as well as nonmaterial (i.e., spiritual) reality. Moreover, because of the existence and self-revealed character of this Creator, who is moral perfection and who has created humankind in his likeness, humans are capable of making moral judgments.

Christian theism therefore insists on the existence of a universal moral impulse and transcendent moral laws that apply to and govern humans irrespective of culture, location, social custom or era. The reality and consequences of such laws are independent of humans' assent to their existence. That humans bear the image of God, and thus are distinguished from the rest of creation, accounts for their capacity to reason, reflect, discriminate, discern and deny themselves. Biblical teaching affirms that human beings are morally free and not mere pawns of deterministic forces, whether psychologically or biologically. A Christian diagnosis of what is awry in the world is spiritual-moral in nature: humans have misused their freedom and are in rebellion against the Creator. The problem is not simply errors in judgment or individual isolated acts of sin; rather, it is a fundamentally depraved nature within that has a *propensity* for rebellion. Ethically speaking, the flaw presupposes the need for divine grace, which begins with repentance and conversion of the will in the direction of the Moral Governor of the universe.

---

[37]Ibid., p. A11.
[38]Thus, contemporary debates over abortion and homosexuality, for example, are a mirror of modernist assumptions at work. Rights, utility and individual choice trump moral standards.

5

Retooling the Evangelical Mindset
Ethics and the Permanent

—

Although Protestant evangelicals, at least in our more recent history, tend not to contemplate those things they hold dear, postmodern culture forces us to revisit and reflect on those basic convictions inherent to a biblical theism. Thus, for example, we need to ask, how do we identify what is moral? And on what basis can we and do we make moral judgments?

Arguing for a morality that is biblically based may seem the proper thing to do, but is such a response meaningful to a society that is biblically illiterate and essentially amoral? First things first.

CONTENDING FOR THE MORAL IMPULSE

While the Ten Commandments (or, literally, the "Ten Sayings") are understood to be God's revelation of an abiding ethical standard to his covenant people, Israel, they are that and more. Their origin 3,300 years ago constitutes a major moral marker in the history of human civilization. Given the fact that the twentieth century was one of the bloodiest, inhumane and barbaric in human history, it is reasonable to question how "civilized" human civilization has become over those thirty-three centuries.

Nevertheless, what sets humans apart from lower forms of biological life is their ability to reflect on their actions, to consider alternatives *before* they act and to be consciously aware of the consequences that accompany their actions.[1] This capacity is in fact the very hallmark of civilized humanity.

Just over two centuries ago, the founders of this nation affirmed the belief that all people, universally, possessed this rational-moral capacity and, hence, were capable of self-government. Individual self-government was understood as the prerequisite for a nation's ability to self-govern and, as a result, to work for the common good of society. This presupposed individual freedom was in no way misconstrued as the freedom to do whatever human urge dictated; rather, it was assumed to be a responsible expression of liberty. Such presuppositions on moral self-restraint are reflected in the words of writer and minister John Wise, writing some eighty years before the penning of the United States Constitution:

> The native liberty of man's nature implies a capability of DOING or NOT DO-ING things according to the direction of his judgments. This liberty does not consist in a loose and ungovernable freedom, or in an unbounded license of act-ing. Such unbridled liberty is inconsistent with the dignity of a civilized being and would make man lower and meaner than brute creatures [animals].[2]

In our own culture children are presently killing children, children are kill-ing parents, parents are killing children, not to mention the myriad patholog-ical ills that plague contemporary American society. One has the right to question whether ours is a civilized age at all. The issue, however, is not whether human beings are moral beings; it is, rather, whether human beings

---

[1]This remains uncontroversial despite rather breathtaking attempts by some theorists to call human per-sonhood in question. One such attempt is that of John Harris, the Sir David Alliance Professor of Bioethics and director of the Institute of Medicine Law and Bioethics at the University of Manchester. Harris recent-ly wrote, "Normally we use the term 'person' as a synonym for 'human beings,' people like us. However we are also familiar with the idea that there are nonhuman persons, and humans who are not, or may not be persons or full persons. . . . Human nonpersons or humans who are not fully fledged [sic] persons may include zygotes and embryos, or individuals who are 'brain-dead,' anencephalic infants, or individuals in a persistent vegetative state" ("The Concept of the Person and the Value of Life," *Kennedy Institute of Ethics Journal* 9, no. 4 [1999]: 293). What is disturbing is that influential secular bioethicists like Harris are mak-ing statements that call for a radical revisioning of our understanding of human personhood. In the same vein, consider the following statement by one of the most respected secular bioethicists of our time: "Al-though nonhuman animals are not plausible candidates for moral personhood, humans too fail to qualify as moral persons if they lack one or more of the conditions of moral personhood" (Tom L. Beauchamp, "The Failure of Theories of Personhood," *Kennedy Institute of Ethics Journal* 9, no. 4 [1999]: 309).

[2]John Wise, "On Liberty," quoted in Robert Sandler, "The Ten Commandments and the Concept of Freedom," *Midstream* 45, no. 7 (1999): 16. Sandler makes a compelling argument for the Ten Com-mandments as a clear philosophy of inner-directed self-restraint. That is, "Thou shalt *not* . . . " means "You shall restrain yourself from . . ."

will acknowledge the moral impulse that makes them truly "human."

The late Allan Bloom began his best-seller *The Closing of the American Mind* with the by now frequently cited—and almost quaint—observation that there is "one thing a professor can be absolutely certain of: almost every student entering the university believes, or says he believes, that truth is relative."[3] Nonetheless, this is, and remains, the order of the day, as philosopher William Irvine has recently testified:

> The first task in any college ethics class . . . is to confront relativism. . . . I confront this epidemic of tolerance every time I discuss value theory in the college philosophy classes that I teach. . . . Those undergraduates who cling to absolutes [face] the scorn of the relativists around them.[4]

But how did we get to this point? How did we as a society move from the affirmation of universal moral givens ("We hold these truths to be self-evident") to the radical relativizing of all moral judgments ("There can be no givens")?[5] Many of the dominant ideologies of the nineteenth and twentieth centuries share the common tendency to substitute personal autonomy (literally, "self-law") for a commitment to the common good of society. Whether skepticism, utilitarianism, evolutionism, existentialism, psychoanalysis, emotivism, situationism or nihilism, each is "antinomian" (i.e., "without or against law") at its core. For each of these, there exists no binding, objective moral standard; ethics reduces to subjective individual choices.[6] What unites all of these "isms" is the central conviction that there are no moral absolutes.[7]

---

[3]Allan Bloom, *The Closing of the American Mind: How Higher Education Has Failed Democracy and Impoverished the Souls of Today's Students* (New York: Simon & Schuster, 1987), p. 25.

[4]William B. Irvine, "Confronting Relativism," *Academic Questions* 14, no. 1 (2000/2001): 42.

[5]To critique ethical relativism is not to deny the fact of moral complexity or the complex nature of certain types of moral decision-making. It is only to emphasize that in denying moral absolutes we thereby render subjective all moral issues, in the end preparing the soil for moral atrocity and terror. That is why, in the context of bioethical debates that are now raging, "quality-of-life" considerations *must not* be allowed to replace *sanctity-of-life* reasoning. Physician-assisted suicide and euthanasia are the *inevitable* result of this reduction of human personhood.

[6]This is the essence of "values clarification." Values clarification poses as a morally neutral method and is radically individualistic, in contrast to traditional education, which is communitarian in character. It conveys the impression that ethics is self-expression and tolerates alternatives that for some are unacceptable, even immoral. But moral education, in the end, cannot be permitted to issue out of self-expression and matters of taste.

[7]This in no way is to maintain that ethical relativism is a new phenomenon. The ancient Epicureans, in their elevation of pleasure over pain (hedonism), encouraged relativism. Likewise, the philosophical school of the Skeptics denied the possibility of being conclusive about moral matters by maintaining that one should suspend judgment since all issues have two sides.

Of course, moral relativism, if followed to its logical conclusion, is self-refuting, since the proposition "There are no absolutes" itself cannot be an absolutely true statement. And yet with stunning creativity relativism continues to don a new appearance with each successive generation.[8]

In chapter three I contrasted the notion of virtue and vice with contemporary usage of the term *values*. This six-letter word is ubiquitous in present-day discourse and serves to conflate everything between personal taste and moral principle, thereby confirming Ludwig Wittgenstein's famous dictum that the limits of one's language define the limits of one's world. In a supremely thoughtful essay that probes the emaciated character of our present moral vocabulary, Terence Ball poses an all-important question: What limits does the language of "values" impose upon our world?[9] And what sort of moral world do we create by speaking in the language of "values"?

In its contemporary usage, the language of values has the effect of homogenizing moral and political discourse. That is, it levels the moral playing field so that critical distinctions are obliterated. In such a world, all people—the neighborhood thug, the porn star, the politician as well as Mother Teresa—have values. In this world of values, all moral choices are personal, legitimate and unassailable. The standard quip "You have your values and I have mine" equates to no more than "One person's mugging becomes another person's good time." Value judgments are, hence, "reports about the psychological state or 'attitude' of the person doing the judging, and say nothing true or false . . . about the thing being judged."[10] Values, then, reduce to lifestyle choices.

Choice, as we all know, is a marvelous function of human existence, that is, within certain limits. Individual liberty is only meaningful in the context of an ordered society, and political liberty—that rare treasure sought the world over—is rendered impossible when moral-social order collapses.[11] Political philosophy is predicated on moral philosophy and, therefore, on a particular

---

[8]To acknowledge with many postmodern theorists that we cannot be certain about knowledge and meaning is to concede that our own understanding is not infallible. But this does not mean that we cannot have *reasonable* grasp of or certainty about some things.

[9]Terence Ball, "What's Wrong with 'Values'?" *New Oxford Review* 63, no. 4 (1996): 6-11. Ball's "genealogy of values" derives primarily from developments in the social sciences, particularly the distinction between "facts" and "values."

[10]Ibid., p. 8.

[11]This is a theme found in several of Pope John Paul II's encyclicals, notably in *Veritatis Splendor* ("The Splendor of Truth").

view of human nature.[12] If there is nothing universal in the moral nature of humankind, then politics truly becomes "war by other means," and culture wars are no mere metaphor.

THE CHALLENGE OF PLURALISM AND ETHICAL RELATIVISM

To a society that previously understood itself—whether rightly or wrongly—to have had Christian influence, it can be disorienting to encounter diverse aspects of radical pluralism that are presently regnant. One writer speaks in terms of "epochal challenges" in considering the radical relativity that postmodernity brings with it.[13] This is especially true as it undermines the Christian church's long-held claim to universal truth. What should be evangelicals' response?

In *The Gospel in a Pluralist Society,* the late Lesslie Newbigin helpfully distinguishes between two senses of "pluralism."[14] First, pluralism as part of creation—that is, the phenomenological reality of different social, cultural, ethnic and linguistic spheres—is to be celebrated as a fact of life.[15] Indeed, redemption encompasses all of creation: saints who have been ransomed by God come from "every tribe and language and people and nation" (Rev 5:9), finding their place around the throne of God.

Second, ideological pluralism, by contrast, calls into question any claims that truth is objective, normative and universal. Such claims, it is argued, are narrow, reductionistic, bigoted and imperialistic. To defend (let alone, advance) Christianity is hereby viewed as an intrusion, and is therefore intolerable, in a multicultural society.

While most people, in their practice, are ethical relativists, what about a theoretical defense of ethical relativism? Can it be upheld by intellectually honest people? It is a long-standing philosophical debate, of course, whether ethics is relative to time, place and culture. One side has argued, with considerable success in the academy, that ethics is the construction and byproduct of

---

[12]James Q. Wilson develops this link quite cogently in "What Is Moral, and How Do We Know It?" *Commentary* 95, no. 6 (1993): 37-43, although he is too tentative in his description of human nature.

[13]Curtis Chang, *Engaging Unbelief: A Captivating Strategy from Augustine and Aquinas* (Downers Grove, Ill.: InterVarsity Press, 2000), pp. 18-39.

[14]Lesslie Newbigin, *The Gospel in a Pluralist Society* (Grand Rapids, Mich.: Eerdmans, 1989).

[15]Very often the term *multiculturalism,* which by itself contains no ideological baggage, becomes something of a Trojan horse for those who wish to undermine established (Western) culture and traditional Judeo-Christian moral authority; thus, in the end, for many, multiculturalism is a means to *multimorality,* whereby objective moral norms are negated.

particular societies and cultures.[16] While one cannot deny that cultures vary in their beliefs and practices, what can one say about their conspicuous similarities? Why are murder, incest, theft, torture, disrespect for parents, child molestation and the like universally proscribed? Simply stated, if morality is merely a convenient way of describing social consensus, then culturally conditioned practices such as burning widows, female genital mutilation, slavery, torture, castration or genocide (to which list one could add abortion and euthanasia), to name but a few, escape any moral censoring whatsoever; they must stand as morally acceptable because of intrasocietal approval.[17]

Were ethical relativism a logically consistent and, therefore, tenable position, it would be impossible to criticize cultures or eras, past and present, on moral grounds. The abolition of slavery cannot be viewed as a *moral* victory, only as a *political* change. The Nuremberg Code, a response by the universal community to German political and medical horrors that occurred during the Third Reich, represents at most a kangaroo court, possessing no universal authority by which to sanction "crimes against humanity."[18] Moreover, if ethical beliefs and practice cannot be assessed or scrutinized, any notion of moral progress (whether conceived of in religious or nonreligious terms) is incoherent and delusory.[19]

In a delightfully insightful essay titled "Confronting Relativism," William Irvine offers this advice after having taught at the university level for many years:

---

[16]While attempts in academic literature to advance the notion of ethical relativism are seemingly endless, a representative case is set forth by Gilbert Harman in "Is There a Single True Morality?" in *Moral Relativism: A Reader,* ed. P. K. Moser and T. L. Carson (New York: Oxford University Press, 2001), pp. 165-84.

[17]A very useful test case that exposes the illogic and inconsistency of ethical relativism *in practice* is found in Loretta M. Kopelman, "Female Circumcision/Genital Mutilation and Ethical Relativism," in *Moral Relativism: A Reader,* ed. P. K. Moser and T. L. Carson (New York: Oxford University Press, 2001), pp. 307-25.

[18]It is significant that in the Nuremberg trials, arguments in defense of those who were accused of "crimes against humanity" were repeatedly and consistently relativist. Consider this one example: "Experiments that time and again have been described in the international literature without meeting any opposition do not constitute a crime from the medical point of view. . . . In view of the complete lack of *written* legal norms, the physician, who generally knows only little about the law, has to rely on and refer to the admissibility of what is generally recognized to be admissible all over the world" (emphasis in original). This is an extract from the Closing Brief for the Defendant [Dr.] Ruff, *Military Tribunal 1,* vol. 1, p. 92, quoted in Ruth Macklin, "Universality of the Nuremberg Code," in *The Nazi Doctors and the Nuremberg Code: Human Rights in Human Experimentation,* ed. George J. Annas and Michael A. Grodin (New York: Oxford University Press, 1992), p. 247.

[19]For a cogent critique of ethical relativism written from an evangelical standpoint, see Francis Beckwith and Gregory Koukl, *Relativism* (Grand Rapids, Mich.: Baker, 1998).

After dealing with student relativism for decades, I have come to the conclusion that it is a view students can fairly easily be talked out of. It is not at all difficult to reveal to students the extent to which they are closet absolutists. It is also not difficult to reveal to them that their fondness for relativism is in large part due to their misunderstanding the nature of absolutism.[20]

Part of Irvine's strategy for "outing closet absolutists" (those are his words) is to point out students' prevalent misconceptions that predispose them toward ethical relativism. What are these misconceptions? Irvine identifies four:[21]

- Only someone coming from a conservative religious background would favor ethical absolutism.
- Absolutists think they have all the answers, ethically speaking.
- Ethical absolutists view the world in black-and-white terms: they regard every action as being either right or wrong and don't allow for cases that are simply outside the realm of ethics.
- Absolutists are intolerant of others.

Irvine's concern is to point out the difference between relativist intolerance, which so frequently masquerades as open-mindedness today, and the persistently occurring notions of fairness and obligation that every self-absorbed undergraduate experiences, which ultimately come from universal and timeless notions of justice.

Much has been written in recent years on the ascent of postmodernity, with its radical relativism in reaction to the fundamental assumptions of modernity. Because numerous Christian writers have offered a critique of postmodernity, it is not my focus to do so here.[22] What I must emphasize, however, in the context of our present discussion—especially for evangelical readers—are these two points:

- The religious and ideological pluralism that accompanies postmodernity is not a new phenomenon.
- Valuable resources, both biblical and historical, stand at the church's disposal as we head into the twenty-first century.

---

[20]Irvine, "Confronting Relativism," p. 51.

[21]Ibid., pp. 43-46.

[22]The amount of literature devoted to postmodernism since 1990 is massive. From an evangelical point of view, highly recommended is Millard Erickson's *Truth or Consequences: The Promise and Perils of Postmodernism* (Downers Grove, Ill.: InterVarsity Press, 2001), which illustrates how theology should be intersecting with philosophy, and, on a less technical level, Gene Edward Veith Jr., *Postmodern Times* (Wheaton, Ill.: Crossway, 1994), which offers the layperson a helpful understanding of the contemporary Zeitgeist.

Renewed contact with saints and strategies of the past will provide us with much-needed wisdom for the present and future task. And to begin with, they will remind us that religious and philosophical pluralism indeed is nothing new.[23]

RETRIEVING NATURAL LAW

Writers such as G. K. Chesterton, Dorothy Sayers and C. S. Lewis, despite their being generations removed, retain immense popularity among American Christians and notably among evangelicals due to their extraordinarily fecund imaginations and lucid defense of Christian basics. But they also have in common the knack for stressing "the permanent things."[24] Consider Lewis, who is not foremost known for his writings on political themes.[25] And yet, we find him addressing topics as wide-ranging as capital punishment, statism, socialism, welfare, crime, the atom bomb, war, censorship, ethics and more. What is striking about the undercurrent of Lewis's thinking is that he consistently seeks to emphasize *the permanent;* hence, his views have lasting value generations later.

In several of his works—notably, in *Mere Christianity* and *The Abolition of Man*—Lewis speaks of the Tao to denote a universal moral code rooted in individual conscience.[26] In "Right and Wrong as a Clue to the Meaning of the Universe," the first of the essays that make up *Mere Christianity,* Lewis presents evidence for the existence of God and contends that every person is born with a moral sense to distinguish between right and wrong.[27] If there is no such

---

[23]An eloquent reminder of this is Robert L. Wilken's essay "Religious Pluralism and Early Christian Thought," originally published in *Pro Ecclesia* 1, no. 1 (1992): 89-103; and reprinted in his *Remembering the Christian Past* (Grand Rapids, Mich.: Eerdmans, 1995), pp. 25-46.

[24]According to one source, already by the late 1980s, more than 70 million copies of C. S. Lewis's works had been sold. As of this book's writing, HarperCollins has announced the purchase rights to Lewis's works, which should guarantee Lewis's place as the best-selling author of all time, if he is not already that.

[25]Political scientist John G. West Jr. deftly calls attention to the political ramifications of Lewis's writings, even when Lewis assiduously eschewed partisan politics during his day. See West, "Politics from the Shadowlands. C. S. Lewis on Earthly Government," *Policy Review* 68 (spring 1994): 68-70.

[26]To the Chinese, moral reality is the Tao (literally, "the way"); to East Asian Indians it is dharma; to Westerners, it is "nature"; and to the apostle Paul, it is "the law . . . written on their hearts."

[27]"One is sometimes (not often) glad not to be a great theologian. One might easily confuse it with being a good Christian," wrote Lewis in *Reflections on the Psalms* (New York: Harcourt, Brace & World, 1958), p. 57, reminding his readers of his acute awareness that he himself was not a theologian. One is tempted to wonder, however, if this disclaimer was more a statement about the elitism that he sensed among most professional theologians. If this in fact is the case, then we can lament with Lewis the fact that very often the language of academic theologians obscures rather than mediates theological truth to the layperson. One of the finest attempts to understand and appreciate Lewis's ability to write for the nontechnical, nonprofessional reader is Gilbert Meilaender's essay "C. S. Lewis and a Theology

thing as right and wrong, no "law of nature," then what, Lewis asks, is the difference between fair and unfair treatment?

> Whenever you find a man who says he does not believe in a real Right and
> Wrong, you will find the same man going back on this a moment later. He may
> break his promise to you, but if you try breaking one to him he will be com-
> plaining 'It's not fair' before you can say Jack Robinson.[28]

Therefore, it would seem for Lewis, we are "forced" to believe in a concept
of right and wrong. For despite our intellectual justifications to the contrary, we
expect to be treated with human decency so much so that one is justified in
calling this expectation a moral "law." What Lewis refers to as the "law of nature" or the "law of oughtness" (i.e., the awareness and expectation within all
people to be treated fairly, justly and decently) is what philosophers and theologians refer to as "judicial sentiment." Conscience, "the law written on the
heart" (cf. Rom 2:15), which both accuses and excuses the individual, is fickle
and can be violated, hardened, seared or ignored; but judicial sentiment is not
fickle.[29] Rather, it appears to be unswerving and wholly consistent.[30] That is,

> whereas our conscience sometimes lets us off the hook when we behave badly
> toward others, our judicial sentiment refuses to let others off the hook when
> they behave badly toward us. In this sense judicial sentiment is virtually unerr-
> ing, unlike our sometimes fickle sentiment of conscience.[31]

Those who object to such a universal moral phenomenon, notes Lewis, perhaps will attempt to argue that morality is a social and cultural convention or
that conventional morality is little more than a herd instinct. To the latter objection it can be said that our varied instincts will, at some point, be in conflict

---

of the Everyday," in *Things That Count: Essays Moral and Theological* (Wilmington, Del.: Intercollegiate
Studies Institute, 2000), pp. 123-44. Meilaender says, "This sense that eternal issues are at stake in the
mundane choices of our everyday life helps, I think, to account for the fact that, in this country [the
U.S.], Lewis has been so popular among evangelical Protestants. . . . Lewis thinks of all the ordinary
decisions of life as forming our character, as turning us into people who either do or do not wish to
gaze forever upon the face of God. It is not just that he appreciates the everyday, however; it is also
that he understands and evokes its significance for our moral and spiritual life" (pp. 131-32).

[28]C. S. Lewis, *Mere Christianity*, rev. ed. (New York: Macmillan, 1960), p. 19.

[29]The phenomenon of judicial sentiment is described by Paul in Rom 2:1-3.

[30]Conscience and judicial sentiment are part of what theology teaches as general revelation: i.e., the
knowledge of the Creator, the self and the universe that is shared by all people at all times and in all
places.

[31]Ted M. Dorman, *A Faith for All Seasons: Historic Christian Belief in Its Classical Expression*, rev. ed.
(Nashville: Broadman & Holman, 2001), p. 6.

with each other; the moral law will adjudicate between and prioritize these competing desires. To the former objection, Lewis reminds us of the simple fact that although conventions are passed on from generation to generation, this does not automatically render them mere cultural constructs. Why is it that most societies, over millennia, transmit moral standards that are remarkably similar? Why are murder, theft, child molestation, incest, property damage and the like *universally* decried by diverse cultures? Such is not the result of democratic consensus; rather, it is evidence of a moral law at work.

This universal law, the law of human nature, tells us what human beings *ought* to do yet fail to do.[32] The existence of such a law invariably leads to the question of the law's origin. Precisely what lies behind this law of oughtness? As a matter of explanation, two contrasting views of reality—the materialist and the religious—offer competing explanations. For materialists, the moral impulse either is a matter of social consensus or is random and evolutionary in nature, the result of chemical processes. For Lewis, this does not give an adequate account of mind, reason, reflection and morality; thus, intellectual honesty demands an openness to the religious explanation.

This universal moral code, what Lewis also calls the Tao, is inescapable and is accessible to all people, independent of their social upbringing, cultural background or private experience.[33] "Natural law," then, may be understood as a consensus that arises through the centuries about notions of right and wrong. The "natural" aspect of natural law reminds us that evidence exists all around us as to *how nature—both physical and human—operates.* The "law" aspect reminds us of the consistency and uniformity of things as they should be. The existence of natural law, it must be emphasized, is independent of faith. That is, regenerate as well as unregenerate people establish laws that impugn child molesters, murderers, thieves, adulterers and the like. Christians and non-Christians draw the same conclusions about behavior that is acceptable and unacceptable. Moreover, both unregenerate and regenerate are held accountable to the temporal judgment that those laws express.

---

[32]Lewis, *Mere Christianity,* pp. 26-30.

[33]One ethicist has put it this way: "Natural law refers to God's revelation of morality from all sources outside of Scripture. In this sense, natural law is general revelation applied to moral values" (Scott B. Rae, *Moral Choices: An Introduction to Ethics,* rev. ed. [Grand Rapids, Mich.: Zondervan, 2000], p. 38). This means that basic moral truth is accessible to Hindus, Buddhists, Muslims, Jews, Taoists and others around the globe. It is basic knowledge that all possess regarding themselves and the nature of things; it is not knowledge, however, that is salvific in nature.

The apostle Paul appears to be assuming this truth in his Areopagus speech (Acts 17:22-31) when referring to the "unknown god" who makes himself known through the created order; who is to be sought after and discovered; who is the one in whom "we live and move and have our being"; and who has set a day of moral reckoning.[34] The "law of nature," what Paul calls "the law written on their hearts" (Rom 2:15), is presupposed, then, in Christianity.[35] Hence natural law may be thought of in terms of general revelation that applies to ethics.[36]

The relevance of general revelation to daily life is evidenced in the fact that many of the peoples of the ancient Near East, including the Israelites, developed particular insights into living—proverbial wisdom—and enshrined them in a corpus of wisdom literature (examples of which in the Hebrew canon are Job, Proverbs and Ecclesiastes). Wisdom proceeds from observations made about physical as well as human nature. Wisdom is not confined to any one people; it is the possession of all who seek it. Consider these intuitions collected from African proverbial wisdom:[37]

- No polecat ever smelled his own stink.
- When it rains, the roof always drips the same way.
- He has the kindness of a witch.
- It is patience that gets you out of a net.
- A butterfly that flies among the thorns will tear its wings.
- The strength of a crocodile is in the water.
- When you marry a beautiful woman, you marry problems.
- The sons of a king do not need to be taught about power.

These insights, it goes without saying, would be regarded as universally true by anyone at any time in any cultural context. Wisdom, then, can be seen as

---

[34]See chap. six, "Biblical Resources for Ethics: The Pauline Model," below, for a discussion of Paul's strategy in Athens.

[35]Paul writes, "When Gentiles, who do not possess the law, do instinctively what the law requires, these, though not having the law, are a law to themselves. They show that what the law requires is written on their hearts, to which their own conscience also bears witness; and their conflicting thoughts will accuse or perhaps excuse them" (Rom 2:14-15).

[36]Scripture does not leave us without an account of this witness to unregenerate humanity; indeed, it presupposes it: see, e.g., Ps 19:1-6; 104:1-30; Acts 14:17; 17:22-28; 26:1-29; Rom 1:18-21, 28; 2:14-15; 1 Cor 11:14. The good news revealed through Christ is predicated on an awareness of the bad news, which is to say, the measurement in a fallen world of ethical norms that we do not keep.

[37]These proverbs have been gathered in Ruth Finnegan's *Oral Literature in Africa* (Oxford: Oxford University Press, 1970), pp. 389-425, and reproduced with commentary in Claus Westermann, *Roots of Wisdom: The Oldest Proverbs of Israel and Other Peoples,* trans. J. D. Charles (Louisville, Ky.: Westminster John Knox, 1995), pp. 145-46.

constituting a common mode of discourse for all people, the world over. In a very practical sense, wisdom shows itself to be a necessary and universally accessible foundation for ethics. The way in which proverbial wisdom bridges morality and social dealings of all cultures and eras is on display in the fascinatingly relevant wisdom sayings of the Old Testament book of Proverbs as well as in the complexities expressed throughout the book of Ecclesiastes. A subtheme of the latter is that "there is nothing new under the sun." The end product of Qoheleth's philosophical musings (the "conclusion to the matter") is that one must revere God and that nothing in life has meaning and purpose outside of a theistic outlook. This philosophical bottom line is intended to express universal truth and have universal application. For that reason, Ecclesiastes remains an invaluable, though much neglected, part of the biblical canon. In neglecting this book Christians rob themselves of much-needed insight into the complexities of their earthly sojourn as they struggle with the vicissitudes of life and find their way among competing worldviews in pluralistic culture.

To the extent that human beings deny or suppress this moral law, they do so at their own peril. Lewis observed already in his own day the trend in the West to reduce—and, in time, eliminate—the essence of what it means to be human. Humans reduce themselves, as Lewis saw it, when they belittle the significance of the Tao both in their own thinking and in the thinking of others. Because the very thing that sets humans apart from the rest of the created order is a conscience rooted in the Tao, a lessening or diminishing of the Tao diminishes human nature. The relativist reduces the Tao by claiming that there are no objective moral standards, that there is no universal truth. Such elimination of humans' ability to judge between right and wrong abolishes the very essence of humanity—hence, the title of what is arguably Lewis's most important work, *The Abolition of Man.*[38]

The approach to moral reasoning illustrated by Lewis—namely, arguing in accordance with the time-honored notion of natural law—speaks in particular to those evangelicals who pride themselves in championing "biblically based morality." It is instructive because of Lewis's belief that natural law as a part of

---

[38]C. S. Lewis, *The Abolition of Man* (New York: Macmillan, 1947). In the appendix to *Abolition*, Lewis gives illustrations of the Tao, or natural law, grouping these precepts according to eight headings: (1) general beneficence, (2) special beneficence, (3) responsibilities to parents and elders, (4) responsibilities to children and posterity, (5) justice, (6) trust and truthfulness, (7) mercy and (8) magnanimity. Given the plethora of ethical and bioethical dilemmas facing contemporary Western culture, *Abolition* should be required reading for every Christian, notwithstanding the fact that it is not an easy read.

general revelation is known to all people based on reason.[39] In one of his lesser-known philosophical essays, titled "On Ethics," Lewis calls into question the popular assumption that Christian ethics introduced to the world a "novel," "new" and "peculiar" set of commands.[40] He maintains that

> the idea . . . that Christianity brought a new ethical code into the world is a grave error. If it had done so, then we should have to conclude that all who first preached it wholly misunderstood their own message: for all of them, its Founder, His precursor, His apostles, came demanding repentance and offering forgiveness, a demand and an offer both meaningless except on the assumption of a moral law already known and already broken. . . .
>
> In a certain sense, it is no more possible to invent a new ethics than to place a new sun in the sky. Some precept from traditional morality always has to be assumed. We never start from a *tabula rasa:* if we did, we should end, ethically speaking, with a *tabula rasa.*[41]

It is noteworthy that in the literature, natural-law thinking presently seems to be staging something of a comeback. This is significant in a climate of postmodernity, which declares that we can make no justified claims to knowing "truth."[42] One "natural lawyer" and cultural critic has observed that in 1998

---

[39]Few will forget the commotion that erupted over natural law at the time of Clarence Thomas's Supreme Court confirmation hearings in 1991. What was all the fuss about? Aside from politics, natural-law theorists differ in significant ways: e.g., in their understanding of what constitutes human nature (dignity or depravity?), human rationality, basic "morality" and the function of law. Harvard's Laurence Tribe, representing a professoriate that was generally enraged that Thomas would rest certain legal convictions on natural law, became unsettled. "Judge Thomas's adherence to 'natural law' as a judicial philosophy could take the Court in [a] . . . troubling direction," Tribe opined in the pages of *The New York Times* (" 'Natural Law' and the Nominee," July 15, 1991, p. A20). Delaware Senator Joseph Biden, fearful that Judge Thomas might have in mind a "moral code," proceeded to lecture Thomas with this misguided piece of advice: "We must never forget that the central natural-law commitment made by this country is the commitment to individual freedom." James Skillen, in the aftermath of the Thomas hearings, wisely reminded us that the either/or depiction of natural law that Senator Biden had created, fully aside from political grandstanding, was a false dichotomy. Freedoms can *only* inhere in a morally ordered society. See James W. Skillen, "Natural Law and the Foundations of Government," *Public Justice Report* 14, no. 4 (1991): 2.

[40]C. S. Lewis, "On Ethics," in *Christian Reflections,* ed. Walter Hooper (Grand Rapids, Mich.: Eerdmans, 1967), p. 46.

[41]Ibid., pp. 46, 53. Lewis does not wish to deny that we find in Christian ethics a deepening or internalization of the existing moral code. He merely wishes to advise the reader that only serious ignorance of Jewish and pagan morality leads one to view Christian ethics as being radically new.

[42]By contrast, Thomas Aquinas believes that human reason *cannot fail* to grasp *some* knowledge of the truth; basic moral principles are knowable, are "inscribed on the human heart"; see, e.g., *Summa Theologica* 1-2.Q.94.4.

and 1999 alone, at least twenty-six books with the term *natural law* in their title had been published in the United States.[43] Appeals to the laws of nature, of course, have been made throughout the entire history of Western civilization. Historically, these have served as an authoritative basis by which to make ethical judgments. In its metaphysical sense, natural law attempts, through reason, to ground human behavior in abiding moral principle that exists by divine design. Natural-law theory assumes there is a common fund of moral knowledge to which all persons have access.

The idea of universal moral truths dates as far back as Socrates and Aristotle. "What is by nature just," writes Aristotle, "has the same force everywhere, and does not depend on what we regard or do not regard as just."[44] This law, he observes, is "universal."[45] In fact, Aristotle believes in and defends the "legislating" of morality. That is, laws—whether *written or unwritten*—help shape character, since men are not born virtuous.[46] Roman writers from Cicero to Marcus Aurelius also comment on laws that issue out of nature.[47] The New Testament presupposes, rather then negates, natural law—a natural law that was expressed in the Ten Commandments: "Ever since the creation of the world his eternal power and divine nature, invisible though they are, have been understood and seen through the things he has made. So they are without excuse" (Rom 1:20). This,

---

[43]J. Budziszewski, "Natural Born Lawyers," *The Weekly Standard,* December 20, 1999, p. 31. One of these volumes was the reissuing of Heinrich Rommen's classic work *The Natural Law: A Study in Legal and Social History and Philosophy,* trans. T. R. Hanley (reprint; Indianapolis: Liberty Fund, 1998). This book was originally published as *Die ewige Wiederkehr des Naturrechts* (Leipzig, Germany: Verlag Jakob Hegner, 1936); it was translated and revised in 1947 by Herder. A renaissance of natural-law thinking seems to have occurred in the 1940s and 1950s, due in no small part to Rommen's work. It is fitting, then, that the Liberty Fund of Indianapolis has recently republished this seminal work. The inspiration for this volume came from Rommen's concern about the rise of Nazi ideology throughout the 1930s. Rommen watched with alarm as the Nazi party attempted a *legal* grasp of power, becoming, in the words of Rommen, "masters of legality" (*The State in Catholic Thought: A Treatise in Political Philosophy* [St. Louis: Herder, 1945], p. 212).

[44]Aristotle *Ethica nichomachea* 5.7 (1134b); Aristotle, *Nichomachean Ethics,* 3rd ed., trans. Martin Ostwald (New York: Macmillan, 1986), p. 131.

[45]Ibid. (1135a).

[46]Ibid. 10.9 (1179b-1180b).

[47]Perhaps the most important early Roman treatise on natural law comes from the Stoic Cicero's *De Republica* 3.22.33: "True law is right reason in agreement with nature, universal, consistent, everlasting, whose nature is to advocate duty by prescription and to deter wrongdoing by prohibition. . . . Neither the Senate nor the People can absolve us from obeying this law, and we do not need to look outside ourselves for an expounder or interpreter of this law. There will not be one law at Rome and another at Athens or different laws now and in the future. There is now and will be forever one law, valid for all peoples and all times" (Cicero, *De Republica, De Legibus,* Loeb Classical Library [Cambridge, Mass.: Harvard University Press, 1951], p. 211).

for Paul, is "the law written on their hearts" (Rom 2:15), corresponding to what
the church variously has referred to as "common grace."

The notion of natural law was central to the church's social teaching during
the medieval period. The great champion of natural law in the thirteenth century was Thomas Aquinas, for whom moral law was natural insofar as it mirrored the order of creation. For Aquinas, a corrective to the Augustinian view
of total depravity was necessary: Aquinas countered that the imago Dei,
though marred, was still intact. Notwithstanding sin's ravages, this law remained self-evident through revelation and reason:

> So it is clear that as far as the general principles of reason are concerned, wheth-
> er speculative or practical, there is one standard of truth or rightness for every-
> body. . . . So we must conclude that the law of nature, as far as first principles
> are concerned, is the same for all as the norm of right conduct and is equally
> well known to all.[48]

The Protestant Reformers, without systematically treating the subject in
their writings, presuppose the notion of natural law, even when they believed
that reason is insufficient due to the effects of sin. Martin Luther describes the
innate awareness of right and wrong behavior in two ways. He speaks of
Naturrecht (natural justice) and *natuerliches Recht* (natural law).[49]

> Thus, "Thou shalt not kill, commit adultery, steal, etc." are not Mosaic laws only,
> but also the natural law written in each man's heart, as St. Paul teaches (Rom.
> 2). Also Christ himself (Matt. 7) includes all of the law and the prophets in this
> natural law.[50]

Referring to the awareness of the so-called golden rule in all people, Luther
writes, "by nature they judge that one should do to others what one wants done
to oneself."[51] Luther believes that natural law exists as a moral standard among
the heathen: "Natural law is a practical first principle on the sphere of morality;
it forbids evil and commands good. The basis of natural law is God, who has

---

[48]Aquinas *Summa Theologica* 1-2.Q.94.

[49]Two of the three primary resources on Luther's understanding of natural law are untranslated from
the German: Ernst Wolf, "Natürliches Gesetz und Gesetz Christi bei Luther," in *Peregrinatio: Studien
zur reformatorischen Theologie und zum Kirchenproblem* (Muenchen: Chr. Kaiser, 1954), pp. 191-223;
and Martin Schloemann, *Natürliches und gepredigtes Gesetz bei Luther* (Berlin: Toepelmann, 1961).
The third is Paul Althaus, *The Ethics of Martin Luther,* trans. R. C. Schultz (Philadelphia: Fortress,
1972).

[50]*Luther's Works,* vol. 40, ed. Conrad Bergendoff (Philadelphia: Fortress, 1958), p. 97.

[51]*Luther's Works,* vol. 27, ed. Jaroslav Pelikan (St. Louis: Concordia, 1964), p. 56.

created this light, but the basis of positive law is civil authority."[52]

Philip Melanchthon, the "quiet reformer," and John Calvin understand natural law in much the same way as Luther. Melanchthon's defense of natural law appears to be based on Romans 2:15: "A natural law is a common judgment to which all men alike assent, and therefore one which God has inscribed upon the soul of each man." Calvin's description is almost identical: "The things contained in the two tables [of the law] are, in a manner, dictated to us by that inner law, which, as has already been said, is in a manner written and stamped on every heart."[53] He also writes that "the activity and insights of conscience are the language in which the law of nature is couched."[54] An "unchangeable rule of right living," natural law, in Calvin's understanding, is "a living law," since it is "the common law of nations."[55]

In his *Of the Laws of Ecclesiastical Polity,* penned in 1594, Richard Hooker observes of the law of nature: "Her seat is the bosom of God, her voice the harmony of the world."[56] Similarly, Nathaniel Culverwel writes in 1652, "By this great and glorious Law every good action was commanded, and all evill was discountenanc'd, and forbidden from everlasting";[57] Culverwel would exercise direct influence on the thinking of a significant political philosopher to come, John Locke.

The eighteenth century witnessed the application of natural law to political philosophy, particularly as a result of Locke's writings.[58] There is a notable shift in emphasis away from the ethical authority of the church and Scripture and

---

[52]*Luther's Works,* vol. 54, ed. T. G. Tappert (Philadelphia: Fortress, 1967), p. 293; cf. also *Luther's Works,* vol. 46, ed. R. C. Schultz (Philadelphia: Fortress, 1967), p. 269.

[53]John Calvin *Institutes of the Christian Religion* 2.8.1 (trans. H. Beveridge [Grand Rapids, Mich.: Eerdmans, 1957]).

[54]Ibid. 2.2.22.

[55]Ibid. 2.2.22, 4.10.16.

[56]Richard Hooker, *Of the Laws of Ecclesiastical Polity,* ed. John Keble et al., 3 vols. (Oxford: Clarendon, 1888), 1:285.

[57]Nathaniel Culverwel, *Elegant and Learned Discourse of the Light of Nature,* ed. Robert A. Greene and High MacCallum (Toronto: University of Toronto Press, 1971), p. 36.

[58]See, e.g., John Locke, *Two Treatises of Government,* ed. Peter Laslett (New York: Cambridge University Press, 1960), esp. the second treatise, secs. 6 and 12; and Locke, *Questions Concerning the Law of Nature,* ed. R. H. Horwitz et al. (Ithaca, N.Y.: Cornell University Press, 1990). Locke's definition of natural law comes to expression in the context of addressing political and individual freedom: "By the foundation of natural law we understand that which supports and upon which are erected, as upon a foundation, all other precepts of this law, even the less obvious, and that from which [these precepts] can be deduced in some manner. As a consequence, these derive their entire force and their binding power from this [foundation] because they are in agreement with primary and, as it were, fundamental law, which is the rule and measure of all other laws which depend upon it" (*Questions,* p. 237).

toward pure reason as the means by which to establish ethical norms. Locke's writings, as it turns out, undergird the American experiment, and the founders appeal to natural law in order to ground the new nation's establishment. Thomas Jefferson appeals to "Laws of Nature and Nature's God," from which issue those self-evident truths spelled out in the preamble of the Declaration of Independence.[59] Locke and the framers of America's charter documents to follow speak of human beings possessing certain inalienable rights.[60]

Although the concept of natural law has long been central to Catholic social thought, contemporary Protestantism, by contrast, has "no comparable coherent framework for grounding its social thought." This is the conviction of theologian Carl Braaten, director of the Center for Catholic and Evangelical Theology, that was recently set forth in an important essay titled "Protestants and Natural Law."[61] Braaten does not hold this conviction alone, however; a similar conviction was expressed a century ago by Dutch Reformed theologian (and former prime minister) Abraham Kuyper, whom Braaten cites.[62] In 1891, on the occasion of the publication of Pope Leo XIII's encyclical *Rerum Novarum,* Kuyper conceded:

> It must be admitted to our shame that the Roman Catholics are far ahead of us in their study of the social question. Indeed, very far ahead. . . . The Encyclical of Leo XIII gives the principles which are common to all Christians, and which we share with our Roman Catholic compatriots.[63]

Kuyper's appreciation of Roman Catholicism on matters moral and social, to which Braaten calls our attention, finds further confirmation seven years later, in the 1898 Stone Lectures that Kuyper delivered at Princeton University. Kuyper praises "the marvelous energy displayed in the latter half of this cen-

---

[59]Jefferson's understanding of natural law represented his own "harmonizing" of the "sentiments of the day, whether expressed in conversation, in letters, printed essays, or the elementary books of public right, as Aristotle, Cicero, Locke, Sydney, etc." (quoted in Paul Ford, ed., *The Writings of Thomas Jefferson,* 10 vols. [New York: Macmillan, 1892-1899], 10:343). While the modernist attack on natural law remains outside the scope of our discussion, multiple perspectives on modern use of natural law can be found in Edward B. McLean, ed., *Common Truths: New Perspectives on Natural Law* (Wilmington, Del.: Intercollegiate Studies Institute, 2000), esp. pt. 2.

[60]Locke, *Treatises,* secs. 6 and 12.

[61]Carl E. Braaten, "Protestants and Natural Law," *First Things* 19 (January 1992): 20-26.

[62]Tireless in his efforts to apply Christianity to every realm of life, Kuyper was the founder of the Free (Reformed) University of Amsterdam in 1880, and from 1901 to 1905 he served as prime minister of the Netherlands.

[63]Kuyper, quoted in Braaten, "Protestants," p. 20.

tury by Rome" and "Rome's successful efforts in social life."[64] He also calls fellow Protestants to acknowledge that "what we have in common with Rome concerns precisely those fundamentals of our Christian creed now most fiercely assaulted by the modern spirit. . . . Now, in this conflict Rome is not an antagonist, but stands on our side."[65]

In both his 1891 and his 1898 remarks Kuyper is addressing two broader tendencies among fellow Protestants: First, relatively speaking, is a sectarian spirit that is unable (or unwilling) to acknowledge Roman Catholics as fellow Christians who confess the same creedal realities in the face of pagan culture.[66] Second is our inability to learn from Roman Catholic social teaching. The "principles . . . common to all" used by Leo and noted by Kuyper relate to natural law—a concept that, in Braaten's words, "serves as a bridge category on ethical and social questions between church and world, between those with *a priori* commitment to sacred Scripture and the Christian creed and those outside the community of faith."[67]

Braaten proposes that Protestants reappropriate the natural-law tradition.[68] This is all the more important in light of the present cultural context, which is radically pluralistic. As it applies to evangelicals, who over the last 125 years

---

[64]Abraham Kuyper, *Lectures on Calvinism,* rev. ed. (Grand Rapids, Mich.: Eerdmans, 1987), p. 183.

[65]Ibid., p. 183. The "fundamentals of our Christian creed" are noted by Kuyper to be "the Trinity, the Deity of Christ, the Cross as atoning sacrifice, the Scripture as the Word of God, and the Ten Commandments as a divinely-imposed rule of life" (ibid., pp. 183-84).

[66]Kuyper is by no means oblivious to the fact that "the Reformation has established a fundamental antithesis between Rome and ourselves." But he does state winsomely, "I for my part am not ashamed to confess that on many points my views have been clarified through my study of the Romish theologians" (ibid., pp. 183-84). Thus, he can see the utter need for common-cause cooperation. To his credit, J. Gresham Machen shared Kuyper's attitude in this regard, thereby distinguishing himself from most of his "fundamentalist" contemporaries. Machen's thinking, on display in his *Christianity and Liberalism* (New York: Macmillan, 1924), appears in the chapter titled "Doctrine" and is both passionate and winsome: "Far more serious still is the division between the Church of Rome and evangelical Protestantism in all its forms. Yet how great is the common heritage which unites the Roman Catholic Church, with its maintenance of the authority of Holy Scripture and with its acceptance of the great early creeds, to devout Protestants today!" (p. 52). Sensing the reader's objection, Machen writes, "We would not indeed obscure the difference which divides us from Rome. The gulf is indeed profound. But profound as it is, it seems trifling compared to the abyss which stands between us and many ministers of our own Church" (ibid.). The implication is that there exists fellowship between differing parts of Christendom, and "specifically Christian fellowship exists only between those to whom the message has become the very basis of all life" (ibid.).

[67]Braaten, "Protestants," p. 25.

[68]His choice of the word *reappropriate* suggests a positive view of natural law among early Protestants. It also means that Protestants should seek to rehabilitate reason. Perhaps the clearest statement on the proper relationship between reason and faith is to be found in the 1998 encyclical by Pope John Paul II, *Fides et Ratio* ("Faith and Reason").

have not exhibited inordinate cultural fluency, the challenge is this: how can the Christian community begin to engage pagan culture, which wholly rejects biblical revelation, if it refuses or is unable to build an apologetic bridge on which both believer and nonbeliever can meet? As Braaten sees it, Protestants who fail to reappropriate the natural-law tradition have two options. Either they parade before a secular audience with a triumphalist theology of glory by which the public square must be conquered, or they withdraw into ghettolike sectarian communities alongside, but outside, the world.

Compounding our dilemma, in Braaten's view, is the fact that some highly visible Christian ethicists reject the very idea of natural law and, thus, are unable, despite their considerable influence, to equip the church effectively in terms of its cultural mandate.[69] Braaten joins a number of thoughtful voices who, while sensitive to the triumphalist error, caution Christians to avoid the opposite error: they must resist any temptation to withdraw from emergent culture.[70]

---

[69]Examples of this category would be ethicists Paul Lehmann, whose "koinonia ethics" amounted to a renouncing of natural-law theory, and John Howard Yoder and Stanley Hauerwas, whose outspoken and forceful Anabaptist critique of Constantinianism excludes the reality of natural law and fails to address the complexities of responsible civil engagement. Braaten is notably (and rightly, in my view) critical of Hauerwas for his rejection of natural-law theory. See, e.g., Stanley Hauerwas, *The Peaceable Kingdom: A Primer in Christian Ethics* (South Bend, Ind.: University of Notre Dame Press, 1983), pp. 11-12, 55-64, and Hauerwas, Richard Bondi and David B. Burrell, *Truthfulness and Tragedy: Further Investigations in Christian Ethics* (Notre Dame, Ind.: University of Notre Dame Press, 1977), pp. 57-70. Hauerwas believes that "Christian ethics theologically does not have a stake in 'natural law' " (*Truthfulness,* p. 58); that reason is insufficient to lead people to basic moral principle (ibid.); that natural-law arguments often take the form of ideological commitments (ibid., p. 214 n. 3); that natural-law thinking is a reflection of the Constantinian era (ibid., p. 214 n. 5); and that natural-law thinking well nigh "perverts" the nature of the Christian life (ibid.).

[70]More recently, ethicist Vigen Guroian has deftly critiqued the "public theology" of Yoder and Hauerwas in *Ethics After Christendom: Toward an Ecclesial Christian Ethic* (Grand Rapids, Mich.: Eerdmans, 1994), notably in pt. 1 (pp. 11-80). While deeming Yoder's position helpful in pointing out the excesses of "re-christianizing America," Guroian also finds it deficient in assisting us in constructing a *public theology.* This is for several reasons, the following of which are among them: its *preoccupation* with denouncing Constantinianism and cultural imperialism, its inability to root "narrative" ethics in the broader streams of historic Christian tradition, and its lack of "eucharistic ecclesiology." In the end, Guroian finds the theology of Yoder and Hauerwas, which is rooted in free-church Anabaptism, lacking a catholic character that is so necessary in today's cultural climate. Guroian, Braaten and Lutheran ethicist Gilbert Meilaender all share the concern that the Yoder-Hauerwas approach to ethics may wittingly or unwittingly discourage responsible Christian participation in society. George Weigel also joins the chorus of skeptics who question how the narrative approach to ethics can help reshape civic discourse and transform "the naked public square" into one that is civil (*Catholicism and the Renewal of American Democracy* [New York: Paulist, 1989], pp. 196-200). Pluralistic society, after all, needs a grammar, a common mode of discourse, that allows all groups to enter conversation with one another. Natural law provides that very vocabulary, for it facilitates a *public* conversation

But why has the tradition of natural law fallen on hard times in Protestant theology?[71] Braaten sees no real discontinuity between the teaching of the Reformers and their predecessors, for whom natural law was assumed as part of revealed truth. Rather, the eclipse of natural-law thinking is to be found in post-Enlightenment philosophical developments.[72] Compounding this secular development is a peculiarly *theological* factor. Some Protestants—and more than a few evangelicals—believe that the *imago Dei* is so thoroughly marred that not even a vestige of the "image" remains. Hence, any discussion of natural law seems, to these people, to commit the fallacy of exalting reason above faith, and therefore it is to be rejected.[73]

Braaten is convinced, and justifiably so, that ecumenical dialogue on the place of natural law in Christian ethics is both necessary and timely "as a kind of counterattack against the wholesale deconstruction of the classical moral and legal principles on which Western culture is founded."[74]

Moral relativism joins with political activism [in the academy] to sabotage the

---

that is based on a common and uniform language. Inter alia, what makes John Paul's encyclical *Veritatis Splendor* ("The Splendor of Truth") so significant is his attempt to demonstrate the relationship of natural law to freedom, reason and conscience. This relationship, the pontiff stresses, is harmonious and not oppositional. For nontechnical commentary on this linkage, see Servais Pinckaers, "Veritatis Splendor: Human Freedom and the Natural Law," *Ethics and Medics* 20, no. 2 (1995): 3-4.

[71]In all fairness, it should be said that Braaten does identify an eclectic band of Protestant theologians who view a positive cooperation between revelation and natural law: among these are Emil Brunner, Paul Althaus, Paul Tillich, Helmut Thielicke and Wolfhart Pannenberg. One could add to Braaten's list the influential ethicist Paul Ramsey.

[72]Braaten, "Protestants," p. 22.

[73]Braaten is understandably critical of Karl Barth, who thought natural law was the self-assertion of human autonomy apart from the living Word of God and, thus, an expression of natural religion. For Barth, the Scriptures alone are to be trusted rather than the "illusions and confessions . . . of the so-called natural law," which is not "derived from the clear law of its own faith" (*Community, State and Church* [Garden City, N.Y.: Doubleday, 1960], p. 165). Any notions of the divine formed outside of Scripture, says Barth, "will not in any way prepare him [the individual] for it. On the contrary, it will keep him from it" (*Church Dogmatics* 2/1, ed. G W Bromiley and T. F Torrance [Edinburgh: T & T Clark, 1957], p. 86). In defense of Barth, the pacifist might argue that Barth's theological position was right since, to his credit, he faithfully resisted Nazism, unlike many of his German counterparts. But it must be said that theology in the service of the Third Reich was less concerned with morality than with *legality*; this is persuasively argued by the German legal scholar and natural-law theorist Heinrich Rommen, who on account of his legal and political views was imprisoned by the Nazis. Thus, there is nothing in natural law per se that contributes to tyranny. When laws are corrupt and authoritarian power commands obedience to those laws, the law of nature has been grossly violated. See Rommen, *The Natural Law*.

[74]Braaten, "Protestants," p. 23. Braaten echoes the conviction of John Courtney Murray: "As a metaphysical idea, the idea of natural law is timeless, and for that reason timely" (*We Hold These Truths: Catholic Reflections on the American Proposition* [New York: Sheed & Ward, 1960], p. 320).

rules and standards needed to implement a societal system ordered by principles of justice and truth. When the normlessness and the nihilistic effects of the
deconstructionist mindset are no longer confined to academia, but invade the
wider public, the way is prepared for the moral collapse of social institutions for
the enthronement of the totalitarian state. . . . Perhaps it is time to expose current relativist and nihilist theories as the underside of totalitarian ideologies and
political authoritarianism. A revival of natural law can be of use in that project.[75]

I am inclined to agree with Braaten. To be sure, most Protestants—indeed,
most Americans—are uncomfortable talking about the "moral collapse of social institutions" or "the enthronement of the totalitarian state." But to speak
in such a way is not to be alarmist; rather, it is to be a realist, in much the same
way that John Paul has called for vigilance in the West against the wedding of
moral relativism and democratic pluralism, the trajectory of which is to breed
a brand of "civil barbarism" and, hence, political tyranny.

At this point it is likely that the reader will object to my use of the word
barbarism. Here I am using the term in the sense that John Courtney Murray
defined it. Barbarism, Murray wrote, is not merely primitive savagery. Rather,
it is also "the lack of reasonable conversation according to reasonable laws." In
using the word *conversation,* Murray means living together and talking together. Society becomes barbarous, he believed,

> when men huddle together under the rule of force and fear; *when economic in-
> terests assume the primacy over higher values;* when material standards of mass and
> quantity crush out the values of quality and excellence; *when technology assumes
> an autonomous existence and embarks on a course of unlimited self-exploitation with-
> out purposeful guidance from the higher disciplines of politics and morals* . . . ; when
> the state reaches the paradoxical point of being everywhere intrusive and also
> impotent; when the ways of men come under the sway of the instinctual, the
> impulsive, the compulsive.[76]

Murray believed that when symptoms like these are seen, barbarism is
afoot. These symptoms indicate that men have ceased talking together according to "reasonable laws," and civility dies with the death of ethical dialogue.[77]
For Murray, the common vocabulary that allowed Americans (and, indeed,

---

[75]Braaten, "Protestants," p. 25.
[76]Murray, *We Hold These Truths*, pp. 13-14, emphasis added.
[77]Ibid.

any free society) to have "conversation" was the language of natural law.[78]

The current revival of natural-law thinking, to which I alluded earlier, is not merely a *theological priority* in which evangelical Protestants should take part; it is also a prerequisite for demonstrating a *viable social ethic* in the face of pagan culture.[79] To affirm natural law is to affirm a transcendent order of which all people have basic knowledge.[80] And it is to realize that political problems, at bottom, are religious and moral problems.

The German legal scholar Heinrich Rommen, whose name is relatively unknown in Protestant circles, understood well the symbiotic relationship between the moral and the political. Rommen's work began to emerge at the time of the dissolution of the Weimar Republic in the 1930s, when Nazi ideology was ascendant. For his legal and political views Rommen was imprisoned by the Nazis, and then in 1938 he fled the Third Reich for the United States. Nazi ideology, as Rommen saw it, aimed "not at a revolution" so much as "a legal grasp of power according to formal democratic processes."[81] Every generation, the historian might observe, finds a new reason for the study of natural law. For those of Rommen's generation, totalitarianism provided that impetus: "When one of the relativist theories is made the basis of a totalitarian state," writes Rommen, "man is stirred to free himself from the pessimistic resignation that characterizes these relativist theories and to return to his principles."[82]

According to Russell Hittinger, who has written an introduction to the recent reissuing of Rommen's *The Natural Law,* Rommen's writings were prompted "by the spectacle of German legal professionals, who, while trained in the technicalities of positive law, were at a loss in responding to what he called 'Adolf Legalité.' "[83] In accounting for the loss of the moral perspective, Hittinger points to Rommen's conviction that legal institutions are mistakenly believed

---

[78]Murray's discussion of natural law (ibid., pp. 109-23, 295-336) belongs to two chapters titled "The Origins and Authority of the Public Consensus" and "The Doctrine Lives: The Eternal Return of Natural Law." The difference between the French Revolution and the American Revolution, writes Murray, was "less a revolution than a conversation" (p. 31).

[79]Although the metaphor of a "culture war" has been overdone in some circles and is counterproductive in policy debates, it nevertheless mirrors the conflict between opposing views of human nature, morality and how society should order itself—all of which play themselves out in the body politic.

[80]The premises of natural law are that all people have a basic knowledge of reality; everything in physical and human nature conforms to this reality; the order of nature is ruled over by the eternal Reason (the Logos); and the order of nature is mirrored in an ordered morality.

[81]Rommen, *State in Catholic Thought,* pp. 48, 212.

[82]Ibid., p. 48.

[83]Rommen, *Natural Law,* p. xii.

by many to serve as a bulwark against governing by raw power, as if they required "only the superintendence of certified professionals."[84] Typically forgotten, Rommen writes, is the fact that "legal institutions themselves can be made the object of the non-legal power struggle."[85] Indeed, already in 1935 Nazi jurist Hans Frank had written, "Formerly we were in the habit of saying: 'This is right or wrong.' Today we ask the question: 'What would the Fuehrer say?' "[86] Frank observed that devotion to Hitler "has become a concept of law."[87] This *Fuehrer Prinzip* justified Hitler's becoming a law unto himself.[88]

The question, then, is unavoidable: Apart from natural law, what argument and protection do we have against evil when it manifests itself?[89]

Certainly the state of the German legal profession in the 1930s rendered Rommen's book timely, but Rommen's book also addresses enduring issues.[90] Because of tyranny's inherent *will to power* (whether in its germinal state or its entrenchment), a necessary defense against both incipient and mature forms of totalitarianism and barbarism is an appeal to justice, to the rule of reason and to an objective body of moral values. Free associations (indeed, free societies) must plead in the name of and on the basis of natural law. It was Rommen's belief that through natural law alone we are able to solve the problem of

---

[84]Ibid.
[85]Rommen, *State in Catholic Thought*, p. 718.
[86]Hans Frank, quoted in Robert Conot, *Justice at Nuremberg* (New York: Macmillan, 1983), p. 79.
[87]Ibid.
[88]The significance of the chasm between morality and legality should not be lost on contemporary Americans. Nazi defendants at the Nuremberg trials and their attorneys presented arguments that resembled that of Gestapo chief Herman Goering: "I am here only to emphasize that I remained faithful to [Hitler], for I believe in keeping one's oath not in good times only, but also in bad times when it is much more difficult" (quoted in Conot, *Justice at Nuremberg*, p. 344). That these defendants were morally guilty of crimes against humanity was strictly *secondary* to their belief that they remained *legally innocent*.
[89]It is here that a purely "narrative" approach to ethics is insufficient to the task. Something concrete and abiding must lie behind—which is to say, be presupposed by—the "story." Meilaender has it right: "Even if Christian moral knowledge is built upon no foundation other than the biblical narrative of God's dealings with his world, *that story itself authorizes us to seek and expect some common moral ground with those whose vision is not shaped by Christian belief*" (*Faith and Faithfulness: Basic Themes in Christian Ethics* [Notre Dame, Ind.: University of Notre Dame Press, 1991], pp. 19-20, emphasis added). What happens when the pagan does not believe in, or does not care to believe, the Christian "story"?
[90]Hittinger's very helpful introduction to *Natural Law* compares Rommen's work with that several other influential European émigrés—viz., Yves Simon, Eric Voegelin, Leo Strauss and Jacques Maritain—who arrived in the United States at about the same time as Rommen. Hittinger also offers a brief assessment of twentieth-century natural-law thinking in the U.S., which is confined almost exclusively to Catholic social thinkers. Hittinger himself holds the Chair of Catholic Studies at the University of Tulsa, where he is also a research professor in the school of law. He is author of *A Critique of the New Natural Law Theory* (Notre Dame, Ind.: University of Notre Dame Press, 1987).

legitimacy of political power as well as the duty of free persons.[91] This is so because natural law—ultimately of divine origin but revealed in the very order of the universe—is "but the rule of reason founded upon the rational and social nature of man. *Veritas facit legem:* law is truth."[92]

Our discussion of natural law or a universal moral sense is by no means an academic exercise, however. Nor is it merely the concern of philosophers, lawyers, theologians or political theorists. It is critical to *every believer, every layperson,* in two unmistakable ways. Most fundamentally, it forms the basis for moral formation and cultivating the virtuous life.[93] It encourages us to ask: How *ought* one to live? What standards of behavior are acceptable and unacceptable? A moral life exists if in fact there is a law of nature.[94] Additionally, and just as importantly, natural law serves as a bridge between Christian and non-Christian morality. In civil society, Christians and nonbelievers conform to the same ethical standard.[95] Given the reality of natural law, believers need not attempt to build a case for biblical ethics that is alien to the unbeliever; we begin with simple observation and reasoning: nature teaches certain moral realities.[96] To minimize or ignore the role that natural law plays is to remove any

---

[91]Not even extreme cases such as that of Dietrich Bonhoeffer negate the fact that sin and the Fall make government necessary. Under "normal" conditions, citizens owe obedience. Only where government usurps its role by making itself sovereign over its citizens and dictating beliefs is disobedience required.

[92]Rommen, *Natural Law,* p. 236.

[93]See in this regard chap. seven, "Biblical Resources for Ethics: The Petrine Model," below.

[94]Thus, the cleft that exists between many virtue theorists and natural-law theorists is most unfortunate. Virtue theorists are prepared to surrender the natural-law framework to legal-political pragmatists, therewith claiming that a linkage of the two realms undermines moral reflection and analysis and distorts the Christian "story." I find this presupposition, to a greater or less extent, in the writings of Alasdair MacIntyre, Edmund Pincoffs, Bernard Williams and Stanley Hauerwas. A helpful analysis of and corrective to this split is found in Joseph Boyle, "Natural Law and the Ethics of Traditions," and Russell Hittinger, "Natural Law and Virtue: Theories at Cross Purposes," both of which are found in *Natural Law Theory: Contemporary Essays,* ed. Robert P. George, rev. ed. (Oxford: Clarendon, 1996), on pp. 3-30 and pp. 42-70, respectively.

[95]Common-ground moral discourse that is rooted in an understanding of natural law will also prevent "Christian ethics" from being reduced to an all-too-common type of Protestant existentialism, whereby meaning is only to be found in one's personal experience.

[96]This is not to deny that reason can be darkened due to sin; it does however acknowledge that all people can observe what nature reveals and, hence, are "without excuse" (Rom 1:20). This is the strength of John Paul's 1998 encyclical *Fides et Ratio* ("Faith and Reason"), which should be required reading for every evangelical Protestant. The pontiff, consistent with historic Christian tradition ("faith seeking understanding"), emphasizes the symbiotic relationship between faith and reason. Reason operates in the service of faith and is not oppositional to it. A proper understanding of this avoids two equal and opposite extremes: rationalism on the one hand, which exalts reason over faith, and fideism on the other, which dispenses with the need for rational reflection. John Paul rightly calls us to appreciate the harmony of faith and reason, all the while cognizant that the two are not to be equated.

common ground between the Christian community and surrounding culture. And surely the more unfortunate manifestations of the absence of common ground are not hard to find around us: self-righteousness among Christian believers, the formation of Christian enclaves that become isolated subcultures (a phenomenon that goes hand in hand with a massive retreat from intellectual and cultural institutions), the inability to articulate one's convictions apart from inherently religious language,[97] and the disdain (at worst) or indifference (at best) toward the workplace, which arises from a false division between the "sacred" and the "secular."[98]

Thus, contemporary evangelicals stand to gain much from a deeper understanding and appropriation of natural law as an expression of general revelation. The currency of natural law and common grace is nowhere more relevant than in evangelicalism's relationship to political power. In terms of long-term strategy, to view political involvement rather than cultural engagement as the highest priority is to err seriously, shortchanging both present and future generations. For this reason, as I have noted in chapter two, the burden of William Wilberforce was a "reformation of manners" in England, not merely social-political activism. Wilberforce, along with a small but influential band of contemporaries,[99] well understood that to change the laws of the land without changing the hearts and minds of the people is to get the cart before the horse.[100] Former deputy attorney general for the state of Indiana, Ian McLean, has stated the matter succinctly: "If our laws are corrupt, it is because our cul-

---

[97]For this reason (and more), the millions—yea, billions—of dollars that are poured into Christian television and (to a lesser extent) Christian radio are largely in vain. Why? Apart from the self-aggrandizing that is so characteristic of much of this enterprise, these media by and large fail to equip the Christian community for *responsible, long-term* involvement in society.

[98]A graphic illustration of this split thinking is the annual (or semiannual) missions emphasis that is found in most evangelical churches and colleges. Representatives from missions organizations routinely lecture congregations, classes and chapel audiences on the high calling of missions or "full-time Christian work" (whatever that is). In so doing they typically reinforce the tragic split thinking that is endemic in much of evangelicalism: namely, *head for the missions field (or the pastorate), but if this is not God's will, then maybe you'll need to get an ordinary job.* Where are the Christian lecturers who will remind us that our gifts and calling to business and finance, nursing, social work, medicine, home-building, acting, writing or teaching are every bit as high and noble in the kingdom of God as are the gifts and calling to missions or the pastorate?

[99]For more on the Clapham sect, see the discussion of Wilberforce in chap. two, above.

[100]Thus, rather than merely condemn homosexuality by arguing that it is *against biblical law,* Christians might be more effective if they were to argue that it is *against nature,* that it is "unnatural" (cf. Rom 1:26, wherein Paul essentially presses this very argument). That is, it defies the very moral order of things in the universe.

ture is corrupt; and our culture thrives only because we nourish it. The reform of man cannot be imposed by law."[101] Legal reform *follows* public opinion, just as water always flows to the lowest terrain.

American evangelicals need first to be consumed with a vision that shapes and molds the contours of culture.[102] This can—indeed, it must—occur regardless of which political parties and agendas are dominant. Faithful and responsible involvement in society will entail the political,[103] but the political will be viable *only* to the extent that it flows out of a deeper vision of incarnational humanism.[104] Moreover, translating moral convictions into public policy, as John West Jr. cautions us, requires more than merely right principles; it requires the virtue of prudence, which has not always been a hallmark of the religious.[105] It is futile to expect government to promote distinctly Christian notions of behavior rather than common dictates that reside in natural law. For religious conservatives,[106] particularly those who are inclined toward political activism, the contemporary implications of the existence of natural law have been eloquently stated by West and are eminently worth pondering:

> The present controversy over religion in politics largely hinges on the assumption that the morality espoused by conservative Christians cannot be justified apart from the Bible, and hence it is illegitimate as a guide to secular policy. But according to [C. S.] Lewis, this is a red herring. One does not need to accept the

---

[101]Ian A. T. McLean, "Criminal Law and Natural Law," in *Common Truths: New Perspectives on Natural Law,* ed. Edward B. McLean (Wilmington, Del.: Intercollegiate Studies Institute, 2000), p. 286.

[102]How "successful" Christians are in bringing about cultural change is beside the point. The Christian community is called first and foremost to faithfulness, not to measured success.

[103]Political-legal solutions can at best only treat cultural symptoms; they are unable to deal with root causes of social pathologies. This is why the teaching of Jesus was so radical—not because there is no place for political involvement (and here the Anabaptist critique needs adjustment, in my view), but because it is the essence and power of the gospel to bring about *moral transformation.* Transformed lives, in turn, leave their imprint on culture.

[104]The term *incarnational humanism* surfaces in the writings of Roman Catholic political philosopher John Courtney Murray (e.g., in *We Hold These Truths,* pp. 189-93) and comes to expression also in the more recent encyclicals of John Paul. One relatively recent (and reader-friendly) reminder of this holistic vision, which should be required reading for every college student, is John F. Crosby's lucid essay "Education and the Mind Redeemed," *First Things* 21 (December 1991), pp. 23-28.

[105]West, "Politics," p. 69.

[106]To speak of a "religious right" is to acknowledge that there exists a religious left as well. Intellectual honesty demands as much; there is no right-of-center without a left-of-center. And without question, the religious left can be just as guilty of politicizing religion as well as of sacralizing politics. Nevertheless, this volume assumes a readership whose theological commitments are rooted in the "great tradition" and who are concerned with preserving the integrity of the gospel (i.e., "evangelicals" in the widest sense).

authority of the Bible to know that theft and slander are wrong, or that honoring one's commitment to a spouse or child is a good thing. Civic morality is not the peculiar domain of religion, and Christians who wish to be politically effective (as well as theologically sound) should drive this point home. It is one of the best ways for them to disarm their critics.[107]

Ultimately, the extent to which evangelicals—for whom the notion of natural law seems strange, academic or removed from day-to-day living[108]—affirm a law of nature will determine the way in which they relate to their surrounding world.[109] If Christian believers have no understanding of natural law, then they are left with an apocalyptic, truncated, future-oriented form of the gospel. This form of discourse, so dominant in the recent history of American evangelicalism, in its essence says, "Jesus is coming back soon, and since society is going to hell in a hand-basket anyway, let's batten down the hatches and hold on until he comes." It goes without saying that this apocalyptic outlook has little or no regard for either moral education or the long-term, multigenerational project of moral persuasion in society.[110]

ON IMPOSING ONE'S MORALITY

One of the most common one-line refutations of traditional morality since the early days of the abortion debate has been the outcry that Christians are trying to "impose their morality" on others. Without question, this slogan has immense evocative power, particularly in a social climate where tolerance has be-

---

[107]West, "Politics." This wisdom should help evangelicals recognize and acknowledge the utter futility of using government and political persuasion to advance expressly Christian standards for behavior. Rather, they should appeal to the common dictates of natural law.

[108]Although there are multiple reasons to help explain Protestant evangelicals' suspicion or neglect of natural law, certainly one is its close association with Roman Catholic thought. One of the benefits of rapprochement between Catholics and evangelicals during the last decade has been the confession, broadly speaking, of a common cultural vision. Consequently, the rediscovery of important aspects of the historic Christian tradition is breathing new life and vigor into evangelical thought-life.

[109]Perhaps the best resource to date that makes a case (in nontechnical, reader-friendly language) for Christian use of natural law is J. Budziszewski, *Written on the Heart: The Case for Natural Law* (Downers Grove, Ill.: InterVarsity Press, 1997), esp. chap. 13 ("A Christian Appraisal of Natural-Law Theory").

[110]Again, I must emphasize that in making this argument for natural law and a common moral grammar I am *not* saying that the efforts of the Christian community guarantee cultural renewal. There are those like Meilaender who believe (with good reason, it seems to me) that "we are witnessing the last gasps of a once-Christian civilization," and thus, "to live in a time of transition and upheaval as Augustine did . . . is to live in a time much like ours" (*Faith and Faithfulness*, p. 33). What does this mean? It means that *we must both embody a distinctly Christian lifestyle amidst a declining civilization and transmit Christian moral culture to coming generations.*

come a cardinal virtue and people are paralyzed for fear of being perceived as insensitive. But the slogan also has a useful function; it forces us to reflect on the deep and inescapable link between morality and public policy.

Frequently, the claim that Christians are imposing their morality on others possesses the clear ring of an indictment that any rational person should accept. Normally assumed, though usually not stated, is that some sectarian or irrational impulse lies behind public promotion of moral standards. And, it follows, religious and sectarian views have no place in democratic pluralism. End of the matter.

Religious conservatives, truth be told, have not been very effective in articulating a response to this sort of "conversation stopper." By way of illustration, Joseph Boyle raises important questions in the context of opposing abortion that will need to be vocalized in the public square:

> Is it a narrowly religious view that the unborn, as living human beings, should be consistently regarded as persons just as all other humans are? Is it only an essentially private and idiosyncratic understanding of justice which implies that in cases of conflict between mother and child the nod should not necessarily and always go to the mother's interests? And, is it merely a religious conviction that utilitarian considerations, often disguised as pubic health and welfare concerns, should not justify abortion any more than they should justify other kinds of killing?[111]

As Boyle observes, these questions—and thoughtfully articulated answers to these questions—are routinely overwhelmed by the repeated incantation, "Don't impose your morals on us."

What may be missing among people of faith is less a philosophically sound argument than the sheer *intestinal fortitude* to demand (respectfully, of course) intellectual honesty of others, as well as the opportunity to speak publicly.

But what applies to abortion also can be applied to the great medical and bioethical debates that currently rage: namely, those surrounding infanticide, physician-assisted suicide and euthanasia, and genetics. Is utilitarianism as a viewpoint really indisputably true and best in all its calculations? So true and good, in fact, that it requires us, for example, to abandon our traditional ethics of health care (offering compassionate care for the dying) and in its place opt for an ethics of assisted death? What does this ethic reveal about our under-

---

[111]Joseph Boyle, "On 'Imposing Morals,' " *Ethics and Medics* 17, no. 9 (1992): 1.

standing of personhood, human nature, human worth and the common good?

Alas, the easy part may be to demonstrate that the assumption of an "imposition of morality" is a patently false one. The difficult part is to move beyond this stage to the place of sustained dialogue.

Let us, however, for the sake of the argument, assume that because a viewpoint is a *minority* viewpoint, it is therefore objectionable (as some will insinuate). But this line of reasoning, when examined, proves to be invalid. Are we to believe that, regarding ethical matters, a *majority opinion* constitutes the *ethical* thing to do? Does might really make right? Or do majoritarians *really* believe that because a viewpoint is a minority view in the public domain, it is therefore irrelevant, irrational or impertinent?[112] What shall we say, then, to other minority views from the past—for example, the views of abolitionists who fought against slavery and the slave trade, civil rights activists or (should we grant their logic) feminists? Minority viewpoints, then, are not excluded *on the grounds* that they are held by a mere minority. When scrutinized, this assumption (usually directed toward the religious viewpoint) collapses under the weight of intellectual honesty.

Perhaps, as some might argue, abortion, euthanasia and even infanticide are private matters and, therefore, are not appropriate realms for the application of public policy or "restrictive legislation." But are they indeed *private*? Traditionally, killing[113] has been viewed by civilized societies as a matter of justice, and justice is an eminently serious and *public* matter that cannot be relegated to *private* preference.

Ultimately, many of the controversial ethical questions of our day revolve around *the nature of personhood;* they are no private matter, even when it is true that the public interest depends on private virtue.[114] Therefore, the viewpoint of our antagonists that debates over what constitutes a person or what constitutes moral atrocity *may not* proceed in the public square is at best arbitrary

---

[112]The argument set forth by Boyle, while it is focused on the abortion issue, is concise and most helpful (ibid., p. 2).

[113]The expressions *assisted suicide* and *euthanasia* themselves are euphemistic.

[114]James Q. Wilson states that conscience and character "are not enough." "Rules and rewards," in his view, must still be publicly employed: "For most social problems that deeply trouble us, the need is to explore, carefully and experimentally, ways of strengthening the formation of character among the very young. In the long run, the public interest depends on private virtue" (*On Character* [Washington, D.C.: American Enterprise Institute Press, 1991], p. 23). Wilson, however, does not spell out *how* such public imposing of rules and rewards is to proceed and on what such rules and rewards are predicated.

and at worst diabolical. Whether or not the unborn, the handicapped neonate, the dying and the comatose are persons possessing inherent worth is a question that *must* be debated in public. There simply exist no questions of greater significance—morally, socially or politically. The alternative is terror.[115]

[115]I have argued elsewhere—drawing from George Orwell's brief but important 1949 essay "Politics and the English Language" (in *The Collected Essays, Journalism and Letters of George Orwell,* ed. S. Orwell and I. Angus, 4 vols. [New York: Harcourt, Brace & World, 1968]) and from Jacques Ellul's work *The Humiliation of the Word,* trans. J. M. Hanks (Grand Rapids, Mich.: Eerdmans, 1988)—that a society's moral corruption is followed by corruptions of language, which in turn are followed by political decay. See my essay "The New Verbal Order," *Modern Age* 38, no. 4 (1996): 321-31. As we sit on the cusp of the third millennium I am more convinced of this argument than ever, particularly as it applies to American culture. While the present volume is not devoted to any sort of prediction of what lies ahead, there is much to be said for the critique offered by legal analyst John Fonte in "Why There Is a Culture War: Gramsci and Tocqueville in America," *Policy Review* 104 (December 2000-January 2001): 15-31. Without discussing the role that religion plays in America, Fonte considers the intellectual histories that have descended from the twentieth-century Italian Marxist Antonio Gramsci, for whom *all* life was *political* (i.e., private life, the work place, religion, social relationships and government), and the nineteenth-century Frenchman Alexis de Tocqueville, for whom the trinity of personal dynamism, religious faith and self-government were notable in early American life. As Fonte observes, Tocquevillians and Gramscians clash on everything that matters. The former affirm objective moral truths applicable to all people at all times; the latter believe that "truths" are multiple, subjective and socially constructed. The former believe that society can and should be remoralized; the latter believe that moral norms are to be subordinate to and an extension of political liberation. The former hold that civil servants such as teachers and police officers possess legitimate authority; the latter holds them to represent power but not legitimacy. Finally, the former believe that each person is responsible and morally accountable; the latter believe that "the personal is political." Fonte does not exaggerate when he notes that "the stakes in this intellectual clash are no less than what kind of country the United States will be in decades to come." A related question poses itself: What will be the nature and influence of religion in decades to come, and what will be the source of moral authority that governs the life of the individual and the community?

6

Biblical Resources for Ethics
The Pauline Model

A basic premise of the preceding chapter was that general revelation, as evidenced by individual conscience and judicial sentiment, serves as common ground between the Christian and unbeliever. Thus, Christians can appeal to pagans on the basis of the law of nature.

ALL THINGS TO ALL PEOPLE?

The New Testament affords us a glimpse into the usefulness of this strategy, for we see this at work in the ministry of the apostle Paul while in Athens (Acts 17), notably in his speech to the Council of the Areopagus. This address (Acts 17:22-31) has been described by one biblical scholar as "the greatest missionary document in the New Testament."[1] The reason for such praise is that Paul's aim was to "exhibit to pagans of a great city in the Mediterranean world what was characteristic of the new religion as concisely as possible."[2]

Curiously, not all New Testament scholars share this enthusiastic assessment of Paul's work in Athens. In fact, some commentators—both liberal and conservative—view Paul's ministry in Athens to have been a failure. Writing a century ago, one biblical scholar gave credence to the view that Paul became

---

[1]Adolf Deissmann, *Light from the Ancient Near East* (New York: H. Doran, 1927), p. 384.
[2]Ibid.

"disillusioned" by his experience in Athens; hence we hear nothing more about the church in this city hereafter.[3] Other commentators call the Areogapus speech "ineffective" and an "unrealistic experiment," since it falls outside of the normal "evangelical" pattern of preaching that we usually find being used by the apostles.[4] A negative view of Paul's work in Athens has even found its way into the notes of the *New Jerusalem Bible*.[5]

The negative appraisal of Paul's ministry in Athens raises several questions. Does Paul's preaching involve compromise with contemporary pagan religious notions? Is Paul sidetracked by a "natural theology" that obscures the distinctives of the Christian message? Is Acts 17:16-34 evidence of Paul's "failure" in Athens? And in Luke's mind, does this account serve as a model or a foil for the reader?

In the book of Acts three of Paul's speeches are recorded: one to a Jewish audience (Acts 13:16-41), one to a Christian audience (Acts 20:17-35) and one to a pagan audience (Acts 17:22-31). This distribution surely is not by chance. Rather, from this the reader might reasonably assume that Luke, as narrator, has some sort of pedagogical aim in mind. This distribution, moreover, illustrates *in practice* what Paul reveals as his personal philosophy of ministry:

> To the Jew I became as a Jew, in order to win Jews. To those under the law I became as one under the law (though I myself am not under the law), in order to win those under the law. To those outside the law I became as one outside the law (not being outside the law of God myself but under the law of Christ), in order to win those outside the law. To the weak I became weak, in order to win the weak. I have become all things to all people, in order that by all means I might save some. I do all this for the sake of the gospel. (1 Cor 9:20-23)

It should be noted that there is nothing in the text of Acts 17:16-34 suggesting that Paul's strategy in Athens is misguided. In fact Luke presents Paul in a way that depicts the apostle as being in line with other noted philosophers of the past who came and "disputed" (*dialegomai*) in the marketplace—among these, Anaxagoras and Protagoras (both mid fifth century B.C.), Socrates and, more recently, the renowned Stoic Chrysippus (first century B.C.). Luke may well have in mind the

---

[3]William M. Ramsay, *St. Paul the Traveller and the Roman Citizen*, rev. ed., ed. Mark Wilson (Grand Rapids, Mich.: Kregel, 2001), p. 194.
[4]See, e.g., C. Munsinger, *Paulus in Korinth* (Heidelberg: Knecht, 1908), p. 5; J. Dupont, *Les Actes des Apôtres* (Paris: Duculot, 1953), p. 157; and M. Dibelius, *Studies in the Acts of the Apostles* (New York: Charles Scribner's Sons, 1956), p. 63.
[5]*New Jerusalem Bible* (New York: Doubleday, 1985), p. 1829.

tradition surrounding Socrates, who was also accused in Athens of introducing "foreign divinities," when he writes of Paul's interaction with Stoic and Epicurean philosophers in the agora: "Others said, 'He seems to be a proclaimer of foreign divinities'" (Acts 17:18).[6] Indeed, not only Socrates but also Anaxagoras and Protagoras were accused of this very crime. From a missiological standpoint, Acts 17 engenders important questions concerning Christian proclamation and the church's relationship to culture—specifically, to educated pagan culture.[7] Some of what confronted Paul and the subsequent Christian community in Athens—the little we know of it—confronts North American Christians as well. What are the lessons to be drawn from Paul's encounter with "cultured paganism"?

PAUL, APOSTLE TO THE CULTURED PAGAN

"I am a Jew, from Tarsus [in the province] of Cilicia, a citizen of an important city" (Acts 21:39). Thus Paul describes himself in one instance of interrogation before the public authorities. Although Saul was trained in Jerusalem, he returned to his home city of Tarsus after his conversion (Acts 9:30). If Paul's family had merely been émigrés from Judea in this city, neither Paul nor his father would have qualified as a citizen (*politēs*); they would have only had the status of resident aliens. It is possible, though by no means conclusive, that Paul's family had been planted there with full rights of *politeia* as part of a colony settled there by one of the Seleucid rulers, who had shown preference to Jewish colonists as they populated Asia Minor.[8] Another possible scenario is that Paul's father or grandfather had been honored for distinguished service to the state.[9] In the first century it was the rule in educated and cosmopolitan society that a man had dual citizenship; thus, the apostle to the Gentiles is at home.

Paul's declaration of his linkage to Tarsus[10] occurs in Acts 21:39, at a time

---

[6]For this we are dependent on the testimony of Xenophon: "Socrates does wrongly, for he does not acknowledge the gods which the state acknowledges; rather, he introduces other new-fashioned gods" (*Memorabilia* 1.1.1).

[7]Not only Acts 17 but Acts 16 as well serves to demonstrate Paul's dictum of being "all things to all men." The apostle's ministry in the region of southern Galatia, where there existed a large Jewish population (cf. Acts 16:3), resulted in a decision to have Timothy circumcised.

[8]On the Jewish seeding by the Seleucids of cities in Asia Minor, see William Ramsey's elaborate discussion in *The Letters to the Seven Churches of Asia and Their Place in the Plan of the Apocalypse* (London: Hodder & Stoughton, 1904), pp. 128-57. Philostratus (*Vita Apollonii* 6.34), writing in the early third century, seems to presume that a significant number of Jews were Tarsian citizens.

[9]These two explanations of Paul's citizenship are offered by William Ramsey (*St. Paul*, pp. 35-36).

[10]To the ancients, "fatherland" applied more to one's city of origin than one's nationality.

(during Jewish hostilities) when confirmation of his Roman citizenship and pedigree was critical. Although the reader must make allowances for Paul's rhetoric, Paul's pride in Tarsian citizenship would make little sense if he had scarcely lived there at all.[11] The Tarsus of Paul's day was a center of government, banking and commerce,[12] and it was one of three "university" cities around the Mediterranean.[13] The apostle-to-be would hence be well acquainted with pagan "high culture"—an acquaintance that, when sanctified, would thrust *him*, not Simon Peter, forward as the "apostle to the Gentiles" (Rom 11:13). Roman citizenship and life in a university city, after all, did have its privileges, and the apostle was not averse to using these when they were needed; this background would aid him enormously during his apostolic work, especially in a city like Athens. The cultural influence of a city like Tarsus may thus be sufficient to help explain the apostle's recourse to poet-philosophers such as Epimenides and Aratus of Soli, a fellow Cilician (Acts 17:28; cf. Tit 1:12).

Is it at all significant that Tarsus was the city that should produce the apostle to the Gentiles? Uniting oriental and occidental cultural and intellectual life, the institutions of Tarsus were uniquely suited to mold Paul's intellectual development.[14] Cicero was governor of Tarsus in the mid-fifties B.C. It was here that Mark Antony met Cleopatra in 41 B.C. Tarsus was the native city of several famous Stoic philosophers: for example, Zeno, Antipater, Athenadorus and Nestor. In the period from 27 B.C. to A.D. 14, during the reign of Augustus, Tarsus achieved renown as a center of intellectual life; Augustus's intended heir to the imperial throne, Marcellus, was tutored by Nestor.[15] Strabo (first century B.C./early first century A.D.) claims that Tarsus as a university city surpassed Athens and Alexandria in terms of zeal for learning.[16]

Prosperous, cosmopolitan and geographically situated literally where East met West, Tarsus would have prepared Paul well for engaging Hellenistic culture.

---

[11]Thus John B. Polhill, *Paul and His Letters* (Nashville: Broadman & Holman, 1999), p. 319.

[12]Although banking was done in all commercial cities, Athens was the leading banking center of the ancient world in the first century. Thus Helmut Koester, *History, Culture and Religion of the Hellenistic Age*, vol. 1 of *Introduction to the New Testament* (Philadelphia: W. de Gruyter, 1984), p. 90.

[13]Athens and Alexandria were the other two cities to which students traveled.

[14]See in this regard David Gill and Conrad Gempf, eds., *Graeco-Roman Setting*, vol. 2 of *The Book of Acts in Its First Century Setting* (Grand Rapids, Mich.: Eerdmans, 1994), esp. chaps. 9 and 12.

[15]Strabo *Geographica* 14.5.14.

[16]Strabo *Geographica* 14.5.13. Strabo notes, however, that Tarsus did not attract as many students from abroad as did Athens and Alexandria.

ATHENS IN PAUL'S DAY

The cradle of democracy, Athens was the foremost among the city-states in the fifth century B.C. Although thirty years of exhaustive strife with Sparta as a result of the Peloponnesian Wars (431-403 B.C.) left Athens weakened politically, the rich cultural heritage of the city remained unsurpassed. Its contributions to sculpture, literature, philosophy and oratory during the fifth and fourth centuries were unparalleled in the ancient world. In addition to being the native city of Socrates and Plato, it became the adopted home of Aristotle, Epicurus and Zeno. Demosthenes, an "unsuccessful Churchill" of the mid fourth century B.C., strove in vain to rouse his fellow Athenians once more to political independence and greatness. Athens was home to the poet Menander, whose New Comedy form of entertainment eclipsed the classical Greek tragedy in the late fourth and early third century B.C.[17]

By Paul's day Athens had lost much of the preeminence it had once possessed. Yet Cicero, writing one hundred years earlier, could observe that in spite of its decline in political power, Athens still enjoyed "such renown that the now shattered and weakened name of Greece is supported by the reputation of this city."[18] People generally came to Athens, Alexandria or Tarsus to study philosophy, rhetoric or general education. In the writings of Strabo and Ovid, Athens is depicted as a tourist center, as the site of great festivals and as a city that attracted itinerant philosophers and mystics. One such traveling teacher-mystic, Apollonius of Tyana, is described by Philostratus in the early third century A.D. as having arrived at Athens about the same time as the apostle Paul.[19] Interestingly, the account mentions that Apollonius was struck by the altars "to unknown gods," corroborating Luke's narrative in Acts 17:23.[20]

Into such a city the apostle Paul enters, adapting himself to the dialectical habits of its inhabitants. Simply stated, for Luke, Athens represents the height of pagan culture. A more careful reading of Acts 17 reveals that he infuses the

---

[17]Paul quotes from one of Menander's comedies in 1 Cor 15:33: "Bad company ruins good morals." On the cultural background of Athens see E. M. Blaiklock, *Cities of the New Testament* (Westwood, N.J.: Revell, 1965), pp. 52-60.

[18]Cicero *Pro Flacco* 26.62 (Cicero, *The Speeches*, trans. L. E. Lord [Cambridge, Mass.: Harvard University Press, 1953], p. 433).

[19]See E. Mayer, "Apollonius von Tyana und die Biographie des Philostratos," *Hermes* 52 (1917): 371-424.

[20]Apollonius's allusion is in the plural ("unknown gods"), in contrast with Luke's reference, which is in the singular.

description of Paul's ministry here with fascinating detail (even when his narrative is concise).

The intellectual atmosphere of first-century Athens might be characterized as mildly promiscuous, in both a religious and a nonreligious sense. At the same time that a growing percentage of the city's population had been initiated into mystery cults, Athenians appear to have had little knowledge of Old Testament revelation.[21] Despite the city's past intellectual reputation, by Paul's day Athens exhibited a somewhat indiscriminate, almost casual, approach to life issues. Several of the church fathers allude to Athens as a city of talkers, a people obsessed with curiosity.[22] According to one ancient source, Athenians were a particularly litigious lot.[23] With hermaphrodites commonplace as statues, and symbols of phallic worship and sexual obsession on public display throughout the city,[24] one can envisage the dislocation in the apostle's spirit as he encounters a culture in moderate decline (Acts 17:16).

MESSAGE AND METHOD IN PAUL'S AREOPAGUS SPEECH

Setting the stage. With the passing of the centuries a canonical twelve gods were thought to hold power on Mount Olympus. Athens was the site of an altar dedicated to this twelve-member pantheon, which included Athena, daughter to Zeus. Religion and politics appear to have been inextricably combined in Athenian society, as evidenced by the surviving literature. One such example is a somewhat turgid speech dating to A.D. 155 by Aelius Aristides at the Panathenaic Festival. In this speech, the author recounts a legal battle of the gods that is significant for an understanding of Athenian history—and for the reader's appreciation of the momentous opportunity that permits Paul to address the Council of the Areopagus. In his pursuit of justice, Poseidon sued Ares over the murder of his son, ultimately winning his case in the presence of all the gods.[25] The record holds that the purported site of disputation took on Ares' name. Hence, throughout Athens's rich cultural history, the Areopagus (literally, "Ares' hill") constituted for many the pinnacle of authority and respect. It was here that jus-

---

[21]This is in spite of the statement by Luke that there was a Jewish synagogue in the city (Acts 17:17).
[22]Compare Luke's statements in Acts 17:18 and Acts 17:21.
[23]Chariton of Aphrodisias *Chaereas and Callirhoe* 1.11.6-7, cited in Luke Timothy Johnson, *The Acts of the Apostles* (Collegeville, Minn.: Liturgical Press, 1992), p. 314.
[24]Pausanius *Description of Greece* 1.14-15.
[25]Aelius Aristides *Sacred Tales* 1.40-48.

tice was to be eternally manifest. Thus it was that Athenians looked to the Areopagus as a source of knowledge, wisdom, reason and justice.

Since the mid third century B.C., the Council of the Areopagus had functioned as an authoritative body in civil-legal and educational matters.[26] The council consisted of about thirty members and was presided over by the president of the assembly, who was charged with conducting official business. In the Roman era the Areopagus was comprised of several committees, one of which was educational and on which Cicero, one hundred years before Paul, is said to have served.[27] Acts 17:22-33 may well be Luke's report of Paul's being led before this elite committee for an informal inquiry.[28] If in fact Paul is being portrayed in the Socratic mold, debating with whoever was in the marketplace (Acts 17:17) and then addressing a select audience (perhaps the education commission of the Council of the Areopagus), Luke may be hitting the apologetic equivalent of a home run with his portrait of Paul. The apostle to the Gentiles is being depicted at his apologetic best, engaged in moral discourse with the cultural elite of his day. In this light, the speech as it is recorded in Acts 17:22-31 reveals the apostle's ability to clothe revelation in relevant arguments that are intelligible to his pagan contemporaries.

Paul's method. By examining Paul's Areopagus speech, we might summarize his goals as being the following:[29]

- to communicate truth in the language of his audience
- to build on pagan concepts and use pagan illustrations—whether philosophical, literary or religious—to express the reality of divine revelation
- to adjust pagan assumptions about the Creator and creation
- to give credence to the Creator's self-disclosure (the cosmos and the resurrection)

---

[26]Cicero informs us that in the Roman period the Areopagus had jurisdiction over criminal matters (*De Natura Deorum* 2.29.74).

[27]We learn this from Plutarch (late first/early second century A.D.). Plutarch, *Lives,* trans. B. Perrin, Loeb Classical Library (Cambridge, Mass.: Harvard University Press, n.d.), p. 89.

[28]One of the best English-language resources on the background of the Areopagus Council is B. Gaertner, *The Areopagus Speech and Natural Revelation,* ASNY 21 (Uppsala, Sweden: Almquist, 1955); see also J. Daryl Charles, "Engaging the (Neo)Pagan Mind: Paul's Encounter with Athenian Culture as a Model for Cultural Apologetics," *Trinity Journal* n.s. 16, no. 1 (1995): 47-62, esp. 51-52. On Paul's Areopagus speech itself, see P. Parente, "St. Paul's Address Before the Areopagus," *Catholic Biblical Quarterly* 11, no. 1 (1949): 144-52; Hans Conzelmann, "The Address of Paul on the Areopagus," in *Studies in Luke-Acts,* ed. L. E. Keck and J. L. Martyn (Nashville: Abingdon, 1966), pp. 218-28; and L. Legrand, "The Areopagus Speech: Its Theological Kerygma and Its Missionary Significance," in *La Notion de Dieu,* ed. J. Coppens (Louvain: Gembloux, 1974), pp. 338-40.

[29]These goals are discussed more fully in Charles, "Engaging," pp. 54-60.

- to move his audience in the direction of repentance by means of rhetorically heightened moral persuasion

Paul's intention is clarified as we consider the specific rhetorical tactics he employs in his address, several of which are conspicuous. First, given the fact that Athens was home to several prominent schools of philosophical thought (Acts 17:18), it is not incidental that Paul's speech touches on core philosophical assumptions of both Stoics and Epicureans: for example, what can be known (Acts 17:23, 30),[30] the cosmos as independent or contingent (Acts 17:24-25) and the universe as solely material or as material and nonmaterial (Acts 17:24-25, 31). Second, the very opening of Paul's speech—whereby he addresses his audience with "men" (*andres*) followed by the designation "Athenians" (*Athēnaioi*)—is thoroughly Greek, allowing his audience immediately to feel at home; yet it reflects the official character of the address.[31] Third, Paul's message incorporates the element of irony. An important subtheme in his address is ignorance (Acts 17:23, 30)—and this in a city of great learning and erudition. Fourth, with the skill of a surgeon, Paul borrows quotations from Epimenides and Aratus of Soli (Acts 17:28-29), two poet-philosophers held in high esteem by Athenians, and employs them selectively in the service of his argument. Last, Paul is conversant with the city's cultural background and uses a public monument (Acts 17:23) as a springboard for his argument based on creation.

Paul's message. The wider relief of Paul's apologetic strategy takes shape as we identify the central components of his message. Three general elements seem to emerge. These are the apostle's appeal to natural revelation, his particular conception of God as Creator and Redeemer and his emphasis on Christian exclusivity against the backdrop of pagan inclusivity.

Although Acts 17:16-31 follows a somewhat different rhetorical pattern from that of Romans 1, which is thought by many to be a primary New Testament text supporting general revelation, Paul identifies in both texts a common apologetic bridge to the pagan mind: nature itself. In Pauline thinking there exists an inseparable connection between creation, the moral order and human accountability. This link, articulated before the Council of Areopagus in the

---

[30]The occurrence of the verb *to know* in Acts 17:23 and cognate forms in the Greek text—e.g., *unknown* in Acts 17:23 and *ignorance* (*agnoia,* from which we get the English *agnostic*) in Acts 17:30—gives the appearance of a wordplay.

[31]Thus C. F. Evans, "Speeches in Acts," in *Melanges bibliques,* ed. A. R. Charne (Paris: Duculot, 1969), pp. 291-92.

idiom of his day, is the core of Paul's speech. Pagans "know" because of creation as well as conscience; in the end, their "ignorance" is "without excuse."

This connection, rooted in the law of nature and discussed at some length in chapter five, above, has an important function in Paul's strategy, since the Athenians—and the men of the Areopagus—have no christological understanding. The apostle's discourse on creation and the cosmos, then, serves as a necessary "pedagogical-missionary preamble."[32] In both Romans 1 and Acts 17 the phenomena of creation are said to be accessible to all;[33] for Paul, this knowledge of the Creator-God is innate. Even pagans without knowledge of Christ have a fundamental awareness of moral accountability; "by nature" they do the moral law, even though they do not have the law (Rom 2:14). For this reason the apostle can assume and speak of universal norms.[34] Whether he is writing to Christians living in the imperial seat of Rome or addressing academics sitting on the Council of the Areopagus, Paul's purpose is to stress that *all people* are morally accountable.

What are the spheres of natural revelation delineated by Paul in his speech? Three realms are noted: creation and the maintenance of the cosmos by God, human dependence on God and human moral accountability before God.[35] Two of these touch commonly recognized Stoic assumptions; hence, Paul can stress continuity. The third is denied by Stoics; hence, Paul's message ends with radical discontinuity.

For the Stoic, the divine essence is *logos,* reason. Stoic thinking maintains that in the structure of the universe itself lie the seeds of knowledge, the *logos spermatikos,*[36] which give rise to the universe. Reason, then, is understood as the highest expression of nature.[37] Paul bridges the chasm between Stoic and Christian thought by appropriating common philosophical ground, asserting

---

[32]This expression has been used by German commentator Philip Vielhauer, "Zum 'Paulinismus' der Apostelgeschichte," in *Aufsätze zum Neuen Testament* (Muenchen: Chr. Kaiser, 1956), p. 13.

[33]According to Rom 1:20, all things are visible for all to see. See H. P. Owen, "The Scope of Natural Revelation in Romans 1 and Acts 17," *New Testament Studies* 5, no. 2 (1958-1959): 142-43.

[34]Note the distinction made by Paul: that pagans *possess* the moral law does not mean they *attain* it.

[35]Gaertner, *Areopagus Speech*, pp. 80-82.

[36]Note in Acts 17:18 the derogatory language used by the Epicureans and the Stoics to describe Paul: the Greek term translated "babbler" is *spermologos.* Luke may be appropriating irony here.

[37]"Right reason" (*logos orthos*), as taught by the Stoic philosopher Zeno, "is the same as Zeus" (*Fragments* 162, quoted in C. K. Barrett, ed., *The New Testament Background: Selected Documents* [New York: Harper & Row, 1961], p. 62). On this aspect of Stoic thought, see E. Zeller, *The Stoics, Epicureans and Skeptics* (New York: Russell & Russell, 1962), pp. 126-66.

that the use of reason can lead to the knowledge of God. To observe the universe is to rouse the individual to seek after God; in truth, this Creator-God is not far removed from humankind (Acts 17:27).

Alluding to God's immanence and human kinship with God places Paul squarely within the Stoic understanding of the divine. Paul exploits theological common ground in citations drawn from two well-known poet-philosophers. The statement "in him we live and move and have our being" (Acts 17:28) expresses the Stoic belief in closeness to and kinship with the divine. Any Stoic worth his salt readily conceded that God "fills" the universe and that a divine-human union exists. This citation is generally attributed to a sixth-century B.C. poet, Epimenides of Crete.

The second citation, "we are his offspring" (Acts 17:28), stems from the third-century B.C. Stoic philosopher Aratus of Soli, who, significantly, hailed from Paul's native Cilicia. Aratus had penned these words in a poem honoring Zeus. Titled *Phaenomena,* the poem is an interpretation of constellations and weather signs. The particular citation reads, "In all things each of us needs Zeus, for we are also his offspring."[38]

Paul does not remain, however, at the level of human reason, even though he will go as far as Greek assumptions will allow him. Creation *ex nihilo* and divine self-disclosure require more from the philosopher. As such, the apostolic message achieves continuity (kinship with God) as well as radical discontinuity (transcendence) with the Hellenistic worldview. Indeed, the structure of Paul's address reflects the movement from the former to the latter. While the materialistic pantheism of Stoic belief corrupts Stoic "theology," Paul first uses the common ground shared by all. Athenian "ignorance" is initially related in a positive manner ("I see how extremely religious you are," Acts 17:22; "I . . . looked carefully at the objects of your worship," Acts 17:23) and then negatively ("God . . . now . . . commands all people everywhere to repent," Acts 17:30).[39]

---

[38]Aratus *Phaenomena* 5. Both Clement of Alexandria (*Stromateis* 1.19) and Eusebius (*Preparation for the Gospel* 13.12.4-8) attribute this citation to Aratus of Soli (third century B.C.) who, like Paul, hailed from Tarsus, but it is possible that the citation may have originated with one of two other third-century sources, the Stoic poet-philosopher Cleanthes and the poet Callimachus, both of whom use near identical language in poetic praise to Zeus. Fragments of these texts are reproduced in H. von Arnim, ed., *Stoicorum Veterum Fragmenta,* 3 vols. (Leipzig: F. Pustet, 1903-1905), 1:537, with an english translation in Barrett, *New Testament Background.*

[39]Ignorance, not worship, is Paul's emphasis. The religious ("superstitious," according to some translations) attitude of the Athenians (Acts 17:22) noted by Paul appears to be a genuine commendation; *deisidaimonia* is praised by some ancient sources as a virtue. This characteristic also surfaces in Acts 25:19.

Paul uses not only literary sources but also the city's cultural history to adjust his audience's conception of the divine. That there were altars to many unknown gods in Athens is established by several ancient writers.[40] Pausanius and Philostratus describe Athens as the scene of innumerable gods, heroes and corresponding altars.[41] Tertullian writes that Paul chose the singular description, "unknown god," over the plural even though the latter is understood.[42] As to the specific identity of the altar referred to by Paul, it is impossible to be conclusive, although one ancient commentator believes that it traces to an Athenian legend, according to which a demon appeared following an Athenian defeat in battle. Out of fear, not wishing to exclude any deity, the Athenians erected an altar "to an unknown god."[43]

In light of the pervasive atmosphere of religious inclusivity, the apostle's strategy is to take what is inclusively "given" and build on it for the purposes of expressing a Christian theism that is exclusive in nature—a strategy referred to by missiologists as "preevangelism." Athenians would not have conceived of Paul's monotheism as the Jews would have.

The materialist and pantheist stamp of the Areopagus address is a clear reflection of Luke's intent to show how the apostolic message engages the pagan mindset. Pagans possess general revelation, by which they know of the Creator-God through creation and conscience. This general knowledge, however, is insufficient to bring them into right relationship with the Creator. Although pagans universally display ignorance of the one true God, the times of ignorance are pronounced by Paul to be past: God now "commands all people everywhere to repent" (Acts 17:30). As evidence that epistemological ignorance is not bliss, the one true God has ordained "a day" on which "the man" Jesus "will have the world judged in righteousness" (Acts 17:31). In this way Paul dismantles the Stoic view of universal continuum, which denies that history as we know it will terminate and that an afterlife, following a day of moral reckoning, exists. The Judeo-Christian understanding of history, begun by and ending with divine fiat, marks a radical discontinuity with the worldview of Paul's audience. One can

---

[40]A vast amount of literature has been devoted to "the unknown god." A summary of the literature can be found in Gaertner, *Areopagus Speech,* pp. 242-47; see also Charles, "Engaging," p. 58 n. 65.

[41]Pausanius *Description of Greece* 1.1.4; Philostratus *Vita Apollonii* 6.3.

[42]Tertullian *Ad nationes* 2.9.

[43]The commentator is Theodore of Mopsuestia, quoted in K. Lake and H. J. Cadbury, *The Beginnings of Christianity, Part 1: The Acts of the Apostles* (reprint; Grand Rapids, Mich.: Baker, 1965), p. 212.

readily imagine that those sitting in his audience, initially inquisitive, move from polite tolerance to seething indignation. While Paul has found common ground in two important realms, in the third, his argument for resurrection[44] and judgment—mediated by a "man"—is nothing short of scandalous!

Summing up Paul's rhetorical strategy at the Areopagus, we may note that he was knowledgeable, dialectical, well-read, relevant and rhetorically skillful. Both his method, which shrewdly draws on subtleties of style, and his message, which presumes and builds on general revelation (creation, knowledge of a Creator, natural law and moral accountability), are appropriate and adapted to his audience. This ability to "become all things to all people" (1 Cor 9:22), and to do so in the language of his audience, is praiseworthy and commends itself as a model to the contemporary reader. Alas, one finds notable affinities between the first and twenty-first centuries. Both are pagan (one being pre-Christian, the other "post-Christian"), both are biblically illiterate, and both require that Christians adapt the gospel in ways that are culturally sensitive yet theologically faithful.

When we view Paul's work in Athens in this light, we are forced to conclude that his ministry was not a failure, as many commentators have thought.[45] To the contrary, a more accurate assessment of Paul's ministry in Athens may be summed up by his own testimony to the Corinthian believers in 1 Corinthians 9:19, 22: "I have made myself a slave to all, so that I might win more of them. . . . I have become all things to all people, that I might by all means save some."

The Apologetic Task in the Twenty-First Century

For the zealous, the impetuous and the "charismatically" oriented Christian, it is worth remembering that Paul, not Peter, was called to be the apostle to the Gentiles. It was Paul who could dispute with philosophers in Athens, argue from the Scriptures with Jews in the synagogue, persuade imperial magistrates

---

[44]Not insignificantly, the resurrection is mentioned three times in Luke's Athens narrative (Acts 17:18, 31-32). Clearly, this suggests that the doctrine of the resurrection is a core piece of effective Christian apologetics, even when "preevangelism" is necessitated. That the focus of Paul's Areopagus speech is not Christology per se is *not* to say that it has no "evangelical" or "evangelistic" thrust.

[45]Nor is it necessary to assume that his not-too-distant reflections about the power of the cross, recorded in 1 Corinthians 1—2, were penned with a wrong apologetic model (i.e., Athens) in mind. Evangelicals have typically pitted rhetorical sophistication against the preaching of the cross; this, however, is a false dichotomy. Paul was not averse to using forceful rhetorical devices to get his message across. Consider by way of example 1 Corinthians 4 and 1 Corinthians 9.

and even procure an audience with the caesar himself. Everything that God had taken away from Saul of Tarsus immediately following his conversion—his pride, his religious zeal, his cultural pedigree, his influence—was restored to the apostle after he lay broken in the presence of Almighty God. Having been sanctified, Paul's past was now to serve the greater purposes of God as the Holy Spirit would see fit.

In many respects Western culture, and North American culture in particular, resembles the culture of Athens in Paul's day. This is true intellectually, religiously and morally. Like first-century Athenians, who had an illustrious past, we have a culture that Alexander Solzhenitsyn has called a "culture of novelty." We are obsessed with that which is novel; truth and its consequences are of little value.

For this reason, Paul's ministry model in Athens beckons us. It invites us to learn at two levels: (1) how to relate biblical truth in culturally relevant ways (i.e., contextualization) and (2) how to formulate a cultural apologetic that retains its theological integrity in the midst of a culture of compromise. Luke's portrayal of Paul's work in Athens is intended to demonstrate Christian *credibility*. Paul has demonstrated a knowledge of and sensitivity to Athenian culture in a way that allows him to accommodate truth positively to the prevailing cultural Zeitgeist. This should be paradigmatic for the church of any era. By first understanding culture, the Christian can effectively and faithfully engage culture with a measure of credibility. Finally, having humbly sought to be a student of culture and an active participant in culture, the believer is able, in the corporate context of the church, to confront the false values that are lodged within culture. Perception, engagement and confrontation necessarily follow—and they do so in this order.[46]

EPILOGUE

The story of Paul's ministry in Athens does not end here, however. We have one more observation to make. It is fair to say that Luke's rather abrupt ending of the narrative (Acts 17:32-34) does not strike the reader as very impressive. Almost as an afterthought, as if to say, "Oh, by the way," Luke appends one sentence mentioning two individuals by name who happened to "believe."

---

[46]Paul's "accommodation" in Athens should in no way be misconstrued as syncretism. Paul accommodates himself, not the message, to the assumptions of his audience. See W. J. Larkin Jr., *Culture and Biblical Hermeneutics: Interpreting and Applying the Authoritative Word in a Relativistic Age* (Grand Rapids, Mich.: Baker, 1988).

One is a woman named Damaris; the other, Dionysius, is said to be a member of the Council of the Areopagus.

Neither Damaris nor Dionysius again appears in the New Testament, and Luke leaves us with no clue as to the significance of either. And yet, a bit of extrabiblical reading changes the complexion of the entire Acts 17 narrative.

Thirty-five years ago historian E. M. Blaiklock wrote of the mix of ancient and modern that strikes the visitor to Athens today. Describing the city more than nineteen hundred years after Paul's visit, Blaiklock was intrigued to find that a street that today runs around the south side of the Acropolis ruins bears the name of Dionysius the Areopagite.[47] Given this sort of legacy, which has endured two millennia, we must ask, what sort of person was this Dionysius, anyway?

The only surviving source that alludes to this convert of Paul is the church father Eusebius's *Church History.*[48] We learn here that Dionysius, a member of the elite Council of Areogapus, converted to Christ through Paul's preaching. Eusebius further mentions that this same Dionysius went on to become a bishop in the church. And not only this—we learn that the self-same Dionysius eventually became a martyr for his faith. Whether Luke was alive and aware of this development is anybody's guess; at any rate, he does not report this in the book of Acts.

Putting Dionysius's influence in further perspective, we are amazed to discover that roughly *one thousand years* after the Areopagite's conversion to the Christian faith, some parts of the Near East were acquainted with a pseudonymous piece of literature, *Pseudo-Dionysius*, that was attributed to Paul's convert. That such attribution persisted for so long raises intriguing questions. One can only guess that this convert of Paul was an extraordinary individual, whose legacy extended in that part of the world for at least a millennium. To the natural eye, Paul's ministry in Athens may have seemed "unsuccessful." Another perspective, however, reminds us that the church did in fact grow in Athens and Greece in the fullness of time. And no one will ever know precisely what role Dionysius the Areopagite played.

---

[47]Blaiklock, *Cities,* pp. 52-55.
[48]Eusebius *Church History* 3.4; 4.23.

7

Biblical Resources for Ethics
The Petrine Model

—

The epistle of 2 Peter is one of those documents that might be viewed as the Rodney Dangerfield of the New Testament. It never seems to get any respect. Paul's epistles? These we prefer. The Gospels? They're familiar to us. Even John's Revelation we've read on occasion; after all, who's not fascinated by prophecy? But have you read 2 Peter? Slim chance. (When is the last time you heard a sermon on the angels who fell, "righteous" Lot, Balaam's ass or the earth disappearing in fervent heat?!)

Along with James, 1 Peter, Jude and 1-3 John, 2 Peter belongs to a part of the New Testament canon designated the catholic or General Epistles—so named because, unlike Paul's letters, which are specifically designated, these epistles lack any specific, localized designations and hence are said to have catholic or universal appeal.[1] One of the great, though little-appreciated, contributions that the General Epistles have made to New Testament study and preaching is their representation of the heart of the New Testament ethical tradition. The documents emphasize the ethics of Christian faith—that is, right living. While it is true that Paul's letters typically end with ethical admonitions,

---

[1]Eusebius *Church History* 2.23.25; 6.14. Jerome appears to be the first to have denominated these epistles as "catholic" (*De Viris Illustribus* 1). Although these letters lack specific addressees and locations, they show evidence of being written to specific groups for specific purposes. In this sense, the designation "catholic" is misleading.

the bulk of his writing is devoted to a definition of Christian belief, hence its *theological* trajectory.

The priority in the General Epistles of ethics over doctrine (which does not minimize their theological content) has important implications for the church. The church's lack of attention to these writings, correlatively, robs us of irreplaceable resources that we need for life and service.

The broader neglect of documents such as 2 Peter has not occurred in a vacuum, however. There are definite reasons for this negligence. One is the tragic fact that biblical scholars and theologians give little attention to them. This neglect was noted in chapter three as it applied to New Testament ethics at the textbook level. And it is no exaggeration to say that in seminaries, where the study of the New Testament should be most concentrated, this neglect in all likelihood will not abate. Such is true in mainline Protestant seminaries, which have devoted themselves primarily to process thought, feminist theology and social activism, as well as in evangelical Protestant seminaries, which, as we noted, have devoted immense curricular attention to personal counseling and church-growth concerns. All this is to say, Rodney Dangerfield, by comparison, should feel very much appreciated! (At least he gets airtime!)

The New Testament's moral vocabulary is most dense in the General Epistles, with the exception of 2-3 John. James, 1-2 Peter and Jude all contain statements about the importance of character and about moral examples from the past as well as strong exhortations toward moral development. James reminds us that true religion (faith) is evidenced by our actions (works). First Peter, a tract written to those who are being persecuted for their faith, admonishes its readers to use Christ as an ethical example. Jude is a brief yet explosive apocalyptic tract that seems to have a Jewish-Christian audience in view; it warns against the perils of apostasy. Second Peter, not unlike Jude, warns against moral lapse in the community, although its recipients are clearly located in a pagan social environment. And the letters of 1-3 John exhort believers that if they really do possess Christian knowledge, their lives and actions will be motivated by the ethics of love and an obedience to the truth.

In 2 Peter the readers are admonished to recall and validate what they already know (2 Pet 1:8-15; 3:1-2, 11, 17). Incomparable divine resources have been placed at their disposal for "life and godliness" (2 Pet 1:3). To concretize the matter, the author uses moral examples or types from the past (2 Pet 2:4-10, 15-16). The angels who rebelled were, in the end, disenfranchised and

have been placed "on reserve," awaiting the day of judgment. Noah's generation was condemned because of hardened moral skepticism, while faithful
Noah, with his family, ultimately experienced deliverance. In similar fashion,
Lot was rescued by the Lord from the judgment that beset the cities of the
plain, thus serving as an example to those who face the daunting challenges of
living in a pagan and amoral society where moral standards are continually
subject to assault and compromise.

That 2 Peter is primarily concerned with *ethical lapse* is seen in the writer's vocabulary: The language reflects the author's burden: "pleasure," "licentiousness,"
"depravity," "lusts of the flesh," "covetousness," "defilement," "lawlessness," "van-
ity," "irrational beasts," "moral corrosion," "adultery," "returning to one's own
vomit," "wallowing in the mud." The writer gives a final admonition to those who
have lapsed ethically, even to the point of hardened moral skepticism and apostasy (2 Pet 2:1-3, 15-16, 20-22; 3:3-5, 17): "Beware that you are not carried away
with the error of the lawless and lose your own stability" (2 Pet 3:17).

Virtue Amidst Vice: Tracing a Petrine Theme

The letter's greeting, the accent of which is received righteousness and grace,
is followed by a catalog of virtues that describe the moral progress incumbent
upon each believer (2 Pet 1:5-7). This catalog is meant to outline the contours
of Christian life and godliness (2 Pet 1:3), to which all should aspire. Possessing these virtues, the readers are told, prevents an ineffective and unfruitful
life; to lack them is to be spiritually blind. At issue is moral self-responsibility
(2 Pet 1:8-9). The moral tenor of the exhortation in 2 Peter 1:12-15 indicates
that the situation in the community is grave.

This gravity is confirmed by the material in 2 Peter 2:1-3, a stinging indictment of certain individuals who are adversely influencing the Christian community. Moral typology as well as a detailed sketch of these individuals
constitute the bulk of 2 Peter 2. These types or examples of moral compromise
from the past reinforce for the reader the reality of divine judgment; they also
serve to encourage the faithful that God is faithful to deliver *them* from their
cultural "furnace."

On the one hand stand the angels who fell and the cities of Sodom and Gomorrah; both examples epitomize the consequences of moral hardness. It is
astonishing to think that the angels who were created by God Almighty as
privileged servants were in fact created with moral agency; even more aston-

ishing is the fact, veiled from human understanding, that some of them *chose* to rebel—a choice that is irreversible. The cities of the plain, by contrast, characterize a moral obduracy that in the end necessitated God's judgment in the present. This judgment, however, did not encompass Lot, despite Lot's obvious weaknesses (cf. Gen 19). Lot, of course, is not Noah. In his weakness he was "tormented" in his soul by unrestrained, lawless men day after day. Thus, the readers should be encouraged that even Lot is described as "righteous"[2] and ultimately is saved amidst the very act of judgment that befell Sodom and Gomorrah, just as the righteous Noah, with his family, also experienced deliverance from cataclysmic judgment. Noah and Lot are types of faithful people who experience divine deliverance despite enormous social obstacles.[3]

A final example should give the readers pause. It graphically demonstrates the corrosive effect of moral compromise. Moral "madness" beset even a prophet, Balaam, whose compact with pagans resulted in a hardness of heart, to the point where, mercifully, the prophet was restrained by a dumb beast (2 Pet 2:16).[4] Whereas Jude contains a brief allusion to Balaam (Jude 11), in 2 Peter the Balaam typology is developed more fully.[5] The language being used strongly suggests apostasy—"have left the straight road and have gone astray," "loved the wages of doing wrong" (2 Pet 2:15)—and comports with the Old Testament characterization of Balaam: the prophet was seduced by pagans, the fruit of which was apostasy for Israel. From the perspective of 2 Peter, the downfall of a prophet of God is a singular phenomenon and one that is highly instructive. Over time Balaam became ethically divorced from the message that he bore. The psychology and nature of apostasy are such that a moral skepticism and cynicism cause one actually to loathe and turn from what was formerly embraced. In the context of Christian community, Balaam's sin acts as a cancer; it threatens everything around it.

The language found in 2 Peter 2:20-22 adds to the picture in a way that should further disturb the readers. The adversaries, who are influencing the

[2]Extraordinarily, Lot is described three times as "righteous" in 2 Pet 2:7-8. It is likely that the 2 Pet text is mirroring the interpretive influence of extrabiblical Jewish traditions surrounding Lot (e.g., Wisdom of Solomon 10:6; 19:17; Philo *De vita Mosis* 2.58) and not Gen 19 directly.

[3]Noah's generation is prototypical of a faithless generation in Jesus' teaching as well (Mt 24:37-39; Lk 17:26-30). In Luke's Gospel, Noah's and Lot's generations appear side by side: they typify life as normal, as unaware of pending judgment.

[4]The writer of 2 Pet may be using irony here, since he described Balaam's opponents as "irrational animals, mere creatures of instinct" (2 Pet 2:12).

[5]The most extensive examination of Balaam typology in Jewish thinking is found in Geza Vermes, "The Story of Balaam," in *Scripture and Tradition in Judaism* (Leiden: Brill, 1973), pp. 127-77.

Christian community by stealth (2 Pet 2:1),[6] are described as having previously escaped worldly defilement but having subsequently become entangled and overcome therein once more—a horrendous state of affairs in which the latter condition eclipses the original. The portrait that follows, though conventional, is meant to shock. A double proverb (2 Pet 2:22), which draws one part from the Old Testament ("the dog turns back to its own vomit," Prov 26:11) and one part from extrabiblical tradition ("the sow is washed only to wallow in the mud"), is employed.[7] The reader is struck by the graphic simplicity of proverbial wisdom; particularly in a pagan social environment, the common stereotyping resonates with the audience.

Second Peter 3:1-13 consists of an exhortation toward remembrance, a caricature of the hardened moral skeptic, the declaration that moral accountability is incontrovertible and pastoral remarks concerning theodicy, followed by concluding admonitions.[8] The material in 2 Peter 3 is the author's calculated response to the current moral state of affairs in which some have forgotten the binding power of Christian claims to moral truth. The author develops a response to the moral skeptic (2 Pet 3:3-7) because the opponents champion moral self-determination and because they "deliberately ignore" (2 Pet 3:5-6) past examples of divine retribution, all of which point to an ultimate day of moral reckoning (2 Pet 3:7).

From the standpoint of the believer, however, the delay in divine vindication is disconcerting and requires a proper perspective (2 Pet 3:8). The faithful, like Noah and Lot, will be rescued at the appointed time. Until then, however, they must resist the social forces at work within culture that would undermine faith and morality. They are to endure because, unseen to the human eye, divine longsuffering is at work with humanity (2 Pet 3:9). For the faithful, patient endurance in a hostile social climate (2 Pet 3:12, 15) is part of God's call to "holiness and godliness" (2 Pet 3:11). The letter's final exhortation clarifies the writer's purpose in writing: "You therefore, beloved, since you are forewarned, beware that you are not carried away with the error of the lawless and lose your own stability" (2 Pet 3:17).

The present situation, perhaps on the eve of the apostle Peter's death (2 Pet

---

[6]This appears to be the case in Jude as well (Jude 4).

[7]The extrabiblical reference is to *The Story of Ahiqar,* the text of which is found in *Apocrypha and Pseudepigrapha of the Old Testament,* ed. R. H. Charles, 2 vols. (Oxford: Clarendon, 1913), 2:772.

[8]Theodicy is a defense of God's justice in the face of evil.

1:13-14), calls for a roundly prophetic and eminently pastoral word of exhortation—exhortation that is meant to enunciate the ethical foundations of Christian faith.

VIRTUE IN 2 PETER: ITS LANGUAGE AND LOGIC

The basis for virtue (2 Pet 1:1-4). The recipients of this epistle are identified as "those who have received a faith as precious as ours through the righteousness of our God and Savior Jesus Christ" (2 Pet 1:1). This faith is described in two ways. First, it has been freely offered by God through Christ's righteousness. That is, it is a righteousness that has been *bestowed*, not achieved. Lest the reader misconstrue the extended ethical admonitions that follow, the writer of 2 Peter is not advocating some form of works-righteousness or of human striving rooted in the power of the human will. Second, this is a "faith as precious as ours." The sense of equality expressed here resonates with the Greek mind, given its importance in law and politics. In Hellenistic thinking, all citizens have the same position and rights; these legal connotations are readily translatable into the covenantal language of New Testament faith. In 2 Peter, this declaration of equal standing is meant to reassure the readers that they stand on the same footing as do the apostles and that they share in the very same provisions. Such a heritage makes no distinctions between apostles and laypersons. The implication is clear: there are no second-class citizens in the kingdom of God.

A key word in the epistle, *knowledge,* appears in its opening. The writer's prayer is that "grace and peace be yours in abundance" (2 Pet 1:2). How does this transpire? Through the knowledge of God (2 Pet 1:2).[9] The implications should not be lost on the readers. First, knowledge of God makes possible—facilitates, serves as the medium for—their growth in grace and peace. Second, through this knowledge the believer experiences "everything needed for life and godliness" (2 Pet 1:3). Not incidentally, the key word, *knowledge,* is also part of the letter's closing exhortation ("But grow in the grace and knowledge of our Lord and Savior Jesus Christ," 2 Pet 3:18).[10]

The catalog of virtues (2 Pet 1:5-7). If 2 Peter is addressed to the Christian

---

[9]The term is *epignōsis*, rendered "full knowledge."
[10]The writer is calling the readers back to what they already "know" (2 Pet 1:12). It would have been better never to have "known" the truth than to "know" it and forsake it (2 Pet 2:20-22).

community in a Gentile social setting, as most commentators suggest,[11] drawing on the concept of virtue would be an appropriate way of countering amo-
rality or moral skepticism. This is particularly true if, according to pagan
moral philosophers, to be rational was to lead a moral life. In the hands of the
writer, Hellenistic ethical ideals are realized in their truest sense by Christian
faith—faith, that is, that culminates in agape love.

For this reason, the writer uses what was a conventional rhetorical device
among moral philosophers of the first century.[12] The recording of ethical lists
in the Hellenistic world extends formally from the Homeric era but reaches its
zenith in the teaching of the Stoics between the third century B.C. and the first
century A.D. The ethical catalog has an important rhetorical function: it is used
to instill in the reader or listener either praise (through a listing of virtues) or
shame (through a listing of vices). As a pedagogical tool, it derives its force
from a standardization of behavioral types.

Schematization of the four cardinal virtues—justice, temperance, prudence
and courage—first appears in Plato's *Republic*. Aristotle distinguishes between
practical, political, social and intellectual virtues in *Nichomachean Ethics*. Vice and
virtue lists are a primary feature of Stoic moral philosophers, who tend to develop
quite elaborate schematizations of each. These lists take a variety of forms and are
used on both an academic as well as a popular level. The dualism between virtue
and vice—what is praiseworthy and what is shameful—is readily adaptable and
incorporated into both Hellenistic-Jewish and Christian literature.[13]

In the New Testament, vice and virtue lists function in different ways. They
may be used for antithesis (e.g., Gal 5:19-23; Jas 3:15, 17), contrast (e.g., Tit

---

[11]This assumption has been most persuasively argued by Tord Fornberg, *An Early Church in a Pluralistic
Society: A Study of 2 Peter,* Coniectanea biblica: New Testament Series 9 (Lund, Germany: Gleerup,
1977), and serves as the basis, more recently, for J. Daryl Charles, *Virtue Amidst Vice: The Catalog of
Virtues in 2 Peter 1,* Journal for the Study of the New Testament Supplement Series 150 (Sheffield,
U.K.: Sheffield Academic Press, 1997).

[12]The commentator J. N. D. Kelly calls 1 Pet 1:5-7 a page out of "current pagan textbook morality" (*A
Commentary on the Epistles of Peter and Jude,* Black's New Testament Commentaries [London: Adam
& Charles Black, 1969], p. 306).

[13]Ethical lists appear frequently in the New Testament. Catalogs of virtue are found in 1 Cor 13:4-7;
2 Cor 6:4-7; Gal 5:22-23; Eph 4:32; 5:9; Phil 4:8; Col 3:12-14; 1 Tim 4:12; 6:11; 2 Tim 2:22; 3:10;
Jas 3:17; 1 Pet 3:8; and 2 Pet 1:5-7. Catalogs of vice appear in Mt 15:19; Mk 7:21-22; Rom 1:29-31;
13:13; 1 Cor 5:10-11; 6:9-10; 2 Cor 6:8-10; 12:20-21; Gal 5:19-21; Eph 4:31; 5:3-5; Col 3:5, 8;
1 Tim 1:9-10; 2 Tim 3:2-5; Tit 3:3; Jas 3:15; 1 Pet 2:1; 4:3, 15; and Rev 9:21; 21:8; 22:15. See in this
regard B. S. Easton, "New Testament Ethical Lists," *Journal of Biblical Literature* 51, no. 1 (1932): 1-
12; and J. Daryl Charles, "Vice and Virtue Lists," in *Dictionary of New Testament Background,* ed. Craig
A. Evans and Stanley E. Porter (Downers Grove, Ill.: InterVarsity Press, 2000), pp. 1252-57.

3:3), polemics (e.g., 1 Tim 1:9-10; 2 Tim 3:2-5) or instruction (e.g., 2 Pet 1:5-7). Occasionally, though not always, alliteration, assonance, cadence or inclusio enhances their rhetorical impact.[14] Usually the elements in these lists do not build on one another, demonstrating any sort of progression, although there are one or two exceptions in the New Testament. The syntactical arrangement of 2 Peter 1:5-7, in which each successive virtue appears to show some relationship to and proceed from the former, suggests an organic whole.

Christian ethics, as evidenced by the catalog of virtues in 2 Peter 1, is rooted in the foundation of faith and climaxes in love. We may assume that the rhetorical effect created by the progression and climax of the virtues mirrors a concrete situation affecting the Christian community in which there has been a fundamental ethical breakdown. In order to address this crisis, the writer of 2 Peter uses a standard rhetorical device to underscore the necessity of the moral life as *proof* of one's profession both to the Christian community and to the world.

Second Peter 1:5 begins, "For this very reason, you must make every effort to support your faith." Of the eight virtues listed in 2 Peter 1:5-7, six of these (moral excellence, knowledge, self-control, perseverance, godliness and brotherly affection) appear in one form or another in comparable pagan ethical lists. This supports the argument that the letter was destined to those living in a pervasively Gentile setting.

The Greek word for "faith," *pistis,* normally conveys in common parlance loyalty or trust. In its Christian sense, it normally means subjective trust placed in the saving realities of the gospel—a faith that is received "through the righteousness of our God and Savior Jesus Christ" (2 Pet 1:1).[15] It is a faith received by and bestowed on the believer. Faith is, therefore, foundational.

To be added to one's faith is "moral excellence," *aretē,* of fundamental importance in all Greek ethical systems. In its classical usage, this term denoted excellence or renown, originally, of the brave or noble warrior.[16] In time, applied to the sphere of ethics, it acquired the sense of moral excellence or virtue.

---

[14]Inclusio is a rhetorical device that employs the same element in a document's opening and closing. In 2 Peter, for example, this is achieved by the key word *knowledge* standing alongside the word *grace* to open (2 Pet 1:2) and close (2 Pet 3:18) the letter; the word *piety* (or *godliness*) is used in a similar fashion (2 Pet 1:3; 3:11).

[15]In Jude 3 it seems to carry the sense of an *objective* trust that is to be preserved and faithfully passed on to others.

[16]In Homer, *aretē* is virtually a synonym for "courage."

Within the structure of Greek society, it came to signify those qualities that typify the outstanding citizen.[17] Moral virtue, observes Aristotle, is "formed by habit [ethos]," for none of the virtues "is implanted in us by nature."[18] Aristotle assumes the conviction that within human nature resides the *capacity* for virtue, although this capacity must be "learned" and subsequently displayed.[19] In fact, Aristotle believes that human nature is equally capable of destroying *and* displaying moral excellence.[20] What applies to moral virtue also applies to a scientist, a skilled craftsman or an athlete: each must "perfect its work." As with the marathon runner or the wrestler, "an expert in any field avoids excess and deficiency."[21] In the end, cultivating virtue is a matter of choice; it entails making priorities, constant repetition and training, and, alas, much hard work. But the acquisition of virtue is such that it "enables its possessor to perform his particular function well."[22]

In the Christian scheme of things, moral excellence in turn leads to "knowledge," *gnōsis*. *Gnōsis* frequently begins or ends pagan ethical lists, reflecting the Stoic belief that the rational person is moral and the unethical person is "ignorant." The placement of knowledge in this list—related to and issuing out of moral excellence—indicates that there is an organic, indivisible link between the two. Where the Christian and Stoic understanding of knowledge differ is that the Christian view prevents knowledge from becoming an end in itself and, thus, an idol. According to Christian morality, knowledge is *part of, but not the goal of,* the ethical life. Apart from faith, knowledge is detrimental.[23] In the context of the Petrine virtue list, knowledge signifies a practical application of what is known to be true.

In the moral progression of 2 Peter 1:5-7, knowledge should lead to greater "self-control" *(enkrateia)* in the lives of the readers. This is an organic connection that is not incidental; both elements go hand in hand, just as their opposites, "ignorance" *(agnoia)* and "lust" *(epithymia),* are closely linked both in

---

[17]See, e.g., Aristotle *Ethica nichomachea* 2.1-9 (1103a-1109b) and 10.9 (1179b-1181lb).

[18]Ibid., 2.1 (1103a).

[19]Ibid., 2.1 (1103a); 2.5 (1106a). This conviction corresponds to the biblical teaching of humans as created in the image of God.

[20]Ibid., 2.1-2 (1103a-1104b).

[21]Ibid., 2.6 (1106b).

[22]This description is given by Martin Ostwald in the glossary of terms appended to his English translation of Aristotle (*Nichomachean Ethics,* trans. Martin Ostwald [New York: Macmillan, 1986], p. 304).

[23]Knowledge alone, writes Paul, puffs up but does not edify (1 Cor 8:1-3, 7-13; 13:2).

pagan ethics and in the New Testament: "Like obedient children, do not be conformed to the desires *[epithymiai]* that you formerly had in ignorance *[agnoia]*" (1 Pet 1:14). Socrates cites self-control as a cardinal virtue;[24] and in his contrast of moral strength and weakness, Aristotle devotes an entire section to its importance.[25] Self-control, as Aristotle conceives it, is understood in its relation to pleasure. Aristotle, however, distinguishes between pleasures of the soul and pleasures of the body, and he understands the need for self-control with respect to the latter.[26] Stoics adopted the same exalted view of self-control,[27] and in Philo (first century A.D.) it is a superior virtue, though linked with asceticism, which marks something of a shift from the classical view.[28] Self-control is perhaps best understood when it is set in juxtaposition to its opposites: incontinence and licentiousness (2 Pet 2:7, 18).[29] It is the inner capacity to restrain one's appetites and to do so in the knowledge of a greater good. Self-control, moreover, is a necessary component in the ethical life to counter any potential misunderstanding of Christian "freedom" or grace—for example, the misunderstanding that might view the struggle against desire and lust as unnecessary.

Self-control, in turn, produces "endurance" *(hypomonē)*. This endurance is active, not passive. For Plato, it takes the form of brave resistance, which is honorable to a man.[30] Also demonstrating endurance's active quality, Aristotle subordinates this virtue to courage,[31] an understanding that is carried over into Stoic thinking. Endurance has two sides: it expresses itself toward the world as well as toward God. As a virtue, it allows the believer to bear up to—or, more literally, "remain under"—difficulty and trial without being moved. Far from being mere willpower, this quality, in the Christian scheme of things, issues out of deep confidence in the divine will and a submission to the hand of God, who will not allow one to be tested beyond one's capacity to stand firm (1 Cor 10:13). A divinely oriented hope allows one to "en-

---

[24]As recounted in Xenophon *Memorabilia* 1.5.4.

[25]Aristotle *Ethica nichomachea* 7.1-14 (1145b-1154b).

[26]Ibid., 3.10.

[27]See, e.g., Stobaeus *Eclogae* 2.61.11 and Diogenes Laertius 7.92.

[28]See Philo *De specialibus legibus* 2.195 and *Legum allegoriae* 3.18.

[29]Alongside "licentiousness" *(aselgeia)* stand other indications of moral squalor in 2 Peter: "corruption" (2 Pet 1:4; 2:12, 19), "lust" (2 Pet 1:4; 2:10, 18; 3:3), and "lawless" deeds (2 Pet 2:7-8; 3:17).

[30]Plato *Theaetetus* 117b.

[31]Aristotle *Ethica nichomachea* 3.9 (1117b).

dure all things" (1 Cor 13:7). To endure, from the perspective of the New
Testament, is to move on into personal maturity (Jas 1:2-4, 12). In so enduring we should remember that we have a model (Heb 12:2-3).[32] In 2 Peter,
the admonition toward *hypomonē* appears alongside the *makrothymia* ("forbearance") of God (2 Pet 3:9, 15); we endure because of God's longsuffering
toward humans.

The connection between self-control, endurance and "godliness" or "piety"
(eusebeia) is logical in the Christian ethical progression. In late Hellenism, *eusebeia* expresses piety or reverence in the broadest sense; it can denote respect for
the gods as well as for family, tradition or the social order.[33] In the wider sense
of the term, it is not an expression of religiosity. In the New Testament it carries
both expressly Christian and broader Hellenistic connotations.[34]

How one relates to God determines how one relates to others; the virtue of
piety, therefore, expresses itself in our relationships with others. Out of the
one's love for God, one learns to love and respect others *(philadelphia)*, both
in the world and in the household of faith. With its synonym *philanthrōpia*,
which frequently appears in pagan literature as well as in the New Testament,
philadelphia describes a kindness or affection to those around us, whether they
are family members or neighbors.[35] Behind the term stands the Greek ideal of
friendship, suggesting duties that attend our relationships.[36] Aristotle helpfully distinguishes between three types of affection or friendship.[37] One type is
that which exists between older people, since in older age people pursue what
is beneficial rather than what is pleasurable. A second is that which exists
among younger people, and this type appears to be based primarily on pleasure. A third type is noted to exist among "good men" who are alike in moral
excellence; each wishes the highest good of the other. Those who wish the other's highest, says Aristotle, are "friends in the truest sense," since their attitude

---

[32]The verb and noun forms of *hypomonein,* "to endure," occur six times in the letter to the Hebrews,
where trials and persecution are being represented.

[33]Werner Foerster, *"Eusebeia,"* in *Theological Dictionary of the New Testament,* ed. Gerhard Kittel and
Gerhard Friedrich, 10 vols. (Grand Rapids, Mich.: Eerdmans, 1964-1976), 7:175-85.

[34]In addition to 2 Pet 1:6, 1 Tim 2:2 seems to employ the term in the wider sense of reverence or respect.

[35]See, e.g., Acts 28:2 and Tit 3:4; cf. Acts 27:3.

[36]See Ulrich Luck, "φιλανθρωπία, κτλ.," in *Theological Dictionary of the New Testament,* ed. Gerhard
Kittel and Gerhard Friedrich, 10 vols. (Grand Rapids, Mich.: Eerdmans, 1964-1976), 9:107-12.

[37]Aristotle presupposes that we cannot have "affection" toward inanimate objects, since inanimate objects do not reciprocate (*Ethica nichomachea* 8.2 [1155b]).

is determined by the friendship itself and not circumstances.[38] True friendship or brotherly affection, so conceived, "appears to consist in *giving* rather than in *receiving* affection"[39] and thus fully accords with Jesus' teaching on neighbor love.[40] For the Christian household, this notion acquires a special meaning,[41] though it can be taken for granted.[42]

The catalog of virtues achieves its climax in authentic Christian "love," *agapē,* which distinguishes the Christian ethos from its counterparts and without which Christian ethics would be incomplete. Christian morality is distinctly a morality of charity. It is the morality of fruit-bearing, whereby one gives evidence of an *internal work of grace;* gratitude is demonstrated through one's actions. Frequently in the New Testament this work of grace is depicted through the imagery of the farmer, the gardener or the vinedresser. God is the cultivator, we are the field (1 Cor 3:5-9). The Christian disciple exists to bear fruit—lasting fruit (Jn 15:1-17; Rom 7:4). The Christian's life, if it is judged to be qualitatively different, must bear the fruit of the Spirit (Gal 5:22-25). It is in this process of fruit-bearing that we please God (Col 1:10) and influence others (Mt 5:16). Inasmuch as *agapē* is the fount and the goal of Christian virtuous action, therein lies the difference between Christian and pagan ethics.[43]

To the contemporary reader the question might naturally arise as to why the writer of 2 Peter does not include the third of the "theological" virtues—hope—or why the many fruits of the Spirit, listed in Galatians 5, are omitted. Or, from the other direction, why did the writer omit three of the four "cardinal" virtues—courage, justice and prudence? Is the list in 2 Peter arbitrary in its selection, as some commentators maintain?

While vice and virtue lists in the New Testament are not all of the same compositional mold, one of their peculiar features—absent from pagan catalogs—is the occasional movement in a list toward crescendo or decrescendo. Prime examples of this are Romans 5:1-5, where the trajectory of grace moves from suffering to hope; 2 Corinthians 6:4-10, a list of hardships moving from

---

[38]Ibid., 8.3-8 (1156a-1159b).

[39]Ibid., 8.8 (1159a), emphasis added.

[40]See, e.g., Mt 5:43; 19:19; 22:39; Mk 12:31, 33; Lk 10:27, 29, 36. Compare also Rom 13:9-10; Gal 5:14; Jas 2:8.

[41]Rom 12:10; 1 Thess 4:9; 1 Pet 1:22; 2 Pet 1:7.

[42]Heb 13:1.

[43]The predominant role of *agapē* can be seen in the fact that it secures a place in the majority of New Testament virtue lists—e.g., 2 Cor 6:6; Gal 5:22; Phil 4:8; 1 Tim 6:11; 2 Pet 1:5-7; Rev 2:19.

general to specific; and 2 Peter 1:5-7, which features an ethical progression that builds toward a climax in *agapē*.[44] The movement of the Petrine catalog of virtues suggests that each virtue, a fruit of the life of faith, facilitates the next; none is independent of the others. Because of this organic unity, the individual virtues are not randomly selected. Their interconnectedness can be stated as follows. Faith produces virtue, which is moral excellence. Because there is a correlation between the character of God and our moral character, faith is a prerequisite. Virtue, if it is to increase in our lives, is affected by what we do with the knowledge of God that comes to us. Greater knowledge of the resources that God has graciously provided through Christ will yield self-control or self-mastery of our appetites. That is to say, grace operative in our lives will curb the human passions arising from within as well as enable us to withstand the forces of surrounding culture from without. An increase in self-control will strengthen our ability to endure, despite the overwhelming social forces that may come against us. Endurance, in turn, will reflect a reverence or piety in our lives. This piety simultaneously pleases God while giving confirming evidence of our faith to those around us through our relationships. These relationships, in turn, will be characterized by mutual affection, which is to say, a sense of kindred belonging that is not pharisaical or sanctimonious, and they will ultimately be governed by the highest virtue and goal of the Christian ethic, *agapē*. Love, after all, is the sign of the kingdom of God.[45]

Although the English translation in 2 Peter 1:5 of the verb *epichorēgeō* ("supplement," RSV; "add," NIV; "support," NRSV) is not inaccurate—"Build upon or add to your faith the following virtues . . ."—the richness of the Greek verb is utterly lost in the translation. The color that this verb adds to the textual commentary is considerable. In Greek theater, large and costly choruses were often employed, requiring the financial support of a wealthy local benefactor, the *chorēgos,* to help defray what were at times exorbitant costs. The

---

[44]Contra some commentators (e.g., Richard Bauckham, *Jude, 2 Peter,* Word Biblical Commentary 50 [Waco, Tex.: Word, 1983], pp. 184-85) who see no logical progression in this virtue catalog, from a uniquely Christian perspective there is indeed a logic, cadence, starting point and climax in this list. This progression, moreover, is suggested by the very syntax of 2 Pet 1:5-7.

[45]This interconnectedness is aptly summarized by commentator J. B. Mayor: "Faith is the gift of God already received; to this must be added (1) moral strength which enables a man to do what he knows to be right; (2) spiritual discernment; (3) self-control by which a man resists temptation; (4) endurance by which he bears up under persecution or adversity; (5) right . . . behavior toward God [piety]; (6) toward the brethren [brotherly love]; [and] toward all [love]" (*The Epistle of St. Jude and the Second Epistle of St. Peter* [New York: Macmillan, 1907], p. 93).

relative extravagance attached to some of these productions is connoted by the verb *chorēgeō,* a strengthened form of which is used in 2 Peter 1:5 *(epichorēgeō).* The readers are not merely to add or supply to their existing faith; they are to *contribute extravagantly* to their own moral development. Lest there be any misunderstanding, however, this is no mere works-righteousness, for two important reasons stated in the text:

- A surplus of grace and divine resources has already been lavished upon believers (2 Pet 1:1-4).
- Entrance into the divine kingdom will be "richly *supplied*" (2 Pet 1:11) by Jesus Christ himself.[46]

The necessity of virtue (2 Pet 1:8-11). The presence of the catalog of virtues leads to the following conclusion: "For if these things are yours and are increasing among you, they keep you from being ineffective and unfruitful in the knowledge of our Lord Jesus Christ" (2 Pet 1:8). Faith received, far from being passive in nature, requires of the believer active cooperation with the grace of God. Progress in one's own moral development does not automatically occur; it is attained, through rigorous struggle and, yes, hard work. This progress, we are told, prevents an "ineffective" *(argos)* life. The same word is also used in two other key New Testament texts, James 2:20 ("Do you want to be shown, you senseless person, that faith apart from works is barren *[argos]*?") and Matthew 12:36 ("I tell you, on the day of judgment you will have to give an account for every careless *[argos]* word you utter").

In the same way, the virtues also prevent one from becoming "unfruitful" or "unproductive" *(akarpos).* In Jesus' parable of the sower, the seed choked out by the cares of the world, the deceit of riches and lust, is accorded the description *akarpos* (Mt 13:22; Mk 4:19). Significantly, the very same linkage of fruit-bearing, good works and the knowledge of God is found in Colossians 1:10: "so that you may lead lives worthy of the Lord, fully pleasing to him, as you bear fruit in every good work and as you grow in the knowledge *[epignōsis]* of God." At issue in 2 Peter, as in the Colossians text, is the matter of *a life worthy of one's calling.*

To be ineffective and unproductive, quite simply, is to cause a Christian scandal. The scandal consists in the fact that the believer has been granted much—everything needed for life and godliness (2 Pet 1:1-4). The coexis-

---

[46]Here the verb *epichorēgeō* is used again!

tence of futility and fruitlessness with "equal" faith, received righteousness and the "full knowledge of God" is a blatant contradiction.

Having stated the conclusion positively, the writer expresses it negatively: "For anyone who lacks these things is nearsighted and blind, and is forgetful of the cleansing of past sins" (2 Pet 1:9). The portrait of blindness is in keeping with imagery used throughout the letter—a simple, striking imagery. The blindness metaphor coincides with the images in 2 Peter 2 of slavery, the dog returning to its vomit and the pig returning to the mud. Its occurrence in the New Testament (e.g., Mt 15:14; 23:16; Jn 9:40-41; Rev 3:17) shows the blindness metaphor to be an integral part of the Christian moral tradition. While a flat translation of "blind and nearsighted" captures the general sense of the admonition, it misses the nuance of "to close the eye" that the Greek text communicates.[47] The nuance created by the writer's choice of words here should not be lost on the reader; emphasis is being placed on *moral self-responsibility*. Some have shut their eyes to the truth, resulting in a blindness that is not inherited but *cultivated*. The same moral dynamic is found in Paul's letter to the Roman Christians. People suppress the truth that is already *known* (Rom 1:18-19); the result is a darkening of their foolish minds. Such is the legacy of apostasy, which is to say, a rejection or suppression of known truth. In 2 Peter this is characterized by denial (2 Pet 2:1), deception (2 Pet 2:3), boldness and willfulness (2 Pet 2:10), a lust for sin (2 Pet 2:14) and seduction (2 Pet 2:14, 18). Those individuals possessing these traits are cast as resembling Balaam (2 Pet 2:15-16), who was seduced by pagans with a view to lead Israel astray.

Some in the community, astonishingly, are said to have "forgotten" that they were forgiven and cleansed of their past.[48] The text of 2 Peter 1:9 literally reads "having received forgetfulness," which offers the faint suggestion of a *voluntary acceptance* of their deceived and darkened condition. Like the dog who returns to its vomit and the pig who returns to the mud after it has been washed, these persons, in a revolting sort of fashion, return to the former way of life from which they had been delivered. They have become slaves to a new tyranny that is worse than the former (2 Pet 2:20-21).

---

[47] The verb *myōpazō* suggests a deliberate "shutting of the eye."

[48] This may be an allusion back to the "cleansing" waters of baptism, though it need not be restricted to that interpretation. Forgetting one's baptism, with its attendant meaning, may stand in the background of Paul's teaching in Rom 6:1-4.

The ethical challenge that follows the line of thinking developed in 2 Peter 1:5-9 has a ring of urgency: "Therefore, brothers and sisters, be all the more eager to confirm your call and election" (2 Pet 1:10). The tenor of 2 Peter has by now shifted from teaching to exhortation, from didactics to warning. The idea of "confirming one's call and election" is a prominent feature of the Pauline epistles (e.g., 1 Cor 1:2; Gal 5:13; Eph 4:1; 1 Tim 6:12).[49] To confirm one's calling is to offer proof—or disproof—of one's profession. As John Calvin aptly puts it, "Purity of life is not improperly called the evidence and proof of election, by which the faithful may not only testify to others that they are the children of God, but also confirm themselves in this confidence."[50]

Moreover, what is striking about the ethical language of 2 Peter is that it preserves the tension between divine sovereignty and human moral agency. The reality of divine grace does not cancel out the necessity of human cooperation. A proper understanding of Christian social ethics is that the two coexist in a necessary (when not wholly explicable) tension, despite the human tendency to negate one or the other pole in this ethical tension.[51] Although God has called people to himself, the believer must respond to that call. While unmerited grace has been extended through the righteousness of Christ, the believer is to demonstrate gratitude by means of a virtuous life. It is plain that in 2 Peter the writer has lapsed Christians in view, which raises particular questions regarding the nature of apostasy. He is not concerned, however, to explore the psychology of apostasy; he only warns that a return to the old life has consequences of a cataclysmic nature. At the heart of moral exhortation in 2 Peter is the balance between divine initiative and human response. On the one hand, great and precious promises have been provided to the believer— indeed, we have received all the divine resources necessary for a life of godliness (2 Pet 1:3-4). On the other hand, the believer is to lavishly support the faith received with a calculated response that, over time, is *measured in terms of ethical quality* (2 Pet 1:5-7). The burden clearly rests on the shoulders of the readers: they must hold up their side of the covenantal agreement. If they are *willing,* they will never stumble (2 Pet 3:17; cf. Jude

[49]It is also implied in 1 Cor 9:27 and Col 3:12, in addition to Heb 9:15, Jas 2:14-26 and 1 Pet 2:21.
[50]John Calvin, *Commentaries on the Catholic Epistles,* trans. J. Owen (reprint; Grand Rapids, Mich.: Baker, 1981), p. 377.
[51]This is the subject of chapter nine, "Toward a Biblical Ethic: Principles in Polarity," below.

24). The guarantee is not that they will not sin, only that they will not *fall*.[52]

The final "promise" extended by the gracious Lord and Savior is to "lavishly provide" entrance into his eternal kingdom. The reward, a full and exceedingly rich provision, awaits those who have "confirmed their calling" by demonstrating a life "worthy of the name" that they bear. Entrance is not *earned*, lest the Petrine ethic be misunderstood. Neither is 2 Peter advocating a "new law," a "new morality" or ascetic rigorism that commentators have supposed. Entrance is by grace, all grace. But the emphasis of the epistle lies on the side of the believer's responsibility. 2 Peter is a call to virtue, and this amidst a world given to vice.

---

[52]The balance between the divine and the human factors is discussed at length in the appendix of my book *Virtue Amidst Vice;* see pp. 159-74 ("Predestination, Perseverance and the Problem of Apostasy").

8

Biblical Resources for Ethics
The Disciple's Model

—

My intention in chapter six was to put Paul on display, advancing Christian truth-claims in a pagan, pluralistic environment. And surely this is Luke's wish in Acts: to show the apostle to the Gentiles in action. Perhaps the apostle's apologetic arsenal strikes the evangelical reader as not very "evangelical." But rather than representing "compromise," as some commentators would have it, Paul's strategy is deliberate and appropriate to a pagan audience, which has little or no knowledge of the Hebrew scriptures.

Chapter seven, in similar fashion, is my attempt to convince the reader that the New Testament is not without resources for the Christian disciple who struggles with pagan cultural surroundings. The social location of the audience to which 2 Peter is addressed shows itself to be relativistic and skeptical in character. The epistle's literary-rhetorical strategy unfolds accordingly.

In the present chapter, I want to draw attention to another New Testament resource. Matthew 5:17-20, unlike Acts 17 and 2 Peter, is framed in the context of *religious* controversy. On display in Matthew's Gospel are competing notions of what the law's role is and how Jesus, a "new Moses" to some, interprets the Hebrew scriptures, particularly the law.

It is of utmost importance in Matthew's Gospel, more so than in the other three Gospel narratives, that the Christian disciple be characterized as a *doer* of the will of God. It is in Matthew that the ethical contours of *righteousness* are accented most heavily. For Matthew, what one *does,* not what one professes, matters most.

The emphasis on ethics is evident from the outset of Jesus' messianic ministry. John the Baptist calls for deeds that befit true repentance (Mt 3:8). Jesus presents himself to John for baptism with the declaration that it is necessary on the basis of "righteousness" (Mt 3:15). Jesus' teaching in the Sermon on the Mount (Mt 5:1—7:29), a description of the ethics of the kingdom, is contextualized and developed only in Matthew. Jesus' stinging denunciation of establishment religion for its failure in *deed* reaches its fullest expression in Matthew (Mt 23:1-36). And Jesus' final exhortation to teach others "to obey everything that I have commanded you" (Mt 28:19-20) is the closing declaration of Matthew's Gospel. For Matthew, then, how the Christian lives is a central motif.

UNDERSTANDING MATTHEW'S BURDEN

The focus on ethics in Matthew's Gospel can be explained by several factors. Among these are a transition in the mid first century from a Jewish-Christian to an increasingly Gentile-Christian church, the early church's relationship to first-century Judaism, and Matthew's desire to present Jesus not only as the fulfillment of Jewish prophecy but also in continuity with the Jewish understanding of the Law (Torah). And if there is one element in the "Jewish-Christian" tradition that is exceedingly difficult to absorb for Gentile Christians, it is the law. What is Jesus' attitude toward the law? What is to be the disciple's relationship to the law? And why is the law mentioned at this stage of the Sermon on the Mount?

What is striking in Matthew is the degree to which Jesus stands in continuity with the Old Testament in general. And while it may surprise many conservative Protestants, early Christianity was united on the fact that Jesus taught and affirmed the Torah. In terms of Jewish theology and Jewish ethics, his teaching—amply on display in Matthew—is orthodox. Without doubt, during Matthew's day, the burning questions among Jews down the street at the synagogue would have been these: Is this Jesus of Nazareth setting aside the Torah? Does he claim to be a new Moses? What about the law? Through the eyes of Matthew, being a Christian and making Christian truth-claims involve some version of self-attestation, particularly in the presence of Judaism, which views the Christian community as a heretical sect. Foremost in Matthew's thinking, then, is the following question: How do the Christian disciples validate themselves as *the* authentic covenant community?

When we begin to probe the reasons behind Matthew's Gospel, taking into account the editorial concerns that distinguish his Gospel narrative from the other three canonical accounts, we grow in our awareness of the debates that must have been raging between Jews and Christians during the first century. And if Matthew is writing to convince Jews that Jesus is the true Messiah and that the Christian community is the true covenant community, then material such as the Sermon on the Mount (Mt 5:1—7:29) is central to his argument. Ethically, the teaching found in Matthew 5:1—7:29 can be legitimately understood as "the fruit of Jewish piety."[1] Consider the assessment of Matthew 5:17-20 by Jewish scholar Pinchas Lapide: "In all rabbinic literature I know of no more unequivocal, fiery acknowledgment of Israel's holy scripture than this opening to the Instruction on the Mount."[2] Within the broader context, this block of teaching can be said to embody the ethical demands of the kingdom of God. The case illustrations recorded in Matthew 5:21-48 (concerning murder, adultery, divorce, making oaths, retaliating and loving one's enemies) amplify the imperatives and warnings of Matthew 5:17-20, material that has been called by one New Testament scholar an "exegetical minefield."[3]

> Do not think that I have come to abolish the law or the prophets; I have come not to abolish but to fulfill. For truly I tell you, until heaven and earth pass away, not one letter, not one stroke of a letter, will pass from the law until all is accomplished. Therefore, whoever breaks one of the least of these commandments, and teaches others to do the same, will be called least in the kingdom of heaven; but whoever does them and teaches them will be called great in the kingdom of heaven. For I tell you, unless your righteousness exceeds that of the scribes and Pharisees, you will never enter the kingdom of heaven.

---

[1]R. E. O. White, *Biblical Ethics* (Atlanta: John Knox Press, 1979), p. 54.
[2]Pinchas Lapide, *The Sermon on the Mount* (Maryknoll, N.Y.: Orbis, 1986), p. 14.
[3]Klyne Snodgrass, "Matthew and the Law," in *SBL 1988 Seminar Papers* (Atlanta: Scholars Press, 1989), p. 536. Snodgrass's essay appears more recently in *Treasures New and Old,* ed. D. R. Bauer and M. A. Powell (Atlanta: Scholars Press, 1996), pp. 99-127.

READING MATTHEW 5:17-20 IN CONTEXT

Even among biblical scholars, Matthew 5:17-20 is considered—and with good reason—to be one of the most difficult texts in the entire New Testament. While more liberal critical scholarship has tended to question the authenticity of this material and the editorial activity of the writer, evangelical commentators have applied their own cut-and-paste approach to these verses. Conservative commentators have tended to interpret these verses by explaining that Jesus "fulfills" the law in the sense that he *supersedes* it—much like he "fulfills" Old Testament prophecy (which, indeed, Matthew wishes to demonstrate elsewhere). But this explanation fails on several counts. It avoids wrestling with the abolish/fulfill antithesis and with the meaning of "the law and the prophets" in Matthew 5:17. It also confuses eschatology for ethics in Matthew 5:18-19, whereby Jesus is emphasizing permanence and duration, not transience or annulment. And it ignores in Matthew 5:20 the contrast introduced by Jesus between genuine righteousness and its Pharisaical counterfeit—a contrast that is developed in the six test cases that follow (Mt 5:21-48).

The case illustrations, it needs to be emphasized, are not negating Old Testament ethics; rather, they affirm Old Testament ethics while adjusting *contemporary rabbinic interpretations of the law*. They show how the law's ethical demands have been tragically circumvented by contemporary religious interpretation. Jesus is in no way setting aside the demands of the law; rather, he is setting aside a wrong interpretation of those ethical demands—an interpretation that originates in the oral tradition of the rabbis ("the tradition of the elders," Mk 7:13).[4] Establishment religion is being indicted for its "making void the word of God through your tradition that you have handed on" (Mk 7:13).

As we read Matthew it becomes clear that the author saw his master not as a new law-giver but as the legitimate interpreter of God's will as contained in the Torah.[5] The true Christian disciple will fulfill the ethical demands that righteousness, revealed in the law, requires. Such obedience is essential to the one seeking to exhibit the "greater righteousness" (Mt 5:20). The disciples are

---

[4]In Mk 7:1-13 Jesus rebukes the scribes and Pharisees for nullifying the commandments of God expressed through Mosaic law by holding to "the tradition of the elders." At issue in the mind of Matthew is not Old Testament law but contemporary misconstruals of the law.
[5]The Torah corresponds to the Pentateuch.

being admonished about their standard of conduct, and this ethical standard *remains fully intact.*

A further clue to properly interpreting of Matthew 5:17-20 lies in its connection to the material that immediately precedes it. Jesus' declarations concerning "the law and the prophets," the law's binding character, obedience to the commandments and the disciples' greater righteousness follow directly on the heels of important ethical imperatives. The disciples are being called to a goal of *good works*:

> You are the salt of the earth; but if salt has lost its taste, how can its saltiness be restored? It is no longer good for anything. . . .
>
> You are the light of the world. A city built on a hill cannot be hid. No one after lighting a lamp puts it under the bushel basket, but on the lampstand, and it gives light to all in the house. In the same way, let your light shine before others, so that they might see your good works and give glory to your Father in heaven. (Mt 5:13-16)

Clearly, Matthew's intent is to frame Jesus' teaching in such a way that it admonishes the Christian disciple about the *durability* and *visibility* of one's lifestyle. *Good works,* depicted by the metaphors of salt (durability) and light (visibility), are the immediate context in which the following imperatives are to be understood. Hence, a distinctive ethic—yet *an enduring ethic*—is the burden of the teaching recorded in Matthew 5:17-20.

Much commentary on these verses, both past and present, attempts to show (or assumes) that Jesus, the true interpreter of the law, is setting aside Mosaic prescriptions. More recently, Frank Thielman, in his important work *The Law and the New Testament,* has argued that in Matthew 5:21-48 the "antithesis" or contrast that exists is between Jesus' teaching and Mosaic law.[6] In fact, Thielman argues that in several cases, Jesus is *forbidding* what Moses *permitted.*[7] In practice, even Mosaic law's proscription of murder, in Thielman's view, becomes "unnecessary."[8] Ethically speaking, Thielman believes that Matthew 5 is stressing discontinuity over continuity and summarizes the Christian disciple's relationship to the law as follows: "The way in which Matthew describes both Jesus' teaching and his role as teacher shows that

---

[6]Frank Thielman, *Law and the New Testament: The Question of Continuity* (New York: Crossroad, 1999).
[7]Ibid., pp. 51-58.
[8]Ibid., p. 52. Thielman writes that Jesus' teaching "obviates the Mosaic law's prohibition" in Mt 5:21-48 (pp. 52-53).

Matthew considered Jesus to be Moses' greater replacement, and believed that his teaching replaced Mosaic law."[9] Thielman asserts that "Jesus has established a new 'law' for his disciples"—a state of affairs that is "clearest" in Matthew's Gospel.[10]

But is this *really* what Matthew is conveying? Does *ethical discontinuity* represent the intent and thrust of Matthew 5:17-20? And is Jesus in fact attempting to set aside the Old Testament sanction against murder? Such a conclusion, if it is true, has enormous ramifications for Christian social ethics. In fact, if Thielman is correct, then public-policy analysts, social scientists, lawmakers and legislators will need to make a quantum shift in their understanding of criminal justice—an understanding that has literally existed for millennia in societies that have sought to maintain any semblance of social order.[11]

The contention by a respected New Testament scholar that Matthew 5:17-20 and Matthew 5:21-48 render the ethical requirements outlined in the Old Testament as "unnecessary" forces an inescapable question on the church. By what ethical standard does the Christian live in the world? That is to say, how is "Christian morality" mediated to a nonbelieving society? Does Matthew present Jesus as truly setting aside the law with its ethical requirements? What, then, is the disciple's relationship to the ethical norms revealed in the Old Testament? *By what standard* are people held morally accountable?

MATTHEW IN LIGHT OF PAUL AND JAMES

As the church, and evangelical Protestantism in particular, reflects on the current moral crisis of our culture, the text of Matthew 5 urgently requires our reexamination. Two equal and opposite errors must be avoided as we seek to interpret the Christian's relationship to the law. One is the theonomist[12] or Christian triumphalist error, which fails to see any discontinuity between the old and new covenants and which mistakenly attempts to apply to the new covenant the his-

---

[9]Ibid., p. 49. Thielman understands Jesus to "deviate" from the law, as recorded in Mt 5:17-48 (p. 170). "Too much of the law," he stresses, "has been omitted or radically reinterpreted for the emphasis to fall on the continuity between law and gospel" (p. 182). This assertion stands in notable contrast to James, in whose thinking there exists a *close connection* between the gospel ("the implanted word that is able to save your souls," Jas 1:21) and the law ("Be doers of the word," Jas 1:22). In keeping the law, according to James, Christians "will be blessed in their doing" (Jas 1:25).

[10]Thielman, *Law and the New Testament,* p. 179.

[11]Thielman is a respected New Testament scholar; thus, his conclusions do not emanate from someone on the religious fringe.

[12]This also goes by the name of Christian reconstructionism.

torical particularities that were intended only for theocratic Israel.[13] The opposite error, however, is more subtle and much more widespread among Protestants, and that is to focus solely or primarily on discontinuity between the old and the new, thereby transforming Matthew 5:17-20 into an abstract ethical entity and modifying Jesus' statements so that they only speak of the "spirit" of the law or that they end up saying the opposite of what was intended.[14]

The challenge of biblical theology, Donald Hagner has rightly reminded us, is "to give proper heed to both the old and the new—not just the old, not just the new, but finding the right balance between the two."[15] And we should not be surprised, in our attempts to discern the right relationship between old and new covenants, to encounter tensions, complexities and paradoxes. But a primary reason for Matthew's account of Christ is to offer an explanation for the *continuity* between the old and the new. In his teaching and in his work, Jesus maintains continuity with the Old Testament scriptures, with the ethical demands of the law and with the message of the prophets. Obedience to the standard of righteousness outlined in the law, a standard reinforced by the prophets, is uniform and maintained.[16]

Historically, Christians have asserted that their morality is rooted in the unchanging cornerstone of the *Judeo-Christian* heritage. Contemporary Protestants, however, have curiously undermined their own foundation by helping to create a false dichotomy between the *Judeo* and *Christian* components. They have more often than not come to perceive Jesus' mission as one of discounting, diminishing and superseding the law as an ethical standard. Accordingly, the New Testament is viewed as fundamentally discontinuous with the Old Testament, as if the ethical standards of the God who revealed himself to Israel are somehow different from those of the God of the New Testament.

---

[13]Although the Protestant Reformers and the Puritans agreed that the moral law is abiding and that it serves as an instrument of civil government to restrain crime and promote civil order, they avoided the theonomist fallacy by distinguishing between ceremonial, civil and moral law in the Old Testament. This is true even though to the modern reader Luther and Calvin seem remarkably uncritical of the political authorities of their day.

[14]More often than not this is the hermeneutical approach of Dispensationalism.

[15]Donald A. Hagner, "Balancing the Old and the New: The Law of Moses in Matthew and Paul," *Interpretation* 51 (January 1997): 20.

[16]Thus, it is not accurate to say with Hagner that obedience to the standard of righteousness revealed in the law is "not direct, but indirect." It is remains every bit as direct and requisite as before. Contra Hagner, Christians are *not* "discharged from obedience to it" (ibid., pp. 27-28), and Matthew is adamant about this point. Salvation was never understood by Israel of old to be predicated on good deeds, even when this distortion was normally associated with Pharisaical Judaism.

To be sure, our concern is not with *covenant ratification,* that is, the manner in which the new covenant has been affirmed or ratified by the Son of God. This distinction is made amply and graphically clear, for example, by the epistle to the Hebrews and by much of Paul's writing. Law does not justify in the presence of God. But the law was *never* meant in the old covenant to justify; faith was *always* requisite. Rather, the law as justification, practiced intentionally or unwittingly, is a distortion of Pharisaical Judaism; and it is this distortion that is denounced by the writers of the New Testament. At the same time that the law does not possess a *salvific* role in either the old or the new covenant, it performs a foremost *ethical* function.[17] Matthew's interest lies herein: that is, in demonstrating the ethical foundation that is *common* to both Jewish and Christian frameworks. He does this against the backdrop of demonstrating *the contemporary religious establishment's failure to live up to its own ethical standards.* But the failure of scribal and Pharisaical religion should *not* be misconstrued as a fundamental setting aside of the standard itself.

There are good (and eminently theological) reasons, however, why contemporary Protestants in the main have viewed the law, as an ethical standard, to be set aside. Our accent on Christian liberty, our fear of legalism and the primacy of faith and grace in Protestant circles cause us to read the apostle Paul and his statements about the law in a very uni-dimensional way. Paul would seem to be *adamant* that the law is no longer in effect, that it functioned only as a tutor until Christ. This assumption would appear to be the basis for his teaching in the letter to the Galatians and in portions of his letter to the Romans.[18] Is this, in fact, the case? And does Paul always use the word "law" (*nomos*) in precisely the same way?

A wider survey of the New Testament as a whole shows that *nomos* is used in a variety of ways. And in the Pauline epistles this usage is *extremely* diverse, often changing without any explanation or qualification. In the New Testament *nomos* can refer to the following:

- the Old Testament as a whole (Acts 18:13; Rom 3:10-19)

---

[17]All of life is ethical and requires an unchanging standard. God's law is perpetual because it reflects the unchanging nature of God. God's law, it must be understood, did not originate with Moses. Universal moral law, as I argued in chap. five, transcends Israel of old.

[18]Admittedly, the problem of the law is one that has vexed not only modern evangelical Protestants: Jonathan Edwards conceded as much among theologians of his day, noting that "orthodox divines do so much differ as stating the precise agreement and differences between the two dispensations of Moses and Christ" (*The Works of President Edwards,* 4 vols. [New York: Leavitt & Allen, 1858], 1:160).

- a rule or principle (e.g., Rom 3:27; 7:21, 23; 8:2, 7; Gal 5:23; Heb 10:16; Jas 2:12)
- "moral law" (e.g., Rom 2:14;[19] 7:12, 22; 1 Tim 1:8-9)
- legalism that is rooted in works-righteousness (e.g., Rom 4:13; 6:14-15; 9:31; 10:4; Gal 2:16, 21; 3:10-13; 5:4, 18; Eph 2:15; Phil 3:6, 9)[20]
- Mosaic legislation as a whole (e.g., Jn 1:17, 45; 7:19; Acts 15:5; 1 Cor 9:9; Gal 3:17; Heb 7:5)
- specifically ceremonial legislation (e.g., Lk 2:22-23; Heb 7:12; 9:19, 22; 10:1, 8)
- the Decalogue (e.g., Rom 13:10)
- the prophets (e.g., 1 Cor 14:21 [cf. Is 28:11-12])
- the Pentateuch or Torah (e.g., Mt 5:17; 7:12; 11:13; 22:40; Lk 24:44; Acts 13:15; 24:14; Rom 3:21).[21]

It is noteworthy that in Matthew's Gospel "law," or *nomos,* carries this latter sense on multiple occasions, notably in the material of the Sermon on the Mount.

Two things strike us, upon an examination of Paul's writings. One is the sheer diversity of meanings and inflections that Paul imports into the term *law* when he uses it. The second is the apostle's burden to emphasize that "the law," either in the sense of Mosaic legislation or legalistic works-righteousness (such as Matthew's Gospel vigorously counters), possesses no *salvific* function: that is, no one can be justified in the presence of God by human effort. Yet, to the surprise of some Protestants, the law never is presented in the Old Testament as having such a function, as we noted above. Salvation in the old covenant was also and always *by faith* and at God's initiative. For this reason the New Testament can speak of Abraham as the "father of faith." Paul himself reasons this way: "For if Abraham

---

[19]Paul's statements in Rom 2:14 and Rom 3:21 illustrate precisely the difficulty we encounter with multiple senses of the word *law.* In his observation about the Gentiles in Rom 2:14, Paul uses *law* both in a specific sense, i.e., what Israel as the covenant people received from God ("When Gentiles, who do not possess the law, do instinctively what the law requires"), and in the general sense of rule or principle (these "are a law to themselves"). In Rom 3:21, the first of two uses of *law* carries the sense of rule or principle whereas the second use refers to the Pentateuch.

[20]Paul's use of *law* seems to shift without any warning to the reader. For example, though he uses it in the sense of legalistic works-righteousness in Gal 3:10-13, in Gal 3:17 he uses it in the sense of Mosaic legislation.

[21]Brice L. Martin is one of the few to make the distinction that *law* as it is used on occasion in the New Testament need not refer to the Old Testament as an entity or to Jewish law. See his "Paul on Christ and the Law," *Journal of the Evangelical Theological Society* 26, no. 3 (1983): 274.

was justified by works, he has something to boast about, but not before God. For what does the scripture say? 'Abraham believed God, and it was reckoned to him as righteousness' " (Rom 4:2-3). All of Romans 4 makes the argument that Abraham is the model, the paradigm, the exemplar of faith. Even Paul's statements in Galatians, many of which are exceedingly harsh due to the legalism he is countering, need some rethinking on our part. While Mosaic law was not given with the intent of imparting righteousness, it does not stand in opposition to the promises of God (Gal 3:21), as Christians have generally assumed.[22] In point of fact, Paul was both *theologically and ethically* "free" in the new covenant to become "as a Jew" (1 Cor 9:20), ceremonially speaking, in order to be more effective among—and to ultimately win—Jews. This indeed occurs in his work among Jewish populations in the region of southern Galatia (Acts 16:1-5). He has his ministry associate Timothy, whose mother was a believing Jew, circumcised "because of the Jews who were in those places" (Acts 16:3). We need to refine our understanding of the "curse" over those "who rely on the works of the law" (Gal 3:10). The curse comes not from the character or substance of the law itself but rather from two inviolable facts:

- No one can "observe and obey all the things written in the book of the law" (Gal 3:10).
- No one can merit right standing before God on the basis of works or achievements (Gal 2:16, 21; 3:10-13; 5:4, 18).

In truth, the law in its character *remains* "holy, righteous and good" (Rom 7:12).[23]

For this reason, we especially need the perspective of the epistle of James; we need it not to counter Paul per se, but rather to counter a *false or lopsided interpretation* of Paul that characterizes so much of conservative Protestantism to the present day. James reminds us, just as he reminded first-century believers, that the law is perfect and intrinsically good; moreover, when understood correctly, law can be expected to bring freedom rather than bondage (Jas 1:25). In James there is no antithesis between law and gospel, between faith and works; rather, a close connection exists between the gospel ("the implanted

---

[22]In fact, ceremonial law is not "abolished" in the sense that it is now wrong to observe or "that it was ever necessary to perform . . . in order to gain life," as Martin correctly points out (ibid., p. 281).

[23]While the law in Pauline writings remains outside the scope of this discussion, more precision regarding this topic can be found in Douglas Moo, " 'Law,' 'Works of the Law' and Legalism in Paul," *Westminster Theological Journal* 45, no. 1 (1983): 73-100, esp. pp. 75-90.

word that has the power to save your souls," Jas 1:21) and the law, so that Christians strive to be "doers of the word" (Jas 1:22). In keeping the law, Christians "will be blessed in their doing" (Jas 1:25).

In retrospect it becomes perhaps easier to understand why Martin Luther was so opposed to the epistle of James. In his erroneous understanding of the message of James (which he decried as "that right strawy epistle"), Luther wrongly supposed that the letter was not sufficiently "christological" and that its message simply returned people to religious and legalistic bondage, from which he had been gloriously freed ("the just shall live by faith"). Hence, James, along with 2 Peter, Jude and Revelation, were excluded from Luther's notion of the New Testament canon. Tragically, the offspring of Luther have carried on this false dichotomy—down to our own day. In elevating the apostle Paul, who champions faith, grace and unmerited favor, Protestants fall prey to the same error: at best they ignore and at worst eschew the message of James (the very message that addresses their weaknesses!). After all, what could be worse than the heretical statement that "a person is justified by works and not by faith alone" (Jas 2:24)? But alas, Abraham, the "father of faith," is also our guide in this respect: "Was not our ancestor Abraham *justified by works* when he offered his son Isaac on the altar?" (Jas 2:21). James, then, does not deny righteousness by faith (Jas 2:23) as a soteriological reality, but he does qualify that faith by saying that *it cannot stand alone.* Authentic faith must be demonstrated, active and "completed," which is to say, *evidenced by attendant works;* otherwise, it is not true faith at all. James's message, as it turns out, sounds remarkably similar to that of Matthew.

Our consideration of Matthew 5:17-20 is necessarily prefaced by these remarks concerning a "misunderstood Paul," since for many believers, statements in Paul and Matthew on the surface appear to be contradictory.[24] For evangelicals who pride themselves in a high view of Scripture, this apparent contradiction is normally satisfied by a reading of Matthew that finds Jesus'

---

[24]Snodgrass ("Matthew," pp. 536-37) does the Christian community a great service by raising the relevant question: Is Matthew in many cases being read from the perspective of a misunderstood Paul? On the differing perspectives of Matthew and Paul that avoid the error of discontinuity described above, see also Snodgrass, "Spheres of Influence: A Possible Solution to the Problem of Paul and the Law," *Journal for the Study of the New Testament* 32 (1988): 93-113, and J. Daryl Charles, "The Greatest or the Least in the Kingdom? The Disciple's Relationship to the Law (Matt. 5:17-20)," *Trinity Journal* n.s. 13, no. 2 (1992): 139-62, esp. pp. 140-47; and more recently my "Garnishing with the Greater Righteousness," *Bulletin for Biblical Research* 12, no. 1 (2002): 1-15.

"fulfillment" of the law (Mt 5:17) as more or less a *canceling of,* or release from, Old Testament precepts.[25] But is Jesus canceling the law, or is he affirming it in its continuity? And what are the stakes of each view? Have we indeed been willing to listen to Matthew and his prescription for Christian discipleship?[26]

Few would deny the fact that the American church has been hamstrung in demonstrating an authoritative, prophetic witness that possesses moral fiber in the context of contemporary culture. Much of this impotence, I would maintain, has to do with a faulty understanding of the function of law—an understanding that has debilitated evangelicals in particular in their attempts (or lack thereof) to develop a "public philosophy." "An erroneous conception of the function of law," wrote the eminent Reformed theologian John Murray,

> can be of such a character that it completely vitiates our view of the gospel; and an erroneous conception of the antithesis between law and grace can be of such a character that it demolishes both the substructure and the super-structure of grace.[27]

In the discussion that follows, it is my hope that "erroneous conceptions" of both law and grace might be brought to light, so that in the end Christian social ethics, particularly as understood by evangelicals, might no longer be "vitiated" or "demolished."

Consider the import of the following. If Jesus' statements in Matthew 5:17-20 about the law's enduring nature are to be understood in light of his previous declaration that the disciples are "the salt of the earth" and "the light of the

---

[25]This solution, of course, is not proposed only by evangelical commentators and laypersons. In the literature, the list of those holding this view is lengthy. Representative are Thielman, *Law and the New Testament;* W. D. Davies, "Matthew 5, 17-18," in *Mélanges biblique: Redignes en l'honneur de A. Robert* (Paris: Blond & Gay, 1957), pp. 428-56; M. Jack Suggs, "Wisdom and the Law in the Gospel of Matthew," in *Wisdom, Christ and the Law in Matthew's Gospel* (Cambridge, Mass.: Harvard University Press, 1970), p. 113; Robert Banks, *Jesus and the Law in the Synoptic Tradition,* Society for New Testament Studies Monograph Series 28 (Cambridge: Cambridge University Press, 1975), pp. 203-26; John P. Meier, *Law and History in Matthew's Gospel,* Analecta biblica 71 (Rome: Biblical Institute Press, 1976), pp. 64, 159; A. Plummer, *An Exegetical Commentary on the Gospel According to St. Matthew* (reprint; Grand Rapids, Mich.: Baker, 1982), p. 76; and Robert Guelich, *The Sermon on the Mount* (Waco, Tex.: Word, 1982), pp. 134-74.

[26]For this reason it is misleading at best and dangerous at worst to say with one commentator that "Paul can write things that Matthew would find unacceptable, and perhaps vice versa" (Hagner, "Balancing," p. 28). While different perspectives of theological truth are emphasized by different writers, there is no contradiction or disagreement between Matthew, Paul and James, even when the history of the Christian church has been littered with such interpretations.

[27]John Murray, *Principles of Conduct: Aspects of Biblical Ethics* (Grand Rapids, Mich.: Eerdmans, 1957), p. 181.

world" (Mt 5:13-16), then does it not follow that the efficacy of our cultural witness stands in direct relationship to our view of the role of law?

"Righteousness" in Matthew: The Primacy of Ethics

In order for the disciples to grasp correctly what righteousness entails, much of Matthew's Gospel is devoted to what it is *not*. As noted above, a sizable amount of the material in Matthew 5:1—7:29 (viz., Mt 5:21-48) contrasts distorted notions of righteousness and what is authentic. By the time the reader arrives at Matthew 23, the relationship between Jesus and establishment religion has reached its climax. This chapter, without parallel in the other Gospel accounts, consists of Jesus' stinging denunciation of the scribes and Pharisees for their failure to perform truly righteous deeds. Seven woes, or curses, are pronounced against the religious leaders; these curses stand in notable contrast to the blessings pronounced earlier by Jesus (Mt 5:3-12). In Matthew's eyes, certain aspects of Pharisaical Judaism already stand judged.[28] Jesus' clash, ultimately, is not with the Torah; it is with establishment religion. In the mind of Matthew, it is the disciples who will replace the scribes and Pharisees as the real transmitters of the faith (Mt 28:16-20).[29]

In Matthew, righteousness is profoundly a matter of *doing*.[30] It is foremost social in character, serving as active leaven in society. Far from invalidating Old Testament law, the test cases in Matthew 5:21-48 reinforce Old Testament ethical standards, even while Jesus adjusts contemporary interpretation of these standards. Popular religious misconstrual of the ethical demands of the law ("You have heard that it was said . . .") is adjusted by the rabbi par excellence so as to reveal the ethical kernel of truth resident in the law.[31] The failure of the scribes and Pharisees was not that they gave alms, prayed, fasted and kept

---

[28]It would be unfair (and inaccurate) to judge all of Pharisaical Judaism of the first century as "hypocritical." Mk 12:28-34 implies what was good in rabbinic Judaism. Nonetheless, Jewish scholar Jacob Neusner maintains that the portrait of the Pharisees we receive in the Gospels is essentially accurate of pre-A.D. 70 Judaism (*Politics to Piety* [Englewood Cliffs, N.J.: Prentice-Hall, 1973], p. xxi.).

[29]See David Garland's excellent volume *The Intention of Matthew 23,* Novum Testamentum Supplements 52 (Leiden: Brill, 1979), esp. pp. 34-63.

[30]The verb *poiein*, "to do," occurs an astonishing eighty-three times in the entire Gospel and is used twenty-two times in Matthew 5:1—7:29 alone.

[31]The formulas "You have heard" and "It was said" (Mt 5:21, 27, 38, 43) are found in rabbinic literature. Examples are cited in Morton Smith, *Tannaitic Parallels to the Gospels,* Journal of Biblical Literature Monographs 6 (Philadelphia: Society of Biblical Literature, 1951), pp. 27-30, and David Daube, *The New Testament and Rabbinic Judaism* (London: Athlone, 1956), pp. 67-71.

certain commandments. In fact, these they "ought to have practiced" (Mt 23:23). Jesus' wrath is directed toward them because they neglected what was ethically basic and essential, "the weightier matters."

Negatively, the disciples' righteousness was not to appear as that which was popularly expounded. Positively, it was to exceed that of the scribes and Pharisees (Mt 5:20). True righteousness consists of "letting your light shine" (Mt 5:14-16), doing visible "good works" (Mt 5:16), doing "every word that comes from the mouth of God" (Mt 4:4), doing "the will of my Father in heaven" (Mt 7:21), serving "the least of these" (Mt 25:44-45) and obeying "everything that I have commanded you" (Mt 28:20). The commandments, then, are to be kept with a proper motive, without which a violation of the law, prohibiting the act, occurs. Far from being arid, formal "legalism," true righteousness is an obedience to divine precepts that issues out of love for God, as the psalmist well understood:

> Happy are those whose way is blameless,
>   who walk in the law of the LORD. . . .
> I will praise you with an upright heart,
>   when I learn your righteous ordinances. . . .
> With my lips I declare
>   all the ordinances of your mouth
> I delight in the way of your decrees
>   as much as in all riches. . . .
> Give me understanding, that I may keep your law
>   and observe it with my whole heart. . . .
> I find my delight in your commandments,
>   because I love them. . . .
> Oh, how I love your law!
>   It is my meditation all day long. (Ps 119:1, 7, 13-14, 34, 47, 97)

Genuine righteousness, then, is based on faith and trust and has nothing to do with legalism. This is true of both the old and the new covenants; in neither is there an antithesis between law and grace.[32] Nearly twenty centuries re-

---

[32]One of the few evangelical writers to correct this widespread misconception among Protestant evangelicals is Old Testament scholar Walter Kaiser, who describes religious motivation in the Old Testament as both "evangelical" and "legal" obedience. That is, Israel was commanded to *love God* with every fiber of being and, as a result, *keep his commandments* ("The Weightier and Lighter Matters of the Law: Moses, Jesus and Paul," in *Current Issues in Biblical and Patristic Interpretation,* ed. Gerald Hawthorne [Grand Rapids, Mich.: Eerdmans, 1985], p. 182).

moved, the reader is apt to miss the significance of *torah* for the first-century Jewish mindset. Firmly rooted in divine covenant, it constituted the visible expression of relationship with God, a supreme gift of divine grace. One biblical scholar has framed it well:

> The idea that underlies the word "Torah" is not primarily the formulation of a series of categorical commands and prohibitions with appropriate sanctions. . . . It is rather a body of instruction regarding man's place in God's world and his duties to God and his neighbor. The "Torah" is divine guidance as to the right way in which man should behave as a subject of the heavenly king.[33]

God's law was present at the dawn of human consciousness and corresponds to created human nature, so that

> fulfilling his requirements we fulfill ourselves, and the gospel of Christ answers to actual human need, as glove fits hand, so that all our responses to God make for our good and no touch of authoritarianism enters into his exercise of authority over us.[34]

His law stands as the external and abiding standard for all human thought and action. All of life is to be guided in one way or another by the law.[35] One may accurately maintain that it is only clarified or illustrated in its historical particularities in theocratic Israel. Matthew's assumption lies at the heart of Jewish and Christian ethics: one "does" because one is a disciple and loves God.

In Matthew 5:19 the disciples are reminded that not only doing but teaching incurs a strict judgment (cf. Jas 3:1). Setting aside the ethical demands of the law *and* teaching others to do the same—whether wittingly or unwittingly—are spoken of in the harshest terms. Those who promulgate such are depicted as "the least in the kingdom." Conversely, those who both do and teach others the commandments are considered "great in the kingdom." In rabbinic terms, Jesus is saying that the disciples' ethical requirements are no less than those expounded by the prophets and Moses before them.

Certainly the gnawing question for many—then as well as now—would be "Is this a new teaching?" It is not incidental that in Matthew's Gospel, Jesus receives

---

[33]T. W. Manson, *Ethics and the Gospels* (New York: Charles Scribner's Sons, 1960). p. 29.

[34]J. I. Packer, *Freedom and Authority* (Oakland, Calif.: International Council on Biblical Inerrancy, 1981), p. 4.

[35]Richard N. Longenecker has rightly pointed out that legalism was never a legitimate part of Israel's religion, whether overt or unintentional ("The Pedagogical Nature of the Law in Galatians 3:19-4:7," *Journal of the Evangelical Theological Society* 25, no. 1 [1982]: 60). The prophets, again and again, denounced legalism.

the title of "Rabbi."[36] Also significant is the fact that in Matthew, Jesus' teaching both begins and concludes with a vigorous accent on the validity of "the law and the prophets" (Mt 5:17; 7:12). Matthew is not portraying Jesus as the "new Lawgiver," nor is Jesus advocating a "new Torah," as some commentators maintain. Rather, Jesus has come to reaffirm God's covenantal requirements.

While the question of whether or not "these commandments" (Mt 5:19) alluded to by Jesus are "fulfillable" is provocative to the modern reader, it was not a question for Matthew. What was commanded could and should be done. In the same respect, Matthew does not allow us the luxury of understanding fulfillment of the law in mere *symbolic* terms. The Old Testament injunctions that begin "You shall not" are not figures of speech; they are to be taken and applied literally. In the New Testament, the character of obedience has not changed. In fact, Jesus' exhortation could not be clearer: only the ones "doing" will "enter" (Mt 7:15-27). The true disciple, then and now, fulfills the ethical demands of the law, for they are now inscribed on the heart.

Matthew, it should be remembered, is waging a war on two fronts: against Pharisaical religion, which distorts the law, on the one hand, and against antinomianism or "lawlessness" *(anomia)*, which discards it, on the other:[37]

> Then I will declare to them, "I never knew you. Depart from me, you who work *lawlessness.*" (Mt 7:23)

> The Son of Man will send his angels, and they will gather out of the kingdom all causes of sin and all who do *lawlessness.* (Mt 13:41)

> So you too appear righteous to others on the outside, but inside you are full of hypocrisy and *lawlessness.* (Mt 23:28)

> And because of the increase of *lawlessness,* the love of many will wax cold. (Mt 24:12)

Without law, one is left with lawlessness. Although Matthew knows that the law can be misused or misunderstood, he recognizes that genuine righteousness will fulfill the ethical demands of the law. For the antinomian, whether that person is religious or not, Jesus has a sharp rebuke: "I never knew you. Depart from me." Future judgment awaits those who disregard the law (Mt

---

[36]*Rabbi* occurs only in Matthew (Mt 23:7-8; 26:25, 49) and John.

[37]It is significant that *anomia* does not occur in the other three Gospel narratives. The antinomian spirit may be libertinistic, gnostic, pragmatic or relativistic in its manifestation.

13:41-42). Interestingly, in Matthew the increase in lawlessness characterizes a drawing near of the end of the age.

Thus, for Matthew, to reject the law is the opposite of righteousness, for then one has no regard for God's law. Practicing lawlessness in turn yields both a temporal and an eschatological harvest.

The influential second-century heretic Marcion was notable for his rejection of the Old Testament and parts of the New. Marcion viewed the God of the Old Testament as harsh and strict over against the "good God" revealed through Christ. Marcion considered the law as spelled out in the Pentateuch ethically inferior and, hence, rejected it as being inconsistent with the morality of the New Testament. In practical terms, the significance of Marcion's error is that he sought to loosen the Christian message from its Jewish heritage. For him, Jesus' coming marked a new *beginning*. Accordingly, Jesus' message had little in common with the Old Testament.[38] A more contemporary version of the Marcionite approach, at least in its approach to ethics, can be seen in the hermeneutics of dispensationalism. Dispensationalists, as their name implies, believe that God worked in different ways during various eras or dispensations of human history. One of these dispensations is referred to as the "dispensation of law," as distinct from the present "dispensation of grace."[39] The interpretive result of this theological assumption is an unfortunate bifurcation between law and grace—a bifurcation that is nonexistent. The church today, as in Marcion's day, must return to Matthew and allow the Matthean perspective to speak once again. In so doing, evangelicals might discover that Matthew 5:17-20 is not that difficult to interpret, given the issues that confronted the writer in the context of a growing, increasingly Gentile church. At the heart, Christian discipleship expresses itself in doing what God has always required, for the ethic of the kingdom is timeless.

THE LAW ANNULLED OR THE LAW AFFIRMED?

What standard of morality guided the early church? It was nothing less than the ethical requirements spelled out in the law and repeatedly enunciated by the

---

[38]Useful English-language resources on Marcion are E. C. Blackman, *Marcion and His Influence* (London: SPCK, 1948), and John Knox, *Marcion and the New Testament* (Chicago: University of Chicago Press, 1942).

[39]Charles C. Ryrie, "The End of the Law," *Bibliotheca Sacra* 124, no. 495 (1967): 239-47. Some dispensationalist theologians, though not all, reject along with Ryrie the threefold division of the law—ceremonial, civil and moral—that the Protestant Reformers maintained.

prophets. Why is it that allusion to "the law and the prophets" (Mt 5:17; 7:12), as I noted above, encircles the central section of the Sermon on the Mount?

The expression *the law and the prophets* is meant to underscore the *ethical* and *unitary* dimension of the law. However, the reversal of this formula, "all the prophets and the law" (Mt 11:13), is designed to emphasize the *prophetic* dimension of the law. Frequently in the Old Testament the prophets were called on to "free," as it were, the Torah from cultic manipulation by upholding a correct interpretation of it. Such seems to be implied in Matthew 7:12 and is expressly stated in Matthew 22:40 ("On these two commandments hang all the law and the prophets"). Making this small yet crucial distinction allows us, then, to define our terms, since we have not yet done so with precision in a way that some readers might wish. The *law* in Matthew would appear to signify the Torah or Pentateuch, which contains both the revelation of a self-disclosing Creator-God (i.e., revelation that is pre-Israel and pre-Mosiac) and the deposit of God's revelatory utterances to his people Israel—utterances made binding by specific commandments and ordinances. The law, representing Israel's standard for good works, was accepted by the Christian community as binding, even when it needed clarification or recontextualization in Jesus' day.

Matthew records two strong "Do not think" declarations in Jesus' ministry. One is meant to shatter the mistaken notion that he brings peace in the context of relationships (Mt 10:34). Anyone supposing that being a Christian will mean being at peace with the world is seriously mistaken. Christian discipleship brings not peace but *a sword* to our existing relationships. The second declaration concerns the ethical requirements of the law (Mt 5:17). The prohibition "Do not think" is to be understood as a rhetorical device in a polemic against popular (or popularly religious) opinion. And what was this opinion? As seen through Matthew's eyes, it was that Jesus' coming was to annul or abolish (*katalusai*) the law and the prophets. To a Jew, significantly, the setting aside or abrogation of the law was the chief mark of a heretic. The force of Jesus' statement recorded in Matthew 5:17, therefore, is this: "Do not begin thinking, do not even consider the possibility, that I am annulling the teaching of the law and the prophets." Such a prohibition has the aim of dealing with a fundamental misunderstanding of his mission.

While some in the Christian community might be inclined to think that the commandments are no longer valid, in the first-century synagogue (Mt 23:2, 6), debates were raging between the schools of Hillel and Shammai regarding the law's interpretation. The New Testament offers us a faint though helpful glimpse into these debates: oral tradition (i.e., the "fence around the law" that ensured one did not actually "break" a commandment) has obscured the true meaning of the commandments (cf. Mk 7:8-13). In a day when oral tradition supported by rabbinic commentary was en route to being absolutized, it was the abrogators of the law who met the fury of Jesus' wrath (Mt 23:1-39). Stringent Pharisaical interpretation of the law, with its distortions (not to mention outright lawlessness), was to be rejected by the Christian disciple. Examples of these distortions are on display in Matthew 5:21-48. The stress on continuity in Matthew 5:17-18 is important for interpreting the test cases in Matthew 5:21-48, since it is not the Torah itself that Jesus sets aside but rather contemporary interpretations that have come to surround and obscure the law.

Much ink has been spilled by biblical commentators in attempts to render precisely the verbs *plērōsai* ("to fulfill") and *katalusai* ("to abrogate," "abolish," "annul" or "loose") in Matthew 5:17. The relationship between the two actions is oppositional and mutually exclusive. The proper sense in which *fulfill* is to be understood derives from its opposite. This sense, coupled with the immediate context (good works that glorify God, Mt 5:16; and the better righteousness, Mt 5:20), does not allow us to understand *fulfill* in the sense of prophecy-verification, transcending or replacement.[40] Jesus' teaching in Matthew 5:1—7:29 is intended to be didactic and not prophetic in its function; its purpose is ethics and not eschatology. Jesus is calling for obedience to the commandments that love for God requires. That is, the guiding principle of love for God is objectively revealed in keeping statutory commandments: "On these two commandments [loving God and loving one's neighbor] hang all the law and the prophets" (Mt 22:40). Matthew's primary concern in this part of the Gospel narrative is the background debate within Judaism over the role of the law, not Jesus as the arrival of the eschatological promise. For this reason, *doing, obeying and keeping* are emphasized. My argument that in Matthew 5:17 to "fulfill" the law is to *do* the law is further buttressed by a passage from the Jewish

---

[40]Contra, e.g., G. Barth, "Matthew's Understanding of the Law," in *Tradition and Interpretation in Matthew* (London: SCM Press, 1963), p. 67; Robert Banks, "Matthew's Understanding of the Law: Authenticity and Interpretation in Matthew 5:17-20," *Journal of Biblical Literature* 93 (1974): 229-33; Banks, *Jesus and the Law*, pp. 210-13; D. A. Carson, *Matthew*, Expositor's Bible Commentary 8 (Grand Rapids, Mich.: Zondervan, 1984), p. 142; and others. These commentators mistakenly understand *fulfill* in Mt 5:17 in an eschatological or prophetic sense because it carries this sense elsewhere in Matthew (e.g., in Mt 1:22-23; 2:15, 17-18, 23; 4:14-16; 8:17; 12:17-21; 13:35; 21:4-5; 27:9-10).

Talmud that shows strong affinities to Jesus' statement: "I have not come to add or take away from the Torah of Moses."[41]

The verb "to annul" (*katalusai*) is set in opposition to the verb "to fulfill" (*plērōsai*) and functions as a flat proscription. Was Jesus setting up a new teaching? And most importantly, was he setting aside the Torah? Such would be the controversy at the local synagogue, in any case. Matthew's aim is transparent: the ethical demands of the law were not to "cease." In accordance with the salt metaphor that had preceded it, Jesus' declaration concerning the law is that it is durative in nature.[42]

What is stated negatively in Matthew 5:17 is declared positively in Matthew 5:18 through the words "For truly I tell you." This introductory formula confirms without exception the certainty of what follows. And as a reflection of its frequent use in the synagogue, it occurs often in Matthew's Gospel.[43] Moreover, Matthew 5:18-19 contains the language of hyperbole—"iota," "tittle" or "stroke," "commandment," "smallest," "least," "everything"—which is aimed at suiting the meticulous expectations of rabbinic scholarship (cf. Mt 23:4, 7-8). This is especially transparent when Jesus speaks in rabbinic terms of *smallness;* both *yod* ("iota"), the tenth and smallest letter of the Hebrew alphabet, and *waw* ("stroke"), the sixth letter, were proverbial for smallness.[44] In emphasizing that not even the smallest detail of the law would "pass away," Jesus is stressing the permanence of the law. Rabbinic literature, before it affirms anything, assumes the permanence of the Torah.[45]

Why, in Matthew's depiction, is Jesus so adamant about the law's detail, and why does Jesus' description of the law conspicuously resemble contemporary legal and theological notions? As seen through Matthew's eyes, to construe Jesus' "coming" as an annulment of the law is to misconstrue his coming altogether.

---

[41]*b. Shabbat* 116b.

[42]The commentary by Calvin in this regard is instructive: "We must not imagine that the coming of Christ has freed us from the authority of the law; for it is the eternal rule of a devout and holy life, and must, therefore, be as unchangeable, as the justice of God, which it embraced, is constant and uniform" (*Commentary on the Harmony of the Evangelists Matthew, Mark and Luke,* vol. 1 [reprint; Grand Rapids, Mich.: Eerdmans, 1963], p. 277).

[43]In Matthew it occurs some thirty times.

[44]H. Strack and P. Billerbeck, *Kommentar zum Neuen Testament aus Talmud und Midrash,* 4 vols. (Muenchen: Beck, 1924), 4:244-47.

[45]The law's permanence is observed in Wisdom of Solomon 18:4; Baruch 4:1; 4 Ezra 9:37; and Philo *De vita Mosis* 2.136.

Being "Least" in the Kingdom

The ramifications of loosening or annulling one of "the least of these commandments" and teaching others to do the same are sobering: according to Jesus, they entail a loss of rank in the kingdom of heaven (Mt 5:19). Among teachers of the law, "light" commandments stood in contrast to "great" or "heavy" ("weighty") commandments. An example of the former was the Pharisaical custom of tithing on herbs and spices (Mt 23:23 par. Lk 11:42). Heavy commandments, on the other hand, included breach of the sabbath (Mt 12:1-13; 28:1), profaning God's name (Mt 26:63-65; Mk 14:61-64; Jn 8:58-59; 10:33) and profaning the temple (Mt 12:6; 21:12-13; 26:61). Scrupulous with respect to details (an ardor not wrong in and of itself, but a monstrosity when contrasted with abrogating the weightier principles of social morality such as justice and mercy; see Mt 23:23-24), Pharisees tithed, as the law required, on "all the increase of your seed which comes year by year from the field" (Lev 27:30; Deut 14:22). They did this, however, to the extent of trifling absurdity. Mint, dill and cummin, for example, were used for medicinal purposes as well as for flavoring. Such inversion of priorities is further illustrated by Near Eastern hyperbole: in seeking to strain out an insect while drinking and thus avoid swallowing what was considered unclean (Lev 11:2-23), they inadvertently swallowed the proverbial camel—another unclean beast. Righteousness, as it turns out, is not to be found by straining gnats!

Smallness, it should be remembered, has its rightful place in the divine economy. One such example is found in Deuteronomy 22:6-7, which contains instructions on one's obligations when coming upon a bird's nest. Indeed, Jesus himself teaches on the value of the sparrow—a small, undomesticated bird—a proverbial symbol of low value (Mt 10:29 par. Lk 12:6-7). Implicit in this teaching is that God values the "least" in his creation. The Old Testament, we do well to observe, does not teach an ethic of either/or. One must regard both small and weighty requirements of the law.

Twice in Matthew 5:19 the verb *to teach* is used, and this in association with the idea of annulling. From Matthew's perspective, *teaching* and *doing* go hand in hand and are indivisible. For the disciples, this unity cannot be overstated. It matters what is transmitted to others; it matters enormously. That the law is not being annulled but that it remains the core of new-covenant ethics for the true disciple is not only a legitimate interpretation of Matthew 5:21-48 but also the implication of Jesus' command in Matthew 23:3 (the context of which is Jesus' denunciation of Pharisaical religion): "Therefore, do whatever they teach you and follow it; but do not do as they do, for they do not practice what they teach." The flaw of establishment religion is foremost *ethical*—hence, the critical link between teaching and doing.

Jews considered losing rank in the kingdom of heaven to be catastrophic. One could not expect the bliss of paradise if one had set aside the Torah.[46] Elsewhere in Matthew, Jesus employs the concept of rank in the kingdom of heaven, notably in his denunciation of scribal religion's preferential treatment of rabbis and teachers:

- the humble are acclaimed great (Mt 18:4)
- the last are made first, and the first are made last (Mt 20:16)
- the great ones are those who become servants (Mt 20:26)
- the greatest will be humbled, and the humble will be exalted (Mt 23:12)

The greatest-least contrast in Matthew 5:19 is clarified, and magnified, in Matthew 23:1-39, where it takes the form of prophetic woe-cries being directed at the teachers of the law (Mt 23:2, 7, 8, 10, 13, 15-16, 23, 25, 27, 29). Both the responsibilities and the consequences that attend *doing* and *teaching* are sobering.[47]

Given the parallelism in Matthew 5:19 between greater and lesser, loss of rank in the kingdom of heaven is best understood as a literary-rhetorical device, or what one commentator calls "poetic justice."[48] But it is more. It entails *literal loss* as well. While Jesus is *not* saying that entering the kingdom of heaven is based on works, he is declaring that by *not obeying,* one suffers loss. Furthermore, based on the vehemence with which Jesus denounces establishment religion in Matthew 23, a literal loss—in the form of divine judgment ("Truly I tell you, all this will come upon this generation," Mt 23:36)—is being forecast.

All told, the elements contained in Matthew 5:19—the whole law, the least parts, teaching, rank in the kingdom of heaven—are Jewish to the core.[49] They underscore what for the disciple is nonnegotiable: all ethical demands of the

---

[46]*m. Sanhedrin* 10:1.

[47]Hence James's exhortation that not many should aspire to be teachers, since they will incur the stricter judgment (Jas 3:1).

[48]R. H. Gundry, *Matthew: A Commentary on His Literary and Theological Art* (Grand Rapids, Mich.: Eerdmans, 1982), p. 82.

[49]See Michael Goulder, *Midrash and Lection in Matthew* (London: SPCK, 1974), esp. pp. 24-27.

law are to be observed. Through both teaching and practice, the law is affirmed and upheld.[50]

THE "GREATER RIGHTEOUSNESS" AND CHRISTIAN DISCIPLESHIP

Matthew 5:20 serves the purpose of introducing the case-illustrations (Mt 5:21-48) and summarizing the preceding statements. Jesus' call is a call for a greater righteousness—one that exceeds the ethics of popular religion. The righteousness of the kingdom, by contrast, is rooted in moral character (Mt 5:3-12) and finds expression in social morality performed from the heart (5:21-48). On this count, scribal Judaism as portrayed by Matthew is found wanting.

But for what reason? Had the Judaism of Matthew's day followed the Torah too closely? By Matthew's account, Jerusalem was lacking the "better righteousness." A generation earlier John the Baptist had delivered a message of warning to that effect. Repentance as preached by John called for a change not in belief but in *deeds* (Mt 3:7-10).

Contemporary Protestants have tended to underestimate greatly the value and role of law within the wider scope of divine revelation. The early Christians, by contrast, traced their ethical teaching back to revelation contained in the Torah—a source and ethical standard reiterated by the prophets.[51] While Matthew is at pains to show that Jesus is the *eschatological* fulfillment of Old Testament prophecy, he is equally meticulous in his attempts to show that the Christian *moral* life is consciously rooted in faithfulness to divine law and stands in continuity with that of Judaism. By making the important distinction between eschatology and ethics, I do *not* wish to argue that the law does not go through significant reinterpretation or recontextualization in the New Testament. Clearly, the concepts of Jerusalem, the temple, the sabbath and sacrifice all undergo redefinition; but the law as *a moral guide,* to which the expression "the law and the prophets" refers, is binding for the Christian disciple.[52] In the mind of Matthew, the question of discipleship could not be divorced from "the core" of Jewish religion, which is *doing righteousness*.

Matthew is not advancing a form of works-righteousness, nor is he portraying

---

[50]This is the conclusion of Jewish commentator Lapide, *Sermon on the Mount,* p. 14.

[51]"Torah" in the Old Testament is essentially "revelation" or "instruction."

[52]Interestingly, based on the ministry of the apostles, the Christian would appear to be "free" to sacrifice, to be circumcised or to engage in the cultic life of the temple, to the extent that faith is not replaced by human achievement or works-righteousness. What is prohibited is making these into *requirements*. Timothy's circumcision, which is intended to facilitate ministry in parts of southern Galatia with large Jewish populations (Acts 16:1-5), illustrates this very point.

Jesus' teaching as some sort of "idealistic," "interim" or even "perfectionistic" ethic, as some commentators have maintained. In Matthew, both lawlessness and legalism incur divine judgment. The ethical demands that are placed on the disciple are presented as both clear and unchanging. Obedience originates in the heart and executes the law's ethical demands.[53] Setting aside the ethical demands of the law and teaching others to do the same are spoken of in the harshest of terms. Those who promulgate such are described as "least in the kingdom." Such a message is applicable to Palestinian "Torah-bound" Jews as well as Hellenistic "Torah-free" factions within the Christian community.

The placement of Matthew 5:17-20 within the Sermon on the Mount shows this material to be a call to do good works. By exhibiting a "better righteousness," the disciple will have the effect of salt and light, thereby validating the Christian community in the presence of its critics.

JESUS' ETHICAL TEACHING

Several important principles that undergird Christian ethics to guide our understanding and interpretation of Jesus' ethical teaching emerge from Matthew 5:17-20 (several test cases of which follow in 5:21-48). First, Jesus stands in continuity with the Old Testament ethical tradition; the law as ethical norm (the core of the ethical corpus) is not being set aside. Second, faithful Christian ethics requires careful observance of and obedience to this standard; neither the wider principles nor the specific details of its content are to be negated. Third, righteousness as befitting the Christian disciple distinguishes itself radically from conventional notions of righteousness that exist in the religious establishment. Jesus' ethical teaching is not intended to deviate from the law and the prophets; it is meant to be distinguished from *contemporary notions* of ethics—notions that had obscured divinely instituted ethical norms.

These guidelines inform Jesus' handling of several test cases, recorded in 5:21-48, which demonstrate his clash with establishment religion. As I have attempted to show, Jesus' use of the formula "You have heard that it was said . . ." is meant to show his contradiction of contemporary interpretation; it is not intended to contrast his own teaching with the Old Testament scriptures.[54] In

---

[53]For this reason it is both inaccurate and misleading to speak of a "new law" in Christ. Christian ethics is, properly understood, *Judeo-Christian* ethics.

[54]As is commonly known, Talmudic literature is laced through and through with the formula "Our rabbis taught" or its equivalent "Rabbi so-and-so said."

what ways, then, was contemporary interpretation flawed?

The initial test case (Mt 5:21-26) concerns the sixth commandment: the prohibition against murder. Rabbinic interpretation had generally restricted its trajectory to the overt act of killing and associated penal sanctions. Jesus is by no means annulling, belittling or underestimating the seriousness of manslaughter; it is and remains clearly the highest crime (cf. Gen 1:26-27; 9:6) and a burning of God in effigy, as it were. Rather, Jesus is deepening our understanding of murder by showing that it has its origin in the recesses of the human heart. The point is not that punishment proportionate to the crime (what some have called an "eye for an eye")[55] is being set aside in the new covenant, as many religious commentators are inclined to tell us.[56] Matthew 5:21-26 is not prescribing a new turn in public policy. It is, rather, warning that the overt act cannot occur unless hatred is already resident in the human heart. At issue are matters of the heart, not matters of the state or public policy. This is clarified by the admonition contained in Matthew 5:23-24, which employs the religious language of fellowship to depict the relationship between two siblings.

In the test case of swearing and oaths (Mt 5:33-37), we do not find Jesus abrogating or proscribing the swearing of oaths. In the Old Testament there are numerous examples of godly persons who voluntarily and solemnly commit themselves in all reverence to particular actions that are not specifically required of the people of God. What Jesus condemns is falsehood, lack of sincerity, untruthfulness and wrong motives. Sincerity, honesty, truthfulness, vulnerability—these are the qualities that distinguish the Christian disciple. Any embellishment of human speech tends to undermine its integrity.

The fifth case-illustration (Mt 5:38-42) reflects a popular understanding and application of the *lex talionis* ("the law of the tooth," i.e., the eye-for-an-eye measurement), which is derived from Pentateuchal legislation directed at personal injury (Ex 21:23-25; Lev 24:19-22; Deut 19:21). It is important to remember that this legislation, designed to ensure restitution based on proportionality (the hallmark of the universal norm of justice), was to oper-

---

[55]Notice that the "eye for an eye" concept is condemned in Mt 5:38-42 (personal dealings with others), not in Mt 5:21-26 (manslaughter).

[56]Gen 9:6 must be regarded as a universal proscription against premeditated murder, affirmed and presupposed in the sixth commandment, and valid for all times and all cultures. Pauline teaching makes this clear: whereas private vengeance ("vigilante justice") is proscribed (Rom 12:17-21), justice and vengeance are placed in the hands of legitimate governing authorities (Rom 13:1-7), who are instituted by the Creator to preserve the moral-social order.

ate within the context of public, not private, affairs. Biblical legislation places the execution and maintenance of justice into the hands of governing authorities, not private parties.[57] This material, far from prescribing passive nonresistance in the face of evil, teaches that at a personal level the Christian disciple is to be characterized by proper motives and not a vengeful spirit. As a guideline it finds its exact parallel in Pauline ethical teaching. Romans 12:17-21 contains ethical imperatives proscribing any sort of vigilante justice and also serves as an introduction to the apostle's prescription for public justice: vengeance and temporal wrath find expression in the hands of governing authorities, who fulfill a divinely instituted role in preserving the moral-social order.[58]

The final case-illustration (Mt 5:43-48), similarly, mirrors mistaken assumptions among Jesus' contemporaries, assumptions in need of revision. Jesus' statement "You have heard that it was said, 'You shall love your neighbor and hate your enemy' " (Mt 5:43) is not pitting a new love ethic against Old Testament teaching. Rather, the element "hate your enemy" adopted by Jesus' enemies is foreign to the Old Testament—"You shall love your neighbor" (Lev 19:18)—and it is a gross ethical distortion. The exhortation to "love your enemies" is rooted both in the reality of God's character and in the reality of humanity as God's image; hence, the disciple is to be like God.

Our own interpretation of Jesus' ethical teaching becomes confused when we view this material as a "radical love ethic" that results in a policy-prescription (viz., pacifistic nonresistance) and dispenses with or abrogates traditional notions of justice. This line of thinking, however, fails to make certain critical ethical distinctions. Chief among these is that the Sermon in the Mount is not intended to address policy matters; rather, Jesus' teaching concerns personal relationships and individual motivation. Pacifism, *while it may be a legitimate dictate of the individual conscience,* cannot be a public policy, as John Courtney Murray correctly emphasizes.[59] The flip side of pacifism's conflation of the personal and the political is that at the theological level it is prone to erect a false

---

[57]John Murray makes the helpful distinction that justice is "vindicatory" but not "vindictive" (*Principles of Conduct,* p. 174).

[58]Tellingly, Paul uses conspicuously religious language in his depiction of the "magistrate": *diakonos* ("deacon") is used twice in Rom 13:4 and *leitourgos* ("minister, servant") once in Rom 13:6.

[59]John Courtney Murray, *We Hold These Truths: Catholic Reflections on the American Proposition* (New York: Sheed & Ward, 1960), pp. 279-82. To illustrate this point, Murray observes that "it is at best a theory of interpersonal relationships and therefore irrelevant to international relations" (ibid., p. 292).

dichotomy between the demands of love and the demands of justice.[60] But love will be careful not to loosen or abolish just standards, just as justice will be motivated by a concern for human dignity.[61] Love, it must be restated, is not inconsistent with the demands of temporal retribution and execution of punishment.[62]

But what about punishment? Isn't punishment—and certainly extreme punishment—inconsistent with Jesus' "love ethic"? Isn't a more humane solution to have lawbreakers undergo therapy and be rehabilitated?

A brief but significant reflection on punishment by C. S. Lewis appears in a collection of essays titled *God in the Dock*.[63] While this volume was published in 1970 by Eerdmans, the essay was originally written thirty years prior and appeared in the little-known *Australian Quarterly Review*. Why was this? Writing to T. S. Eliot and explaining his frustration, Lewis confided that he simply could "get no hearing" for his point of view in England. What was his unpopular position? That we affirm human dignity and worth *precisely when* we hold individuals, who are moral agents created in the image of God, consistently

---

[60]This false dichotomy is related to a deeper theological error that hinders the Christian community, an error on which the teaching of Mt 5:17-20 bears directly. It concerns the relationship of law and grace. A mistaken understanding of this relationship is so grave that it wholly undermines the realities of both law and grace. Failing to ponder the fact that Paul uses the term *law* in several ways, evangelicals, in their zeal to avoid the Galatian aberration of legalism and works-righteousness—with its associated warnings such as "If justification comes through the law, then Christ died for nothing" [Gal 2:21] and "You are not under law but under grace" [Rom 6:14])—are prone to read Matthew through the lens of a misunderstood Paul. The main disposition of the old covenant is not law while that of the new is grace. Both grace and law are operative in both covenants; and faith alone justifies in both covenants. Abraham, father of the old covenant, is the exemplar for faith (Rom 4:1-25; Heb 11:8-12), just as the law, revealed in the old covenant, remains an abiding ethical standard in the new. There has been no clearer or more cogent depiction of this theological tendency among religious conservatives than that offered by John Murray: see his *Principles of Conduct,* esp. the chapter titled "Law and Grace" (pp. 181-201).

[61]Insofar as the death penalty *in the case of premeditated murder* is proportionate to the crime (which is my position), it is just and theologically defensible, though by no means a test of Christian fellowship. I have presented this argument variously elsewhere in "Outrageous Atrocity or Moral Imperative?: The Ethics of Capital Punishment," *Studies in Christian Ethics* 6, no. 2 (1993): 1-14; "The American Bishops and Capital Punishment: A Response," *Social Justice Review* 85, nos. 11-12 (1994): 172-77; "Sentiment as Social Justice," *Christian Research Journal* 85, no. 7 (1994): 16-23; "Rights and Mass Murderers," *Social Justice Review* 87, nos. 1-2 (1996): 15-17; and, more recently, "The Sword of Justice: On Revenge and Retribution," *Touchstone* 15, no. 2 (2001): 12-15.

[62]Thus, the use of force in itself is not to be viewed as illegitimate or as motivated by hatred; it is legitimately rooted in a love for, and a desire to maintain, justice. To the extent that there can be an unjust war or violence, there can also exist an unjust peace.

[63]C. S. Lewis, *God in the Dock: Essays on Theology and Ethics* (Grand Rapids, Mich.: Eerdmans, 1970), pp. 287-94.

and proportionately accountable for their actions. In challenging the materialist ("humanitarian") and abolitionist view of punishment held by his contemporaries, Lewis argued that to abandon the criteria for *just* punishment is to
abandon criteria for *all* punishment:

> This is why I think it essential to oppose Humanitarian theory of punish-
> ment, root and branch, wherever we encounter it. It carries on its front a sem-
> blance of mercy which is wholly false. . . . The error . . . stands noble, and
> was indeed the error of a noble mind. . . . The older view was that mercy and
> justice had met and kissed. The essential act of mercy was to pardon; and par-
> don in its very essence involves the recognition of guilt. . . . If crime is only
> a disease which needs cure and not sin which deserves punishment, it cannot
> be pardoned.[64]

In the Christian moral tradition, then, truth and love "kiss"; they dare not be
severed.[65]

What shall we then say to summarize the Christian disciple's relation to the
law? We may tease out of Matthew 5:17-48 a general, underlying assumption:
the law creates the moral atmosphere in which human beings understand—
and exhibit—divine standards of ethical conduct. It remains essential to matters of conscience, presupposing universal moral law that has been revealed in
the human heart and particularized in the Mosaic code.

While the distinction between law as redemptive covenant (in theocratic Israel) and law as moral guide confronts the Christian community with a valid

---

[64]Ibid., p. 292.

[65]The aforementioned confusion regarding Jesus' ethical teaching, which frequently pits Jesus' so-
called radical love ethic over against the responsibility of governing authorities to maintain justice,
was abundantly on display in the aftermath of the September 11, 2001, terrorist attacks on the World
Trade Center buildings and the Pentagon. Following these attacks, which left multiple thousands of
innocent civilians dead, the responses of not a few clerics, religious leaders and academics were highly irresponsible. Much of this politically jaundiced ("Blame Amerika first") and theologically naive
("We must forgive our enemies") reaction can be attributed to a lack of serious thinking about—and
understanding of—the role that government plays in preserving the social order. Whether events of
extraordinary magnitude like this are part of God's sovereign economy and the outworking of his
judgments on the earth is beside the point and not in question here; clearly all such events are, but
a finer point needs to be made (though it would be a valid topic in another context). Pacifistic nonresistance as a policy-prescription in this situation is an illegitimate reading of Mt 5:21-48, even when
it remains a legitimate conviction of individual conscience. For a biblically and theologically informed response to the events of September 11, see Keith J. Pavlischek, "Just War Theory and Terrorism: Applying the Ancient Doctrine to the Current Conundrum," *The Witherspoon Fellowship
Lectures 21* (2001): 1-21 (which is a transcript of the Witherspoon Fellowship Lecture that was delivered by Pavlischek in Washington, D.C., on October 26, 2001).

hermeneutical issue, the pathetic disregard for the law that characterizes American evangelicalism is reflected by the blight of antinomianism endemic to its culture. For this reason serious theological reflection is in order. What is the *basis* for an ethic that calls itself *biblical?* And what guidelines inform the Christian community regardless of its cultural context?

9

Toward a Biblical Ethic
Principles in Polarity

—

I n the beginning of this book I made the observation—a rather painful one—that Protestant evangelicals do not tend to be found serving in great numbers in particular vocational settings: for example, ethics, social- and public-policy analysis, the social and behavioral sciences, economics, and the media (both electronic and print). To be sure, part of this regrettable absence has something to do with notions of culture that stem from the phenomenon of "fundamentalism" in recent evangelical history, as the recent work of George Marsden, Mark Noll and James Davison Hunter abundantly demonstrates.[1] Part of it, some would argue, has to do with a free-church reading of history, which advocates separation as a response to the distortions of church and culture.[2] But part of the dilemma is of a theological nature, and it is to this factor that the present chapter is devoted.

---

[1] I am not one of those, however, who is obsessed with the "fundamentalist" bogeyman, as if it somehow explains all the problems that can be found in Christendom. Such a tack—which is pervasive in the scholarly literature (among mainline writers as well as some evangelicals)—is distorted, and in some cases, dishonest.

[2] See, e.g., Vigen Guroian, *Ethics After Christendom: Toward an Ecclesial Christian Ethic* (Grand Rapids, Mich.: Eerdmans, 1994), pp. 21-27; Gilbert Meilaender, *Faith and Faithfulness: Basic Themes in Christian Ethics* (Notre Dame, Ind.: University of Notre Dame Press, 1991), pp. 19-34, 114-50; George Weigel, *Catholicism and the Renewal of American Democracy* (New York: Paulist, 1989), pp. 196-200; and Carl E. Braaten, "Protestants and Natural Law," *First Things* 19 (January 1992): 20-26.

Protestant evangelicals have prided themselves in their faithfulness to the *sola*'s of their Reformational forebears. One of our strengths, down to the present day, is our commitment to the realities of faith and grace. A consequence of this primacy of faith and grace, intended by some and unintended by others, has been to emphasize discontinuity with respect to law and Old Testament ethical norms. One of the unintended consequences of stressing discontinuity over continuity is the raising of false dichotomies. Several of these false dichotomies overlap and, thus, resist neat compartmentalization.[3] For example, modern Dispensationalism in particular has set up a sharp antithesis between the dispensation of law and the dispensation of grace. The theological error herein is twofold: law and grace are pitted against one another and viewed as mutually exclusive; moreover, within the sphere of grace, law tends to be wrongly understood.[4] This dualistic thinking, to be sure, pervades much (if not all) of Christendom, but it is particularly entrenched in evangelicalism and thus requires additional commentary. It is a viewpoint that fails to see any connection between love for God and the law of God (despite universal evidence to the contrary), and as a result it misunderstands the nature of covenant. And yet,

> before there was any human action in response, this love [of God] chose the people for God's own possession and gave them the law as a token of their special position of favor. To obey the law thus becomes man's response of love to the divine act of election.[5]

God's grace, hence, can be seen as preceding the giving of the law. Obedience issues out of love (Deut 4:37-40; 7:6-11). For this reason, the psalmist can speak in language that baffles most Christians: "LORD, how I delight in your law!" (Ps 119:16, 24, 47, 70, 92, 97, 143; cf. Ps 1; 19).

Another common misconception is the idea that the Old Testament knows only bodily circumcision whereas the New Testament emphasizes circumcision of the heart, an idea that suggests Israel in the old covenant had no spiritual union and fellowship with God. For true Israel, as reiterated by the

---

[3]The very candid remarks by one Old Testament scholar mirror how widespread these distortions are among evangelicals. See Kenneth L. Barker, "False Dichotomies Between the Testaments," *Journal of the Evangelical Theological Society* 25, no. 1 (1982): 3-16.

[4]Though, admittedly, Paul's varied use of *nomos* easily produces confusion in and of itself and has been the subject of considerable scholarship.

[5]Walter Eichrodt, *Theology of the Old Testament*, 2 vols. (Philadelphia: Westminster Press, 1961), 1:94.

prophets, circumcision in the flesh was merely an outward sign and witness to an inner reality: that is, the surrender of one's whole life to Israel's sovereign God (Deut 10:16; Jer 4:4; Ezek 44:9).

A related and equally false dichotomy is the notion that whereas the New Testament reveals the *spirit* of the law, the Old Testament presents only the *letter* of the law. As I argued in the previous chapter, not infrequently interpreters cite Matthew 5:21-48 as evidence that Jesus is superseding the law with a new interpretation. What he is setting aside is a false understanding among *contemporary* interpreters ("You have heard . . . but I say to you"), an understanding that obscures the intent of the law from the beginning. The contrast is between Jesus' teaching and pharisaical externalism, not between his teaching and Old Testament scriptures. Moreover, the proper interpretation of Jesus' teaching is clarified by statements recorded in Matthew 5:17-20. As I previously argued, at issue is the need to address a popular misconception and adjust pharisaical distortions of the law. That misconception is that the law was being set aside ("Do not think that I have come to abolish the law or the prophets," Mt 5:17). Jesus wishes to affirm the abiding validity of the law as an ethical standard.

The Christian ethic can only be understood against the background of the Old Testament and the notion of covenant, both of which presuppose natural law. The God of creation chooses Israel as a people, and he requires that they obey his will. This motivation for ethics, which emerges out of divine revelation, distinguishes itself sharply from the sundry forms of humanistic ethics that have shaped contemporary moral philosophy. That Yahweh chooses to reveal to Israel his ethical norms does not negate the universality and impartiality of those standards of moral law. The prophets of the Old Testament insist that God makes the same demands on all people and will judge them on the same basis—by their obedience and disobedience to these demands. Israel's chosen status, granted through covenant, does not entitle it to special *privilege* in the sense of a *different moral standard,* although it does entail unique *responsibilities.* To stress ethical continuity between the old and new covenants is not to deny the difference between the two covenants. Discontinuity relates first and foremost to the manner of covenant ratification and not to a change in the ethical standards required of humanity.

These observations are not meant to minimize the complexity of approaching ethics in the Bible, especially Old Testament ethics. Walter Kaiser, author of an Old Testament ethics primer, candidly points out some of the knotty is-

sues one has to confront.[6] Among these are the following:
- modern uneasiness with an underlying rationale for ethical principles
- the problem of particularity and specificity in Old Testament laws
- the diversity of seemingly contradictory ethical material

But these perplexities should not be allowed to give the impression that the New Testament promotes a different ethic than the Old does. While the church rightly observes the reality of discontinuity between the covenants, evangelical preaching frequently portrays Jesus and Paul as ushering in a "new and better" ethic. Categories of justification and ethics are frequently conflated, with the result being disastrous, theologically and ethically. The evangelical mode of predominately discontinuous thinking has resulted in an ethical dualism. While God's method of ratifying his covenant (i.e., justification) is indeed new and better, his character (which is to say, his moral essence) and, hence, what God requires ethically of humans, remains unchanged. One is warranted in distinguishing between the mode of covenant ratification, which unfolds within salvation history, and the timelessness of God's ethical standards.

POLARITIES THAT CONSTITUTE BIBLICAL ETHICS

Because our finite minds cannot grasp infinitude, divine truth, as it comes to us through revelation, tends to be paradoxical. Such, however, is not to say that it is antithetical; rather, it is more accurate to speak of this truth as being refracted to us in complementarity or polarity. That truth is comprehended by humans in pluriform fashion or in multiple dimensions is evidenced by the sheer inability of human logic to penetrate the concept of trinitarianism. After exhausting the various analogies that might account in human language for the Godhead as three persons, we are left to confess that God, who is one in essence, is nevertheless multiple persons. Thus, we have a model, rooted in our understanding of the Godhead itself, for attempting to understand moral truth: principles or elements that appear to be contradictory, antithetical or paradoxical are in fact not so; rather, they may be thought to represent two sides of the same coin.[7]

To view principles undergirding a biblical ethic in terms of complementarity is to demonstrate their essential interdependence. The tension that exists

---

[6]Walter C. Kaiser Jr., *Toward Old Testament Ethics* (Grand Rapids, Mich.: Zondervan, 1983), pp. 289-92.
[7]Similarly, J. I. Packer uses the term *antinomy* to speak of the seeming contradiction between two reasonable principles (*Evangelism & the Sovereignty of God* [Downers Grove, Ill.: InterVarsity Press, 1961, 1991], pp. 18-19).

between two ethical poles can be illustrated by the tension between sovereignty and free will. Any construal of this relationship that negates or effectively cancels one side does irreparable harm to our theology and our ethics.

What follows is a listing (representative, not exhaustive) of complementary principles that inform and undergird our attempt to construct a biblical ethic. It is understood that many of the pairs are overlapping; thus, for the purposes of the present investigation, they elude strict precision with regard to terminology and definition.

VERTICAL POLARITIES

1. Transcendence/perfection and condescension. The Old and New Testaments leave little room for doubt that the God of the universe is a self-revealing Creator who has made his existence known through his creative cosmic works and through a universal moral impulse implanted in all human creatures. This Creator-God has neither cause nor criteria. His will and his design establish the basis for what is moral. The certainty of this moral standard is rooted in his own unchanging nature—if, in fact, this Creator-God is moral perfection ("Be perfect, therefore, as your heavenly Father is perfect," Mt 5:48). Because there is "no variation or shadow due to change" with this God (Jas 1:17), he demonstrates his moral perfection. His moral law, therefore, is a *"perfect* law, the law of liberty" (Jas 1:25).

And yet this God of moral perfection reveals himself through condescending acts that are designed to deliver humankind from sin, grief, despair and suffering. The wonder of the incarnation is precisely this:

> Though he was in the form of God
> > he did not regard equality with God
> > as something to be grasped;
> rather he emptied himself,
> > taking the form of a servant,
> > being born in human likeness.
> And being found in appearance as a man,
> > he humbled himself
> > and became obedient to the point of death. (Phil 2:6-8)

Christian theism distinguishes itself dramatically from Islamic theology on this very point. Islamic theology posits a God who is absolutist and transcendent but not condescending. The ethical implications derived from either system are clear. In biblical morality there is a balance between God's reputation and the creature's need for illumination. The God of moral perfection, in the end, is concerned to reveal himself in ways that are humanly meaningful. Hence, it stands to reason that there is no doctrine of the incarnation in Islamic theology.

2. *Holiness and accommodation.* The transcendent is rooted in the reality of God's uncompromisingly holy character. High moral demands placed on humankind are due to the holiness of God. The Judeo-Christian God is perfect holiness ("For I am the LORD your God; sanctify yourselves therefore, and be holy, for I am holy," Lev 11:44-45; cf. 1 Pet 1:16). Divine holiness demonstrates an unremitting concern for moral purity; hence, the Old Testament has exceedingly harsh sanctions for those who dared enter the realm of the holy ill-prepared.[8] The God of the Bible is a consuming fire (Heb 12:29).

The compassion and mercy with which the biblical God shows himself is neither sentimentality nor softness; neither is it predicated on the worthiness or the desired gratitude of the recipient. Rather, it sees and responds to human need. Thomas Burke has stated the contrast well:

> On the one hand, the Bible presents God as being of incomparable holiness, unable to abide the least taint of moral lassitude, a God who is so uncompromising and unrelenting in his concern with moral impeccability that He pursues transgressors with unparalleled indignation. But on the very next page, He is presented as a God of infinite mercy and compassion who willingly sacrifices Himself for the sake not only of the downtrodden and weak, but the undeserving and wicked.[9]

3. *Justice and mercy.* The term *justice* is perhaps one of the most prostituted words of the English language as we enter the twenty-first century. In the United States every conceivable minority or political-interest group locates its interests in the nebulous, albeit all-encompassing, authority of "social justice." But because its purportedly objective points of reference are illusory, as Richard Neuhaus has noted, the definition of justice is subject to the whims of whoever invokes it: " 'Justice' is the greed of the poor and the self-protection of the rich."[10]

---

[8]Graphic examples of these sanctions in the Old Testament narrative are found in Lev 10:1-11; 2 Sam 6:5-11; 2 Chron 26:16-21.

[9]Thomas J. Burke, "The Fundamental Principles of Biblical Ethics," in *The Christian Vision: Man and Morality,* ed. Thomas J. Burke (Hillsdale, Mich.: Hillsdale College Press, 1986), pp. 31-32.

[10]Richard John Neuhaus, *Time Toward Home: The American Experiment as Revelation* (New York: Seabury, 1975), p. 168.

But justice is not a fluid entity; it has no independent existence. Justice is developed philosophically both in the Judeo-Christian moral tradition and in pre-Christian philosophy (Plato's *Republic* is dedicated to this theme); hence, it is a "cardinal" virtue. Historically, justice has been defined as that which is due each person—a definition affirmed from Aristotle to Cicero to Aquinas.[11] The language of justice fills the entire Bible, giving one the clear impression that it is a hallmark of biblical ethics. And correctly so, since justice describes how people associate with one another and, therefore, how society functions. While Scripture agrees with the pre-Christian philosophical tradition that justice is that which is due, it also provides the rationale of *why* this is so. In Scripture the people of God are commanded to execute justice precisely because God himself does so. Justice is cognizant of the fact that humans bear the image of God. While the Hebrew term for "justice," *mišpaṭ*, occurs in numerous Old Testament contexts (and thus eludes precision), it generally refers to God-given principles that govern how humans related to one another.[12] These rules are of a moral nature.[13] They discriminate between righteousness and wickedness as well as between guilt and innocence (e.g., Gen 18:25, "Will not the Judge of all the earth do what is just *[mišpaṭ]*?"; Is 5:20-24), they erect protection for those without a voice (e.g., Ex 23:6-9; Lev 19:9-10), they seek to prevent injustice from arising (e.g., Lev 19:11-14), and they rectify injustice (e.g., Is 10:1-2). This justice, moreover, is to be impartial. It is worthy of note that a perversion of justice occurs when there is partiality to *either* rich or poor (Ex 23:3; Lev 19:15).

The Pentateuch defines the contours of justice, the book of Psalms extols God for his inherent justice, and the prophetic literature calls Israel to repent and do justice. The Christian moral tradition, following Thomas Aquinas, has generally maintained that biblical justice can manifest itself in differing ways: it can be punitive or vindictive; it can be distributive; and it can be restorative, compensatory or creative.[14] The cardinal virtue of justice, then, may be defined as the capacity to fulfill one's moral duties and, thus, a wider

---

[11]Aristotle *Ethica nichomachea* 5.1-11 (1129a-1138b); Cicero *De officiis* 1.5.15; Thomas Aquinas *Summa Theologica* 2-2.Q.58.

[12]David Jones, *Biblical Christian Ethics* (Grand Rapids, Mich.: Baker, 1994), p. 83.

[13]See Jones's very helpful discussion of these moral guidelines (ibid., pp. 79-86).

[14]A brief but excellent overview of mainstream Christian teaching on justice is found in Ted Rebard, "Justice: Moral Virtue in Society," *Ethics and Medics* 19, no. 12 (1994): 1-2.

moral condition of right relations.

Mercy presupposes the abiding nature of justice.[15] The inseparability of justice and mercy can be seen in revelation given to Moses on Mount Sinai:

> The LORD, the LORD,
> a God merciful and gracious,
> slow to anger,
> and abounding in steadfast love and faithfulness,
> keeping steadfast love for the thousandth generation,
> forgiving iniquity and transgression and sin,
> yet by no means clearing the guilty,
> but visiting the iniquity of the parents
> upon the children
> and the children's children,
> to the third and the fourth generation. (Ex 34:6-7)

Although mercy presupposes justice, it is not obligatory in the sense that justice is. The wonder of mercy lies in its voluntary aspect. Once again, our model for this is divine and covenantal:

> But God, who is rich in mercy, out of the great love with which he loved us even when we were dead through our trespasses, made us alive together with Christ—by grace you have been saved—and raised us up with him and seated us with him in the heavenly places in Christ Jesus. (Eph 2:4-6)

Mercy is accentuated as it finds application in the sphere of covenantal obligation and law. It commutes the sentence, as it were, that is incurred when one violates truth and justice. Salvation history monitors this dynamic as it moves toward its climax of divine mercy in Christ, whose death is vicarious and substitutionary. Christ's atonement—necessary but free—is for sins that condemned humanity. What evangelicals at times forget, or do not comprehend, is that mercy does not remove the consequences of ethical violations. Consequences still must be faced, whether in the heavenly realm ("For if the message declared through angels was valid, and every transgression or disobedience received a just penalty, how can we escape if we neglect so great a sal-

---

[15]The Hebrew *ḥesed* is normally rendered "mercy" or "lovingkindness" in the Old Testament. Jones writes, "The distinctive quality of the *divine ḥesed,* and that which warrants its normal translation as 'mercy,' is expressed in the climactic defining clause . . . 'bearing [taking away] iniquity, transgression, and sin' " (*Biblical Christian Ethics,* p. 90).

vation?" Heb 2:2-3) or in the earthly realm, for violations ranging from speeding to stealing to strangulation.[16]

Consider the important address delivered by South African Justice Richard Goldstone at the U.S. Holocaust Museum in Washington, D.C., on January 27, 1997. Goldstone, who had previously been chief prosecutor of the International Criminal Tribunals for the former Yugoslavia and Rwanda, underscored in his lecture—titled "Healing Wounded People"—the typically false notion of justice that people have. Goldstone observed that "too infrequently is justice looked at as a form of . . . therapy for victims who cannot really begin their healing process until there has been some public acknowledgment of what has befallen them."[17] He continues,

> The one thing I have learned in my travels to the former Yugoslavia and in Rwanda and in my own country is that where there have been egregious human rights violations that have been unaccounted for, where there has been no justice, where the victims have not received any acknowledgment, where they have been forgotten, where there's been a national amnesia, the effect is a cancer in the society. It's the reason that explains, in my respectful opinion, spirals of violence that the world has seen in the former Yugoslavia for centuries and in Rwanda for decades, to use two obvious examples. . . . So justice can make a contribution to bringing enduring peace.[18]

Given that which he has witnessed worldwide, what specific contributions can the application of justice make, in Goldstone's view? Which is to ask, what are the marks of bona fide justice? He identifies several inherent principles:[19]

- the exposure of the truth of individual guilt and avoidance of general collective guilt (an example of which was the trial of Nazi criminals at the Nuremberg for specific, and not general, crimes against humanity)
- the recording of truth for the historical record (which counters attempts

---

[16]While, practically speaking, most Christians would never think of arguing on the basis of theological justification through Christ that a highway patrol officer *not issue the speeding ticket they had just earned,* many Christians—both evangelical and non-evangelical—have a tendency to conflate justification and ethics in the sphere of law and public policy. Criminal justice is impossible if standards of justice are not fixed. In the ethical realm, biblical justice requires that payment always be made for a violation and that this payment be proportional to the offense; hence, the catchword *restitution* that occurs frequently in the Pentateuch. Biblically speaking, the only category of ethical offense for which no restitution exists is premeditated murder (cf. Num 35:6-33, esp. Num 35:29-33).
[17]Richard Goldstone, "Healing Wounded People," *Washington Post,* February 2, 1997, p. C4.
[18]Ibid.
[19]Ibid.

by the guilty or their defenders—Holocaust deniers, for example—to fabricate and avoid guilt)

- the public acknowledgment of the loss endured by the victims (who, as broken and terrified people, want and need justice)
- the deterrent nature of criminal justice (since human nature and potential criminals are deterred by the fear of apprehension and punishment)

4. *Law and grace.* Luther made a proper theological distinction between law and the gospel, but in contrast to some of his offspring, he did so without separating the two concepts. While law and gospel describe two different modes of God's activity, law exists prior to gospel not only in salvation history but also in human experience. Law is the means by which God mediates his moral demands. It is the universal instrument by which God is at work with all nations; it expresses itself both in written codes of conduct for all people in all places but also in unwritten codes that explain the structure of creation.[20] Law is like a recipe: it specifies what *ought* to be done.[21] Historically, the Judeo-Christian moral tradition has referred to the absolute or universal character of law as natural law. Viewed theologically, natural law is understood as existing in relationship to God the Creator and, thus, can be spoken of as divine law. In the words of Carl Braaten, who writes out of the Lutheran tradition, God's activity

is not dependent on or limited to human awareness and knowledge. God carries out his purposes in the world through leaders, events, institutions, whether they know it or not; there is no sphere of life where he is not active through the law to promote his will.[22]

Law is, therefore, universal and inescapable. Moreover, it is intuited by

---

[20]Carl E. Braaten, "Natural Law and Catholic Moral Theology: A Response," in *Preserving Grace: Protestants, Catholics and Natural Law,* ed. Michael Cromartie (Washington, D.C.: Ethics and Public Policy Center; Grand Rapids, Mich.: Eerdmans, 1997), p. 37. Both thorough and accessible to the religiously and nonreligiously inclined is Heinrich A. Rommen, *The Natural Law: A Study in Legal and Social History and Philosophy,* trans. T. R. Hanley (Indianapolis: Liberty Fund, 1998). Rommen, a Roman Catholic legal theorist at the time of the rise of Nazism, believed that the crisis of World War II provided an opportunity to reconsider natural law, which is ultimately of divine origin but revealed in human rational and social nature. In the unity of truth and justice the words "And the truth shall make you free" are applicable to the community of all people under law (pp. 236-37).

[21]Thus Timothy F. Sedgwick, *The Christian Moral Life: Practices of Piety* (Grand Rapids, Mich.: Eerdmans, 1999), pp. 98-99.

[22]Braaten, "Natural Law," p. 37. The contributors to *Preserving Grace,* while having theological disagreements, all agree that natural-law theory must not be separated from theology, since secular theory does not take into account the presence and activity of a Creator-God who makes concrete demands on human beings.

atheists, skeptics and agnostics who do not believe in any form of special revelation.[23]

Grace, it should be observed, appears as foundational to Old Testament ethics, not just to ethics of the New Testament. The basic motivation propelling ancient Israel to live and act ethically was their gratitude for God's revelatory and saving activity on her behalf. Stephen Charles Mott correctly observes that the structure of ancient Near Eastern covenant treaties assumes the presence of grace and law: the conduct mandated in the laws is understood as a *response* to what God has done.[24] This is grace.

Grace, moreover, can be seen in the giving of the law. This symbiotic relationship is expressed frequently in the New Testament. Grace empowers us to act ethically. It creates that inner affectation to obey, to keep God's ethical demands: "You shall love the LORD your God with all your heart, and with all your soul, and with all your might. Keep these words that I am commanding you today in your heart" (Deut 6:5-6). The summary of the law is understood in terms of love, a work of interior grace. This basic assumption lies behind Jesus' admonition "If you love me you will keep my commandments" (Jn 14:21; 15:10; cf. 1 Jn 5:3). The apostle Paul concurs, writing that love keeps the ethical demands of God, and thus "love is the fulfilling of the law" (Rom 13:10).[25] This also agrees with Jesus' summary of our moral duty, which he gave when asked which commandment was the greatest: "On these two commandments [i.e., loving God with one's whole being and loving one's neighbor as oneself] hang all the law and the prophets" (Mt 22:40). The ethical command to love one's neighbor, significantly, is a quotation from Leviticus 19:18. It is this concern—the tendency to interpret Jesus' teaching as setting aside the ethical requirements of the law—that seems to be in Matthew's mind. Hence, following his admonition to "let your light shine before

---

[23]The categorizing of selected Old Testament laws as moral and symbolic (as per Augustine) or as ceremonial, civil and moral (as per Luther and Calvin) is necessary to highlight developments within redemptive history. This classification, however, is not without difficulties, since there are within the corpus of the Pentateuch many timeless *moral* laws that are applicable to people at all times. See chap. six, "Biblical Resources for Ethics: The Pauline Model," above, for a fuller discussion of the relationship between the Christian and the law.

[24]Stephen Charles Mott, *Biblical Ethics and Social Change* (New York: Oxford University Press, 1982), p. 25. On the structure of ancient Near Eastern treaty covenants, see George E. Mendenhall, *Law and Covenant in Israel and the Ancient Near East* (Pittsburgh: Biblical Colloquium, 1955).

[25]The "law of the Spirit" (Rom 8) is not a new code of law; it is rather an impulse to do the law and honor God's ethical standards.

others, so that they may see your good works and give glory to your Father in heaven" (Mt 5:16), Jesus is recorded as dispelling what evidently was a widespread misconception: "Do not think that I have come to abolish the law or the prophets" (Mt 5:17). The purpose of this block of teaching is to strengthen the case for the law as an ethical guide. The six case-illustrations in Matthew 5:21-48 serve notice that *law as the ethical norm* remains in force.[26] In the same way, James can write that "dead faith," or faith "alone," is insufficient, to the extent that ethics always validates authentic Christian faith (Jas 2:20, 24).

The Christian must avoid two extremes—legalism and antinomianism—both of which are a perversion of the relationship of law and grace and both of which are common to evangelicals. Legalism, to which most of us react quite strongly, is part of our recent legacy. But perhaps more prevalent among us as we enter the third millennium is our tendency toward antinomianism. This should come as no surprise, given the (relatively) lawless state of contemporary culture. Significantly, Arnold Toynbee detected a pattern of lawlessness dominating civilizations in the process of decline.[27] The antinomian erroneously views laws and freedom as oppositional. This error, it should be remembered, finds expression among both religious and nonreligious persons. The New Testament informs us, grace notwithstanding, that disdain for the law leads to slavery, not freedom (2 Thess 2:9; Jas 1:25-27; 1 Pet 4:3; 2 Pet 2:19; cf. Mt 5:17-19), just as love fulfills the law (Rom 13:10), which is to say, keeps the commandments. The Christian disciple should, like the psalmist (Ps 119:16, 24, 47, 70, 92, 97, 113, 119, 143, 159, 167) and Paul (Rom 7:22), delight in the law, for the law is holy, righteous and good (Rom 7:12). Evangelical Christians especially should beware lest they contribute—through bad theology—to a lawless society.

Keeping the relationship between law and grace in balance,[28] realizing that

---

[26]For a fuller examination of Jesus' attitude toward the law as it applies to ethical living, see J. Daryl Charles, "The Greatest or the Least in the Kingdom? The Disciple's Relationship to the Law (Matt. 5:17-20)," *Trinity Journal* n.s. 13, no. 2 (1992): 139-62, and more recently my "Garnishing with the Greater Righteousness," *Bulletin for Biblical Research* 12, no. 1 (2002): 1-15.

[27]Arnold J. Toynbee, *A Study of History,* ed. D. C. Somervell, 2 vols. (New York: Oxford University Press, 1947-1957), 1:440-42.

[28]John Murray has stated the deficiencies in our understanding of law and grace quite well: "An erroneous conception of the function of law can be of such a character that it completely vitiates our view of the gospel; and an erroneous conception of the antithesis between law and grace can be of such a character that it demolishes both the substructure and the superstructure of grace" (*Principles of Conduct: Aspects of Biblical Ethics* [Grand Rapids, Mich.: Eerdmans, 1991], p. 181).

the two *may not be severed,* will help preserve us from both ethical extremes, legalism and antinomianism.[29]

HORIZONTAL POLARITIES

1. Truth and love. The apostle Paul admonishes the Christians in Ephesus to speak the truth in love (Eph 4:15). This polarity suffers from neglect perhaps more than any other, and yet the fruit of its divorce borders catastrophic. *Agapē,* as already noted, is neither sloppy sentimentalism nor unencumbered antinomianism. Unlike many North American Protestants, it has a high regard for truth.

It is not uncommon to find Christian ethicists maintaining that love and truth or love and justice stand in opposition to one another. It is thus assumed that truth is cold, harsh, unbending and inflexible, whereas compassion manifests the opposite characteristics and has the person's best at heart. Therefore, a society of those who try to love their neighbors must dispense with justice as mediated by the courts and the state. Unhappily, this contrast tends to produce a false dichotomy in the minds of many religious people. In the end, love is given the highest priority (normally buttressed theologically by Jesus' so-called love ethic gleaned from the Sermon on the Mount and by Paul's statement in 1 Cor 13:13 that "the greatest of these is love"), with the unfortunate consequence that love is disengaged from moral content and the character of God. A recent volume published by Cambridge University Press titled *Love Disconsoled* illustrates this unfortunate tendency:

> These words [Mt 5:38-48] override the *lex talionis* and call for an extremely stringent life of charity. . . .
>
> Strong agape treats love as the primary human source and end, a "metavalue." . . .
>
> Matthew is notoriously ambivalent as to whether Jesus is best seen as fulfilling the old Torah or as supplanting it with a new one. . . .
>
> My more modest thesis is that a future heaven and/or hell ought not to play much of a role in ethics. . . . So, in quasi-Rortian fashion, charity tends to change the subject when the topic of heaven arises. . . .
>
> Love . . . is the greatest good; it does trump in cases of conflicting values.

---

[29]For a wide range of interpretations as to the utility of the law for the Christian, see Greg L. Bahnsen et al., *Five Views on Law and Gospel* (Grand Rapids, Mich.: Zondervan, 1996).

Charity is beyond both certainty and morality.[30]

But this sort of thinking is disastrous when imported into the realm of ethics. Love is not beyond morality; that idea is as pernicious as it is heretical. Rather, love and truth inform one another; they presuppose one another.[31] Truth, like justice, is the consequence, the expression, of love. Justice might be seen as an instrument of love. To have an exalted view of justice is to take seriously loving one's neighbor by honoring laws that safeguard the neighbor.[32] To avoid the truth is not to love in the genuine sense; that would reduce love to spineless sentimentalism. Love calls us and others to respond to what is ultimate, what is true, what is commensurate with the moral character of God. Love does not shy away from doing the ethically right thing, even when this means offending our modern, liberal sensibilities. There is no dualism between love and justice. In the end, it is impossible to achieve justice among people who will not love their neighbor. In this sense, the "relevance" of Christian love to the problems of society, as Reinhold Niebuhr puts it, is demonstrated by its effects on the system of justice.[33] Love and truth are inextricably bound up in one another.

The social evils and suffering of our time require that the Christian community not be complacent concerning norms for "social justice." Although every cultural sub-group imaginable appeals to social justice as a category, thus requiring some redefinition, the basic assumption of this writer is that, biblically speaking, social justice corresponds to the unity or convergence of truth and love: that is, because we love God, we love our neighbor accordingly. Moreover, Jesus' teaching indicates that not social institutions per se but individuals who make up those institutions are simultaneously the flaw and the remedy.

---

[30]Timothy P. Jackson, *Love Disconsoled: Meditations on Christian Charity* (Cambridge: Cambridge University Press, 1999), pp. 5, 20, 89, 155, 169, 174, 176. Richard Hays, in an otherwise fine volume on New Testament ethics, offers this rather remarkable comment on Mt 5:38-48 (the passage cited by Jackson above): "This extraordinary change of emphasis constitutes a paradigm shift that effectually undermines the Torah's teaching about just punishment for offenders" (*The Moral Vision of the New Testament* [San Francisco: HarperSanFrancisco, 1996], pp. 324-25).

[31]Similarly, Reinhold Niebuhr argues that the relationship of love and justice is best understood dialectically (*Human Destiny*, vol. 2 of *The Nature and Destiny of Man* [New York: Charles Scribner's Sons, 1943], pp. 244-56).

[32]To have a healthy view of laws that support justice is not to be uncritical of or oblivious to the limitations of law or to abuses of power by the state. The Christian faith has always viewed power as a means and has resisted power as an end in itself.

[33]See Reinhold Niebuhr, *An Interpretation of Christian Ethics* (New York: Harper's, 1935), esp. chap. 4.

(This is *not* to say that we should not work for justice at the social or societal level.) To work for social justice is to apply biblical principles in a way that takes into account the complementarity of biblical ethics. For example, loving one's neighbor does not require that we dispense with criminal justice, contrary to the views of many Christian ethicists. Nor does it mean that proportionate punishment be set aside when a crime is committed.

The loving (and just) thing to do is always to *honor truth*. This will entail holding people accountable in proportionate measure for their actions, the biblical term for which is *restitution*. To hold people accountable is to treat them with dignity, to treat them as moral agents created in the image of God.

2. *Dignity and depravity.* It was Aquinas who succinctly summarized the twofold constitution of biblical anthropology, observing that humankind is simultaneously the jewel of creation and the scum of the earth. As with the other polarities, dignity and depravity must be held in balance lest a flawed anthropology, disastrous when applied to ethics, will emerge. It is the testimony of Scripture that human beings are preeminent among creatures. This is made clear by the text of Genesis 1. God created humans in his own image and entrusted to them dominion over all living things (Gen 1:27-28), hence the language of praise on the part of the psalmist:

> When I look at your heavens, the work of your fingers,
> the moon and the stars that you have established;
> what are human beings that you are mindful of them,
> mortals that you care for them?
> Yet you have made them a little lower than God,
> and crowned them with glory and honor.
> You have given them dominion over the works of your hands;
> you have put all things under their feet,
> all sheep and oxen,
> and also the beasts of the field,
> the birds of the air, and the fish of the sea,
> whatever passes along the paths of the seas. (Ps 8:3-8 NRSV)

On what ground does the psalmist give such an exalted view? It is a dignity that originates not in humans themselves, but rather in their relation to the Creator. As the image of God, they reflect the nature of their Maker—a nature that is spiritual, moral and psychological in its constitution.

Alongside this portrait of humanity is a strikingly realistic view of human nature. This finds expression in Jesus' teaching (e.g., "If you then, *who are evil,* know how to give good gifts to your children," Mt 7:11, emphasis added) and is developed at length in Pauline theology (esp. Rom 3; 6—7). It is a universal realism attested to by historic Christian tradition.[34] The assumption of a depraved nature presupposes the need for redemption.

The challenge to Christians in a therapeutic age—when psychological, social and biological factors are cited to justify human deviancy—is to reaffirm both anthropological poles of the Christian moral tradition. Human dignity and worth extend to every person, regardless of religious background, station in life or quality of existence. At the same time, the realities of moral standards, guilt and social stigma must be reaffirmed as a reminder to society that people are held morally accountable for their every action (Acts 17:30-31; Rom 14:10; 2 Cor 5:10; 2 Pet 3:3-10).

3. Tolerance and absolutism. The rejection of or indifference to absolute ethical values is a salient feature of contemporary culture. Postmodern thinking is right in its rejection of "absolutism" as a modernist value, to the extent that the error lay in an exaggerated view of human reason. Apart from divine grace, reason inevitably and inescapably succumbs to the centripetal forces of human fallenness. From the Christian vantage point, however, it is necessary to *postulate* absolutes, even when it is impossible to *possess* them. Modernism's error is not assuming the existence of such values but assuming that these values are attained by human agency.

An equal and opposite distortion may emerge: namely, the denial of the possibility of absolute value. The equation of indifference and tolerance is, simultaneously, a moral-philosophical error and a popular error that is used to permit all manner of injustice and evil in American society. In such a cultural climate, tolerance is an end. The secularist argues that tolerance, in the broadest sense, is possible—indeed, desirable—given the presupposition that there are no moral absolutes. Although the fruit of tolerance-as-highest-virtue thinking is relativistic in the extreme at the end of the twentieth century, its epistemological assumptions have been formulated over the last 250 years.

As I noted in chapter one, tolerance originally meant a policy of patient forbearance in the presence of something disliked. As a political virtue, it denoted a government's readiness to permit a wide variety of religious beliefs, based on the

---

[34]Christian theology affirms the radical, universal, personal and intrinsic nature of sin.

fundamental assumption of truth's existence.[35] When we speak of tolerance today, our reference point is not the state but the individual's lifestyle choices. Tolerance ceases to be a virtue and becomes a vice when it is indifferent to truth, ignores what is morally good and holds contempt for the values that uphold the community.[36] Tactically, tolerance becomes pernicious when it abdicates moral responsibility, encourages indulgence in sentimentalism or uses intimidation and emotional appeal to subvert and destroy critical judgment.[37] A typical strategy for moral leveling proceeds by quoting Jesus' words in Matthew 7:1: "Do not judge, so that you may not be judged." This citation is used to intimidate and silence by intimating that people should not condemn the faults of others, especially when they have faults of their own. The Christian should respond to this brand of intellectual dishonesty by noting that Christ does not condemn all judging; he condemns only what is hypocritical. Moreover, Paul exhorts the Christians in Corinth to "clean out the old yeast" as it touches the community (1 Cor 5:7). As it turns out, this bit of "yeast" is a case of deviant sexuality, to which the apostle asks rhetorically, "Is it not those who are inside [the church] whom you are to judge?" (1 Cor 5:12). His answer leaves little room for false consolation: "Drive out the wicked person from among you" (1 Cor 5:13).[38]

The challenge both for individual Christians and for the Christian community as a whole is learning how to be tolerant without being relativistic and discerning when and how to draw the line between private behavior and norms for public policy (since public policy makes the private normative).[39]

4. *Freedom/autonomy and responsibility/stewardship.* The popular concept of freedom is being released from something—from past experience, restraints,

---

[35]See the section "An Intolerable Tolerance" in chap. one, above (p. 39).

[36]A good example of this is the widespread use of the term *compassion* in a prostituted sense by which it condones evil or denies the effects thereof. A typical scenario in which one can observe this linguistic-moral dishonesty at work is the public reaction to AIDS. A flood of sympathy is unleashed toward AIDS victims, which automatically is employed as a wedge for the purposes of normalizing homosexuality. The effect of this is that people then ignore the moral, physical and psychological degradation of sodomy. Cogent analyses of tolerance as vice are found in Kent Weber, "How Far Is Tolerance a Virtue?" *re:generation quarterly* 2, no. 1 (1996): 29-31; Nikolaus Lobkowicz, "The Vice of Tolerance," *New Perspectives Quarterly* 15, no. 1 (1998): 56-59; and John Attarian, "In Dispraise of Tolerance, Sensitivity and Compassion," *The Social Critic,* spring 1998, pp. 14-23.

[37]Attarian, "Dispraise of Tolerance," p. 14.

[38]Compare the repeated admonition in Deut 17:7; 19:19; 21:21; 22:21, 24; 24:7: "So you shall purge the evil from your midst."

[39]On the moral assumptions informing tolerance as virtue and vice, see J. Budziszewski, "The Illusion of Moral Neutrality," *First Things* 35 (August-September 1993): 32-37.

obligations or inhibitions. Freedom is thus seen as involving a rejection of authority in one form or another. And no era is marked by a crisis in authority as much as the one in which we presently live. Since Immanuel Kant, philosophers have spoken of autonomy (literally, "self-law") as a form of liberty in which individuals determine their course of action based on choice. *Freedom, liberation, choice, rights* and *empowerment* have become the most revered words in the contemporary moral (and civic) lexicon. Behind these terms stands a basic assumption that our social relationships and arrangements exist to nurture the self.[40] North American culture has been increasingly seduced into worshiping autonomy, which undermines the very moral, social and civil infrastructure on which society rests.[41]

And yet, paradoxically, there is no freedom apart from external authority. In Pauline terms, one is either a slave to God's righteousness or a slave to one's sin (Rom 6:15-23). To contend that I am autonomous, that I am my own authority, is to succumb to the worst sort of bondage. Only moral freedom can bow before an authority. Authentic freedom is freedom *to* something, not merely *from* something.

But what is authority? How are we to define it? In the realm of belief, authority corresponds to what is ultimate and true. In the sphere of behavior, authority stands in relation to moral law.[42] Genuine authority is to be distinguished from authoritarianism, which makes morally unjustified or false demands, whether in the form of outright totalitarian evil or simply in the context of day-to-day social relationships. We cannot avoid authority.[43]

Improperly understood, autonomy is destructive to human good; an autonomous being is able to justify rebellion against its Creator, yet it is unaware

---

[40]See the section "The Therapeutic Model" in chap. one, above. Though not written from the standpoint of faith, two books by author and critic Wendy Kaminer are very much worth reading, if for no other reason than enjoying the sheer wit and humor with which the author satirizes therapeutic society: *I'm Dysfunctional, You're Dysfunctional* (New York: Addison-Wesley, 1993) and *It's All the Rage* (New York: Vintage, 1995). Due to my own interest in criminal justice, I have reviewed the latter volume, which takes up a critique of the criminal justice system, though it does so in ways that require some modification. See my review, "Beyond the Therapeutic State," *First Things* 66 (October 1996): 64-66.

[41]Not coincidentally, autonomy is one of three "cardinal" virtues that govern bioethical discourse (and increasingly, the one that assumes a primary status).

[42]See J. I. Packer, *Freedom and Authority* (Oakland, Calif.: International Council on Biblical Inerrancy, 1981), pp. 7-9.

[43]It is clear from the development of Paul's thought in Rom 13 that authority is woven into the fabric of creation, an institution of the Creator (Rom 13:2). This agrees with Jesus' all-inclusive claim that "all authority in heaven and on earth has been given to me" (Mt 28:18).

that without the Creator it would cease to exist altogether. Properly understood, autonomy harmonizes with the will of God, cognizant that humans are
called to be stewards of the Creator-God. Today's unwillingness to acknowledge biblical authority—indeed, any external authority whatsoever—has resulted in the disintegration of both individuals and society as whole. Sadly,
Protestant churches in exceeding numbers have lost touch with the principle
of authority to such an extent that even when they bemoan the cultural drift
toward antinomianism, they are impotent to stop the cultural dry rot. The
growth in evangelicalism of "independent" churches, while it may in part represent a rejection of denominational authoritarianism, has the effect of diluting
evangelicalism's authority. Why is this the case? Because evangelical churches
by and large do not stand accountable to any ecclesiastical authority; more often than not they pursue paths that detract from the unity of Christ's body
rather than contribute to it. It is this absence of moral and ecclesiastical authority that has resulted in significant numbers of evangelicals joining the Roman Catholic and Orthodox churches.

I am *not* hereby advocating Roman Catholic or Orthodox ecclesiologies
(whatever their merits), inasmuch as they pose significant theological obstacles for Protestants. Nor do I advocate that one become docile under church
authority. Rather, Christians must affirm scriptural authority *while* acknowledging (as Protestants have *not* been inclined to do) that the church in consensus interprets Scripture. This task is to be done not by individuals in their
private closets but corporately *in consensus with Christ's church.* The options are
not limited to two mutually exclusive alternatives, either biblicism or traditionalism. Scripture controls Christian ethics, and the commitment to this
truth must be nonnegotiable, but this control must involve the subordination
of our interpretation to the church's consensus, both past and present.

To the extent that freedom and autonomy measure themselves against the
background of authority, stewardship acknowledges its awareness of responsibility and accountability before authority. Stewardship can be defined as the
state by which humans exercise their God-given autonomy for the benefit of
others and not merely for self. The steward has free range of action, yet this
freedom is not unlimited. Stewards are stewards insofar as they possess their
identity in relation to a master.

Properly understood, the term *dominion* is able to capture both of the aforementioned elements: a limited autonomy (which acknowledges divine sover-

eignty) and stewardship (which acknowledges ultimate accountability for goods or services rendered). *Dominion* brings together both concepts to show that human beings share in the creative action of God in the world (Gen 1:28-30; 2:19-20).

How far does this dominion extend? To what extent is this creative action shared? Simply stated, God never ceases being God. Dominion must never be confused with total control, especially in matters of life and death. As Pope John Paul II observed in his encyclical *Evangelium Vitae* ("The Gospel of Life"), "There exists in contemporary culture a certain Promethean attitude which leads people to think that they can control life and death by taking decisions about them into their own hands."[44] Given the place of freedom among contemporary idolatries, we must qualify our definition of freedom.[45]

Freedom that extends to human creatures is never unlimited. It must cease at the tree of the knowledge of good and evil and accept the moral law of God the Creator. The law of God does not reduce, much less do away with, human freedom; rather, it promotes and preserves authentic freedom. As already noted, freedom is an inner state that has movement to something, not merely away from something.[46] Here we encounter particular tendencies in contemporary approaches to ethics that focus on an alleged conflict between freedom and law.[47] Frequently, under the guise of freedom, moral autonomy would attempt to lay claim to absolute sovereignty. Such a position is incompatible with the Christian moral-philosophical tradition. Genuine freedom is manifest in our being created in—and in our exercising—the *imago Dei.* Human reason and God's moral law are called to intersect. (This is sometimes referred to as "natural law," since our use of reason in recognizing this intersection is specific to human nature; cf. Rom 2:15). In the end, a freedom that refuses to acknowledge this intersection dehumanizes and contributes to what C. S. Lewis described more than fifty years ago as "the abolition of man."

God never ceases being God, and we never cease being creatures. Human

---

[44]John Paul II, *Evangelium Vitae,* par. 15.

[45]Nowhere is the distinction between limited and absolute autonomy more important than in contemporary bioethical debates, wherein autonomy of the patient inevitably trumps justice and nonmaleficence.

[46]Packer calls attention to several aspects of freedom: it is integrated, spontaneous and contented, which is to say, it is pure, voluntary and desirous of the divine will (*Freedom and Authority,* p. 13).

[47]John Paul devotes considerable attention to this distortion in his 1993 encyclical *Veritatis Splendor* ("The Splendor of Truth"); see esp. sec. 35-64.

nature is indecipherable apart from reference to the God who creates and shares his dominion with his sons and daughters.[48]

Humans have been created expressly for communion with God as well as with their fellow human beings. Although each individual has intrinsic value based on the imago Dei, no individual retains dignity in life isolated from the human community. For this reason, the most powerful witness in culture to divine truth is that of the redeemed community (hence the myriad biblical metaphors that are *corporate* in nature). For that reason the marks of the church can only be those features that are eminently corporate in their essence—heralding of the Word, the sacraments and discipline.

THE IMPLICATIONS OF COMPLEMENTARY THINKING FOR ETHICS

We have examined a prevailing tendency of the evangelical mindset toward polarized theological thinking. This inclination, when applied to the sphere of ethics, significantly undermines evangelical witness. In its essence, polarization mirrors an inability to reflect on divinely revealed truth as it appears in complementary theological and anthropological poles.

Numerous examples of contemporary moral issues might be cited as evidence of dualistic or polarized ethical thinking on the part of evangelicals as they engage broader culture. Bioethical debates proceed over the place of autonomy in relationship to beneficence and justice. The abortion issue tests the Christian community's commitment to both truth and love. Growing support for euthanasia tests our ability to reconcile autonomy and stewardship. The vastly complex issues related to criminal justice (including the death penalty) test our understanding of law and grace as well as our understanding of tolerance and absolutism. In the political realm, we in the United States have witnessed over the last several years unparalleled moral shenanigans, with their attendant moral justifications, in the White House, where incomparable political, financial and legal resources have been marshaled to hide behind the argument—an argument furthered by the electronic and print media—that public and private morality require two different standards. How do we respond to the public-private dichotomy? Are Christians called to tolerate private deviant behavior in others? To what extent? Are we called to tolerate it

---

[48]A most helpful and concise commentary on these related concepts is Germain Kopaczynski, "Stewardship, Dominion and Autonomy," *Ethics and Medics* 20, no. 9 (1995): 1-2.

among those who hold public office?[49] And how might the balance of tolerance and absolutism affect the normalizing of deviant sexuality in the culture at large, a shift that will challenge the Christian community increasingly in the years ahead? And does it really matter?

Moral persuasion more often than not proceeds as a slow, tedious, long-term project, without any immediate visible results. There are occasions, however, when the Christian community is required, as it were, to draw lines in the sand. If we are inadequate to either task (whether long-term education or critical spontaneous proaction), it can be argued that we ourselves are contributing to a collapse of the social order around us. But before we can argue coherently and effectively in culture at large, it is imperative that moral order first visit the household of faith (cf. 1 Pet 4:17-18). This can only begin with serious reflection on theological and anthropological truth, from which a biblically faithful standard of ethics can then emerge.

---

[49]An indispensable resource for assessing Christian ethical responsibility as it relates to political use and abuse of religion is Gabriel Fackre, ed., *Judgment Day at the White House: A Critical Declaration Exploring Moral Issues and the Political Use and Abuse of Religion* (Grand Rapids, Mich.: Eerdmans, 1999).

10

Thinking with
the Church

—

Cultural critic Os Guinness identifies what he believes to be strategic or "tactical" errors that are recurring in evangelical attempts to develop a "public witness." Evangelicals, he notes, have frequently concentrated their efforts in domains that are peripheral to society rather than central. Correlatively, they have relied heavily on populist strengths and rhetoric rather than addressing "gatekeepers" of contemporary culture. Moreover, and critical to the viability of an evangelical social ethic, we have sought to change society through political and legal means rather than contending in the marketplace of ideas at the intellectual level. Thus, evangelicals have tended to rely on "a rhetoric of protest, pronouncement, and picketing"[1] rather than on moral persuasion.

While there is nothing inherently wrong in a "rhetoric of protest"—indeed there are seasons in which the Christian community is called to such a strategy—there is doubtless something to be said for Guinness's concern. The relative inattention to winning a person's mind and way of thinking, an inattention that tends to depreciate a long-term strategy of building relationships and addressing moral-philosophical complexities, has lasting results that are counterproductive to evangelicals' mission to the world.

---

[1]Os Guinness, *Fit Bodies, Fat Minds: Why Evangelicals Don't Think and What to Do About It* (Grand Rapids, Mich.: Baker, 1994), pp. 17-18.

If one argues that moral persuasion is necessary in society, one must also assume that the church has undertaken the task of moral education. This may be assuming too much, however, particularly when one considers the character of contemporary evangelicalism and evangelicals' approach to educating their own. Even when it is not a major part of present-day evangelicalism's repertoire, education in virtue and character, coupled with a public theology that outlines the contours of social ethics, has historically been at the heart of Christian ethics. But bridging the past and the deficiencies of the present is a tall task, one that will require concerted and committed effort. More fundamentally, however, it will require *vision*. And to instill vision one must provide education—education that is deliberate, conversant with the past and relevant to the present. Gilbert Meilaender compares this education to learning a new language; this sort of learning, as anyone who has lived abroad knows, is slow, continuous, deliberate and constantly under alteration. Observes Meilaender, "Communities . . . that do not inculcate virtuous habits of behavior will utterly fail at the task of moral education. . . . In short, the development of true virtue requires both grace and a community dedicated to shaping character."[2]

Grace *and* community? A community *dedicated to shaping character?* How will the evangelical "community" respond to the sort of notion that Meilaender proposes? By instituting another outreach program? With more sermonizing on religious television? Perhaps with more alternative Christian music? Or maybe by planting more seeker-friendly churches? No, the business at hand calls for evangelicals to move into uncharted waters. The "task of moral education," the "development of true virtue," "a community dedicated to shaping character"—these concepts, truth be told, are foreign to many of us. And Meilaender is right: we will need to learn a new language.

But let us leave evangelicalism aside for a moment. Entering the third millennium, Protestants of all stripes are more likely than not to define virtue as a strictly private entity, divorced from its public dimensions. Vigen Guroian, writing from within the Orthodox tradition, calls attention to the debilitating implications of the private-versus-public dichotomy when he warns that our neglect of moral education—by which we witness to the good through our

---

[2]Gilbert C. Meilaender, *Faith and Faithfulness: Basic Themes in Christian Ethics* (Notre Dame, Ind.: University of Notre Dame Press, 1991), pp. 5, 51.

lifestyle—"jeopardizes not only the salvation of neighbors and strangers" but "the common good of society" as well.[3]

THE EVANGELICAL LEGACY: HOW WILL WE EQUIP OUR OWN?

The responsibility for equipping the saints (Eph 4:7-16), however daunting, confronts the church with questions of the highest priority. Who is training the trainers? How are we presently training and preparing Christian leadership? How will we train the emerging generation of Christian leadership? And what will be the core priorities in that training? Practically speaking, primary responsibility for teaching and training falls to local churches and parishes and also to Christian institutions of higher education that affirm biblical orthodoxy: that is, those institutions in which the emerging generation of Christian leadership is being shaped. To the extent that congregational leaders—pastors, priests, rectors and lay leaders—are receiving some form of seminary training, seminary education is critical for imparting moral vision.[4] If the average pastor by way of education has had limited exposure to moral philosophy, the moral life, the study of virtue and Christian social ethics, the seminary will need to confront the possibility that while it is doing a commendable job teaching exegetical and homiletical skills, inculcating useful counseling techniques and

---

[3]Vigen Guroian, *Ethics After Christendom: Toward an Ecclesial Christian Ethic* (Grand Rapids, Mich.: Eerdmans, 1994), p. 97.

[4]Although it is not universally so, there is in some evangelical circles a bias against seminary education. This bias rests on the mistaken assumption that education (i.e., training that strongly emphasizes theory, method, reflection and interpretation) is intrinsically opposed to the operation and empowering of the Holy Spirit. While it is true that some people compromise their faith in the process of their education, this compromise is not inevitable; in fact, today it is rare, and in the seminary context it is virtually nonexistent. As it turns out, this assumption is predicated on an overly pietistic approach to faith and life, and it erects a false dichotomy between faith and reason, between the devotional and cognitive dimensions of faith. Indeed, the case can be made that people who despise education tend to lose their minds and an ability to think critically and creatively; consequently they are rendered ineffective in their cultural witness. Perhaps the most forceful argument for stewardship of the mind as intrinsic to Christian discipleship—written by an evangelical to evangelicals—is Mark A. Noll's *The Scandal of the Evangelical Mind* (Grand Rapids, Mich.: Eerdmans, 1994). Anyone who is considering entering the pastorate, indeed, anyone who through calling and gifting has a teaching ministry at any level, should consider *some level of seminary education* indispensable. Typically, the student in most evangelical seminaries sits under men and women who have dedicated their entire lives to the study of Scripture, to significant interpretive issues, to the study of the church's history and to an understanding of the Judeo-Christian moral tradition. To glean from these godly mentors in a particular season of our lives and then seek application of these insights into our personal ministries is *not* to quench the Spirit's power or ability; to the contrary, such becomes an avenue through which the Spirit can use us as we return to our local congregations and parishes and invest ourselves in the lives of other parishioners.

imparting strategies for church growth, it may be lagging in the task of moral formation and imparting a vision of moral education that can be transferred from pastors, priests and lay leaders to their congregations.

A survey of standard M.Div. and M.A. programs currently being offered by evangelical seminaries might illustrate the matter of priorities. I examined the catalogs of six evangelical seminaries—five that are well-established and one that has emerged recently—with a view to determine the role of moral formation and Christian ethics in the seminary curriculum. In one school, neither the M.Div. program nor the M.A. program (the latter of which offered *eight* different concentrations) had a required ethics course; mentoring was the closest thing offered. "Social Ethics," "Issues in Social Ethics" and "Philosophical Ethics" were, however, offered as electives in that seminary's "Philosophy of Religion" track. At a second institution, one course in "Christian Ethics" was required of both M.Div. and M.A. students. Similarly, at a third, one course in "Christian Social Ethics" was required of M.Div. and M.A. students. At a fourth, neither the M.Div. program nor the M.A. program (with *six* different areas of concentration) required any course in ethics, although "Theological Formation" and "Pastoral Formation" were part of the curriculum. At a fifth institution, neither the M.Div. program nor three concentrations in the M.A. program required any course in ethics. Finally, the sixth institution required one course, "Survey of Christian Ethics," at both the M.Div. and M.A. level.

If the critique of evangelicalism I have offered in this volume is accurate and to be taken seriously, then evangelical training institutions, where formal leadership of the church is being developed, will need to rethink some of their present priorities with regard to theological education.

Perhaps evangelical liberal arts colleges and universities, unlike the seminaries, are doing an adequate job of inculcating moral formation in the liberal arts curriculum. A perusal of the catalogs of five member institutions of the Coalition of Christian Colleges and Universities suggests that this is not the case.[5] It should be said in fairness to these schools that, based on statements made in their catalogs, all five share certain Christian core commitments—notably, the pursuit of truth based on a commitment to Scripture, the integration of faith and knowledge and preparation of the student for a life of service. And yet, notwithstanding these central convictions, *none of the five* includes in its

---

[5]Three of these schools are considered top-tier institutions.

core curriculum a *required course* devoted specifically to moral formation, moral reasoning, character ethics or Christian social ethics—even though Bible and theology classes were required at all five institutions. In two of the five, elective religion courses addressed character and moral education; in both cases this course was offered jointly with the philosophy department.

In contrast to this state of affairs, it is interesting to note that all five institutions spelled out in their catalogs lengthy behavioral stipulations for students—a listing of rules and regulations on particular behaviors that were prohibited on campus or categorically prohibited for students and staff. Quite telling, and indicative, of evangelical ethics, based on published information in the college catalogs, is the combination of the *absence of moral education* in the curriculum and an approach to Christian ethics that is defined by *what is not done,* that is, by what behaviors the community must avoid.[6]

To be sure, while Scripture knows prohibitions ("Thou shalt not . . ."), declaring negatively what behaviors are unacceptable or destructive, it also prescribes in a positive manner a standard of ethical living that corresponds to faith, delineating the shape of that lifestyle. Consider by way of illustration the practical wisdom that emerges from the book of Proverbs. The God-fearing person learns of the contours of individual virtues that are indispensable for living—for example, wisdom, discretion, prudence, industry, self-mastery, modesty, honesty, moral excellence, faithfulness, hospitality, moderation, truthfulness, integrity, a teachable spirit, guidance, stewardship, justice, humility and discernment. In the New Testament, virtues or "beatitudes" lie at the heart of Jesus' teaching regarding Christian discipleship (Mt 5). Both Paul (1 Cor 13) and Peter (2 Pet 1) advise their readers on the indispensability of "theological" virtues (faith, hope and love) as well as the relationship between theological virtues and their "natural" counterparts (knowledge, moral excellence, self-control, endurance, piety and brotherly affection), respectively.

One of the great strengths of a Christian liberal arts education is that it prepares the student not only for a job in the marketplace but also *for life* in the broadest and best sense. There are certain aspects of the educational enterprise that simply cannot be measured by factors issuing from the marketplace or the economic sphere. And honestly, doing what is ethical and standing for what is

---

[6]This observation remains valid even when we acknowledge the need for each institution to "draw boundaries" for the collective good of the campus community.

right will not always be in one's best economic interests. Indeed, life situations may necessitate one's going against the economic or financial grain and defying conventional wisdom. Where will this fundamental "life lesson" be inculcated and learned if not in a liberal arts education rooted in Christian vision? And what resources will help form the moral vision of a young adult in such a way that this vision will serve the individual life-long? Given the growing trend in higher education to tie colleges and universities to corporate and business interests, economics is becoming the bottom line and surely will influence future curricular decisions. There is no reason not to think that even at Christian institutions, curricular matters in the days ahead will be driven by economic rather than philosophical or pedagogical questions. After all, most trustees serving on the boards of colleges and universities are businesspeople and not teachers, philosophers or ethicists.[7]

But supposing that the mythical Christian college decides that *life preparation,* and not *finance,* dictates the bottom line of the curriculum, what might a required course for all students resemble? Perhaps this hypothetical course might be titled "Virtue Amidst Vice," "Living in the Twenty-First Century," "Christian Moral Formation" or "Faith and Society." Course objectives, infused with but a small amount of imagination, might include the following:

- To observe and learn from interaction between Christian and non-Christian ethical theory
- To learn how to construct a biblical worldview[8]
- To understand how basic philosophical assumptions inform one's worldview
- To examine basic moral reasoning

---

[7]It is worth noting that, by contrast, in the nineteenth century, ethics was typically a capstone course required of all senior college/university students, and it often was taught by the institution's president. Over time the study of ethics became relegated to an elective course and is rarely a required course. Philosopher Christina Hoff Sommers believes that courses in moral philosophy reached an all-time low in the 1960s. She points out, however, that within a decade a turnaround was evident, due to an emphasis on "applied ethics" (see "Teaching the Virtues," *The Pubic Interest* 111 [spring 1993]: 5-6). Nevertheless, where ethics is currently studied in the academy, it typically consists primarily of questions of social policy and "social justice." Personal morality is notably absent. This is true of both religiously affiliated and state-affiliated institutions.

[8]In truth, I would highly recommend that the mythical Christian college include a second required course: "Anatomy of a Biblical Worldview." This course would be devoted specifically to the construction of a Christian view of reality as well as to a comparison of major competing worldviews. Words such as *integration* and *worldview* are frequently tossed about at Christian colleges with the underlying assumption that students know what they mean. They may not. In fact, we may be assuming too much when we assume that *most faculty members* understand how to integrate their respective disciplines or construct a biblical worldview.

- To compare different approaches to moral reasoning
- To understand character formation
- To examine selected readings from the Christian moral tradition
- To acquaint oneself with biblical resources for character formation

And what might be required reading for such a course being offered at the mythical Christian college? The student would be exposed to a smattering of writers—ancient and modern, Christian and non-Christian—who have reflected on the essence of human behavior. Basic readings might be drawn from Plato and Aristotle, Augustine and Aquinas, Immanuel Kant and John Stuart Mill, as well as important contemporary Christian ethicists, including Alasdair MacIntyre, Oliver O'Donovan, Arthur Holmes, Gilbert Meilaender, Stanley Hauerwas, Stephen Charles Mott and Vigen Guroian. A valuable supplement would include readings from significant social thinkers—such as Gertrude Himmelfarb, Michael Novak, Leon Kass, Jean Bethke Elshtain and David Novak, to name but a few—whose writings offer a discerning commentary on the moral fabric of American society.[9] Some exposure to social thinkers and ethicists a generation or two removed would also be invaluable, especially to help counter the twin nemeses of evangelical amnesia and postmodern arrogance, both of which are disinterested in the fruit and labor of previous generations; this list might include people such as Paul Ramsey, H. Richard Niebuhr, Dietrich Bonhoeffer, Joseph Pieper, John Courtney Murray, Christopher Dawson and Jacques Ellul. Students would be required to read parts of the Pentateuch, Wisdom literature (Proverbs, Job, Ecclesiastes), the Sermon on the Mount (Mt 5—7), Pauline instructions on private and civic responsibilities (Rom 12—13) and the General Epistles (James and 2 Peter in particular).

The above-mentioned readings, which can be used judiciously in teaching undergraduates, are easily incorporated into seminary education alongside biblical exegesis, biblical theology, philosophical hermeneutics and biblical ethics. The latter would benefit from a "covenantal" perspective by which the *continuity* between the ethical demands of the two covenants at least equals, if not supersedes, the emphasis on their *discontinuity,* which in recent evangelical history has been the dominant hermeneutical assumption

---

[9]The undergraduate needs to be exposed to ethical theory without being overwhelmed by the technical language and jargon that are so typical of philosophical discourse.

governing any teaching of biblical ethics.[10]

Furthermore, in addition to readings in classical texts,[11] seminary students should probe natural-law thinking (as understood by both Catholic and Protestant social thinkers) and the implications of general revelation for ethics (as distinct from a secular approach to natural law).[12] Required reading should be drawn from among Protestant, Catholic and Orthodox thinkers. Given the prolific rate with which Pope John Paul II has issued major encyclicals during his tenure of twenty-plus years, and given the fact that his professional training is in moral philosophy, seminary students should be exposed to recent papal encyclicals that have addressed the nature of truth, our present "culture of death," the relationship between faith and reason and pressing bioethical issues confronting contemporary culture. *Veritatis Splendor* ("The Splendor of Truth," 1993), *Evangelium Vitae* ("The Gospel of Life," 1995) and *Fides et Ratio* ("Faith and Reason," 1998), in particular, should be required reading.[13]

Especially in the context of seminary education it is critical to acknowledge, and counter, the false dichotomy between theology and philosophy that has characterized and hindered evangelical thinking—a false choice

---

[10]Much of twentieth-century American evangelicalism has been molded by dispensationalist hermeneutics, which stresses discontinuity over continuity. In this regard, John Murray's *Principles of Conduct: Aspects of Biblical Ethics* (reprint; Grand Rapids, Mich.: Eerdmans, 1991) offers the needed theological adjustment and remains the standard.

[11]See, e.g., Aristotle *Ethica nichomachea* 2.2, Augustine *Confessions* and Thomas Aquinas *Summa Theologica* 1-2.Q.27, 51, 90-114, esp. 94.

[12]An excellent place to start is J. Budziszewski's *Written on the Heart: The Case for Natural Law* (Downers Grove, Ill.: InterVarsity Press, 1997). Another very helpful resource, written in a nontechnical style with the layperson in mind, is George J. Marlin, *The Politician's Guide to Assisted Suicide, Cloning and Other Current Controversies* (Washington, D.C.: Morley, 1998), esp. pt. 1 (pp. 3-62). Despite the book's title, almost one-third of the volume is devoted to the role that natural law has played in America's past moral crises and must play in present and future bioethical dilemmas. Of a more technical nature but indispensable are Edward B. McLean, ed., *Common Truths: New Perspectives on Natural Law* (Wilmington, Del.: Intercollegiate Studies Institute, 2000); Heinrich Rommen's classic *The Natural Law: A Study in Legal and Social History and Philosophy*, trans. T. R. Hanley (Indianapolis: Liberty Fund, 1998); and Robert P. George, ed., *Natural Law Theory: Contemporary Essays*, rev. ed. (Oxford: Clarendon, 1996).

[13]Also indispensable for the seminary student should be the 1984 apostolic letter by John Paul II titled *Salvifici Doloris* ("The Christian Meaning of Human Suffering"), the text of which is reproduced in *Origins* 13, no. 37 (1984): 609-24. This letter has the twin purpose of articulating distinctly Christian attitudes toward suffering and what John Paul calls the "apologetic" function of suffering in the world. I have elsewhere attempted to underscore the significance of *Salvifici Doloris* in "John Paul II and the Meaning of Suffering: Protestant Reflections on *Salvifici Doloris*," *National Catholic Bioethics Quarterly* 2, no. 1 (2002): 1-12.

that is notorious in the congregation at the lay and popular levels. Pastors
and priests need resources to counter this split thinking so that laypeople
do not view faith and the intellect as diametrically opposed. Although the
church's motto historically has been *fides quaerens intellectum* ("faith seeking understanding"), many evangelicals are deeply suspicious of the mind,
as if faith is inevitably undermined by intellectual growth, probing and
stimulation. This pitting of piety over against reason, of the heart over
against the head, is most unfortunate. While it is true that faith and reason
are not synonymous, and while it is also true that reason operates in the
service of faith, it must be acknowledged and reaffirmed that the relationship between the two is harmonious. The believer need not degenerate
into rationalism on the one hand or fideism on the other; both extremes
can and must be avoided.[14]

The seminary would also be a proper context in which to critique what theorists like Philip Rieff, Paul Vitz, Christopher Lasch and cultural critics like
Charles Sykes, among others, have called "therapeutic culture."[15] As I noted in
chapter one, already three decades ago sociologist Rieff, in attempting to describe the moral reconfiguration of contemporary culture, observed that ours
had become a postcommunal and "therapeutic" society, characterized by "self-
worship" and by having "nothing at stake beyond a manipulatable sense of
well-being."[16] Psychologist Vitz has contended that a "new priesthood" has
supplanted the old one: whereas the traditional notion of priesthood had existed for the purpose of helping people toward the *confession of sin* and *doing
good*, the new priesthood consists of an emergent caste of therapists who assist
people in the direction of *self-actualization* and *feeling good*. Vitz's penetrating
critique, titled *Psychology as Religion: The Cult of Self-Worship,* has become
something of a classic since its publication in 1977 and was reissued by Eerdmans in 1995. Correlatively, exposure to the writings of cultural critics as di-

---

[14]I have not encountered any better explanation of the symbiotic relationship between faith and reason
than in John Paul's encyclical *Fides et Ratio* (delivered at Saint Peter's Basilica in Rome on September
14, 1998, on the occasion of the Feast of the Triumph of the Cross; published October 15, 1998).
The text of the encyclical is found in *Origins* 28, no. 19 (1998): 317-48.

[15]Philip Rieff, *The Triumph of the Therapeutic: Uses of Faith After Freud* (New York: Harper & Row, 1966);
Paul C. Vitz, *Psychology as Religion: The Cult of Self-Worship,* rev. ed. (Grand Rapids, Mich.: Eerdmans,
1995); Christopher Lasch, *The Culture of Narcissism: American Life as an Age of Diminishing Expectations* (New York: W. W. Norton, 1978); Charles Sykes, *A Nation of Victims: The Decay of American
Character* (New York: Free Press, 1991).

[16]Rieff, *Triumph,* p. 13.

verse as Helmut Thielicke,[17] Michael Novak,[18] J. Budziszewski[19] and John Paul[20] is also invaluable in attempting to reckon with the cultural Zeitgeist;[21] all have written on the problem of nihilism in contemporary culture. More recently, James Davison Hunter has added commentary to this socially pervasive

---

[17]Helmut Thielicke, *Nihilism: Its Origin and Nature with a Christian Answer,* trans. J. W. Doberstein, rev. ed. (New York: Schocken, 1969) and *Death and Life* (Philadelphia: Fortress, 1970).

[18]Novak's personal journey is noteworthy. See, e.g., his introduction to the 1969 revision of Thielicke's *Nihilism;* his work published one year later, *The Experience of Nothingness* (New York: Harper & Row, 1970); his important book *Belief and Unbelief: A Philosophy of Self-Knowledge* (New Brunswick, N.J.: Transaction, 1994), which more or less chronicles his turn to faith from nihilism; and "Awakening from Nihilism," Novak's address presented on May 5, 1994, when he became the twenty-fourth recipient of The Templeton Prize for Progress in Religion, the text of which is reproduced in *First Things* 45 (August-September 1994): 18-22. Novak's analysis of culture is penetrating. For the average Protestant reader, who is unfamiliar with Novak, consider the following excerpt from *Belief and Unbelief,* in which he describes the contradictions embodied in the work of Richard Rorty, perhaps the most popular postmodern philosopher in the American academy. I cite at length his observations about Rorty (cf. my allusion to Rorty in the section "Rediscovering the Wheel," in chap. one, above) to give the reader a taste of Novak, whose personal return from nihilism and trenchant critique of contemporary forms thereof are exceedingly helpful to the Christian community as we attempt to engage the current Zeitgeist head-on: "One of the most ironical characteristics of those who, like Professor Rorty, call themselves nihilists is that they write books. They claim to believe in nothingness, a bedlam in which truth cannot be distinguished from nontruth, a swirling sea of impressions and events for which there is neither top nor bottom, foundation nor direction, but only contingency, accident, hazard, idiotspeak, and randomness all the way down. And yet they dedicate their days . . . of bright . . . skies with the sun streaming through the yellow and red leaves of maples and oaks on campus with a glory that makes one's heart shout . . . to sitting at their writing machines pecking away messages for people in remote climes and times, in full faith that there will be enough rightness about things for those distant others to understand exactly what they are saying. . . . [These] are . . . our nihilists. . . . [Yet they] have a stronger sense of truth than they let on. They value . . . the courage it takes to sit on one's bottom for hours typing, risking hemorrhoids and worse, fighting off stiff necks and weary wrists and sore backs, rubbing one's eyes to remove the ache and to change focus for a moment's blessed relief. All this they do, craving praise for their honesty (and no doubt their solidarity with others), in a world which, as they have elsewhere shown, cares not a fig for their honesty; indeed, permits no possibility of such a thing (nor its opposite, either)" (Novak, *Belief and Unbelief,* p. xxi).

[19]See, e.g., J. Budziszewski, *Written on the Heart* (cited earlier), a nontechnical history of the idea of natural law and its significance for today, and *The Revenge of Conscience* (Dallas: Spence, 1999), a delightfully written account of the author's philosophical journey and retreat from nihilism.

[20]Notably, John Paul's *Veritatis Splendor, Evangelium Vitae* and *Fides et Ratio* contain cogent critiques of, and responses to, the postmodern, therapeutic, antinomian and nihilistic tendencies of contemporary culture.

[21]To the list of sturdy cultural critiques should be added Herbert Schlossberg's *Idols for Destruction: The Conflict of Christian Faith and American Culture,* rev. ed. (Wheaton, Ill.: Crossway, 1990). In this well-researched volume, the author, who is a historian, analyzes American culture under the rubric of "idolatry." Idolatry in its wider meaning is "properly understood as any substitution of what is created for the creator. People may worship nature, money, mankind, power, history, or social and political systems instead of the God who created them all" (p. 6). This process, notes Schlossberg, connotes "turning away from the worship of God while ignoring the fact that something is being turned *to* in its place" (ibid.). The author examines each of these contemporary idols—history, humanity, mammon, nature, power and religion—in the context of contemporary American culture.

phenomenon, speaking of present-day American culture in terms of the present "psychological regime."[22] Finally, requisite reading for laypeople and religious leaders alike would be the writings of theologians Lesslie Newbigin and Alister McGrath, who in creative and thoughtful ways examine the relationship between Christian faith and pluralistic culture.[23]

Given both the challenges imposed by the current social climate as well as the responsibilities of pastors and priests to preserve the traditional notion of priesthood in their congregations and parishes (i.e., helping people toward repentance, forgiveness,[24] faith and a life of sanctification), the aforementioned works would be essential reading.

Assuming that seminary education should supply those who have pastoral responsibilities with resources to equip their congregations, what sort of courses might a seminary offer? Possible course titles might include the following:

- "Evaluating Moral Theory: A Synopsis"
- "Moral Reasoning: Christian and Non-Christian Approaches"
- "The Christian Moral Tradition"
- "Torah as Ethical Guide"
- "Covenantal Perspectives on Christian Social Ethics"
- "Doctrine and Ethics: Differing Hermeneutical Perspectives"
- "Cultivating Virtue in a Therapeutic Culture"
- "Virtue Amidst Vice: The Christian Call to Character Formation"
- "Learning from the Wisdom Perspective"
- "Wisdom in an Age of Information"
- "A Biblical Basis for Christian Social Ethics"
- "The Virtues: A Study in Christian Character"
- "The Virtuous Life"
- "The Christian Stake in Contemporary Ethics"

---

[22]James Davison Hunter, *The Death of Character: Moral Education in an Age Without Good or Evil* (New York: BasicBooks, 2000), esp. chap. 5.

[23]See especially Newbigin's *Foolishness to the Greeks: The Gospel and Western Culture* (Grand Rapids, Mich.: Eerdmans, 1986) and *The Gospel in a Pluralist Society* (Grand Rapids, Mich.: Eerdmans, 1989), and McGrath's *Evangelicalism and the Future of Christianity* (Downers Grove, Ill.: InterVarsity Press, 1995) and *A Passion for Truth: The Intellectual Coherence of Evangelicalism* (Downers Grove, Ill.: InterVarsity Press, 1996).

[24]A volume that should be in every Christian's personal library (especially those with pastoral responsiblities) is Avis Clendenen and Troy Martin, *Forgiveness: Finding Freedom Through Reconciliation* (New York: Crossroad, 2002).

- "The Christian Stake in Contemporary Bioethics"[25]

It is important to emphasize that moral education transcends lists of behavior that are deemed acceptable or unacceptable. That is, moral education is a study of the contours of virtue, sometimes referred to as character ethics; it subsists in the pursuit of becoming good and not merely treating behavior that is symptomatic. Such a pursuit entails studying the great classical texts on Christian ethics that are a part of the "great tradition" as well as being exposed to the grand themes and important texts of the Bible (both Old and New Testaments) that serve as a guide for Christian living. *Every believer,* whether butcher, baker or candlestick-maker, is called to this pursuit; it is not a calling reserved only or primarily for those in the academic guild or for theologians, philosophers and technicians. In this regard, both the pastor and the layperson would benefit immensely from very accessible books on character and virtue written by people such as Peter Kreeft, Donald DeMarco and David Gill.[26] While the works by these three authors are delightful, the books by DeMarco and Gill deserve particular note because of the similarity with which they describe and contextualize for the reader particular virtues in the Christian life; DeMarco writes from a Catholic perspective, Gill from a Protestant. The following books should also be required reading for seminarians: Stanley Hauerwas's *A Community of Character,* Alasdair MacIntyre's *After Virtue,* Oliver O'Donovan's *Resurrection and Moral Order,* the collection of essays edited by Richard John Neuhaus titled *Virtue: Public and Private,* Gilbert Meilaender's *Faith and Faithfulness* and *The Theory and Practice of Virtue,* Vigen Guroian's *Ethics After Christendom* and Timothy Sedgwick's *The Christian Moral Life.*[27] Together,

---

[25]My suggestions for this chapter have fully omitted recommended readings in the sphere of bioethics. Nevertheless, bioethics is presently—and will be in the immediate future—*the* battleground on which competing notions of human personhood, i.e., the very *foundations of ethical thinking,* are clashing. Absolutely critical to evangelical awareness of bioethical issues, and requisite responsible involvement, are the writings of Gilbert Meilaender, Nigel Cameron, John Kilner, Leon Kass, Wesley J. Smith, as well as Paul Ramsey (whose work, though a generation removed, nevertheless contained near-prophetic insight).

[26]Peter Kreeft, *Back to Virtue* (San Francisco: Ignatius, 1992); Donald DeMarco, *The Heart of Virtue* (San Francisco: Ignatius, 1996); and, most recently, David Gill, *Becoming Good: Building Moral Character* (Downers Grove, Ill.: InterVarsity Press, 2000).

[27]Stanley Hauerwas, *A Community of Character* (Notre Dame, Ind.: University of Notre Dame Press, 1981); Alasdair MacIntyre's *After Virtue: A Study in Moral Theory,* 2nd ed. (Notre Dame, Ind.: University of Notre Dame Press, 1984); Oliver O'Donovan's *Resurrection and Moral Order: An Outline for Evangelical Ethics* (Grand Rapids, Mich.: Eerdmans, 1986); the collection of essays edited by Richard John Neuhaus titled *Virtue: Public and Private* (Grand Rapids, Mich.: Eerdmans, 1986); Gilbert Meilaender's *Faith and*

these works offer the student, pastor, priest and layperson a reflective and roundly ecumenical challenge to take seriously the church's ethical mandate in a "post-everything" culture.

CONVERSING WITH CULTURE FROM
WITHIN THE GREAT TRADITION

Implicit in every chapter of this book is the operating assumption that contemporary evangelicals have relatively little engagement with the writings and resources of the church's "great tradition," especially those of the early and medieval church. And yet these resources are important—indeed, they are indispensable—for faithful Christian living in the present. We neglect such resources at our own peril. Evangelical Protestants, at least in their more recent history, are notoriously amnesiac, and too much of our leadership has forgotten or has been blissfully unaware that we are part of a continuum: our faith and our identity rest on what we have received from prior generations of faithful.

Compounding this tendency toward amnesia is the very ethos of postmodernism in which we presently find ourselves. The spirit of the age, which worships today, at best is indifferent to yesterday and at worst loathes the past. Hence, the challenge is great. Given our propensity for shortsightedness and the prevailing cultural climate, evangelicalism may very well transmute into something that scarcely resembles historic Christian faith—quite possibly within the next generation.

It has been said that, theologically, we are like dwarfs sitting on the shoulders of giants. Every successive generation must faithfully transmit to the coming generation the deposit of Christian truth. The tradition which we have received, from which we partake, and which we must hand on to those who follow us is historic Christian orthodoxy. Only because of others, those who faithfully preserved and transmitted the tradition, do we ourselves partake of the bounty of that tradition. Whether the current leadership within Protestant evangelicalism will be faithful to the tradition remains to be seen. But it is critical that those in positions of pastoral and teaching service ponder this question: What will evangelicalism look like twenty-five years from now?

Faithfulness (cited earlier) and his The Theory and Practice of Virtue (Notre Dame, Ind.: University of Notre Dame Press, 1984); Guroian's Ethics After Christendom; and Timothy Sedgwick's The Christian Moral Life: Practices of Piety (Grand Rapids, Mich.: Eerdmans, 1999).

In his important book *American Evangelicalism: Conservative Religion and the Quandary of Modernity,* sociologist James Davison Hunter raises important questions about evangelicalism in its *present* and not future form. He writes,

> While Evangelicalism has not thrown in the towel, as it were, it has conceded a great deal in its encounter with modernity. . . . Whether this cultural accommodation will eventually result in doctrinal compromise remains to be seen. . . . The future strength of the Evangelical movement and the purity of the Evangelical world view are . . . dubious. Popular support will undoubtedly lessen in the long run. It is also reasonable to predict that the Evangelical world view will undergo still further mutations that will make it even less similar to the historic faith than it already is.[28]

Hunter, of course, writes as a sociologist; yet in the end, he is not a critic of evangelicalism but rather one who shares its basic theological convictions. It is significant, moreover, that two decades have passed since he wrote these words—two decades that have brought significant change in the character of evangelical churches. Not all of these changes, it is safe to say, would be applauded by Hunter as we cross the threshold into the new millennium.

No amount of talk about "thinking ethically" or "moral education" or "Christian social ethics" will have any lasting effect without a corresponding and thoroughgoing vision that undergirds and animates moral persuasion. Nor will mere Bible knowledge per se suffice in the critical task of integration. The reason that Protestant evangelicals are not known for their embodiment of a Christian social ethic is largely due to two stubborn factors: our failure to reflect seriously on the social implications of Christian faith and our inattention to, or disavowal of, tradition.[29] To their credit, evangelicals have in their recent history stressed spiritual experience, faith and grace, scriptural inerrancy, and missionary zeal—often in contrast to liberal Protestants and Roman Catholics. Equally to their credit, evangelicals (for the most part) have left their fundamentalist trenches, re-entering the cultural mainstream in the latter half of the twentieth century. In so doing, however, evangelicalism stands at the point of losing its theological distinctiveness. One contemporary critic worries, and with considerable justification, that

---

[28]James Davison Hunter, *American Evangelicalism: Conservative Religion and the Quandary of Modernity* (New Brunswick, N.J.: Rutgers University Press, 1983), p. 133.

[29]Historian Jaroslav Pelikan calls this "a refusal to remember" (*The Vindication of Tradition* [New Haven, Conn.: Yale University Press, 1984], p. 24).

evangelicalism is presently largely defined by social and cultural factors and not theological or historical ones.[30]

If this is true, it should be cause for serious reflection. Although evangelical expansion is evident in the church around the world, and although evangelical churches in America demonstrate extraordinary church growth, one is justified in asking whether, at least at home, the term *evangelical* refers to *form or method* rather than *content*. Is it an exaggeration to say that the very content of contemporary Protestant Christianity is up for grabs, given the prevailing attitude among evangelicals that Christian doctrine and history should no longer inform "faith" and practice?[31]

DRINKING FROM THE STREAM OF THE GREAT TRADITION

As we evangelicals navigate the twenty-first century, we must learn to overcome our inclination toward amnesia, which is only worsened by the contemporary Zeitgeist. In order to take ethics seriously, it behooves us to learn how to think historically and theologically; over the last thirty years, our re-entry into the cultural mainstream notwithstanding, we have been known for neither.

Teaching university undergraduates who represent "pan-evangelicalism," I am confronted on a daily basis by evangelicalism's relative indifference to history and theology, a trait that is often *magnified* in congregational life. Not long ago my wife and children and I took in yet another performance of *Fiddler on the Roof*—this time at a dinner theater on the outskirts of Indianapolis. Regardless of how often one has seen the play, one cannot help but be struck by the importance of its central theme—a theme that comes to full expression when the characters, Tevye in the lead, are dancing in a circle, with their hands above their heads, singing "Tradition." Tevye's character is only meaningful in light of the awareness that tradition is what gives him, his family and

---

[30]D. H. Williams, *Retrieving the Tradition and Renewing Evangelicalism: A Primer for Suspicious Protestants* (Grand Rapids, Mich.: Eerdmans, 1999), pp. 3-4.

[31]This is Williams's conclusion (ibid., pp. 25-26). The content of teaching and preaching in most evangelical congregations would seem to confirm this impression. After we have announced the endless array of programs we offer and engaged in our "happy-clappy" approach to worship, our pulpits offer little more than pablum—a mirror of our desire to be "seeker-friendly" and not offend (a state of affairs that Old Testament prophets would have described as a famine of the word of the Lord; see Amos 8:11; cf. Prov 29:18). It is a simple fact, however tragic, that many if not most pastors of evangelical churches fear a straightforward exposition of the biblical text. "Seeker-friendly" topical sermons are the order of the day. Catechetical instruction in historic Christian faith is virtually nonexistent.

his people their fundamental sense of identity. For this reason, then, when the church is assembled on the sabbath, our confessing of the Apostles' Creed or the Nicene Creed is (or at least should be) a profoundly moving expression of public worship. In these moments the believer realizes that *everything* we believe has been *inherited*—inherited *from* God and *through* others as instruments of God.

Doubtless the absence of theological and ethical guidance in evangelical churches has created a vacuum that is being filled by new gimmicks and techniques in facilitating "outreach" and "ministry." Few have described this lamentable state of affairs within contemporary evangelicalism as lucidly as has D. H. Williams in his important recent book *Retrieving the Tradition and Renewing Evangelicalism*. For this reason I quote Williams at length:

> New trends for church growth or the establishment of "seeker sensitive" settings have replaced the church's corporate memory for directing ecclesial policies and theological education. Pragmatics in ministry threaten to swallow the necessity for theology and marginalize the craft of "reflective understanding" about God which ought to have its primary place of exercise in the church. While pastors have become more efficient administrators and keepers of the institution, along with being excellent performers, they are losing their ability to act as able interpreters of the historic faith. Likewise, biblical exegesis is too often guided by no other authority than the marketplace of ideas and the social and emotional agenda of the congregation. Interpretation of the text is far more indebted to the latest trends in interpersonal dynamics, effective communication style, or popular pastoral psychology. And all the while, the issue of determining Christian identity has lost its way in the mists of emotionally charged and professionally orchestrated worship. . . . This situation, in turn, has led to a loss of coherency within the church as the very content of faith (*fides quae creditur*) no longer informs the central task of the church. Preaching easily slips into the mode of moralizing or entertaining, and eventually the flock of God can no longer stomach the diet which exposes them to or causes them to think deeply about the content of the Christian faith. Congregations are well schooled in neatly dividing the faith into practical and theoretical aspects, believing that only the former is of concern to them.[32]

Happily, increasing numbers within our ranks are growing weary of the seemingly interminable shallowness that characterizes broader evangelical-

---

[32]Ibid., pp. 10, 25. Used by permission.

ism. It is possible to detect in some circles a growing hunger to live, worship and serve with a greater historical-theological awareness that expresses itself in Christian moral formation and a distinctly Christian social ethic. Yet this transformation will not (indeed, it cannot) occur without a conscious and conscientious rediscovery of those resources that constitute the "center" or mainstream of historic Christian belief. The moral education of our own, not to mention moral persuasion aimed toward broader culture, depends on it.

Tradition, as Williams warns, is not something that evangelicals can view as optional.[33] To make any claim for orthodox Christianity means that "the evangelical faith must go beyond itself to the formative eras of that faith, apostolic and patristic, which are themselves the joint anchor of responsible biblical interpretation, theological imagination, and spiritual growth."[34] By "going beyond itself," evangelicalism recognizes that the Christian faith extends far deeper than and is richer than its own frame of reference, important as that frame of reference might be. But given the fact that the evangelical ethos is largely activistic, populist, pragmatic and utilitarian, it inherently allows little room for a broader and deeper intellectual growth, since, as Mark Noll has chronicled with considerable care, it is consumed by the exigencies of the moment.[35] Dynamic, we must remember, should never be a substitute for con-

---

[33]Jaroslav Pelikan helpfully distinguishes between tradition and traditionalism. Whereas the former can be described as the living faith of the dead, the latter can be understood as the dead faith of the living (*Vindication*, pp. 54-61).

[34]Williams, *Retrieving the Tradition*, p. 13. David Wells's much acclaimed *Losing Our Virtue: Why the Church Must Recover Its Moral Vision* (Grand Rapids, Mich.: Eerdmans, 1998) is a fine example of incisive cultural criticism, much in line with his two previous volumes, *No Place for Truth, or, Whatever Happened to Evangelical Theology?* (Grand Rapids, Mich.: Eerdmans, 1993) and *God in the Wasteland* (Grand Rapids, Mich.: Eerdmans, 1994). What the reader misses in *Losing Our Virtue*, however, is any interaction with the considerable resources for moral theology that antedate the Protestant Reformation. It is not an exaggeration, nor is it inflammatory, to contend that there exists no Protestant Christian social ethic, even when Protestants can offer important or unique perspectives on the church's ethical mandate. In the end, Wells does not treat the sickness that he himself so eloquently identifies. I have proposed specific recommendations, in response to Wells, in "Losing Our Moral Theology," *First Things* 89 (January 1999): 50-54. This assessment of Wells's book, it should be pointed out, is shared by Williams, who writes: "It may be rightfully asked . . . whether his [Wells's] tentative solution goes far enough. . . . To point us in the direction of the origins of Protestantism is not a return to Christian roots. For the Reformers were themselves seeking to restore the church in accordance with the model of the early Fathers that they accused medieval Catholicism of having abandoned." Williams believes that "Wells offers no cure for the disease he has diagnosed" (*Retrieving the Tradition*, p. 25).

[35]Noll, *Scandal*, pp. 29-35, 241-53.

tent.[36] If it fails to think historically and to value tradition, evangelicalism, regardless of its numerical growth, will surely devolve intellectually, theologically and socially into a large sect or an American subculture, all the while accommodating itself to and being absorbed by common culture. There is a point, then, at which evangelical Protestants no longer bear anything remotely resembling "Christian identity."[37]

FOR A RENEWAL OF CULTURE

Alister McGrath sounds an optimistic (though realistic) note concerning the future of evangelicalism.[38] McGrath believes that despite our weaknesses,[39] we are "ideally placed" to chart a course that avoids both "a modernism without foundations" as well as "a fundamentalism without modernity."[40] Undergirding McGrath's confidence is the belief that resident within evangelicalism are the seeds of renewal. This ability to experience renewal is predicated at least in part on evangelicalism's continuity with the historic Christian tradition. This tradition, we do well to remember, is not merely a fixed set of ideas or doctrines. It also entails a distinctive ethical tradition or, in the words of Williams, "a bond which defines *the way of faithfulness* throughout the passing ages of the world."[41]

Moral formation does not take place in a social vacuum; it requires the presence of a subculture that *not merely tolerates but actively and tenaciously facilitates* moral development. A recovery of Christian ethics—in the seminary, in the liberal arts curriculum, in the congregation—will need to proceed before any cultural renewal is actualized.[42] Such a project, it goes without saying, is

---

[36]This is forcefully argued by Williams in *Retrieving the Tradition,* pp. 208-14.

[37]While it might be argued that Roman Catholics emphasize continuity of tradition to a fault, evangelicals are inclined to ignore it altogether, dogged by the persistent assumption that Scripture and tradition are mutually exclusive. Evangelicals simply *will not* submit to *any* authority outside the congregational level. This attitude alone may be their undoing, rendering them a large religious sect that is irrelevant both to the purposes of God and the needs of culture.

[38]McGrath, *Evangelicalism and the Future of Christianity.*

[39]These weaknesses are thought to be, inter alia, the curse of the personality cult, legalism, chronic guilt and self-doubt, and a dogmatic spirit with regard to nonessential convictions (ibid., pp. 139-58).

[40]Ibid., p. 51.

[41]Williams, *Retrieving the Tradition,* p. 206, emphasis added.

[42]One might raise the objection that I am placing too much faith in training institutions, since moral formation begins in the home. This I indeed grant: the home is crucial to a child's moral development. But when families live in a cultural environment that actively, even militantly, works against this foundation, those "mediating institutions" that through Christian vision God has called into being alongside the local church play a decisive and necessary role in the equipping process.

long-term in nature; there is no quick fix. Any social movement that has ever set out to capture the hearts and minds of human beings has done so on the basis of a firmly entrenched system of beliefs and deeply held convictions about human nature. After all, as we are frequently reminded, ideas *do* have consequences.

In her wonderful little classic *Creed or Chaos?* Dorothy Sayers minces no words when addressing those who desire a "respectable" Christianity that possesses no ethical teeth:

> The thing I am here to say to you is this: that it is worse than useless for Christians to talk about the importance of Christian morality, unless they are prepared to take their stand upon the fundamentals of Christian theology. It is a lie to say that dogma does not matter; it matters enormously. It is fatal to let people suppose that Christianity is only a mode of feeling; it is vitally necessary to insist that it is first and foremost a rational explanation of the universe. It is hopeless to offer Christianity as a vaguely idealistic aspiration of a simple and consoling kind; it is, on the contrary, a hard, tough, exacting, and complex doctrine, steeped in a drastic and uncompromising realism.[43]

Sayers is frank and unsparing in her critique of the Christian ethics contemporary to her own day. Much of what she has to say could well be applied to American Christians two generations later:

> The brutal fact is that in this . . . country not one person in a hundred has the faintest notion what the Church teaches about God or man or society or the person of Jesus Christ. There are the frank and open heathen, whose notions of Christianity are a dreadful jumble of rags and tags of Bible anecdote and clotted mythological nonsense. There are the ignorant Christians, who combine a mild gentle-Jesus sentimentality with vaguely humanistic ethics. . . . Finally, there are the more or less instructed churchgoers, who know all the arguments about divorce and auricular confession and communion in two kinds, but are about as well equipped to do battle on fundamentals against a Marxist atheist or a Wellsian agnostic as a boy with a peashooter facing a fanfare of machine guns. Theologically, this country is at present in a state of utter chaos, established in the name of religious tolerance, and rapidly degenerating into the flight from reason and the death of hope.[44]

---

[43]Dorothy L. Sayers, *Creed or Chaos?* (reprint; Manchester, N.H.: Sophia Institute Press, 1974), p. 31.
[44]Ibid., pp. 31-32.

In *After Virtue,* MacIntyre challenges his readers to help construct local forms of community by which the intellectual and moral life might be sustained through the "dark ages" that he believes to be already upon us. That community, it goes without saying, must be nourished by ways of thinking and acting that are distinctly Christian. Only by means of persistence and creative energy that anchored in *an abiding tradition* can we faithfully transmit the Christian deposit to the next generation.[45] One may or may not accept MacIntyre's thesis that a new "dark age" is present. But whether or not MacIntyre is right, whether a new "dark age" is already with us or whether it perhaps lies in the future, evangelicals will need a moral vision—a vision rooted in the classical mainstream of the "great tradition"—*if* their witness is to remain viable in neopagan culture.

---

[45]Robert Wilken is correct: "For the task of handing on the faith, the warm heart is insufficient," important as evangelical piety and fervency might be ("Memory and the Christian Intellectual Life," in *Reasoned Faith,* ed. Frank F. Birtel [New York: Crossroad, 1993], p. 165).

Epilogue

A recurring theme in the encyclicals of Pope John Paul II has been the necessity of freedom's harnessing to truth. Speaking from the vantage point of one who has had intimate acquaintance with political tyranny, John Paul addresses those of us who live in a "free" society by reminding us that the wedding of democratic pluralism and moral relativism constitutes a thinly veiled totalitarianism.[1] Indeed, the historical record would seem to vindicate the pontiff: the century immediately behind us constitutes a sobering reminder that freedom is capable of annihilating itself; this occurs when human freedom is no longer tethered to moral principle.

In chapter three I suggested that when moral vision fails, the door is open for the totalitarian option. This "option," it needs to be stressed, requires preparation—preparation that is facilitated by a reconfiguration of the way people

---

[1]Thus, for example, *Veritatis Splendor,* par. 101. Gene Edward Veith Jr. critiques the wedding of democratic pluralism and moral relativism in terms of a "democratic tyranny," that is, a tyranny that though presided over by cultural elites is nevertheless willed into existence by the broader population. See his *Postmodern Times: A Christian Guide to Contemporary Thought and Culture* (Wheaton, Ill.: Crossway, 1994), pp. 166-67. The "end of democracy" debate that surfaced several years ago among some political and legal theorists, though controversial and offensive to some, nevertheless raised questions that demand our consideration. There is a form of tyranny that democratic pluralism is capable of engendering, precisely when it is wed to the ethical relativism against which John Paul warns. See "The End of Democracy: The Judicial Usurpation of Politics," *First Things* 67 (November 1996): 18-42, and "The End of Democracy? A Discussion Continued," *First Things* 69 (January 1997): 19-28.

think about life and death, moral agency and personhood. What sort of world our children and our children's children inherit is inextricably linked to this reconfiguration. For this reason, one cannot overestimate the nature of what is at stake in current ethical debates as well as the importance of present and future Christian involvement in the public square. Western societies, highly secularized though they are, still retain humane features. Yet, as Glenn Tinder observes, our position is morally precarious, for good customs and habits need a spiritual base; if such a base is lacking they will gradually—or perhaps suddenly, in some crisis—disappear. To what extent are we now living on moral savings accumulated over many centuries but no longer being replenished?[2]

Only a half-century removed, we Westerners—and we Americans, in particular—seem to have forgotten a most disturbing fact of recent history: *moral atrocity, couched in medical and scientific justification, is the end result of the encroachment on ethics that implants itself in the realm of medical science.* Consequently, we are increasingly comfortable with speaking of "death with dignity," "compassionate release" and "merciful exit preference" for those we deem "no longer worthy of life itself."[3] This utilitarian strain of thinking, perhaps dormant for several brief decades, would appear to have emerged once more in full force.

Perhaps because I married into a German family and spent the early years of marriage living and studying in (former West) Germany, where the first of our children was born, I am all the more interested in exploring the history of ideas as they refract in contemporary ethical debates. (Unquestionably, the older I become, the more aware I am of the truism that ideas do indeed have consequences, and if there is one legacy I would like to leave with my students, it is precisely this awareness.) My own experience and close identification with German culture doubtless have created a greater sensitivity than I otherwise would have known to recent history and to the character of moral atrocities that lie in the not-too-distant past. And contemplating lessons to be learned, I am struck by several observations; foremost among these are the following:

- The beginnings of scientific and medical depravity are small, marked by subtle shifts in the way personhood is defined and law is defined.

---

[2]Glenn Tinder, *The Political Meaning of Christianity—The Prophetic Stance: An Interpretation* (San Francisco: HarperSanFrancisco, 1991), p. 51.
[3]Recall the attempts to redefine personhood by prominent bioethicists as noted in n. 1 of chap. five, above.

- Given the fact that scientific "progress" invariably outpaces our ability to reflect ethically on that progress, it is critical that the church not remain silent in the face of present or potential evil.

Part of the ethical task, then, is to discern and expose utilitarian ethics when it surfaces.

THE BIOLOGICAL AND ECONOMIC ARGUMENTS

One of the tragic legacies of social Darwinism is that it assisted in giving justification to the elimination of *lebensunwertes Leben,* life that is unworthy of living, or in the language of Darwinists, life that is simply unfit.[4] While it is commonly assumed that the moral atrocities associated with the Holocaust were the exclusive domain of Adolf Hitler and those loyal to him (people such as Joseph Goebbels, Hermann Goering, Heinrich Himmler and Albert Speer), this was only the final act.[5] Indeed it would appear, as authors with such diverse backgrounds as Alexander Mitscherlich, Robert Jay Lifton, Robert Proctor, Michael Burleigh and Wesley Smith have documented, the path to medical evil was prepared long before Nazism was even a cloud on the German horizon.[6]

In addition to the ascendancy of biological determinism,[7] an important step in legitimizing the killing of the weak, the infirm, the terminally ill and the incom-

---

[4]What writer Hugh Gregory Gallagher rather succinctly states as the essence of Darwinian thinking a century ago could very easily be applied to our own day: "The eugenicists and Darwinists, for all their pretensions, made no distinctions within the fitness category. Crooks and prostitutes, the blind, the paralyzed, the retarded, all were degenerate, all were unfit. These were people with weak genes. The degeneracy of their character, as well as the flawed nature of their bodies, was seen to be inherited" (*By Trust Betrayed: Patients, Physicians and the License to Kill in the Third Reich,* rev. ed. [Arlington, Va.: Vandamere, 1995], p. 50).

[5]Perhaps the best resource for understanding not only the indispensable role that Hitler's assistants played in propping up the Third Reich, but also the psychology of totalitarianism as it was played ethically out in their individual lives, is Guido Knopp's *Hitlers Helfer* (Muenchen: Wilhelm Goldmann Verlag, 1996). Unfortunately, this book remains untranslated from the German.

[6]Alexander Mitscherlich and Fred Mielke, *Doctors of Infamy: The Story of the Nazi Medical Crimes* (New York: Henry Schuman, 1949); Robert Jay Lifton, *The Nazi Doctors: Medical Killing and the Psychology of Genocide* (New York: BasicBooks, 1986); Robert Proctor, *Racial Hygiene: Medicine Under the Nazis* (Cambridge, Mass.: Harvard University Press, 1988); Michael Burleigh, *Death and Deliverance: "Euthanasia" in Germany Circa 1900-1945* (Cambridge: Cambridge University Press, 1994); Wesley J. Smith, *Forced Exit: The Slippery Slope from Assisted Suicide to Legalized Murder* (New York: Times Books, 1997) and, more recently, *Culture of Death: The Assault on Medical Ethics in America* (San Francisco: Encounter, 2000).

[7]It is telling that National Socialist leaders commonly referred to the phenomenon of National Socialism (Nazism) as "applied biology." An example of this in the literature is Fritz Lenz, *Menschliche Auslese und Rassenhygiene* (Muenchen: Beck, 1931), which remains untranslated from the German. (The title of this volume translates "Human Selection and Race-Based Health.") Significantly, the 1931 version of Lenz's book was already its *third* edition.

petent was the shift in ethos among medical doctors and psychiatrists several decades prior to World War II. Proctor has argued persuasively that the Nazi experiment was rooted in pre-1933 thinking about the essence of personhood, racial hygienics and survival economics; he has also maintained that physicians were instrumental both in pioneering research and in carrying out this program.[8] In fact, Proctor is adamant that scientists and physicians were pioneers and not pawns in this process. By 1933, however, when political power was consolidated by the National Socialists, resistance within the medical community was too late. Proctor notes, for example, that most of the fifteen-odd journals devoted to racial hygienics were established long before the rise of National Socialism.[9]

Few accounts of this period are more thoroughly researched than Burleigh's *Death and Deliverance: "Euthanasia" in Germany Circa 1900-1945*. Particularly important is Burleigh's discussion of psychiatric reform and medical utilitarianism during the Weimar period.[10] During the years of World War I, it is estimated that over 140,000 people died in German psychiatric asylums.[11] This would suggest that about 30 percent of the entire pre-war asylum population died as a result of hunger, disease or neglect.[12] Following the war, evidence indicates that a shift in the moral climate was in progress. In the spring of 1920, the chairman of the German Psychiatric Association, Karl Bonhoeffer, testified before association members at the annual meeting that "we have witnessed a change in the concept of humanity"; moreover, he said,

> in emphasizing the right of the healthy to stay alive, which is an inevitable result of periods of necessity, there is also a danger of going too far: a danger that the self-sacrificing subordination of the strong to the needs of the helpless and ill, which lies at the heart of any true concern for the sick, will give ground to the demand of the healthy to live.[13]

[8]Robert Proctor, "Nazi Doctors, Racial Medicine and Human Experimentation," in *The Nazi Doctors and the Nuremberg Code: Human Rights in Human Experimentation*, ed. George J. Annas and Michael A. Grodin (New York: Oxford University Press, 1992), pp. 19-31.

[9]Ibid., p. 20.

[10]The Weimar Republic corresponds to the period extending from 1919, the year of a German constitutional assembly at Weimar, to 1933, when the republic was dissolved with Hitler becoming chancellor.

[11]Hans-Ludwig Siemen, *Menschen bleiben auf der Strecke: Psychiatrie zwischen Reform und Nationalsozialismus* (Guetersloh, Germany: Guetersloher Verlag, 1987), pp. 29-30.

[12]This is Burleigh's calculation (*Death*, p. 11).

[13]Karl Bonhoeffer's address was published in the *Allgemeine Zeitschrift fuer Psychiatrie* 76 (1920-1921); the citation is from p. 600 (an English translation of which appears in Burleigh, *Death*, pp. 11-12).

According to Burleigh, Bonhoeffer went on in the 1930s to offer courses that trained those who in time would be authorized with implementing sterilization policies introduced by the National Socialists.[14]

Already in the 1890s, the traditional view of medicine—that physicians are not to harm but only to cure—was being questioned in some corners by a "right-to-die" ethos. Voluntary euthanasia was supported by a concept of negative human worth: the combined notion that suffering negates human worth and that the incurably ill and mentally defective place an enormous burden on families and surrounding communities. It is at this time that the expression "life unworthy of being lived" seems to have emerged and was the subject of heated debate by the time World War I had ended.[15]

One notable "early" proponent of involuntary euthanasia was influential biologist and Darwinian social theorist Ernst Haeckel. In 1899 Haeckel published *The Riddle of the Universe,* which achieved an enormous amount of success and became one of the most widely read science books of the era.[16] One of several influential voices contending for the utility of euthanasia, Haeckel combined the notion of euthanasia as an act of mercy with economic concerns that considerable money might be thereby saved.[17]

Further justification for euthanasia in the pre-World War I era was provided by people such as social theorist Adolf Jost and Nobel Prize-winning chemist Wilhelm Ostwald. According to Ostwald, "In all circumstances suffering represents a restriction upon, and diminution of, the individual and capacity to perform in society of the person suffering."[18] In his 1895 book *Das Recht auf den Tod* ("The Right to Death"), Jost set forth the argument—almost forty years in advance of Nazi prescriptions—that the "right" to kill existed in the context of the higher rights possessed by the state, since all

---

[14]Burleigh, *Death,* p. 12.

[15]This is the view of historians Burleigh (*Death,* pp. 12-13) and Proctor ("The Destruction of 'Lives Not Worth Living,'" chap. 7 of *Racial Hygiene,* pp. 177-222).

[16]According to historian Daniel Gasman, Haeckel's *Riddle* sold more than 100,000 copies in its first year, went through ten editions by 1919, had sold over 500,000 copies by 1933, and in time was translated into twenty-five different languages (*The Scientific Origins of National Socialism: Social Darwinism in Ernst Haeckel and the German Monist League* [New York: American Elsevier, 1971], p. 14). Gasman has called Haeckel "Germany's major prophet of political biology" (p. 150).

[17]See Walter Schmuhl, *Rassenhygiene, Nationalsozialismus, Euthanasie: Von der Verhuetung zur Vernichtung "lebensunwerten Lebens" 1890-1945* (Göttingen: Vanderhoeck & Ruprecht, 1987), esp. p. 109.

[18]This was part of an exchange that was published in Wilhelm Boerner, "Euthanasie," *Das monistische Jahrhundert* 2 (1913): 251-54. An English translation of this text appears in Burleigh, *Death,* p. 14.

individuals belong to the social organism of the state:[19] Furthermore, this was couched in terms of "compassion" and "relief" from one's suffering. Finally, the right to kill compassionately was predicated on biology, in accordance with the spirit of the age: the state must ensure that the social organism remains fit and healthy.[20]

THE LEGAL AND MEDICAL ARGUMENTS

Well before the outbreak of World War I, multiple influential voices appear in the literature agitating for a legalization of assisted death. One such legal proposal is spelled out as follows:[21]

1. Whoever is incurably ill has the right to assisted death.
2. The right to assisted death will be established by the patient's petition to the relevant judicial authorities.
3. On the basis of the petition, the court will instigate an examination of the patient by the court physician in association with two qualified specialists.
4. The record of the examination must show whether the examining doctors were scientifically convinced that the illness was more likely to follow a terminal course than that the patient would recover permanent ability to work.
5. If the examination finds that a terminal outcome is the most probable one, then the court should accord the patient the right to die. In contrary cases, the patient's request will be firmly denied.
6. Whoever painlessly kills the patient as a result of the latter's express and unambiguous request is not to be punished, provided that the patient has been accorded the right to die under clause 5 of the law, or if posthumous examination reveals that he was incurably ill.
7. Whoever kills the patient without his express and unambiguous request will be punished with hard labor.
8. Clauses 1 to 7 are equally applicable to the elderly and crippled.

---

[19]Adolf Jost, *Das Recht auf den Tod: Sociale Studie* (Göttingen: Dietrich'sche Verlagsbuchhandlung, 1895).

[20]English-language assessments of Jost can be found in Lifton (*Nazi Doctors,* p. 46) and Burleigh (*Death,* pp. 12-15), with a more thorough untranslated examination in Klaus Doerner, "Nationalsozialismus und Lebensvernichtung," *Vierteljahrshefte fuer Zeitgeschichte* 15 (1967): 121-52.

[21]This "draft" was originally published in *Das monistische Jahrhundert* 2 (1913): 170-71. A written translation appears in Burleigh, *Death,* pp. 13-14.

In many respects the most significant contribution to the debate over euthanasia[22] was the publication in 1920 of *Die Freigabe der Vernichtung lebensunwerten Lebens: Ihr Mass und ihre Form*, by esteemed law professor Karl Binding
and psychiatrist Alfred Hoche.[23] By 1920 the subject of euthanasia was no longer
merely a matter of academic debate. Binding and Hoche argued with considerable precision that the medical profession had the responsibility not only to
promote health but, where necessary, to facilitate death (*Sterbehilfe*) as well. The
Binding-Hoche book is significant for several reasons. One is the way in which
the authors seek to mainstream the distinction between *lebenswertes Leben* ("life
worth living") and *lebensunwertes Leben* ("life not worth living").[24] Binding attempts to extrapolate from what he believes to be a "weakness" in the German
criminal code by suggesting that certain life (e.g., someone who is "deathly ill
or fatally wounded")[25] "no longer merits full legal protection."[26] Binding laments the fact that distinguishing between worthwhile and unworthwhile life

---

[22]This is the view of American Holocaust historian Lifton (*Nazi Doctors,* pp. 46-48), German historian
Christian Pross ("Nazi Doctors, German Medicine and Historical Truth," in *Nazi Doctors and the
Nuremberg Code: Human Rights in Human Experimentation,* ed. George J. Annas and Michael A. Grodin
[New York: Oxford University Press, 1992], p. 40), American historian Proctor (*Racial Hygiene,* pp.
177-80), British historian Burleigh (*Death,* pp. 15-21), writer Gallagher (*By Trust Betrayed,* p. 60) and
writer/legal expert Smith (*Forced Exit,* pp. 73-75).

[23]Karl Binding and Alfred Hoche, *Die Freigabe der Vernichtung lebensunwerten Lebern: Ihr Mass und ihre
Form* (Leipzig: Felix Meiner Verlag, 1920). The title is usually translated from the German as "The
Permission to Destroy Life Unworthy of Life." This translation, cited in most accounts of this period
(see, for example, the following footnote), does not adequately capture the nuance and the euphemism in the German original. A better rendering would be "Release for the Extermination of Life Unworthy of Being Lived." The German verb *freigeben,* from which the noun *Freigabe* is derived, can
mean "permit," but more often than not it carries the sense of "release" or "set free." (In my research
I came across only one historical source that rendered *Freigabe* as "Release": Proctor's *Racial Hygiene,*
p. 178.) Hence, in the title of Binding and Hoche's volume, this word is probably intended to convey
a *therapeutic* nuance and not merely descriptive or prescriptive function; from the standpoint of euthanasia advocates, people are "released" or "set free" by the act of "mercy killing." *Freigabe* in this
context is a partner-term standing alongside another German euphemism, *Gnadentod* ("mercy
death"). This language, it should be emphasized, comports perfectly with the ethos of contemporary
euthanasia advocates.

[24]The expression "life unworthy of living" occurs regularly throughout *Freigabe* and is never qualified
or questioned: e.g., Binding and Hoche, *Freigabe,* pp. 24, 51 and 53. See the English translations of
these passages on pp. 244, 258 and 260, respectively, of Karl Binding and Alfred Hoche, "Permitting
the Destruction of Unworthy Life," trans. W. E. Wright and P. G. Derr, *Issues in Law and Medicine* 5,
no. 2 (1992): 231-65. (One of the translators received his medical degree from the Johann Wolfgang
von Goethe University of Frankfurt in 1925, where he attended lectures in neurology and psychiatry
by co-author Hoche. Reprints of this translation can be obtained by writing to The Editor, *Issues in
Law and Medicine,* P.O. Box 1586, Terre Haute, IN 47808.)

[25]In the German this reads *"einer Todkranker oder toedlich Verwundete"* (Binding and Hoche, *Freigabe,* p. 24).

[26]Ibid., pp. 24-25.

"has made no progress"[27] in the actual practice of German criminal law, although in the academic literature it has "gained a lively reception."[28]

What's more, the authors stress that ending "life unworthy of living" had a *therapeutic* goal. But in what instances was the facilitation of death necessary? Binding and Hoche carefully reasoned that certain categories of persons were living "unworthy" lives but also that assisting in their death was ethically, medically and economically justifiable. These categories included the retarded, the deformed, the mentally ill[29] and the severely disabled.[30]

Freigabe consists of two essays, the first being a "legal explanation" by Binding, whose reflections followed forty years of teaching law at the university level; the second is a "medical explanation" by Hoche. What follows is a summary of their twofold argument—an argument that is remarkably similar to the one being advocated by present-day proponents of assisted death.[31]

Binding, one of Germany's leading constitutional scholars, restates a question that has "much occupied" his thinking for many years "but which most people timidly avoid because it is seen as delicate and hard to answer."[32] His question is this: "Should permissible taking of life be restricted, except in emergency situations, to an individual's act of suicide as it is in current law, or should it be legally extended to the killing of fellow human beings, and under what conditions?"[33] Binding is a passionate and deeply committed secularist. Foreclosing any debate, he asserts unequivocally:

> Religious reasons have no probative force in law for two reasons. First, in this instance, they rest on a wholly unworthy concept of God. Second, law is thor-

---

[27]Here the English translation ("has had no continuation," p. 245) is awkward and misses the sense of the German original: "hat . . . im Reichsstrafgesetz keinen Fortgang . . . gefunden" (Binding and Hoche, *Freigabe*, p. 25).

[28]Binding and Hoche, *Freigabe,* p. 25.

[29]In a remarkable comment confined to a footnote, Binding insinuates that death would prevent the "mentally dead" person, or "idiot," from having to endure the shame of being a public spectacle and the mistreatment that results from other people's verbal abuse. "The life of such poor people is an unending invitation to die" (my translation of *Das Leben solcher Armen ist ein ewiges Spiessrutenlaufen,* ibid., p. 26).

[30]These individuals Binding calls *die unrettbaren Kranken,* "the hopelessly ill" (e.g., ibid., p. 34).

[31]My own commentary on the Binding-Hoche book is based on the German original, but for the benefit of the reader I locate most of the citations in the English translation of *Freigabe* cited in n. 24, above. Where the Wright-Derr translation is weak or misses particular nuances of the authors' language, I allude in the footnotes directly to the pages of the German original. (In addition, it is somewhat distracting that the translators' enumeration of footnotes does not follow that of the authors.)

[32]Ibid., pp. 231-32.

[33]Ibid., p. 232.

oughly secular and is focused on the regulation of our external common life. Additionally, the New Testament says nothing about the problem of suicide.[34]

Binding's prejudice against religion allows him to re-cast traditional Christian morality as the true villain, thereby paving the way for a universal "right to die":

> After an extended, deeply unchristian interruption in the recognition of this right [the right to end one's life] (an interruption demanded by the church and supported by the obscene idea that the God of love could wish that human beings not die until they undergo endless physical and spiritual suffering) . . . it has now been fully reestablished (except in a few backward countries) as an inalienable possession for all time. Natural law would have grounds for calling this freedom the primary "human right." . . . For the law, nothing else remains except to regard the living person as the sovereign of his own existence and manner of life.[35]

Based on the above presuppositions, Binding reasons that the right of persons to kill themselves is to be protected legally.[36] Moreover, this "right" is "transferable" to "all so-called accomplices who act with the suicide's express consent."[37] The practical rationale for euthanasia is that it "replaces a death which is painful . . . with a less painful death."[38] To reassure his audience, Binding adds, "This is not 'an act of killing in the legal sense' but is rather the modification of an irrevocably present cause of a death which can no longer be evaded. *In truth it is a purely healing act.*"[39] Such "healing intervention" must extend even to "unconscious patients," since, according to Binding, "the permission of the suffering patient is not required."[40]

THE "COMPASSION" ARGUMENT

Anticipating his readers' objections, Binding assures them that "in truth it [the previous question] arises from nothing but the deepest sympathy."[41] "The act

---

[34]Ibid., p. 233.
[35]Ibid., pp. 233, 237. This statement is staggering not only for its hubris but its distortion of language, its distortion of Christian belief and its distortion of natural-law thinking.
[36]Binding acknowledges that in 1885 he had written from the opposite viewpoint, arguing that assisted death should remain illegal (*verboten;* see Binding and Hoche, *Freigabe,* p. 19 n. 32). Binding's sole objection to the legality of suicide is the possible loss of potentially valuable members of society.
[37]"Permitting the Destruction," pp. 236-37. In fact, Binding asserts that "this act must be considered as not legally forbidden even when the law does not explicitly recognize it" (ibid., p. 241).
[38]Ibid., p. 240.
[39]Ibid., emphasis in original.
[40]Ibid., p. 241.
[41]Ibid., p. 246.

of euthanasia," he intones, "must be a consequence of free sympathy."[42] Thus, given the combination of his illustrious career teaching law and his thinking about "the hopelessly ill," which is motivated by the "deepest sympathy," Binding seems well-positioned to pose questions that "raise an uneasy feeling in anyone who is accustomed to assessing the value of individual life."[43] One such question is this: "Are there human lives which have so completely lost the attribute of legal status . . . that their continuation has permanently lost all value, both for the bearer of that life and for society?"[44] Binding's own response has the ring of authority as well as common sense:

> It is impossible to doubt that there are living people to whom death would be a release, and whose death would simultaneously free society and the state from carrying a burden which serves no conceivable purpose, except that of providing an example of the greatest unselfishness.[45]

Binding's reflections compel him to tread—and agitate—where German society heretofore has not legally trod:

> Is it our duty actively to advocate for this life's asocial continuance . . . or to permit its destruction under specific conditions? One could also state the question legislatively, like this: Does the energetic preservation of such life deserve preference . . . ? Or does permitting its termination, which frees everyone involved, seem the lesser evil?[46]

Because his logic appears to be airtight, Binding is resolute:

> I cannot find the least reason—legally, socially, ethically or religiously—not to permit those requested to do so to kill such hopeless cases who urgently demand death; indeed I consider this permission to be simply a duty of legal mercy (a mercy which also asserts itself in many other forms).[47]

Binding then proceeds to discuss "the necessary means" of carrying this "duty of legal mercy." "With good reason," he observes, "permission always presupposes a clinical diagnosis." This diagnosis, moreover, "requires competent objective verification, which cannot possibly be placed in the agent's own

---

[42]Ibid., p. 252.
[43]Ibid., p. 246.
[44]Ibid.
[45]Ibid.
[46]Ibid., pp. 246-47.
[47]Ibid., p. 248.

hands."[48] He recommends two steps:

- "The initiative must take the form of an application for permission from a qualified applicant."[49]
- "This application goes to a government board, whose primary task is limited to investigating whether the presuppositions for permission are met."[50]

According to the Binding prescription, each case was to be evaluated by a three-person panel consisting of a physician, a psychiatrist and a lawyer, who "alone have the right to vote."[51] This "Permission Board" shall decree that

> after thorough investigation on the basis of current scientific opinion, the patient seems beyond help; that there is no reason to doubt the sincerity of his consent; that accordingly no impediment stands in the way of killing the patient; and that the petitioner is entrusted with bringing about the patient's release from his evil situation in the most expedient way.[52]

Death, according to this process, was to be "expertly" administered by a physician, in whom the right to grant death was a "natural extension of the responsibilities of the attending physician"; the "final release must be completely painless, and only qualified persons are justified in applying the means."[53]

And what about the possibility of error? Binding is confident that scientific consensus operates beyond the realm of error. Of course, he realizes that despite the morally promiscuous era of which he is apart, objections to "mercy killing" will be many. Proof of "alleged error by the Permission Board would be very difficult to come by," he assures the potential Permission Board member; nonetheless, "the possibility of error by the Permission Board is undeniable."[54] Indeed,

> error is possible in all human actions, and no one would draw the foolish conclusion that, considering this possible defect, we must forego all useful and

---

[48]Ibid., p. 251. Note, as well, that this diagnosis cannot be placed in the hands of family members or spiritual leaders.

[49]Instigation of the request, however, may originate with relatives or the person's doctor.

[50]Ibid., p. 252.

[51]Ibid.

[52]Ibid.

[53]Ibid. The authors use several German words in the text therapeutically and euphemistically to speak of the patient's "release." The term here is *Erloesung*, which can be translated "solution" or "salvation" as well as "release."

[54]Ibid., p. 254.

wholesome activities. Even the physician in private practice can make errors which have serious consequences, but no one would bar him from practice because he is capable of erring. *What is good and reasonable must be done despite the risk of error.*[55]

Ultimately, however, even the possibility of fatal mistakes should not stand in the way of carrying out Binding's "good and reasonable" prescription, which is the elimination of "life unworthy of living." Professor Binding's self-proclaimed "deepest sympathy" for "valueless lives" comes to full expression at the conclusion of his essay: "But humanity loses so many members through error that one more or one less really scarcely matters."[56]

In the second essay of *Freigabe,* Hoche examines the medical relationship of physicians to their patients and the physicians' relationship to killing. Hoche opens the essay by observing that a "code of medical ethics is nowhere explicitly established":

There is no medical moral law set out in paragraphs, no *Moral Service Regulations.* The young physician enters practice without any legal delineation of his rights and duties—especially regarding the most important points. Not even the Hippocratic Oath, . . . with its generalities, is operative today.[57]

In practice, what physicians "may do, or ought to do, emanates from peer opinion." Indeed, writes Hoche, in some instances physicians "are compelled to destroy life"—for example, in "killing a living child during delivery for the purpose of saving the mother, terminating a pregnancy for the same reason." This is done "in the interest of serving a higher good."[58] Furthermore, "in all surgical procedures, one tacitly counts on a certain percentage of fatal outcomes," and these "can never be wholly avoided. Our moral sensibility is completely reconciled to this."[59]

One recurring "inner dilemma" that "not infrequently touches the physician" is whether or not, through "passive acquiescence," to yield to the "temptation to let nature run its course" in matters of dying. Hoche is convinced that in certain cases such "passive acquiescence" to natural death is to be resisted. For example, "when the patient is incurably mentally ill," then "death is at all

[55]Ibid., emphasis in original.
[56]Ibid.
[57]Ibid., p. 255.
[58]Ibid., p. 256.
[59]Ibid.

events preferable."[60] Hoche emphasizes how "immensely complicated it has already become for doctors to balance, in daily life, the rigid basic principles of medical ethics and the demands of a higher conception of life's value"; and when these two stand in conflict, the physician "must recognize" that "he has no absolute relation to this [latter] obligation in all circumstances."[61] Rather, "this relation is merely relative, alterable under new conditions, and always open to question." Medical ethics, as Hoche understands it, "cannot be viewed as an eternally fixed pattern."[62] For example,

> If killing incurables or eliminating those who are mentally dead should come to be recognized (and generally acknowledged) as not only unpunishable, but as desirable for the general welfare, then, from that very moment, no opposing grounds for excluding this could be found in medical ethics.[63]

Hoche is not unmindful of practical concerns as he ponders the ethical duties of the medical profession. Extreme cases of "hopeless illness" that require the continuation of life, in Hoche's view, render "nonsensical" the need for life-saving measures. In posing the question, "Is there human life which has utterly forfeited its claim to worth . . . that its continuation has forever lost all value both for the bearer of that life and society?" Hoche answers "with certainty: Yes." One example of this is what Hoche calls "mental death": that is, the condition of people who are deemed "complete idiots," those "whose existence weighs most heavily on the community."[64]

WHEN ALL ELSE FAILS: ECONOMICS AS TRUMP CARD

Hoche instinctively moves to the economic dimensions of caring for those who are said to "burden the community." He calculates, based on the number of "complete idiots" cared for in German institutions in his day, the amount of money and resources that would be saved. His calculations show that, were Binding's recommendations acted upon, "it is easy to estimate what *incredible capital* is withdrawn from the nation's wealth for food, clothing, and heating—for an unproductive purpose."[65] This great loss due to

---

[60]Ibid., p. 257.
[61]Ibid.
[62]Ibid., pp. 257-58.
[63]Ibid., p. 258.
[64]Ibid., p. 260.
[65]Ibid., pp. 260-61.

"such dead weight" of "valueless lives" calls for "the liberation of every available power for productive ends."[66]

Hoche is not naive in realizing that overturning conventional thinking, especially at the popular level, takes time and conditioning. Legislative as well as religious roadblocks serve as an additional impediment to the advancement of scientific thinking. Hoche waxes realistic:

> The enormous difficulty of trying to address these problems legislatively will continue for a long time. Likewise, the ideas of gaining relief from our national burden by permitting the destruction of wholly worthless mentally dead persons will (from the start and for a long time) encounter lively, strident, and passionately stated opposition. This opposition will draw its strength from many different sources: resistance to the new and unfamiliar, religious ideas, sentimental feelings, and so on.[67]

Up to now, he laments, when the "the individual's subjective right to exist" has clashed with "objective expediency and necessity," the former has typically won. This "difficult" problem has been a result of "the essential participation of Christian ideas." But "alien perspectives" should not prevent us from realizing—and acting on the conviction—that "valueless lives" and "dead-weight existences" are a drain to society as a "civil organism."[68]

PUTTING EUTHANASIA IN PERSPECTIVE: THE PREPARATION OF AN IDEA

In 1933, with the accession of the National Socialists to power, two developments that had reached their critical mass were promptly codified into law. One was the long-discussed sterilization program, which had been debated but had not achieved majority support. The second was authorized euthanasia. The proposal, issued by the German Ministry of Justice, was reported on the front page of *The New York Times*: "It shall be made possible for physicians to end the tortures of incurable patients, upon request, in the interests of true humanity." Moreover, the Ministry ensured, "no life still

---

[66]Ibid., pp. 261, 262. Hoche's sheer arrogance and inhumanity are breathtaking. He writes: "Naturally no doctor would conclude with certainty that a two- or three-year-old was suffering permanent mental death. But, *even in childhood,* the moment comes when this prediction can be made without doubt" (ibid., p. 265, emphasis in original).
[67]Ibid., p. 261.
[68]Ibid., p. 262.

valuable to the state will be wantonly destroyed."[69]

Andrew C. Ivy, M.D., asked in 1946 by the Board of Trustees of the American Medical Association to serve as a consultant at the Nuremberg trial of Nazi physicians who had been indicted for "crimes against humanity," reflected on his difficult experience with the following observation:

> It was inconceivable that a group of men trained in medicine and in official positions of power in German governmental circles could ignore the ethical principles of medicine and the unwritten law that a doctor should be nearer humanity than other men. . . . We had assumed that the sacred aspects of medicine and its ethics would certainly remain inviolate.[70]

Although, according to Ivy, "fewer than two hundred German physicians participated directly in the medical war crimes," it became clear to Ivy that these atrocities were only "the end result" of the "complete encroachment on the ethics and freedom of medicine" by those in positions of influence.[71]

Two or three generations removed, this utilitarian strain of thinking, perhaps dormant for several brief decades, is once again dominant as we stand before scientific breakthroughs. Utilitarian thinking about ethics is ubiquitous; it is the air we breathe, propagated by ethicists, health-care practitioners, social theorists and sundry consultants, all of whom weigh the value of personhood against the economics of health care and the cumulative "burden" on society.[72] Lacking any strong commitment to the sanctity of life, utilitarian ethicists and practitioners adopt a "quality-of-life" ethic. The inevitable question that follows is this: At what point does an individual no longer have a "quality of life" that is "worthy of life" itself? With justification, bioethicist Leon Kass has warned, "There is the very real danger that what constitutes a 'meaningful life' among the intellectual elite will be imposed on the people as the only standard by which the value of human life is measured."[73]

Consider the following dilemma, "Problem 97," found in a German mathematics textbook published in 1935:

---

[69]"Nazis Plan to Kill Incurables to End Pain: German Religious Groups to Oppose Move," *New York Times,* October 8, 1933, p. 1.
[70]Quoted in the foreword to Mitscherlich and Mielke, *Doctors of Infamy,* pp. ix-x.
[71]Ibid., pp. x-xi.
[72]See, e.g., Daniel Callahan's book *Setting Limits: Medical Goals in an Aging Society* (New York: Simon & Schuster, 1987) as well as the rather breathtaking essay by John Hardwig, "Is There a Duty to Die?" *Hastings Center Report* 27, no. 2 (1997): 34-42. (Callahan edits the *Hastings Center Report.*)
[73]Leon Kass, in a personal interview with author Wesley Smith, cited in Smith, *Culture of Death,* p. 9.

A mental patient costs about 4 RMS [i.e., 4 Reichmarks] a day to keep, a cripple 5.50 RMS, a Criminal 3.50 RMS. In many cases a civil servant only has about 4 RMS, a salaried employee scarcely 3.50 RMS, an unskilled worker barely 2 RMS for his family. (a) Illustrate these figures with the aid of pictures. According to conservative estimates, there are about 300,000 mental patients, epileptics, etc., in asylums in Germany. (b) What do they cost together per annum at a rate of 4 RMS per person? . . . How many marriage loans at 1,000 RMS each could be awarded per annum with this money, disregarding later repayment?[74]

The solution to "Problem 97" follows:

Assuming an average daily outlay of 3.50 RMS there hereby results:
a daily savings of RM 245.955
an annual saving of RM 88,543.98
assuming a life expectancy of ten years . . .

Eight hundred and eighty-five million four hundred and thirty-nine thousand eight hundred Reichmarks . . . will have been, or has already been, saved by 1 September 1951 by reason of the disinfection of 70,273 persons which has been carried out to date.[75]

Proctor has argued that the primary impetus for forcible euthanasia in the 1930s was economic: assisted death was justified as a kind of "preemptive triage" to free up beds.[76] Persons who were considered a burden on German society included handicapped infants, the mentally ill, the terminally ill, the comatose and the criminal element. By 1941, euthanasia had become part of normal hospital routine.[77] This disposal, or "disinfection," of human lives, however, was to be done "humanely and economically."[78] But let it be empha-

---

[74]Adolf Doerner, ed., *Mathematik im Dienste der nationalpolitischen Erziehung mit Anwendungsbeispielen aus Volkswissenschaft, Gelaendekunde und Naturwissenschft* (Frankfurt am Main: Fischer, 1935), p. 42. (An English translation of the title would be "Mathematics in the Service of National Political Education with Examples Drawn from Social Science, Folk Art and Natural Science." An English translation of this math problem, with the title untranslated, appears in Burleigh, *Death*, p. ix.)

[75]From a digest found in 1945 at Schloss Hartheim, one of six killing centers where organized euthanasia was being performed on adults during the war. This is Exhibit 39T-1021, Heidelberger Dokumente, Roll 18, Item 000-12-463, of the National Archives, Washington, D.C.

[76]Proctor, "Nazi Doctors," p. 24.

[77]Ibid.

[78]Lest we think that was then but this is now, in 1942 an article was published in the *Journal of the American Psychiatric Association* that called for the killing of retarded children ("nature's mistakes"). Elsewhere Proctor has noted that until reports of wholesale Nazi exterminations began to appear in American newspapers in 1942, the merits of forced euthanasia were being vigorously debated in various American scholarly journals. See his *Racial Hygiene*, pp. 179-89.

sized that most of the people advocating assisted death at this time were, relatively speaking, ordinary, good, hard-working, loyal people who surely thought of themselves as engaged in the service of mankind through a philosophically neutral practice of science and medicine.[79]

Writing in 1989, the late Cardinal John O'Connor of New York City, an ardent pro-life advocate, predicted that euthanasia would "dwarf the abortion phenomenon in magnitude, in numbers, in horror."[80] When one considers the sheer number of abortions that are performed each year and that have been performed over the last three decades, this statement borders on fantastic. But Cardinal O'Connor's are not the words of someone given to exaggeration. While there is nothing inevitable about human predictions, O'Connor's words are haunting. What is it that can hinder this "prophecy" from coming to pass?[81]

Such, I dare say, will be the true test of our moral vision in the days ahead.

---

[79]And if this be the case, surely Gilbert Meilaender is right when he warns that "it is always fair, appropriate, and important to ask what kind of bioethics can best protect us against the possibilities for evil that may lie within us" (*Body, Soul and Bioethics* [Notre Dame, Ind.: University of Notre Dame Press, 1995], p. 105), for after all, we who live two or three generations removed from unspeakable atrocity are convinced that *we too* are ordinary, good, hard-working, loyal people engaged in serving humankind through our own philosophically neutral practice of science and medicine.

[80]John Cardinal O'Connor, "A Cardinal's Chilling Warning," *New Covenant*, May 1989, pp. 23-24.

[81]Following a public referendum in the state of Washington that turned back the permission to assist death, but before Oregon's approval of the same, the Ramsey Colloquium of the Institute on Religion and Public Life in New York City produced an eloquent statement of the Jewish and Christian understanding of euthanasia. The colloquium, consisting of Jewish and Christian theologians, ethicists and philosophers—and named after Paul Ramsey (1913-1988), the distinguished Protestant ethicist who was a pioneer in the field of contemporary medical ethics—issued a declaration that was published in the journal *First Things* 20 (February 1992): 45-47, and appeared in abbreviated form in the November 27, 1991, issue of the *Wall Street Journal*.

Bibliography

Arendt, Hannah. *Eichmann in Jerusalem: A Report on the Banality of Evil.* Rev. ed. New York: Viking, 1964.

———. *The Origins of Totalitarianism.* Rev. ed. New York: Harcourt, Brace & World, 1966.

Aristotle. *Nicomachean Ethics.* 3rd ed. Translated by M. Ostwald. New York: Macmillan, 1986.

Attarian, John. "In Dispraise of Tolerance, Sensitivity and Compassion." *The Social Critic,* spring 1998, pp. 14-23.

Bahnsen, Greg L., Walter C. Kaiser Jr., Douglas J. Moo, Wayne G. Strickland, and Willem A. VanGemeren. *Five Views on Law and Gospel.* Grand Rapids, Mich.: Zondervan, 1996.

Ball, Terence. "What's Wrong with 'Values'?" *New Oxford Review,* May 1996, pp. 6-11.

Beckwith, Francis, and Gregory Koukl. *Relativism.* Grand Rapids, Mich.: Baker, 1998.

Berman, Morris. *The Twilight of America Culture.* New York: W. W. Norton, 2000.

Berman, Ronald, ed. *Solzhenitsyn at Harvard: The Address, Twelve Early Responses, and Six Later Reflections.* Washington, D.C.: Ethics and Public Policy Center, 1980.

Bloesch, Donald G. *The Evangelical Renaissance.* Grand Rapids, Mich.: Eerdmans, 1973.

Braaten, Carl E. "Eschatology and History." In *New Directions in Theology Today.* Volume 2, *History and Hermeneutics,* pp. 160-79. Philadelphia: Westminster Press, 1966.

———. *No Other Gospel! Christianity Among the World's Religions.* Minneapolis: Fortress, 1992.

———. "Protestants and Natural Law." *First Things,* May 1992, pp. 20-26.

———. *The Two Cities of God: The Church's Responsibility for the Earthly City.* Grand Rapids, Mich.: Eerdmans, 1997.

Budziszewski, J. "The Illusion of Moral Neutrality." *First Things,* August/September 1993.

———. *The Revenge of Conscience: Politics and the Fall of Man.* Dallas: Spence, 1999.

———. *True Tolerance: Liberalism and the Necessity of Judgment.* New Brunswick, N.J.: Transaction, 1992.

Burke, Thomas J., ed. *The Christian Vision: Man and Morality.* Hillsdale, Mich.: Hillsdale College Press, 1986.

Chang, Curtis. *Engaging Unbelief: A Captivating Strategy from Augustine and Aquinas.* Downers Grove, Ill.: InterVarsity Press, 2000.

Charles, J. Daryl. "Blame It on the Beta-Boosters: Genetics, Self-Determination and Moral Accountability." In *Genetic Engineering: A Christian Response,* edited by T. J. Demy and G. S. Stewart, pp. 241-58. Grand Rapids: Kregel, 1999.

————. "Engaging the (Neo)Pagan Mind." *Trinity Journal,* n.s. 16 (1995): 47-62.

————. "Evangelicals and Catholics: One Year Later." *Pro Ecclesia* 5, no. 1 (1996): 73-90.

————. "Garnishing with the 'Greater Righteousness': The Disciples' Relationship to the Law (Matthew 5:17-20)." *Bulletin for Biblical Research* 12, no. 1 (2002): 1-15.

————. "Losing Our Moral Theology." *First Things,* January 1999, pp. 50-54.

————. "Two Evangelical Manifestos." *Regeneration Quarterly,* spring 2001, pp. 37-39.

————. "Vice and Virtue Lists." In *Dictionary of New Testament Background,* edited by Craig A. Evans and Stanley E. Porter, pp. 1252-57. Downers Grove, Ill.: InterVarsity Press, 2000.

————. *Virtue Amidst Vice. JSNTSS* 150. Sheffield: Sheffield Academic Press, 1997.

Charry, Ellen T. "The Moral Function of Doctrine." *Theology Today,* April 1992, pp. 31-45.

Chesterton, G. K. *Orthodoxy.* Rev. ed. Wheaton, Ill.: Harold Shaw, 1994.

————. *Saint Thomas Aquinas: The Dumb Ox.* New York: Doubleday, 1956.

Conyers, A. J. *The Long Truce: How Toleration Made the World Safe for Power and Profit.* Dallas: Spence, 2001.

Cromartie, Michael, ed. *Preserving Grace: Protestants, Catholics and Natural Law.* Grand Rapids, Mich.: Eerdmans, 1997.

Crosby, John F. "Education and the Mind Redeemed." *First Things,* December 1991, pp. 23-28.

Cutsinger, James S., ed. *Reclaiming the Great Tradition: Evangelicals, Catholics and Orthodox in Dialogue.* Downers Grove, Ill.: InterVarsity Press, 1997.

Delattre, Edwin J. *Education and the Public Trust: The Imperative for Common Purposes.* Washington, D.C.: Ethics and Public Policy Center, 1988.

DeMarco, Donald. *The Heart of Virtue.* San Francisco: Ignatius, 1996.

Dulles, Avery. *The Survival of Dogma.* Rev. ed. New York: Crossroad, 1987.

Ellul, Jacques. *The Humiliation of the Word.* Translated by J. Hanks. Grand Rapids, Mich.: Eerdmans, 1985.

————. *The Subversion of Christianity.* Grand Rapids, Mich.: Eerdmans, 1986.

————. *To Will and to Do: An Ethical Research for Christians.* Philadelphia: Pilgrim, 1969.

Elshtain, Jean Bethke. *Democracy on Trial.* New York: BasicBooks, 1995.

Erickson, Millard J. *Truth or Consequences: The Promise and Perils of Postmodernism.* Downers Grove, Ill.: InterVarsity Press, 2001.

Fackre, Gabriel. *Judgment Day at the White House: A Critical Declaration Exploring Moral Issues and the Political Use and Abuse of Religion.* Grand Rapids, Mich.: Eerdmans, 1999.

Finnis, John. *Aquinas.* Oxford: Oxford University Press, 1998.

Foster, Richard. *Celebration of Discipline.* San Francisco, Calif.: Harper & Row, 1978.

George, Robert P., ed. *Natural Law Theory: Contemporary Essays.* Rev. ed. Oxford: Clarendon Press, 1996.

Gill, David W. *Becoming Good: Building Moral Character.* Downers Grove, Ill.: InterVarsity Press, 2000.

Glendon, Mary Ann. *Rights Talk: The Impoverishment of Political Discourse.* New York: Free Press, 1991.

Glendon, Mary Ann, and David Blankenhorn, eds. *Seedbeds of Virtue*: New York: Madison, 1995.

Guinness, Os. *Fit Bodies, Fat Minds: Why Evangelicals Don't Think and What to Do About It.* Grand Rapids, Mich.: Baker, 1994.

Guroian, Vigen. *Ethics After Christendom: Toward an Ecclesial Christian Ethic.* Grand Rapids, Mich.: Eerdmans, 1994.

Haas, John M., ed. *Crisis of Conscience.* New York: Crossroad, 1996.

Hauerwas, Stanley. *A Community of Character.* South Bend, Ind.: University of Notre Dame Press, 1981.

Hays, Richard B. *The Moral Vision of the New Testament.* San Francisco: HarperSanFrancisco, 1996.

Henry, Carl F. H. *Remaking the Modern Mind.* Grand Rapids, Mich.: Eerdmans, 1946.

———. *The Uneasy Conscience of Modern Fundamentalism.* Grand Rapids, Mich.: Eerdmans, 1947.

Himmelfarb, Gertrude. *The De-moralization of Society: From Victorian Virtues to Modern Values.* New York: Alfred A. Knopf, 1995.

———. *On Looking into the Abyss.* New York: Alfred A. Knopf, 1994.

———. *One Nation, Two Cultures.* New York: Alfred A. Knopf, 1999.

Hofstadter, Richard. *Anti-intellectualism in American Life.* New York: Alfred A. Knopf, 1963.

Holmes, Arthur F. *Ethics: Approaching Moral Decisions.* Downers Grove, Ill.: InterVarsity Press, 1984.

Hunter, James D. *American Evangelicalism: Conservative Religion and the Quandary of Modernity.* New Brunswick, N.J.: Rutgers University Press, 1983.

———. *Culture Wars: The Struggle to Define America.* New York: BasicBooks, 1990.

———. *The Death of Character.* New York: BasicBooks, 2000.

Imber, Jonathan B. "American Therapies and Pieties." *The American Enterprise,* May/June 1993, pp. 18-22.

Irvine, William B. "Confronting Relativism." *Academic Questions,* winter 2000/2001, pp. 42-49.

Jenson, Robert W. "The Kingdom of America's God." In *Essays in Theology and Culture,* pp. 50-66. Grand Rapids, Mich.: Eerdmans, 1995.

John Paul II. *Evangelium Vitae* ("The Gospel of Life"). Reproduced in *Origins,* April 6, 1995, pp. 689-725.

———. *Fides et Ratio* ("Faith and Reason"). Reproduced in *Origins,* October 22, 1998, pp. 315-47.

———. *Veritatis Splendor* ("The Splendor of Truth"). Reproduced in *Origins,* October 14, 1992, pp. 297-334.

Jones, David. *Biblical Christian Ethics.* Grand Rapids, Mich.: Baker, 1994.

Kaminer, Wendy. *I'm Dysfunctional, You're Dysfunctional.* New York: Wesley-Addison, 1993.

Keller, E. F. *Refiguring Life: Metaphors of Twentieth Century Biology.* New York: Columbia University Press, 1995.

William Kilpatrick. *Why Johnny Can't Tell Right from Wrong: Moral Illiteracy and the Case for Character Education.* New York: Simon & Schuster, 1992.

Kirk, Russell. *Redeeming the Time.* Edited by Jeffrey O. Nelson. Wilmington, Del.: Intercollegiate Studies Institute, 1996.

Kmiec, Douglas. "America's 'Culture War': The Sinister Denial of Virtue and the Decline of Natural Law." *Saint Louis University Public Law Review* 13, no. 1 (1993): 183-205.

Kuyper, Abraham. *Lectures on Calvinism.* Rev. ed. Grand Rapids, Mich.: Eerdmans, 1987.

Lapide, Pinchas. *The Sermon on the Mount.* Maryknoll, N.Y.: Orbis, 1986.

Larkin, William J., Jr. *Culture and Biblical Hermeneutics: Interpreting and Applying the Authoritative Word in a Relativistic Age.* Grand Rapids, Mich.: Baker, 1988.

Lasch, Christopher. *The Culture of Narcissism: American Life as an Age of Diminishing Expectations.* New York: W. W. Norton, 1978.

Lewis, C. S. *The Abolition of Man.* New York: Macmillan, 1947.

———. "On Ethics." In *Christian Reflections,* edited by Walter Hooper, pp. 44-56. Grand Rapids, Mich.: Eerdmans, 1967.

———. *God in the Dock: Essays on Theology and Ethics.* Grand Rapids, Mich.: Eerdmans, 1970.

———. "Right and Wrong as a Clue to the Meaning of the Universe." In *Mere Christianity,* rev. ed., pp. 15-39. New York: Macmillan, 1960.

Lindbeck, George. *The Nature of Doctrine.* Philadelphia: Westminster Press, 1984.

Lobkowicz, Nikolaus. "The Vice of Tolerance." *New Perspectives Quarterly,* winter 1998, pp. 56-59.

Machen, J. Gresham. *Christianity and Liberalism.* New York: Macmillan, 1924.

MacIntyre, Alasdair. *After Virtue: A Study in Moral Theory.* Notre Dame, Ind.: University of Notre Dame Press, 1981.

———. *Three Rival Versions of Moral Inquiry.* Notre Dame, Ind.: University of Notre Dame Press, 1990.

Markham, Ian. *Plurality and Christian Ethics.* Rev. ed. New York: Seven Bridges Press, 1999.

Marsden, George M. *Fundamentalism and American Culture: The Shaping of Twentieth Century Evangelicalism, 1870-1925.* New York: Oxford University Press, 1980.

McLean, Edward B., ed. *Common Truths: New Perspectives on Natural Law.* Wilmington, Del.: Intercollegiate Studies Institute, 2000.

McGrath, Alister E. "The Challenge of Pluralism for the Contemporary Christian Church." *Journal of the Evangelical Theological Society* 35, no. 3 (1992): 361-73.

———. "Doctrine and Ethics." *Journal of the Evangelical Theological Society* 34, no. 2 (1991): 145-56.

———. *Evangelicalism and the Future of Christianity.* Downers Grove, Ill.: InterVarsity Press, 1995.

———. *The Genesis of Doctrine: A Study in the Foundations of Doctrinal Criticism.* Oxford: Basil Blackwell, 1990.

————. *A Passion for Truth: The Intellectual Coherence of Evangelicalism.* Downers Grove, Ill.: InterVarsity Press, 1996.

McInerny, Ralph. *A First Glance at St. Thomas Aquinas.* Notre Dame, Ind.: University of Notre Dame Press, 1990.

Meilaender, Gilbert C. *Faith and Faithfulness: Basic Themes in Christian Ethics.* Notre Dame: University of Notre Dame Press, 1991.

————. *The Taste for the Other: The Social and Ethical Thought of C.S. Lewis.* Rev. ed. Grand Rapids, Mich.: Eerdmans, 1998.

————. *The Theory and Practice of Virtue.* Notre Dame, Ind.: University of Notre Dame Press, 1984.

————. *Things That Count: Essays Moral and Theological.* Wilmington, Del.: Intercollegiate Studies Institute, 2000.

Moser. Paul K., and T. L. Carson, eds. *Moral Relativism: A Reader.* Oxford: Oxford University Press, 2001.

Mott, Stephen Charles. *Biblical Ethics and Social Change.* Oxford: Oxford University Press, 1982.

Moynihan, Daniel Patrick. "Defining Deviancy Down." *The American Scholar,* winter 1993, pp. 17-30.

Murray, John. *Principles of Conduct: Aspects of Biblical Ethics.* Rev. ed. Grand Rapids, Mich.: Eerdmans, 1991.

Murray, John Courtney. *We Hold These Truths: Catholic Reflections on the American Proposition.* New York: Sheed & Ward, 1960.

Nash, Ronald. *Worldviews in Conflict: Choosing Christianity in a World of Ideas.* Grand Rapids, Mich.: Zondervan, 1992.

Neuhaus, Richard John, ed. *Virtue: Public and Private.* Grand Rapids, Mich.: Eerdmans, 1986.

Neuhaus, Richard John, and George Weigel, eds. *Being Christian Today: An American Conversation.* Washington, D.C.: Ethics and Public Policy Center, 1992.

Newbigin, Lesslie. *The Gospel in a Pluralist Society.* Grand Rapids, Mich.: Eerdmans, 1989.

————. *Truth to Tell: The Gospel and Public Truth.* Grand Rapids, Mich.: Eerdmans, 1991.

Niebuhr, H. Richard. *Christ and Culture.* New York: Harper, 1951.

Niebuhr, Reinhold. *An Interpretation of Christian Ethics.* New York: Harper, 1935.

————. *The Nature and Destiny of Man.* Vol. 2, *Human Destiny.* New York: Charles Scribner's Sons, 1943.

Noll, Mark. *The Scandal of the Evangelical Mind.* Grand Rapids, Mich.: Eerdmans, 1995.

Noll, Mark, Cornelius Plantinga Jr., and David Wells. "Evangelical Theology Today." *Theology Today,* January 1995, pp. 495-507.

Novak, David. *Jewish-Christian Dialogue: A Jewish Justification.* New York: Oxford University Press, 1989.

Novak, Michael. "Awakening from Nihilism: The Templeton Prize Address." *First Things,* August/September 1994, pp. 18-22.

————. *Belief and Unbelief: A Philosophy of Self-Knowledge.* New Brunswick, N.J.: Transaction, 1994.

Oden, Thomas C. *After Modernity...What? Agenda for Theology.* Grand Rapids, Mich.: Zondervan, 1990.

———. *Two Worlds: Notes on the Death of Modernity in America and Russia.* Downers Grove, Ill.: InterVarsity Press, 1992.

O'Donovan, Oliver. *Resurrection and Moral Order: An Outline for Evangelical Ethics.* Grand Rapids, Mich.: Eerdmans, 1986.

Orwell, George. "Politics and the English Language." In *The Collected Essays, Journalism and Letters of George Orwell,* edited by S. Orwell and I. Angus, 4:127-40. New York: Harcourt, Brace & World, 1968.

Oosterhoff, F.G. *Postmodernism: A Christian Appraisal.* Winnipeg: Premier, 1999.

Packer, J. I. *Freedom and Authority.* Oakland, Calif.: International Council on Biblical Inerrancy, 1981.

Pelikan, Jaroslav. *The Vindication of Tradition.* New Haven, Conn.: Yale University Press, 1984.

Pieper, Josef. *The Four Cardinal Virtues.* Notre Dame, Ind.: University of Notre Dame Press, 1966.

Postman, Neil. *Amusing Ourselves to Death.* New York: Viking, 1985.

Prager, Dennis, and Jonathan Glover. "Can We Be Good Without God? A Debate at Oxford University." *Ultimate Issues* 9, no. 1 (1993): 3-22.

Rae, Scott B. *Moral Choices: An Introduction to Ethics.* Rev. ed. Grand Rapids, Mich.: Zondervan, 2000.

Ramsey, Paul. *Ethics at the Edges of Life: Medical and Legal Intersections.* New Haven, Conn.: Yale University Press, 1978.

———. *Fabricated Man.* New Haven, Conn.: Yale University Press, 1970.

———. *The Patient as Person: Explorations in Medical Ethics.* 2nd ed. New Haven, Conn.: Yale University Press, 2002.

Ratzinger, Joseph Cardinal. *Introduction to Christianity.* Translated by M. Kohl. San Francisco: Ignatius, 1990.

Rieff, Philip. *The Triumph of the Therapeutic: Uses of Faith After Freud.* New York: Harper & Row, 1966.

Rommen, Heinrich A. *The Natural Law: A Study in Legal and Social History and Philosophy.* Translated by T. R. Hanley. Indianapolis: Liberty Fund, 1998.

Sayers, Dorothy L. *Creed or Chaos?* 1949; reprint, Manchester, N.H.: Sophia Institute Press, 1974.

Schlossberg, Herbert. *Idols for Destruction: The Conflict of Christian Faith and American Culture.* Rev. ed. Wheaton, Ill.: Crossway, 1990.

Sedgwick, Timothy F. *The Christian Moral Life: Practices of Piety.* Grand Rapids, Mich.: Eerdmans, 1999.

Sire, James W. *Habits of the Mind.* Downers Grove, Ill.: InterVarsity Press, 2000.

———. *The Universe Next Door: A Basic Worldview Catalog.* 3rd ed. Downers Grove, Ill.: InterVarsity Press, 1988.

Sorokin, Pititim, and Walter Lunden. *Power and Morality: Who Shall Guard the Guardians?* Boston, Mass.: Porter Sargent, 1959.

Stout, Jeffrey. *Ethics After Babel: Languages of Morals and Their Discontents.* Boston: Beacon, 1988.

Sykes, Charles. *A Nation of Victims.* New York: Free Press, 1991.

Thielecke, Helmut. *Nihilism: Its Origin and Nature with a Christian Answer.* Rev. ed. Translated by J. W. Doberstein. New York: Schocken, 1969.

———. *Theological Ethics.* Vol. 1, *Foundations.* Philadelphia: Fortress, 1966.

Toby, Jackson. "Medicalizing Temptation." *The Public Interest,* winter 1998, pp. 64-78.

Veith, Gene Edward, Jr. "The Ethics of Vocation." In *God at Work.* Wheaton, Ill.: Crossway, 2002.

Vitz, Paul C. *Psychology as Religion: The Cult of Self-Worship.* Rev. ed. Grand Rapids, Mich.: Eerdmans, 1995.

Walsh, Brian J., and J. Richard Middleton. *The Transforming Vision: Shaping a Christian Worldview.* Downers Grove, Ill.: InterVarsity Press, 1984.

Webber, Robert. *Common Roots: A Call to Evangelical Maturity.* Grand Rapids, Mich.: Zondervan, 1978.

Weber, Kent. "How Far Is Tolerance a Virtue?" *Regeneration Quarterly,* winter 1996, pp. 29-31.

Weigel, George. *Catholicism and the Renewal of American Democracy.* New York: Paulist, 1989.

Wells, David F. *No Place for Truth: Or, Whatever Happened to Evangelical Theology?* Grand Rapids, Mich.: Eerdmans, 1993.

Werpehowski, William, and Stephen D. Crocco, eds. *The Essential Paul Ramsey: A Collection.* New Haven, Conn.: Yale University Press, 1994.

Wilberforce, William. *A Practical View of Christianity.* Edited by K.C. Belmonte. Peabody, Mass.: Hendrickson, 1996.

Wilken, Robert L. "The Durablity of Orthodoxy." *Word and World* 8 (1988): 124-32.

———. *Remembering the Christian Past.* Grand Rapids, Mich.: Eerdmans, 1995.

Wilkens, Steve. *Beyond Bumper-Sticker Ethics: An Introduction to Theories of Right and Wrong.* Downers Grove, Ill.: InterVarsity Press, 1995.

Willard, Dallas. *The Spirit of the Disciplines.* New York: Harper & Row, 1988.

Williams, D.H. *Retrieving the Tradition and Renewing Evangelicalism: A Primer for Suspicious Protestants.* Grand Rapids, Mich.: Eerdmans, 1999.

Wilson, James Q. *On Character.* Washington, D.C.: American Enterprise Institute Press, 1991.

———. *The Moral Sense.* New York, N.Y.: Free Press, 1993.

Witten, Marsha. *All Is Forgiven: The Secular Message in American Protestantism.* Princeton, N.J.: Princeton University Press, 1993.

Wolfson, Adam. "What Remains of Toleration?" *The Public Interest,* winter 1999, pp. 37-51.

Wolters, Albert M. *Creation Regained: Biblical Basics for a Reformational Worldview.* Grand Rapids, Mich.: Eerdmans, 1985.

Index of Names